BRUNEI

IRASEC-NUS Press Publications on Contemporary Southeast Asia

Pierre-Arnaud Chouvy and Joël Meissonnier, *Yaa Baa: Production, Traffic and Consumption of Methamphetamine in Mainland Southeast Asia* (2004)

Guy Faure and Laurent Schwab, *Japan-Vietnam: A Relation under Influences* (2008)

Andrée Feillard and Rémy Madinier (Wong Wee, trans.), *The End of Innocence? Indonesian Islam and the Temptations of Radicalism* (2011)

Benoît de Tréglodé, *Heroes and Revolution in Vietnam* (2012)

Renaud Egreteau and Larry Jagan, *Soldiers and Diplomacy in Burma: Understanding the Foreign Relations of the Burmese Praetorian State* (2013)

Vatthana Pholsena and Oliver Tappe, eds., *Interactions with a Violent Past: Reading of Post-Conflict Landscapes in Cambodia, Laos and Vietnam* (2013)

BRUNEI

From the Age of Commerce to the 21st Century

Marie-Sybille de Vienne

Translated by Emilia Lanier

NUS PRESS
SINGAPORE

IRASEC
INSTITUT DE RECHERCHE SUR L'ASIE DU SUD-EST CONTEMPORAINE
RESEARCH INSTITUTE ON CONTEMPORARY SOUTHEAST ASIA

Published by NUS Press in association with IRASEC

Published by:

NUS Press
National University of Singapore
AS3-01-02, 3 Arts Link
Singapore 117569

Fax: (65) 6774-0652
E-mail: nusbooks@nus.edu.sg
Website: http://nuspress.nus.edu.sg

ISBN 978-9971-69-818-8 (Paper)

First edition 2015
Reprint 2016

National Library Board, Singapore Cataloguing-in-Publication Data

Vienne, Marie-Sybille de, 1954–
Brunei: from the age of commerce to the 21st century/Marie-Sybille de Vienne; translated by Emilia Lanier. – Singapore: Published by NUS Press in association with Research Institute on Contemporary Southeast Asia, [2015]
pages cm
Includes bibliographic references and index.
ISBN: 978-9971-69-818-8

1. Brunei – History. 2. Brunei – Economic conditions. 3. Brunei – Politics and government. 4. Brunei – Social life and customs. I. Lanier, Emilia, translator. II. Title.

DS650.54
959.55 — dc23 OCN 890685085

First published in French by CNRS Editions in 2012.

Cover image: 59th birthday of the Sultan of Brunei, 15 July 2005
(GA794247_019 © Alain Benainous/Gamma)

Printed by: Markono Print Media Pte Ltd.

Anakanda pakulun ratna tempawan
Jangan sekali berhati sawan
Jalan yang salah mesti dilawan
Hendaknya jangan mahu ditawan.

Oh you precious and tested hearts
Do refrain from all fear
The path of error, you need to face it
May your wishes not be hindered.

Sultan Omar Ali Saifuddin III
Sya'ir Perlembagaan Negeri Brunei
[*Poem for the institutionalisation of Brunei*], 1959

Contents

List of Graphs

List of Maps

List of Tables

List of Figures

Acknowledgements

The writing of this book would not have been possible without the support of all those who in various ways have helped me to bring it to term, and in particular the Universiti Brunei Darussalam (UBD), which regularly welcomed me.

In Brunei, I would like to thank:

Pehin Dato Seri Setia Lim Jock Seng, Second Minister of Foreign Affairs and Trade;

Pehin Dato Hj Mohd Jamil Al-Sufri, director of the Pusat Sejarah, for his many illuminating writings, which made me regret that his time constraints did not allow him to meet me;

Pengiran Dato Paduka Haji Idriss bin Pengiran Temenggong, former ambassador of Brunei Darussalam in France and president of the Alliance Française of Bandar Seri Begawan;

Haji Rozan bin Dato Paduka Haj Mohammed Yunus, permanent secretary, Ministry of Culture, a connoisseur of the history and culture of Brunei;

Dr Amin Abdullah Liew, former permanent secretary, Ministry of Industry and Primary Resources;

Dr Haji Zulkarnain bin Haji Hanafi, vice-chancellor of Universiti Brunei Darussalam (UBD);

Dato Paduka Haji Mohammed Nor, assistant permanent secretary, Ministry of Foreign Affairs;

Dr Siti Norkhalbi Hj Wahsalfelah, director, Academy of Brunei Studies, UBD;

The director of the UBD Library, Dr Haji Suhaimi Bin Haji Abdul Karim and the whole team on the third floor (Bruneiana Collections);

Pengiran Hahaj Suryani Binti Pg Hj Damit, Brunei Museum Library;

Dr B.A. Hussainmiya, associate professor, UBD, for his foreword and his friendship;

Dr Mariam Ali, former senior lecturer, UBD;
Dr Johannes L. Kurz, senior lecturer, UBD;
Dr Frank Fanselow, former senior lecturer, UBD;
Ignatius Stephen, journalist, prematurely deceased;
Pierre Imhof, General Manager of Baiduri Bank and president of the French Bruneian Business Association (FBBA);
Glenn Rase, former ambassador of the United States to Brunei Darussalam, then director of Citibank at Bandar Seri Begawan;
Louis Heuzé and Yves Grosjean, successively directors of Total E&P Borneo B.V., for their interest in this project;
H.E. Louis Le Vert, former ambassador of France (2008–12) to Brunei Darussalam, for his hospitality and help;
H.E. Jean-Yves Berthault, former ambassador of France (2012–14) to Brunei Darussalam for his hospitality in 2013.

In Bangkok:

The whole team at the Research Institute on Contemporary Southeast Asia (IRASEC) and in particular its directors and deputy-directors, successively Guy Faure, Benoît de Tréglodé, François Robinne, Arnaud Leveau and Jérémy Jammes.

In Singapore:

Lena Qua, NUS Press, for her accurate supervision of the English edition.

In Paris:

National Institute for Oriental Language and Civilisations (INALCO), for having financed several research missions to Brunei and part of the English translation;
Jean-Louis Sabouret, senior research fellow at Centre National de la Recherche Scientifique (CNRS), executive director and financial officer of Réseau Asie (Asian Network), for the French edition of the present work;
Jérôme Samuel, associate professor in Indonesian-Malaysian at INALCO for having reviewed the translations from Malay;
Wong Wee for her wonderful copyediting work;
The smallest *clergeonnet du Roi* for having launched the barque as an adventure before it was finally secured by the *shahbandar*;
and all (*Syndicaliste* included) who, in one way or another, by their comments, curiosity, patience, annoyance, re-reading or criticism, contributed to the midwifery of this book.

Foreword

Despite being a tiny state in Southeast Asia perched on the north-west corner of Borneo, the third largest island in the world, Brunei Darussalam, an oil-rich country, has emerged as an interesting political and international entity in the contemporary world. It has been exercising some degree of influence in regional political and economic bodies such as ASEAN, OIC, Association of Commonwealth Nations and various other international groupings. The Sultan of Brunei, His Majesty Hassanal Bolkiah, regularly takes part in APEC meetings and hosts important area meetings in his country. He also entertains regular visitors from among the heads of states and other global VIP guests. As an oil- and gas-producing state, Brunei has conserved a fair amount of financial reserves mostly invested around the world through multiple strategies. Deriving wealth from this, plus oil income, the citizens of Brunei enjoy a comfortable standard of living on the whole, and have access to education, health and many social services, with the largesse of the state. The country has also long emerged from its image as a backwater in Southeast Asia. In short, Brunei's importance is on the rise although its political and social institutions are ensconced within a traditional monarch who also wields executive power. On the whole, those who read and write about Brunei are always fascinated by it. Unfortunately few books on Brunei have hit the shelves, especially of late. Many excuses have been put forward by aspiring researchers. Local intellectuals, who do not necessarily enjoy official support, remain reluctant to write about their own country and delve into sensitive issues while foreigners may have genuine difficulties in accessing proper and appropriate sources to make a free analysis of Brunei history and institutions. Despite some setbacks, books and research publications do appear periodically to enlighten us about the country and its progress, although one would expect more publications to appear given the importance of Brunei Darussalam as a contemporary monarchic state.

Professor Marie-Sybille de Vienne's latest work on Brunei, appearing in its English version (translated from the original French), is a most welcome addition to the dwindling literature on the subject of Brunei. Not only does the book fill an important lacuna on the early history of the Sultanate, it also serves as an analytical tool to understand the modern government in Brunei. It is truly remarkable that Professor de Vienne, though far away in France, has produced such a deeply penetrating analysis of the country. Indeed she has made several visits to Brunei to collect critical material and interview people concerned in the higher echelons of education and government. She has left no stone unturned, to say the least, in her search for sources and facts.

Her book is quite comprehensive in scope and treatment, as the readers would agree—a compendium of salient aspects of the history, government, economics, politics and society of Brunei from the past to the present. While being short of encyclopedic in its treatment of various topics, the book nonetheless provides rare insights on the nature of the contemporary Brunei government and its operations, from the ideological to operational level. Being a practising and leading French economic historian, Professor de Vienne has produced umcommon insights into the inner workings of a modern monarchic state. That makes her book more interesting and valuable for Brunei watchers. She is daring and forthright in her analysis, rather than presenting mere facts and figures. More importantly, her work is up to date as she races to "cover the story" up till the time the book goes to press!

Aside from interesting discussions, the author embellishes her work with important tools for our easy understanding—easily readable graphs and statistics. Her special qualifications as an economic historian thus come in handy for her approach to Bruneian economic issues in particular; her skillful analysis is hardly matched by others who write on the subject.

One other appreciable attribute of this book is its comprehensive bibliography. Unlike other books, this work divides the bibliographic references according to relevant subjects. It also demonstrates the painstaking efforts by the author to differentiate between overlapping issues.

The tenor of the book is daring as well as candid and it treads at times on sensitive issues, especially the way in which the current monarchic system seeks sustenance in Malay Islamic Monarchic (MIB) ideology for its survival. I am not sure to what extent these discussions will be palatable for intellectual consumption within Brunei, but for outsiders, it is critical to understand Brunei's true ethos without fear or favour. That is what this book achieves. No doubt the book will be welcomed by Brunei specialists and others as an important contribution to the study of monarchic Brunei—an ancient country but a modern state.

Professor B.A. Hussainmiya
Historical Studies, Universiti Brunei Darussalam (UBD)

I

PROLOGUE: BRUNEI VERSUS BORNEO

An Apparently Unfavourable Geography

Situated some 300 km southwest of the southern extremity of the Island of Borneo (Kudat) and close to the equator (400 km to the north),[1] Brunei is today a modestly sized country (5,765 km^2, or the equivalent of

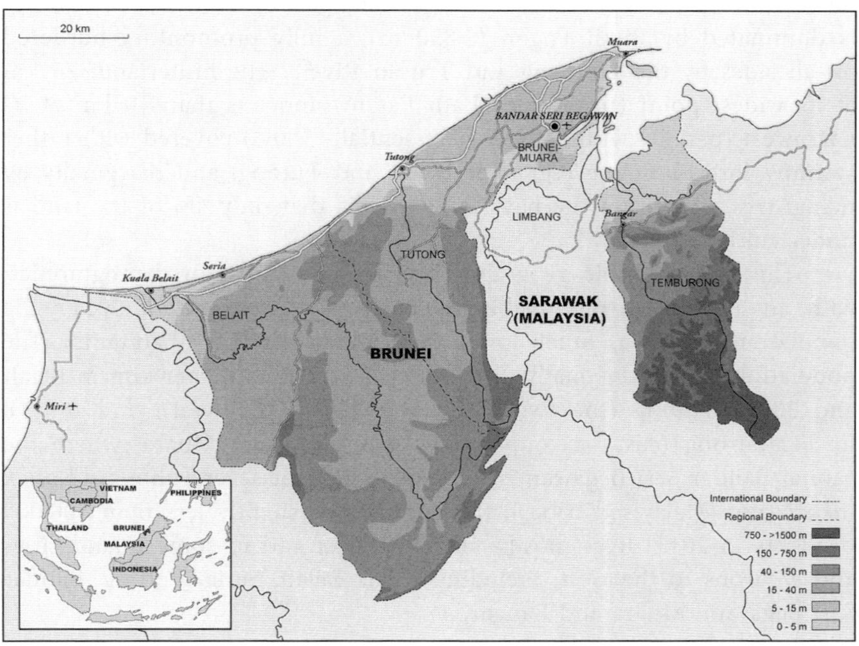

Map 1. Brunei

[1] Latitudes 4°00'N and 5°05'N; longitudes 114°06'E and 115°22'E.

the state of Delaware in the United States and more than double the size of Luxembourg), embedded in the Malaysian state of Sarawak. In addition to its small size, its territory is cut in two, since Sarawak, with which Brunei shares 381 km of land border, owns the bottom of the "little bay" of Brunei (the southwest portion of the Brunei Bay, into which the river of the same name flows): the division of Limbang, a band some 7 km wide along the coast, whose surface area measures less than 3,978 km^2 but which is almost as large (four-fifths) as that of the sultanate.

Brunei has 269 km of coastline, of which a slender and sandy two-thirds borders the southern China Sea; the other third, along the Brunei Bay, is remote and muddy. Formed in large part of alluvial plains, Brunei includes three important water networks: to the west, the Belait (143 km) and the Tutong (120 km); to the east, the Temburong (70 km); the Brunei River, essentially an estuary, extends only 35 km.

The western coastal plain is raised towards the east by the spurs (less than 350 m high) of Mount Madu, which culminates at 2,370 m on the other side of the border. The eastern part of Brunei (Temburong) is dominated by Bukit Pagon (1,850 m), a hilly promontory bordered on all sides by the Limbang and Trusan Rivers. The hinterland, 75 km at its widest point (near Bukit Batu Patam) and less than 10 km at its narrowest (parallel with Muara), is essentially (80%) covered with rather swampy forests, in the region of Belait and Tutong, and marginally by mangroves, in part of the bay. The result is that only 4% of the land is under cultivation.

This unfavourable geography has repercussions on demographics: with an average of 68 inhabitants per km^2 at the end of 2011,[2] the population density is much lower than Malaysia's (81 inhabitants). The population is very unequally distributed: 24 inhabitants per km^2 in Belait and 38 in Tutong (the two forest districts to the west), and only 8 in Temburong (east), as opposed to 473 in Brunei Muara, where the capital Bandar Seri Begawan is located. Except for several thousand *puak sakai*[3] (non-Malayised tribes), the population (slightly less than 400,000 residents in 2013) lives mostly near the coast and in some inland cities and environs to the west, including Kuala Belait, Seria, Tutong, Bandar Seri Begawan, Muara and Bangar.

[2] *Brunei Darussalam Statistical Yearbook 2011*, BSB, JPKE, 2014, p. 13.

[3] The expression *puak sakai* is typically Bruneian. *Puak* means "group" in Malay and *sakai*, etymologically, means "savages", "the non-civilised", "people of inferior status". See "Lexicon" under Appendices for the Malay terminology.

The Best Port in West Borneo

The territory of Brunei can only be fully grasped when seen as integrated into the vast network of river mouths that carve up the 2,700 km-long west coast of Borneo. A bird's eye view of the coast shows an abundance of watercourses, of which a dozen constitute important hydrological networks—the rivers flowing from east to west such as the Sarawak, Sadong, Lupar, Rajang, Tatau, Kemena, Baram, Limbang and Padas.[4] However, the west coast of Borneo contains few harbours propitious for the agglomeration of Malay peoples of a riparian tradition, whose matrix is that of trading posts on the estuaries; the harbours of the rivers mentioned above, starting with the vast delta of the Rajang, are for the most part formed of flooded and swampy lands that are full of silt. Kuching (ex-Sarawak) and Bintulu are trading centres more than 500 years old; Kota Kinabalu (ex-Jesselton), the capital of Sabah, is a pure colonial creation.

Borneo is scarcely better endowed with harbours that are sheltered from cyclones. It has only two in its western part: the Marudu Bay to the north, in the current state of Sabah, and that of Brunei. Comparing the two sites reveals that the Brunei Bay (2,500 km^2, similar in size to the bays of Manila and Tokyo) is by far the best potential port on the island's west coast, as it is formed of two enclosed structures (see map 3). In addition, the secondary bay to the southwest of the main bay is like a natural fort protected by two rocky escarpments of the Brunei River

[4] The main rivers, *sungai* (s., stream) or *batang* (b., river) are: s. Sarawak, 120 km long, basin 2,459 km^2; b. Sadong, 150 km; b. Lupar, 275 km; b. Rajang, 760 km, basin 51,237 km^2; b. Tatau, 270 km; b. Kemena, 190 km; b. Baram, 635 km, basin 22,209 km^2; s. Limbang, 275 km; b. Trusan, 205 km; s. Padas, 420 km. See River Basin Information System (RBIS), "River basin of Sarawak", Department of Irrigation and Drainage Sarawak, http://www.did.sarawak.gov.my/rbis/map-html/basins-table.htm [accessed March 2010].

(see map 2),[5] whose access is guarded by a series of islets, which bore fortifications at Keingaran and Pulau Chermin, dating from the end of the 17th century.[6]

The Brunei Bay has long been coveted by many, resulting in it being shared today between three political entities: Brunei Darussalam to the west, Sarawak in the centre, and Sabah to the east (to which the island of Labuan was attached before becoming Malaysian federal territory in 1984).

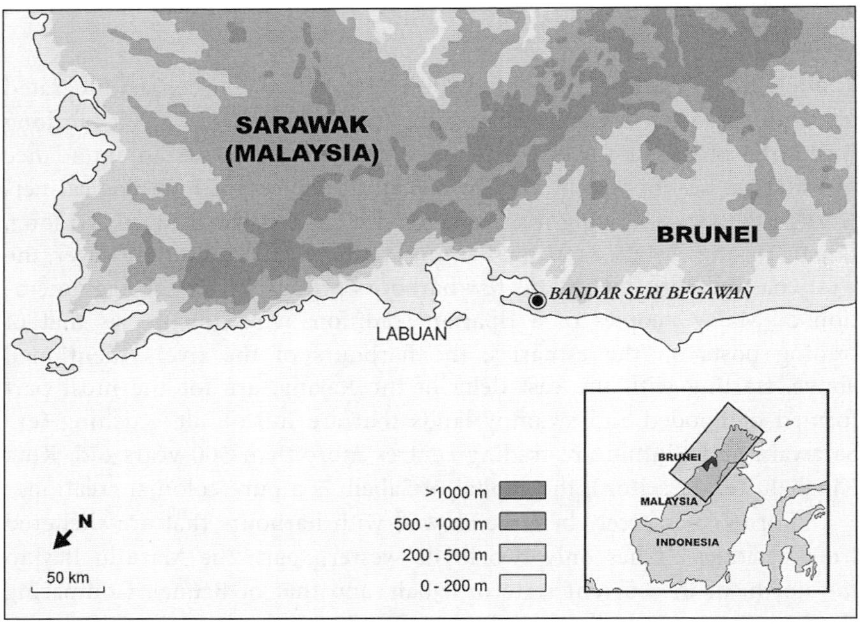

Map 2. Topography of the Brunei Bay

However, the meagre portion of the Brunei Bay controlled by the sultanate (50,000 km^2, or one-fifth)[7] has proved to be the only one to

[5] Map drawn from a sketch by J. Népote.

[6] Robert Nicholl, "Relations between Brunei and Manila A.D. 1682–1690", *BMJ* 4 (1977): 128–76.

[7] "Brunei Bay", ASEAN Regional Centre for Biodiversity Conservation, http://www.arcbc.org.ph/wetlands/brunei/brn_brubay.htm; "Brunei Darussalam", ramsar.wetlands.org/Portals/15/Brunei.pdf, website of the Ramsar Convention [Iran] on wet zones, signed in 1971 [accessed Feb. 2010].

combine management of a secondary bay and a port. Thus it is not surprising that the kingdom's capital was established there since at least the 14th century (as shown by the vestiges of Kota Batu and the tomb of Sultan Bolkiah, c. 1473–1521). This modest merchant town was sufficiently strategic to dominate the whole western and southern coast of Borneo until the second half of the 18th century, when the Marudu Bay escaped its grasp and went under the control of the sultanate of Sulu.

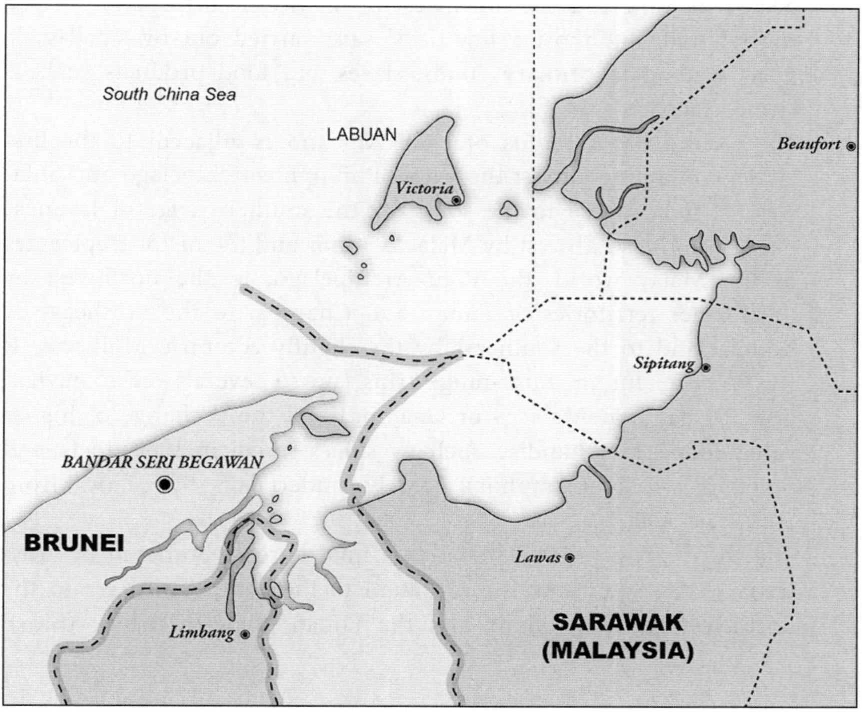

Map 3. Brunei Darussalam and the Brunei Bay

The value of Brunei was not limited to its bay; the territory is also part of a several-thousand-year-old commercial network that can be discerned intermittently through Indian and Chinese sources[8] from the

[8] See, for example, Paul Wheatley, *The Golden Khersonese* (Westport: Greenwood Reprinting, 1973), 388 p.

first century CE[9] (the toponyms *Boni/Foni* appears in Chinese accounts at the start of the Song era).[10] This network can be modelled in the form of three concentric circles starting from Brunei (see map 4):

1. The first, with a radius of 1,000 km, is bordered on the south by Banjermasin; to the north by Palawan, the southern tip of the Philippines archipelago; to the east by Zamboanga and to the west by Pontianak. It covers almost the totality of Borneo, the archipelago of Sulu and the northwest of Sulawesi, corresponding to a coastal trade (at most a few days' sail) carried out by small-scale boats trading in primary goods, slaves and food products such as rice or sago.
2. The second has a radius of 1,500 km and is adjacent to the first circle, containing almost the whole Philippine archipelago and Sulawesi. It is bordered to the south by the southern edge of Javanese Pasisir; to the southwest by Malacca-Johor and the historic epicentre of the Malay world, the Riau Archipelago; to the northwest by the former territories of Funan and Champa; to the northeast by Manila; and to the southeast by the slightly eccentric Moluccas. It was the site for medium-range trips (up to several weeks' navigation, 30 days for Malacca or Champa) and the exchange of higher value-added merchandise such as spices, medicinal products and precious woods (camphor), largely undertaken by sailors from Southeast Asia.
3. The third circle (2,500 km) adds a final aureole bordered by Australia to the south, Aceh and Patani to the west, Ayutthaya to the northwest, Taiwan, Amoy and the Fujian ports to the northeast;

[9] Vestiges of Han potteries from the first century CE have been discovered in the east of Borneo (J. Népote, *Histoire de l'Asie du Sud-Est en fiches*, ca 1996, unpublished, In-4°, 82ff + 70 cartes, f. 45).

[10] The toponyms *Boni* 渤泥 and *Foni* 勃泥 cited by Johannes L. Kurz, *Boni in Chinese Sources: Translations of Relevant Texts from the Song to the Qing Dynasties* (unpublished, 2008), may be transcribed—in conformity with the pronunciation of the period, on the basis of pronunciations recovered by Bernhard Karlgren, Edwin G. Pulleyblank and William H. Baxter—as "*but nei* in the Tang era, or *p(h)ut nei* in the Song era, which appears to me to transcribe Barunei rather well" (personal communication in French from Michel Ferlus, 28 January 2009). See Michel Ferlus, "L'intérêt linguistique des transcriptions chinoises concernant le Cambodge ancien [Fou-nan et Tchen-la]", *Bulletin de l'AEFEK* 15 [January 2009], http://aefek.free.fr/pageLibre00010944.html [accessed 3 May 2011].

the southern Moluccas, Ambon and Banda, and New Guinea to the east. Via the Andaman and South China Seas, it bound the Chinese and Indian "empires", which were both markets and reserves of cultural and technological expertise. This third circle corresponded to long-distance trade in products of higher technological content such as textiles, ceramics, lacquerware and utensils, and which operated at places that once required several months of navigation, along itineraries joining the South China Sea to the Persian Gulf and the Red Sea.

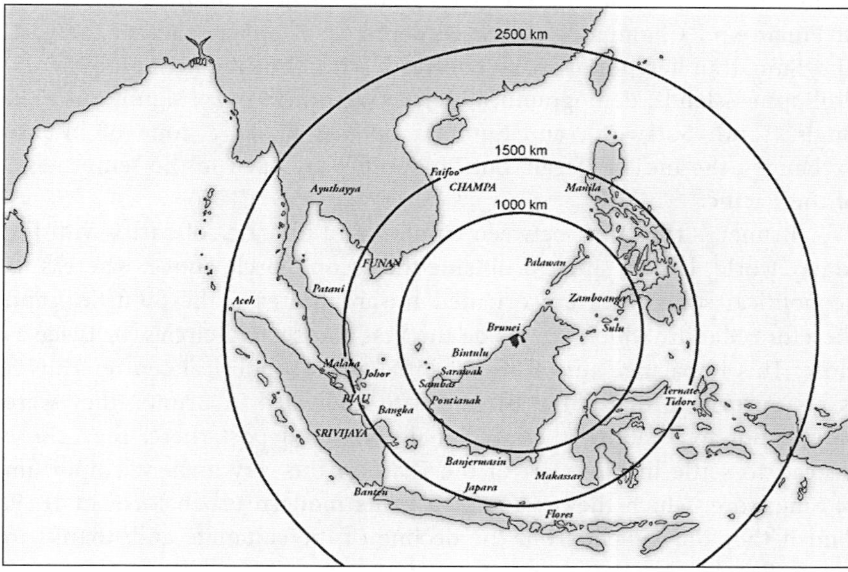

Map 4. An Age-old Commercial Network

Brunei is thus at the heart of a network in which all points on a north/south axis (from Canton at the top, down to Flores) correspond in pairs to the focal points of trade of the South China Sea. To the north-west, the straits and isthmuses of the Sea of Andaman, Penang Island, the Straits of Malacca and Sumatra, correspond to a northeast axis, with Taiwan, Philippines, Luzon and its focal point Manila, the Visayas and Mindanao. Java and the ports of Pasisir (in the southwest) can be paired with the Bugis and Makassar (Sulawesi) lands to the southeast. The Riau pirate networks in the west correspond to those of the east, Sulu-Jolo.

This Southeast Asian pattern of exchanges has been endlessly recomposed over the last millennium with the upsurge of new actors and the emergence or disappearance of trading centres and posts, but after the great maritime innovations of the Song, its material elements (the prevailing winds, primary material and techniques of naval construction) scarcely changed between the 12th and 19th centuries.

This symmetrical interpretation does not, however, totally stand up to examination, for the western half of the diagram counts for much more—historically and commercially—than the eastern half. The epicentre of the thalassocracy of Srivijaya (7th–13th centuries) was situated around the Riau, while there was no equivalent in Sulu; the same is true of Funan and Champa, which were deprived of appendages to the east. The Sumatran territorial mass contrasts with the fragmentation of the Philippine islands; demographically, Java was much more significant than Bugis (south Sulawesi); and Sumatra opened up as a zone of intense exchanges, the Indian Ocean, but Philippines lay open to the "emptiness" of the Pacific.

Brunei is thus torn between cultural and historic solidarity with the Malay world, largely situated outside the second circle above, whereas its geopolitical solidarities are oriented toward the east, the Sulu Sea, and therefore Manila, which are inside the first and second circles, or twice as close. This imbalance cut off its potential as a geopolitical centre. Thus it is not surprising that if the British were interested in Brunei, they were careful not to establish their regional command post there; they chose instead to settle in the heart of the Riau, in the very ancient emporium of Singapore, which they re-founded in its modern urban form in 1819. And if they did benefit from the decline of the sultanate and, thanks to James Brooke, laid hands on its western coast (Sarawak) and obtained Labuan in 1847, with Brunei losing nine-tenths of its riverbank lands in the course of the 19th century, the advent of steam navigation and the digging of the Suez and Panama Canals, by increasing the links between China and Europe, put them in even closer contact with the Malay Peninsula. British control was at the origin of the privileged connection between Brunei and Singapore, which has grown consistently up to modern times.

A Relatively Strategic Site

Brunei, this second-rank site, has been endowed in the contemporary era with an additional economic dimension that reaches far beyond the regional framework, conferred by its possession of a key resource—hydrocarbons—first petroleum, whose exploitation started in 1932 in Seria, then natural gas, whose production became significant in the 1970s. But far from being an oil emirate transplanted to the China Sea, Brunei, as shown by its urban typography (absence of a business district, under-occupation of the waterfront, etc.) has made choices opposite to those of the Persian Gulf states from the beginning of its modernisation.

So what are the political and ideological foundations of the Bruneian mode of development? Since the sultanate, due to its prosperity and peacefulness, has remained largely ignored by the social sciences and has not been the subject of much social debate, it is necessary to ground our analysis in historical data gathered over a long timeline, in order to understand the contemporary stakes and propose perspectives for the future.

II

FROM THALASSOCRACY TO RENTIER STATE

Introduction: Sources and Methodology

In a more marked manner than in the rest of Southeast Asia, where archaeological and epigraphic information compensate (at least partially) for the paucity of written sources, historical sources are cruelly lacking in Brunei up until the middle of the 19th century.

Textual Sources

Malay textual sources[1] are of three types, listed below in decreasing pertinence to the history of Brunei:

1. The genealogies of the sultans of Brunei, or *silsilah*. Today they are accessible in two published series of documents written in Jawi (Arabo-Malay) and compiled between the first half of the 18th century and the start of the 19th. The first is the English translation of a genealogy and a historical synopsis made by Hugh Low in 1880;[2] the second is the transliteration into Romanised Malay of two manuscripts conserved in London and published by Amin Sweeney in 1968.[3] Evidence suggests that at least ten *silsilah* have been conserved by the royal family and at least one by the National University of Malaysia, but the sensitivity of the subject is such that they remain inaccessible. To these *silsilah* should be added the genealogical synopsis engraved on the tomb of Sultan Muhammad

[1] Geoffrey Gunn, *Language, Power and Ideology in Brunei Darussalam* (Athens: Ohio University Center for International Studies, 1997), pp. 53–4.
[2] Hugh Low, "*Selesilah* (Book of Descent) of the Rajas of Bruni", *JMBRAS* 5 (June 1880): 1–36.
[3] Amin P.L. Sweeney, "Silsilah Raja-Raja Berunai", *JMBRAS* 41, 2 (1968): 1–82; "Errata and Short note", *JMBRAS* 42, 2 (1969): 222–4.

Jemal-ul-Alam (*Batu Tarsilah*, dated 1807), also translated by Hugh Low.[4]

2. The long epic poem relating the myth of the foundation of Brunei, the *Sya'ir Awang Simawn* [*Simaun*], which was still being recited in the first half of the 20th century. Eight different versions have been transliterated and studied by Allen Maxwell,[5] and there are supposedly several others conserved in Brunei. Since the epic integrates the Spanish attack of 1578 and several other events of the first half of the 18th century, in its actual form, it could not have predated the 1770s. The *Dewan Bahasa dan Pustaka* (DBP) has just published a version in transliterated Malay based on a manuscript held by the Muzium Brunei (Museum), but unfortunately it is deprived of any critical tool.[6] To this might be added the *Sya'ir Rakis*[7] composed in 1846 after the recognition of British rights over Labuan.
3. Some of the Malay annals and genealogies which contain incidental material with information about the history of Brunei, even though its toponym is scarcely mentioned, for example, the *Sejarah Melayu*,[8] the *Hikayat Hang Tuah*,[9] the *Hikayat Bandjar*[10] (Banjermasin), the

[4] Low, "*Selesilah*"; translation used by P.M. Shariffudin and Abdul Latif Hj. Ibrahim, "'Batu Tarsilah', the genealogical tablet of the Sultans of Brunei", in *Papers Relating to Brunei*, ed. Cheah Boon Kheng (Kuala Lumpur: MBRAS, 1998), pp. 159–67.

[5] Allen R. Maxwell, "Who is Awang Simawn?", in *From Buckfast to Borneo: Essays Presented to Father Robert Nicholl on the 85th Anniversary of his Birth, 27 March 1995*, ed. Victor T. King and A.V.M. Horton (Hull: Centre for South-East Asian Studies, 1995), pp. 178–206; A.R. Maxwell, "Accessing the Epic Status of the Brunei Malay Sya'ir Awang Simawn", paper presented at the *Tenth International Conference on Linguistics, 17–20 January 2006, Puerto Princessa* (Palawan), http://www.sil.org/asia/Philippines/ical/papers.html, pp. 20ff [accessed May 2010].

[6] *Syair Awang Simaun* [*Koleksi Muzium*] (BSB: DBP, 2010), 247 p; unlike Allen Maxwell, the museum chose to spell the name of the eponymous hero as Simaun and not Simawn.

[7] Written in 1846 by Pengiran Shahbandar Indera Mahkota Mohd Salleh ibnu Pengiran Sharmayuda (referred to in Western sources by his title *Indera Mahkota*), after the loss of Labuan.

[8] T.D. Situmorang and Andries Teeuw, *Sedjarah Melayu menurut terbitan Abdullah* [*Ibn Abdulkadir Munsji*] (Jakarta: Djambatan, 1952), 359 p.

[9] P.-Y. Manguin and Ian Proudfoot, *Hikayat Hang Tuah* (*a Malay text of the 17th century after the edition printed by Dewan Bahasa dan Pustaka, 1975*), electronic edition (1,305 Ko, 171,000 words), and a revised and enlarged edition of the printed text for the Malay Concordance Project, 1994, 224 p.

[10] J.J. Ras, *Hikajat Bandjar: A Study in Malay Historiography* (The Hague: Bibliotheca Indosinica, Martinus Nijhoff, 1968), 651 p.

genealogies of the princely families of Sulu and Kalimantan, notably that of Sambas[11] and the *Sya'ir Saribas*;[12] the *Silsilah Melayu dan Bugis dan Sekalian Raja Raja nya*[13] and *Tuhfat al-Nafis*,[14] etc., of which none is prior to the start of the 17th century. Overall these contain a few lines relating to the sultanate.

For the period prior to the 19th century, we thus have, by current publishing standards, at most 400 pages of Malay sources, largely redundant and split essentially in terms of interest between the various published versions of the royal genealogy and the variants of the *Sya'ir Awang Simawn*.

As for sources in foreign languages, which today in terms of page volume constitute nine-tenths of the sources accessible until the 1950s, they are of three types:

1. Chinese sources, which are both older and extend over a greater period of time, from the *Manshu*[15] (late ninth century, under the Tang Dynasty), which mentions for the first time the toponym *Boni*, up to the *Official History of the Ming Dynasty*,[16] a compilation of Ming sources completed in 1739, with the qualification that they include at most about 100 pages concerning more or less the

[11] E.U. Kratz, "Silsilah raja-Raja Sambas as a source of history", *Archipel* 20 (1980): 255–67.

[12] Bob Reece, "The Sya'ir Saribas Project", *Borneo Research Bulletin* (henceforth *BRB*, see the list of acronyms in Appendix III, Bibliography), 2 February 2002, electronically published.

[13] [*Genealogy of the Malays, Bugis and all kings*] by Raja Ali Haji Ibn Ahmad, translated by Hans Overbeck, *JMBRAS* 4, 3 (1926).

[14] Raja Ali Haji Ibn Ahmad, *Tuhfat al-Nafis* [*The Precious Gift*], trans. by Virginia Matheson Hooker and Barbara Watson Andaya (Kuala Lumpur: Oxford University Press, 1982), 476 p.

[15] Fan Chuo 樊綽, *Manshu jiaozhu* 蠻書校注, translated in Johannes L. Kurz, *Boni in Chinese Sources: Translations of Relevant Texts from the Song to the Qing Dynasties*, p. 6.

[16] *Mingshi* 明史, translated in Kurz, ibid., pp. 66ff; *Ming Shi-lu* 明實錄, in Geoff Wade, trans., *Southeast Asia in the Ming Shi-lu: An Open Access Resource*, Asia Research Institute and the Singapore E-Press (NUS, 2005), http://epress.nus.edu.sg/msl; Carrie C. Brown, "Two Ming texts concerning King Ma-na-je-chia-na of P'o-ni", *BMJ* 3, 2 (1974): 222–31; W.P. Groeneveldt, "Notes on the Malay Archipelago and Malacca compiled from Chinese sources", Batavia, *Verhandelingen van het Bataviaasch Genootschap van Kunsten en Wetenschappen* 39 (1880), 111 p.

polity,[17] that is, a dozen pages per century until the end of the Ming Dynasty—and again, provided that they refer to one and the same entity.

2. Meagre Arab sources (less than one page in total), where the toponym Brunei appears for the first time with certitude in 1462,[18] then again (1511) in a nautical route chart.[19]
3. Western sources—only Iberian sources for the 16th century,[20] to which should be added Dutch sources for 17th and 18th,[21] and British sources[22] since the end of the 18th century. The total is about 180 pages for the years from 1500–1800 (some 60 pages per century), except for unpublished documents that may lie in the Spanish archives—largely tapped by R. Nicholl—and occasional

[17] Refers to the sources published by Liu Xinsheng 刘新生, *Zhong guo yu Wen Lai guanxi shi ke jiang bian* 中国与文莱关系史科江编 [*The collection of historical documents related to bilateral relations between China and Brunei Darussalam*] (Beijing: World Affairs Press 世界知识出版社, 2006). To please official ideology, Liu added some documents from Tang sources concerning Poli 婆利, when this toponym, for whatever reason, could not refer to Brunei, cf. Roderich Ptak, "Possible Chinese References to the Barus Area [Tang to Ming]", in *Histoire de Barus, Sumatra: le site de Lobu Tua, vol. I, Études et documents,* ed. Claude Guillot (Paris: Cahiers d'Archipel, 1998), pp. 120–5.

[18] Shihab al-Dīn Aḥmad bin Mājid mentions the sea of *Barnī*, see G.R. Tibbets, *A study of the Arabic texts containing material on Southeast Asia* (Leiden: Brill, 1979), pp. 195, 198, 207, 255; and especially, J.V. Mills, "Arab and Chinese Navigators in the Malaysian waters in about A.D. 1500", *JMBRAS* 47, 2 (1974): 1–82.

[19] Sulaiman b. Aḥmad al-Maḥri c. 1520, *Barānī*, in Tibbets, ibid., pp. 195, 217, 225, 255.

[20] The main ones are: Robert Nicholl, ed., *European Sources for the History of the Sultanate of Brunei in the Sixteenth Century* (BSB, 1st ed. 1975, 3rd ed. 2007), 119 p; John S. Carroll, "Berunai in the *Boxer Codex*", *JMBRAS* 55, 2 (1982): 1–25. Note that the *Boxer Codex* contains the most detailed description of Brunei to be found in the 16th century.

[21] Published for the 17th century by L.C. van Dijck, "Relations of the East Indian Company with Borneo (Brunei), the Sulu Archipelago, Mindanao, etc.", *BMJ* 5, 4 (1984): 6–34.

[22] For example, the syntheses of J.R. Logan, "Borneo"; "Notices of European intercourse with Borneo Proper prior to the establishment of Singapore in 1819"; "Traces of the origin of the Malay Kingdom of Borneo, with notices of its condition when first discovered by Europeans, and at later periods"; "Notices of Chinese intercourse with Borneo Proper prior to the establishment of Singapore in 1819", *Journal of the Indian Archipelago and Eastern Asia* [*JIAEA*] 2 (1848): 495–7, 498–512, 513–27, 611–5; "The piracy and slave trade of the Indian Archipelago", *JIAEA* 3 (1849): 581–8, 629–36; 4 (1850): 45–52, 144–62, 400–10, 617–68, 734–46; 5 (1851): 374–82.

mentions of Brunei in the *Dagh Registers* (daily accounts) of the *Vereenigde Oost-Indische Compagnie* (VOC) covering the period 1683–1799, currently unpublished.

Apart from being highly heterogeneous in both purpose (being written by princes, merchants, adventurers, missionaries of various orders, *conquistadores* and colonials, who did not have the same aims in the territory as Malay historiographers)[23] and in form (from a few sinograms in the first Chinese sources to hundreds of pages in the British reports), these textual sources are discontinuous and full of lacunae—and contradictory on more than one occasion.

Archaeological Sources

In the absence of any architectural vestiges other than scraps of the mural of Kota Batu,[24] archaeological data[25] are currently limited to modest traces of fabrics and ceramics[26] and other minor objects, plus some 40 Islamic epigraphs, the latter collected near the historic heart of the current capital and at a handful of other sites.[27]

Overview of the Sources

In light of this inventory of sources, compared to a Southeast Asian history that is traditionally conceived in terms of "classic" sources—

[23] As noted by J.C. van Leur in *Indonesian Trade and Society: Essays in Asian Social and Economic History,* 2nd ed. (Leiden: KITLV, 1983), p. 261, the history of Insulindia is written "from the deck of the ship, the ramparts of the fortress, the high gallery of the trading house".

[24] Tom and Barbara Harrisson, "Kota Batu in Brunei (Introductory Report)", *SMJ* 23 (1956): 283–318; on the need to pursue archaeological inquiry, see Matussin bin Omar, "Archaeology and the reconstruction of Brunei's Early History", *BMJ* 9, 1 (1994): 1–12.

[25] Matussin bin Omar, *Archaeological excavations in protohistoric Brunei* (BSB: Muzium Brunei, 1981), 116 p.

[26] Roderich Ptak, "From Quanzhou to the Sulu Zone and Beyond: Questions Related to the Early Fourteenth Century", *JSAS* 29, 2 (1998): 269–94; Michel L'Hour, *La mémoire engloutie de Brunei: une aventure sous-marine*, 3 vols. (Paris: Textuel, 2001), 142 p, 175 p, 47 p.

[27] Ludwik Kalus and Claude Guillot, "Les inscriptions funéraires islamiques de Brunei", *BEFEO* 90–91 (2003–04): 229–72; ibid., "Les inscriptions funéraires islamiques de Brunei (2ème partie)", *BEFEO* 93 (2006): 139–81.

archaeological (including epigraphy) and Indianised, or literary and Sinicised—the history of Borneo and *a fortiori* that of Brunei can scarcely be presented until the end of the 18th century except in the form of a series of hypotheses, whose contradictions would arise *lato sensu* from the divergent interests of those (mostly foreigners) who have passed down these sources. The first periodical (apart from the official yearbooks published since 1906), the *Government Gazette,* appears in Brunei only in 1951, and the first private magazine, *Salam Seria*, in 1952.[28] In this respect, the situation is representative of that prevailing in the equatorial zones of insular Southeast Asia, where it is very difficult to find traces of permanent and stable settlements of a certain importance, either in the first millennium of our era or in prehistoric times.[29] However, once reintegrated into Southeast Asian generality, the temporality proper to Brunei that can be glimpsed through these materials proves to be meaningful.

On this basis, one hypothesis may be formulated about the constitution of the Bruneian entity as follows.[30] Descended from an Austronesian proto-historic substratum similar to those of other societies from western Borneo, three polities followed one another in Brunei, in response to the evolution of maritime trade until the end of the 19th century: (1) a merchant chiefdom that controlled the Brunei River and gradually became Indianised from the second half of the first millennium of the Common Era; (2) an Islamised thalassocracy radiating largely beyond both sides of the bay to as far as Palawan and Sambas; (3) an evanescent sultanate reduced to the confluence of the Kedayan and Brunei Rivers.

---

[28] Rozan Yunus, "History of Brunei Newspapers", *Brunei Times*, 7 July 2007.

[29] Peter Bellwood, *Man's Conquest of the Pacific: The Prehistory of Southeast Asia and Oceania* (New York: Oxford University Press, 1979), p. 126.

[30] See a brief glimpse of the confrontation between the ideas of Mohd. Jamil Al-Sufri and of Robert Nicholl in A.V.M. Horton, *Turun-temurun: A Dissection of Brunei Darussalam*, 2nd ed. (Bordesley: A.V.M. Horton, 1998), pp. 162–4.

PREMISES AND EMERGENCE OF THE BRUNEIAN THALASSOCRACY

First Settlements and End of the Ice Age (40,000 BCE–600 CE)

End of the Ice Age

The prehistory of Borneo, from which Brunei emerges, can be surmised through the vestiges of the oldest stratum of the Niah cave in Sarawak.[1] They testify to the presence of Australo-Melanesians around 40,000 BCE, during the Ice Age when Borneo and Palawan were linked to the continent west of the Wallace-Huxley Line which separated the former continents of Sunda[2] and Sahul. The following stratum of the site reveals the presence of "pre-Hoabinians", characterised by a more elaborate lithic industry that was maintained until around 16,000 BCE,[3] which marks a glacial paroxysm. Then began a long process of water rising for more than 10,000 years, which gradually led to the creation of Southeast Asia

[1] Located 110 km west of Miri, at the border of the current territory of Brunei, in a region formerly controlled (at least on its coastal and river shores) by the sultanate.
[2] See J. Allen, J. Golson and R. Jones, *Sunda and Sahul: Prehistoric Studies in Southeast Asia, Melanesia and Australia* (London and New York: Academic Press, 1977), 647 p.
[3] Bellwood, *Man's conquest of the Pacific: The Prehistory of Southeast Asia and Oceania*, p. 83.

in two parts, insular (Nusantarian)[4] and peninsular (Indochinese), reducing by 40% the emergent land and increasing by four-fifths the length of the coasts.[5] Thus the affected populations had no choice but to go on the move. The gradual submersion[6] touched the Hoabinians (proto-Melanesians characterised by a diet composed partially of food they grew and by a new type of stone-working) of the Nusantarian world, which lasted until around 8000 BCE in Borneo (Niah sites) and in the Malay Peninsula (Gua Cha). The societies of the future Insulindia appeared relatively conservative at the time, with respect to the Neolithic revolution that spread from the lower valley of the Huanghe to southern China, then to the Indochinese Peninsula around 5000 BCE, although it is impossible to speak with certainty of the spread of techniques from one point to another, or their concomitant emergence.

Austronesian Migrations

Then began the descent of the coastal populations from south of the Yangzijiang toward Taiwan, which can be detected thanks to their microliths. One group reached Philippines, then Borneo via Palawan, while others headed toward Sulawesi and the Indonesian east, and yet others to Java. These "proto-Austronesians" migrated between 4000 and 3000 BCE.[7] With respect to land routes, a Neolithic proto-agriculture descended along the Peninsula, introduced by immigrants probably of Mongoloid stock, as evidenced by the Gua Kecil site near Pahang (the appearance of pottery),[8] signifying the end of the Melanesian "Bacsonians".[9] In synchrony, for the archipelagos, the Neolithic usage of ceramics and cultivation of rice reached the Austronesian populations of

---

[4] From *Nusantara*, defined as "archipelago" in W.J.S. Poerwadarminta, *Kamus umum bahasa Indonesia* [*Indonesian General Dictionary*] (Jakarta: Balai Pustaka, 1976), p. 679.

[5] Jacques Népote, *Histoire du Champa* (Paris: unpublished, 1999), p. 54 n. 123.

[6] Ian C. Glover, "Agricultural origins in East Asia", in *The Cambridge Encyclopaedia of Archaeology*, ed. Andrew Sherratt (Cambridge: Cambridge University Press, 1980), p. 152.

[7] See the historical map of Austronesian migrations in Peter Bellwood, "The Austronesian Dispersal and the Origin of Languages", *Scientific American* 7 (July 1991): 70–5.

[8] Per Sorensen, "La Préhistoire de la Thaïlande", in *Grand Atlas de l'Archéologie*, ed. C. Flon (Paris: Encyclopedia Universalis, 1985), p. 252.

[9] Present essentially in South China and the Indochinese Peninsula, the "Bacsonians" are characterised by the polishing of stone tools.

Philippines around 2500 BCE, then Palawan,[10] Borneo (c. 2300 BCE)[11] and the rest of Insulindia. The Austronesians (or Malayo-Polynesians in J. Wisseman Christie's terms)[12] developed the elements of a cosmology that conveyed the appearance of megalithism,[13] linked to worship of the earth and revealing the start of social structuration (appearance of a society of ranks)[14] and a "fixing" of land (people began to settle down), while their sociocultural identity and organisation[15] remained linked to material circulation and exchange, as illustrated by the evidence of proto-historic navigation[16] and the recurrence of the ship theme in iconography and in funeral rites,[17] especially in Borneo.

---

[10] Site of Tabon III; see Florent Détroit et al., "Upper Pleistocene *Homo sapiens* from the Tabon cave (Palawan, The Philippines): Description and Dating of New Discoveries", *Comptes rendus Palevol* 3, 8 (2004): 705–12.

[11] P. Beavitt, E. Kurui and G. Thompson, "Confirmation of an early date for the presence of rice in Borneo: preliminary evidence for possible Bidayuh/Asian links", *BRB* 27 (1996): 29–37.

[12] Jan Wisseman Christie, "State Formation in Early Maritime Southeast Asia: A Consideration of the Theories and the Data", *Bijdragen tot de Taal-, Land- en Volkenkunde* 151, 2 (1995): 240.

[13] Bellwood, *Man's Conquest of the Pacific: The Prehistory of Southeast Asia and Oceania*, p. 106. While megalithism is still active on the Island of Nias, western Sumatra, there are traces of it everywhere: one of the most remarkable traces in several Southeast Asian cultures is the practice of double inhumation, first in jars (deriving directly from stone funerary urns), followed by cremation (Theravada Buddhism) or burial (Malay world).

[14] Christie, "State Formation in Early Maritime Southeast Asia", quoting the work of A. Wurm and B. Wilson, *English Finderlist of Reconstructions in Austronesian Languages* (*Post-Brandstetter*) (Canberra: Department of Linguistics, Research School of Pacific Studies, Pacific Linguistics, Ser. C. no. 33, ANU, 1975), xxxii, 246 p.

[15] The political vocabulary retains a memory of this mode of constituting society beyond the proto-historical period, cf. Pierre-Yves Manguin, "Shipshape Societies: Boat Symbolism and Political Systems in Insular Southeast Asia", in *Southeast Asia in the 9th to 14th Centxuries*, ed. D.G. Marr and A.D. Milner (Singapore: ISEAS and Canberra: ANU, 1986), pp. 187–213; Denys Lombard, "Le thème de la mer dans les littératures de l'Archipel", *Archipel* 20 (1980): 317–28.

[16] Many fragments of boats have been found on sites from 500 BCE to the 400–500 CE (ibid., p. 244); and Pierre-Yves Manguin, "Research on the Ships of Śrīvijaya [and of First Millennium AD Southeast Asia]", in *SPAFA Consultative Workshop on Archaeological and Environmental Studies on Śrīvijaya, Final Report* (Bangkok: SEAMEO, 1985), pp. 291–306.

[17] From one end of the archipelago to the other and over a long period, wooden sarcophagi evoke the boat theme, of which the best known are those of the Torajas in Sulawesi and the coffins in the form of a dugout canoe in the Niah cave, dated about 780 CE (B.A.V. Peacock, "Recent Archaeological Discoveries in Malaysia", *JMBRAS* 38, 1 [1965]: 248–55).

In Indochina a regional cultural complex appeared about 600 BCE, revolving around a Bronze Age civilisation that is usually called by default the "Dongsonian"[18] (cult of the Mountain King and diffusion of bronze drums from Yunnan and Tonkin on dual north-south and west-east axes, from Burma to New Guinea), which coincides on the maritime front with megalithic cults. The synchronic arrival in Southeast Asia of iron (which first penetrated the Peninsula by means of trade with India)[19] and of bronze between 500 and 200 BCE[20] marked the lingering end of the Neolithic, while the Indian Maurya emperors launched in the third century BCE a missionary Buddhist project targeting the Peninsula. While their enthusiasm quickly subsided, the intensification of exchanges with the Mediterranean Sea pushed India to procure spices at their sources, which at the start of the Christian era accounts for the presence of Greco-Roman objects in the Malay Straits (Palembang, Sunda) and in Patthalung (southeast of current Thailand). And with the resumption of the imperial thrust under the Han Dynasty around 120 BCE, which stimulated trade and resulted in the official opening of routes with India and Southeast Asia, Insulindia, whose sailors regularly frequented the coasts of Dravidian India,[21] became the "toll barrier" for inter-Asian trade. One of its articulations was the Isthmus of Kra, which ensured the transhipment of merchandise between the two seas. Among the sought-after merchandise was copper, present in abundance in parts of the Peninsula, Philippines, Sumatra and Timor, which circulated from one pole to the other. And in the other direction, Southeast Asian bronze was exported to India, as evidenced by the presence of bronzes with a high pewter content coming from U Thong (current Thailand) in Taxila (north Pakistan).[22] Borneo, situated on the route leading from Philippines

[18] Note that the term "Dongsonian", when used to refer to the Bronze period regardless of ethnic identities, is merely a historical "catch-all" (Népote, *Histoire du Champa*, p. 54 n. 123).
[19] Népote, ibid., p. 60.
[20] Bellwood, *Man's Conquest of the Pacific: The Prehistory of Southeast Asia and Oceania*, pp. 106, 127.
[21] All the shipwrecks found in Southeast Asia dating from the proto-historic age and the first centuries CE are Southeast Asian (P.-Y. Manguin, "Research on the Ships of Śrīvijaya [and of First Millennium AD Southeast Asia]", 1985).
[22] Ian C. Glover, *Early Trade between India and Southeast Asia: A Link in the Development of a World Trading System* (Hull: University of Hull Occasional Paper no. 16, 1990), pp. 29ff.

to the Peninsula and possessing (like Sumatra) a series of small deposits of lateritic iron, was already integrated into the "great" Southeast Asian trade: many beads of glass or stone, of Indian provenance, have been discovered in various megalithic sepulchres, as well as bronze drums of a Dongsonian type, in Sambas[23] and more than ten other sites.[24]

Funan and Indianisation

At the end of a century-and-a-half of accelerated trade, a thalassocracy centred on the Mekong Delta took shape, capable of managing exchanges between India and China: Funan,[25] which sent embassies to the Han Court in 89 and 105. Thus Indianisation moved along the coasts of the future Champa (today Central Vietnam), where appeared a first series of Sanskrit inscriptions (first to third centuries).[26] Judging by the epigraphy, by the start of the fourth century, Indianisation had in turn reached the Malay Peninsula (Penang, Kedah, Perak); in parallel, it was confirmed in the north-east of the Peninsula with the constitution in Champa of a Shivait kingdom. Chinese trade opened a second route through the archipelagos, running along Luzon, Palawan, the west coast of Borneo and the Sunda Strait (Chinese sources report a Ko-Ying[27] chieftainship in west Java, where Hellenistic objects from the first three centuries CE have been found). Crossing by the Isthmus of Kra was finally abandoned in the fifth century, in favour of passage through the Malacca Strait, and inscriptions along it multiplied. Funan, at its apogee, exercised a form of suzerainty there.

Along this second route, via Borneo and the Sunda Strait, are located the oldest Sanskrit inscriptions of Insulindia.

---

[23] Heger I type (E.E. McKinnon, "The Sambas hoard: bronze drums, and gold ornaments found in Kalimantan in 1991", *JMBRAS* 67 [1994]: 9–28).

[24] John N. Miksic, "Evolving Archaeological Perspectives in Southeast Asia, 1970–95", *JSAS* (March 1995): 46–62.

[25] See the medallion of the Roman Emperor Antonius Pius (152) found at Oc-eo. For an overview, see Michael Vickery, "Funan Reviewed: Deconstructing the Ancients", *BEFEO* 90, 1 (2003): 101–43; and quite recently Éric Bourdonneau, "Réhabiliter le Funan—Óc Eo ou la première Angkor", *BEFEO* 94 (2007): 111–58, which contests the hypothesis of a pure thalassocracy based on findings from new archaeological digs.

[26] Those of Võ Cạnh, cf. Jean Filliozat, "L'inscription dite de Võ Cạnh", *BEFEO* 55 (1969): 107–16, and of Kauthara (end of the fourth century).

[27] Annals of Liang—see the most recent translation by Richard L. Davis, ed., *Historical Records of the Five Dynasties* [*by Ouyang Xiu*] (New York: Columbia University Press, 2004), 736 p.

First, in Borneo, on the Kutai site (east coast, relatively far inland and without any other vestige), a group of seven *yūpa* (ceremonial pillars) bear a series of Sanskrit inscriptions, in a kind of writing that originated in South India. These mention an Austronesian name relating to a "chieftainship of the vegetal" (*Kundungan*, *kundung* refers to a tree in Iban)[28] among the royal lineage, which attests to the presence of an indigenous Indianised political entity.[29] At Batu Pahat[30] (West Kalimantan), near the source of Tekarek (a tributary of Kapuas) in a region that exported gold, were found Buddhist epigraphs of the fifth century very similar to those discovered in Kedah between the valleys of Merbok and Muda. Their semantics and orthodoxy suggest the presence of Indian rather than Indianised communities. Finally an epigraph of the same type as that of Batu Pahat was discovered in Brunei very near the coast, which also suggests an "Indian" presence.

Second, in Java, five inscriptions show the existence of an Indianised kingdom in Taruma (in the region of Jakarta today), situated not far from the port settlements used during the first half of the first millennium where objects originating in southern India have been discovered.

By the time Indianisation reached the east of Java in the sixth century, followed by Bali—that is to say, the zones with the strongest demographic concentrations in the archipelago—it could be considered to be well established in insular Southeast Asia.

At the Intersection of Archaeological and Textual Data, A Hypothesis about the Entry of Brunei in History

In the light of both the paucity of data and the Bruneian myth of foundation (the first ten episodes[31] of the *Sya'ir Awang Simawn* [*Epic of the Ancient One*]), it is possible to reconstruct the origins of the *Barunay*,

[28] Kuṇḍuṅga, grandfather of the king Mūlavarman; see Christie, "State Formation in Early Maritime Southeast Asia": 262.

[29] S. Supomo, "Indic Transformation: The Sanskritization of Jawa and the Javanization of the Bharata", in *The Austronesians: Historical and Comparative Perspectives*, ed. Peter S. Bellwood, James J. Fox and Darrell T. Tryon (Canberra: ANU, 1995), pp. 310ff.

[30] See H.G. Quaritch Wales, *The Making of Greater India*, 3rd ed. (London: Bernard Quaritch, 1974), pp. 99ff.

[31] These episodes take place solely in the western part of the Brunei Bay and in Labuan (A.R. Maxwell, "Accessing the Epic Status of the Brunei Malay Sya'ir Awang Simawn").

whose ethnonym (independently of contemporary and mythographical re-interpretation)[32] evokes the vegetal, in the manner of the Cham clans of the areca[33] and the coconut palm trees or the epigraphy of Kutai.[34] Similarly the Bisayah/Murut group, who are established in the environs of Temburong and live off fishing and other sea products, is presented as coming from Nature. According to the myth,[35] the *Barunay* entered history after the female elements of society met with a foreign masculine element[36] that carried the "cultural" novelty of an alliance among masculine networks, represented by solidarity among the 14 sons of the paternal ancestor. After a race in dugout canoes, the founders are said to have secured the best port location of the bay, the Brunei River, and from this base, brought together various communities established in its perimeter by setting up a chain of riverbank tributaries. This archetypal dimension of the myth and the matrilineal substratum of society are illustrated by the fact that the *Sya'ir Awang Simawn*[37] was usually recited (until two decades ago) by women during marriage rituals.[38] On this

---

[32] The discoverer of the site is said to have cried "*Baru nah!*" or "Here it is!". This is constantly evoked in contemporary mythography, for example, "Treasuring Brunei Past", *Brunei Times*, 3 March 2007.

[33] Story 21 in Aristide Marre, *Sadjârah malâyou, le Livre des chroniques malaises depuis les origines jusqu'à la conquête de Malaka par les Portugais, en 1511*, Vaucresson, 1900, In-8°, pp. 81–311.

[34] Myth aside, the Malay word *berunai* (Iban: *berenai*) refers to a specie of euphorbia, *antidesma neurocarpum*, a shrub of the secondary forest that grows in alluvial soil after 40 years of pruning and has edible fruits. It is commonly found on the heights bordering the Brunei River. See Endela Tipot, Jacqualine Henry and Chai P.K. Paul, *Management of the Pulong Tau National Park—resource use by the Penan Communities*, Sarawak, National Tropical Timber Organization, Sarawak Forest Department, Sarawak Forestry Corporation, ITTO Project PD 224/03 Rev. 1, s.d. [c. 2007], p. 75; and *Flora of Merimbun Heritage Park*, BSB, Tutong no. 13063 (collected in 2000).

[35] See a synoptic analysis of the two Malay myths of foundation present in *Sejarah Melayu* and in *Hikayat Banjar* by J.J. Ras, *Hikajat Bandjar: A Study in Malay Historiography* (The Hague: Bibliotheca Indosinica, Martinus Nijhoff, 1968), pp. 173–201.

[36] Descended from a heavenly egg (D.E. Brown, *Brunei: The Structure and History of a Bornean Malay Sultanate* [Brunei: Brunei Museum, 1970], p. 134), he begot 14 sons of different mothers, including Awang Simawn. On symbolism of the egg, see D.E. Brown, "Hiranyagarbha, the Hindu cosmic egg—and Brunei's Royal line", *BMJ* 4, 4 (1980): 30–7.

[37] Maxwell, "Who is Awang Simawn?", p. 188.

[38] The Sakai of Kampung Saba (in Kampung Ayer) being considered as the genuine owner of the myth (Brown, *Brunei: The Structure and History of a Bornean Malay Sultanate*, p. 53).

basis, the proto-Bruneians must have entered into contact with the Dongsonian, either directly or via their various epigones, as evidenced even today by their mastery of bronze techniques.[39]

After several centuries of absence from proto-history, Brunei Bay was becoming (from the fifth century at least) fully implicated in the Southeast Asian port network, as indicated by the presence of Indian merchants on its coast (shown by the inscription mentioned above), who were attracted by the trade in camphor and other medicinal products, although there is no evidence of any actual Indianisation of the site.

[39] One illustration of this is the multiplication of *bedil* (bronze cannons) exported from Brunei to the Malay Peninsula, cf. Tom Harrisson, "Brunei cannons—their role in Southeast Asia", *BMJ* 1, 1 (1969): 94–118.

Brunei from Srivijaya to the Ming Dynasty (7th–15th Centuries)

The Southeast Asian maritime networks were reconfigured again at the end of the sixth century after the disappearance of Funan, which came under attack from its former Khmer vassals of Chenla. This paved the way for new centres of power.

First the point of intersection of the Indian Ocean and the China Sea networks, southeast of Sumatra in the region of Palembang, where the kingdom of Srivijaya was established, whose sovereigns took on the Funanese title of "Mountain King".[39] The growing importance of straight navigation made rounding the Malay Peninsula the favoured trade route between the Chinese empire (at the time the largest market in the world) and the Indian Ocean, and from there to the Middle East, along a series of relays leading from Canton to the Pallava Kingdom (in southeast India), via Champa and/or Borneo. Indian and Chinese presences are evident at the start of the Tang era along the west coasts of Borneo, especially in the delta of the Sarawak River.[40] Around 670 CE, Srivijaya, whose influence extended as far north as Ligor,[41] ceded to the demands

[39] Christie, "State Formation in Early Maritime Southeast Asia": 273.

[40] Barbara Harrisson, "Recent Archaeological Discoveries in Malaysia, 1962–1963, Borneo", *JMBRAS* 37, 2 (1964): 192–200; F.E. Treloar, "The Composition of Gold Artefacts from Santubong and Gedong, Sarawak", *SMJ* 25, 46 (1977): 9–17.

[41] Georges Cœdès, *Les États hindouisés d'Indochine et d'Indonésie* (Paris: E. de Boccard, 1964), p. 170.

of Chinese diplomacy and became a tributary of Tang China.[42] The upheavals caused by the trade boom were such that in south Borneo, the peoples south of the Barito River took part (or were forced to take part) in a vast emigration movement that would take them all the way to Madagascar.[43]

Then in Java, where Chinese sources describe a new entity of Buddhist allegiance, Holing,[44] at the start of the eighth century, began the process of forming a Javanese kingship. This translated into rivalry among the princely houses, which built Indo-Buddhist monuments scattered across central Java. For example, the Sailendra, which took on the same Funanese title as Srivijaya,[45] erected the vast stupa of Borobudur c. 760 and pushed back their rival, the Shivait dynasty of Sanjaya, to the east. A decade later, the Javanese were able to destroy the Cham capital of Po Nagar (774), then carry out a series of raids on Cambodia.[46] The decline of the Sailendra paved the way for the Kingdom of Mataram,[47] which seemed to have succeeded in unifying the island at the end of the ninth century.

---

[42] Srivijaya sent embassies in 695, 702, 724, 728 and 742 (Gabriel Ferrand, *L'empire sumatranais de Çrīvijaya* [Paris: Imprimerie nationale, 1922], pp. 7ff).

[43] These groups were already in contact with Indianised peoples, see Claude Allibert, "Migration austronésienne et mise en place de la civilisation malgache", *Diogenes* 218 (2007/2): 7–16; and Alexander Adelaar, "The Indonesian Migrations to Madagascar: Making Sense of the Multidisciplinary Evidence", in *Proceedings of the International Symposium*, ed. Truman Simanjuntak, Ingrid H.E. Pojoh and Mohammad Hisyam (Jakarta: LIPI, 2006), electronic edition, http://www.santafe.edu/events/workshops/images/6/6d/IndonesianMigrations.pdf.

[44] This identification is contested by Roland Braddell, "Notes on Ancient Times in Malaya", in *The Study of Ancient Times in the Malay Peninsula and Straits of Malacca* (Kuala Lumpur: MBRAS, 1980), who considers that Holing must have been located on the west coast of Borneo. However, since the well-known Chinese pilgrim I Ching states that Poli is located east of Holing, this raises the problem of locating Poli. The polity could not be Brunei, given Chinese historical linguistics and the fact that the *Universal Geography of the Taiping Era, Taiping huan yu ji* 太平環宇記 (written in 976–983) states that Boni was absent from the census up till that point.

[45] Cœdès, *Les États hindouisés d'Indochine et d'Indonésie*, p. 168.

[46] For the controversy on the interpretation of the events, see Michel Ferlus, "Localisation, identité et origine du Javā de Jayavarman II", *Aséanie* 26 (2010): 65–81; Arlo Griffiths, "The problem of the Ancient Name Java", *Archipel* 85 (2013): 43–81.

[47] Construction of the Prambanan complex.

Entry of Brunei into the Orbit of Srivijaya

In this context of growing competition between Srivijaya's well-established thalassocracy,[48] which maintained diplomatic relations with both India and China in the tenth century (embassies were resumed c. 904), and a rising Javanese power in the hands of Mataram for the time being, and the resultant recurrent wars, appeared a polity located in the Brunei Bay.[49] At the end of the tenth century, the *Universal Geography of the Taiping Era*[50] (written in 978) mentions sending a first embassy from *Boni* (渤泥[51]) in 977, named a "country" in collateral sources,[52] specifying that the said entity had hitherto been absent from geographical recensions.[53] Carried by a Sino-Muslim ship, the emissaries brought gifts of camphor, tortoiseshell, sandalwood and six elephant tusks to the emperor.

Where was this *Boni*? Equidistant from Champa, the principal trading power of the Indochinese Peninsula important enough for the South China Sea to be called in Chinese and Arab sources the "Champa Sea", and from Mindoro, this excludes locating *Boni* southwest of Borneo, which is half as close to Champa as to Mindoro, if we stick to Chinese sources, which have been documenting Champa[54] since the start

---

[48] Srivijaya destroyed the Cham capital of Indrapura in 982.

[49] Excavations of the site of Barus (Sumatra) dismiss the hypothesis of Robert Nichol, *JSSA* 14, 1 (March 1983): 32–45, that the toponym mentioned by Abu Dulaf ("... then I went to the Country of Camphor which is a high mountain, where the towns overlook the sea, including *Qamrūn* from which comes a delicate aloe wood called *Mandal al-Qamrūnī*..."), cited in G.R. Tibbetts, *A Study of the Arabic Texts Containing Material on Southeast Asia* (Leiden: Brill, 1979), p. 40, must be Brunei, since the description corresponds much more to the site of Barus-Lobu Tua than to various archaeological sites in Brunei. See C. Guillot, ed., *Histoire de Barus (Sumatra), Le site de Lobu Tua—Vol. I: Études et documents*, 284 p; *Vol. II: Étude archéologique et documents*, 342 p (Paris: Cahiers d'Archipel, 1998 and 2003).

[50] For a critical study of the texts, see Kurz, *Boni in Chinese Sources*.

[51] For the transliteration of 渤泥 "*Boni*" as Brunei, based on historical linguistics, see Frédéric Pain, "Note", unpublished, 2009.

[52] *Boni guo* 渤泥國, in Li Tao 李濤, *Xu Zizhi tongjian changbian* 續資治通鑑長編, which resumes the annals lost today, quoted in Kurz, *Boni in Chinese Sources*, p. 16.

[53] Fan Chuo 樊綽 mentions a *Boni* 渤泥 in the *Manshu* 蠻書 c. 890, that is, a century earlier, but provides no further details.

[54] R.A. Stein, "Le Lin-yi. Sa localisation, sa contribution à la formation du Champa et ses liens avec la Chine", Pékin, *Han-hiue, Bulletin du Centre d'études Sinologiques de Pékin* 2, 1–3 (1947): 334 p; Georges Maspero, *Le royaume de Champa*, 2nd ed. (Paris: EFEO, 1988), 278 p.

of the first millennium CE). *Boni*[55] is described in these sources as a group of 14 geo-administrative lands, hilly and very humid, whose population grows rice, is ignorant of ceramics and buries its dead (at least the adults) in the surrounding hills. This description might have applied to more than one site in Borneo or Philippines, except that: (1) soldiers wear tubular armour of bronze (such armour is mentioned by the Spaniards in 1578[56]), which favours the identification of *Boni* with the actual Brunei; and (2) the number of "prefectures"—to use the Chinese term—of Brunei corresponds to the number of brothers, who were each in charge of a territory situated around the Brunei Bay, in the Bruneian myth of foundation *Sya'ir Awang Simawn*, whereas outside Brunei, only Srivijaya (then designated *Shi Li Fo Shi*[57] in Chinese sources) in the tenth century comprised the same number of territorial components.[58] Add to these data the fact that camphor is produced only in Baros (northwest of Sumatra) or in the northwest of Borneo, the latter region, moreover, possessing till today a variety of elephants that are smaller than their equivalents in the Peninsula.

Whether or not it was located where the current Brunei capital lies, a political entity did exist around the Brunei Bay in the tenth century. It was more or less subservient to Srivijaya, whose territorial network it copied. Trading with Champa and Mindoro (via Sulu), and in contact with the Indo-Persian trade networks[59] as well as—judging by Chinese

---

[55] The excavations led by P.-Y. Manguin ("Palembang et Sriwijaya: anciennes hypothèses et recherches nouvelles [Palembang Ouest]", *BEFEO* 76, 1 [1987]: 366) have enabled a reconstitution of the riverbank site of Palembang, which refutes the hypothesis of Robert Nicholl ["The Sribuza of Capitain Buzurg", *BMJ* 5, 2 (1982): 1–11] that the Sribuza described by Abū Zayd (Ferrand, Gabriel, *Relations de voyages et textes géographiques arabes, persans et turks relatifs à l'Extrême-Orient, traduits et annotés par* [Paris: E. Leroux, 1913], p. 84) might have been located on the Brunei Bay.

[56] John S. Carroll, "Francisco de Sande's invasion of Brunei in 1578: An Anonymous Spanish Account", *BMJ* 6, 2 (1986): 55.

[57] *Shi Li Fo Shi* 尸利坲誓.

[58] *Xin Tang Shu* 新唐书, cited by O.W. Wolters, *The Fall of Śrīvijaya in Malay History* (Kuala Lumpur: Oxford University Press, 1970), p. 9.

[59] A Persian gold coin of 960, identified as such by the British Museum, was discovered among later objects of the 13th–14th centuries among the "treasure of Limbang" at the end of the 19th century, but it disappeared inadvertently from the Sarawak Treasury during World War Two (Tom Harrisson, "The Golden Hoard of Limbang", *BMJ* 1 [1969]: 59). Moreover, the first embassy from *Boni* to the Chinese Court was sent after the coming of the Arab merchant Puluxie 蒲盧歇 (Kurz, *Boni in Chinese Sources*, p. 4).

sources—with sandalwood-producing zones from East Java to Timor,[60] Brunei was regularly frequented by Sino-Muslim ships sailed by people who had mastered the routes to and from China, unlike those living around the Bay.

The taking of the capital of Champa by the Kinh,[61] then the expeditions of the rival maritime empire Chola (Tanjore) against Srivijaya in 1017 and 1025, and the capture of the sovereign c. 1070,[62] turned away a portion of its trade. Coupled with the Chinese commercial decline caused by the end of the Tang and the rise of the Northern Song,[63] this entailed a drop in "indigenous" Southeast Asian exchanges: over the course of 70 years, Srivijaya sent only 5 embassies to China.[64] So it is not surprising that Brunei[65] waited until 1082 to dispatch another embassy, following in the footsteps of Srivijaya,[66] which rushed three diplomatic missions to Kaifeng in that year.[67]

After the dislocation of its main competitor, the Indian Chola empire, c. 1150 and the rising competition from Southern Chinese whose naval innovations allowed both the building of high-seas junks and straightforward navigation,[68] Srivijaya reorganised its trade. The consequence was the take-off of Quanzhou[69] at the nexus of itineraries that

---

[60] Paul Wheatley, "Geographical Notes on some commodities involved in Sung Maritime Trade", *JMBRAS* 32, 2 (1959): 1–139, fig. 4.

[61] Champa moved its capital a few dozen kilometres to the south and henceforth protected its borders.

[62] Hermann Kulke, K. Kesavapany and Vijay Sakhuja, eds., *Nagapattinam to Suvarnadwipa: reflections on Chola naval expeditions to Southeast Asia* (Singapore: ISEAS, 2009), 337 p.

[63] Under the Song, the income from maritime customs rose from 0.5 million *guan* (貫, ligature of 1,000 *sapeques*) at the start of the 11th century to 65 million *guan* in 1189 (Jacques Gernet, *Le monde chinois* [Paris: Armand Colin, 1972], p. 285).

[64] 1028, 1067, 1082, 1083, and yet another between 1094 and 1097 (G. Ferrand, *L'empire sumatranais de Çrīvijaya*, p. 22; and Claudine Salmon, "Srivijaya, la Chine et les marchands chinois", *Archipel* 63 [2002]: 57–78).

[65] *Boni* 勃泥, *Song huiyao* 宋會要 [*Institutions of the Song*], Kurz, *Boni in Chinese Sources*, p. 14.

[66] *Sanfoci* 三佛齐.

[67] A few years later, at the height of its glory due to the erosion of the Cholas, Srivijaya established a monopoly on sandalwood by increasing the prices (So Kee-Long, "Dissolving hegemony or changing trade pattern? Images of Srivijaya in the Chinese sources of the twelfth and thirteenth centuries", *JSAS* 29, 2 [1998]: 295–308).

[68] J. Gernet, *Le Monde chinois*, pp. 287ff.

[69] Roderich Ptak, "From Quanzhou to the Sulu Zone and Beyond: Questions Related to the Early Fourteenth Century", *JSAS* 29, 2 (1998): 269–94.

enabled either direct access to the source of spices and sandalwood in the Moluccas and Timor (avoiding Srivijaya), or access to the Malay straits via Palawan and Borneo. During the first half of the 13th century, the erosion of Srivijaya power, whose northern tributaries in the Malay Peninsula also rejected tutelage,[70] and the maritime routes of the Malay straits, benefited Javanese thalassocracies that were closer to the spices, such as the kingdom of Singhasari, founded in 1222.

Brunei was increasingly frequented by merchants from South China. This is corroborated by the mention of *Boni* twice in Chinese sources (c. 1151 and 1206)[71] for its eagle wood (aloes) and especially its camphor. Recent (2002) archaeological data reveals an abundance of coins and artefacts of the Song period, particularly at Sungai Limau Manis,[72] about 30 km from the present-day capital, where the number of shards is

---

[70] Cœdès, *Les États hindouisés d'Indochine et d'Indonésie*, p. 336.

[71] So Kee-Long, ibid.

[72] Pg. Dr. Karim bin Pengiran Haji Osman, *Sungai Limau Manis: Tapak Arkeologi Abad Ke-10-13 Masihi* [*Sungai Limau Manis, archaeological remains from the 10th–13th centuries CE*], BSB, Jabatan Muzium-Muzium Brunei, Kementerian Kebudayaan, Belia dan Sukan, 2004, 175 p. See also the synopsis of the exhibition "The Islamic Sultanate of Brunei: Past and Present Culture" at SOAS of London in early 2009, http://www.soas.ac.uk/gallery/brunei/. The "capital" status of Limau Manis seems corroborated by the account published by Carroll, "Francisco de Sande's invasion of Brunei in 1578", p. 52, which mentions a first capital situated a little less than 25 km upstream from today's Bandar Seri Begawan. Limau Manis is also mentioned in the *Sya'ir Awang Simawn* (3rd part), Maxwell, "Accessing the Epic Status of the Brunei Malay Sya'ir Awang Simawn", p. 14. We can get an idea of the site's importance by comparing it to Santubong (Sarawak). About 49,600 shards of Song terra cotta pottery and more than 1,000 bronze coins were found in Limau Manis (Pg. Dr. Karim bin Pg. Haji Osman, ibid., p. 19), across a length of 1,156 m (on both sides of the river) and some 50 m from the banks, on an explored zone of some 2 km^2. About 49,400 shards of Tang and Song pottery and stone jars (Cheng Te-k'un, *Studies in Chinese Archaeology* [Hong Kong: Chinese University Press, 1982], p. 46) were found on the principal site of the Santubong dig, Bongkissam, across a length of 800 m. In comparison, only 1,312 shards were discovered in West Palembang, cf. P.-Y. Manguin, "Palembang et Sriwijaya: anciennes hypothèses et recherches nouvelles (Palembang Ouest)", *BEFEO* 76, 1 (1987): 359. Given the quantity of shards and vestiges of habitation found on the site, it is obviously not a funerary site. And despite the presence of some dozens of whole pieces shown by Pg. Dr. Karim bin Pg. Haji Osman, the hypothesis of the wreck of a Song trading junk is not likely either in view of the very shallow river (judging by the various Chinese accounts, junks traditionally dropped anchor at the entry to the Brunei river).

double that found in Kota Batu[73] (although it should be noted that it is difficult to compare the sizes of the two excavations which are separated by half a century). This completes the remains found on secondary sites such as Tanjung Batu[74] or Sungai Lumut.[75] The importance of Brunei in maritime networks was reasserted 20 years later (1225) by the fact that a controller from the maritime customs of Quanzhou (at the time the most important Chinese port for Southeast Asian trade), Zhao Rugua, included it in his compilation of trade data.[76] Comparison with the first tenth-century descriptions showed that in just two-and-a-half centuries, Brunei had prospered and was becoming "Indianised". Protected by a wooden palisade, it possessed 100 war pirogues[77] and included some 10,000 inhabitants (1,500–2,000 homes), who were essentially Buddhists. Its principal resources were camphor and tortoiseshell,[78] which were traded for textiles, gold and ceramics. Trade was subjected to a royal monopoly, under personal supervision of the sovereign; as in Srivijaya,[79] wealth—manifested by the use of silk and golden utensils[80]—was

[73] The first excavations show that two-thirds of the Chinese coins and most of the monochromes (apart from celadons) found in Kota Batu are from the Song era (Tom and Barbara Harrisson, "Kota Batu in Brunei", *SMJ* 23 [1956]: 283–318).

[74] Matussin bin Omar, "A preliminary account of surface finds from Tanjong Batu beach, Muara", *BMJ* 3 (1973): 158–74.

[75] Barbara Harrisson, "Sungai Lumut: A 15th century burial ground", *BMJ* 1 (1969): 24–56.

[76] Zhao Rugua 趙汝適, *Zhufanzhi* 諸蕃志 [*Record of all Barbarian countries*], translated by F. Hirth and W.W. Rockhill, *Chau Ju-kua: On the Chinese and Arab trade in the twelfth and thirteenth centuries, entitled Chu-fan-chi*, 2nd ed. (Amsterdam: Oriental Press, 1966), pp. 153ff.

[77] Pirogues 2, 5–3 m wide and 13–15 m long, crewed by 30–40 men; see François Valentyn, "A description of Borneo and our trade there", *BMJ* 4, 2 (1978): 79.

[78] More than 20 samples were discovered at the site of Limau Manis.

[79] Wolters, *The Fall of Śrīvijaya in Malay History*, pp. 13ff and Zhao Rugua, quoted by Ferrand, *L'empire sumatranais de Çrīvijaya*, pp. 10ff. Ibn Khurdādhbih and Abū Zayd state that each day the Maharaja of Srivijaya threw a gold ingot into a pool situated opposite the palace. Upon his death, the ingots were shared among the royal family, the dignitaries and the people (Ferrand, *Relations de voyages et textes géographiques arabes, persans et turks relatifs à l'Extrême-Orient*, p. 84, and K. Hall, *Maritime Trade and State Development in Early Southeast Asia* [Honolulu: University of Hawaii Press, 1985], pp. 80ff).

[80] Zhao Rugua, quoted in Kurz, *Boni in Chinese Sources*, p. 9.

indissociable from political power.[81] And by means of Quanzhou, the Zaitun of Arab merchants, Brunei increased contact with Muslim Chinese traders: the first Islamic epigraph of Brunei[82] is the stele of Pu Zongmin, originally from Quanzhou, who died in 1264.[83] This anteriority of Muslim presence in Brunei is corroborated by a Spanish source of 1578, which states that "there has been a mosque in Brunei for three centuries, and six 'Moorish' kings of that lineage",[84] claiming that locals and some Chinese residing in Brunei were the first to convert. This Islamic presence is also attested to by the genealogy of the sultans of Brunei. The five accessible *silsilah* mention the Chinese alliance, with two versions: the

[81] The *Sya'ir Awang Simawn* (Maxwell, "Accessing the Epic Status of the Brunei Malay Sya'ir Awang Simawn", stanza 55–7) relates a similar myth as that of Kutai (P.-Y. Manguin, "The Merchant and the King: Political myths of Southeast Asian coastal polities", *Indonesia* 52 [October 1991]: 44), where victory in cockfighting is a source of wealth, except that the loser in Brunei is not a Chinese merchant but a Majapahit prince.

[82] W. Franke and T'ieh-fan Ch'en, "A Chinese tomb inscription of A.D. 1264, discovered recently in Brunei", *BMJ* 3, 1 (1973): 91–9.

[83] As shown by W. Franke and Ch'en T'ieh-fan, 1973, ibid., p. 92, "there can be no doubt about the date". We cannot say the same about *Xishan zazhi* 西山杂志 by Cao Yongjian 蔡永蒹, which links Brunei's Pu Gongbei to the famous Pu family of Quanzhou. According to the *Xishan zazhi*, the Pu family served the Song for five generations but rebelled at the end of the Southern Song era, with the result that one of its branches settled in the Philippines. The presumed chief censor, Pu Zongmin, born in Quanzhou, was sent to *Boni* in 1247. His oldest son, Pu Ying, was said to have settled in Brunei and the second son to have been responsible for trade with the Western Ocean (K.H. Hall, "Sojourning Communities, Ports-of-Trade, and Agrarian Based Societies in Southeast Asian Eastern Regions, 1000–1300" [University of Hawaii, Center for Southeast Asian Studies, 26 October 2007], f. 4, www.hawaii.edu/cseas/download/pdf/UHM.CSEAS.Brownbag.20071026). But Xie Fang 谢方, "Ye tan Wen Lai Pu Gongbei yu xi shan za zhi Pu Cuo de guan xi 也谈文莱《蒲公碑》与《西山杂志蒲厝》的关系 [Relations between "Pu Gongbei" discovered in Brunei and the "Pu cuo" of *Xi Shan Za Zhi*]", *Hai Jiao Shi Yan Jiu* 海交史研究 [*Maritime History Studies*] 1 (1998): 104–8), stressing the significant anomalies in the *Xishan zazhi*, already demonstrated that it was composed around 1880 and that no serious link could be established between the Pu Zongmin of the Fujian sources and the Pu Gongbei of Brunei (many thanks to Claudine Salmon for having drawn my attention to the doubtful historicity of the *Xishan zazhi*). On the discovery of the *Xishan zazhi* of Cao Yongjian by Lin Shaochuan, and photographs of the manuscript, see *Xiamen wanbao* 厦门晚报, 26 June 2006, http://wap.qzwb.com/qzx/content/2006-08/16/content_2162309.htm?COLLCC=2621617060&..

[84] Carroll, "Francisco de Sande's invasion of Brunei in 1578", p. 51.

first states that the second sultan married the daughter of a Chinese "official"[85] while the second, that the first sultan was succeeded by his Chinese son-in-law.[86]

The Double Game of Tribute and Islam

Pax Mongolica and the Growing Importance of Brunei

In reopening land trade routes, then engaging in the conquest of south China, the advent of the Mongols (Yuan) radically upset regional geopolitics. In order to ensure control of the Indochinese Peninsula, they put the Thai populations (who formed most of their land troops in the southern Empire) on the move, resulting in the formation of the kingdoms of Lan Na and Sukhothai. The latter extended rapidly over the Malay Peninsula to the detriment of Srivijaya, which also had to deal with the desire for autonomy of the kingdom of Melayu (Jambi, in Sumatra), which did not hesitate to enter into direct contact with the Yuan (1275) following a Javanese attack.[87] The Yuan then tried to take control of the maritime routes in the south via expeditions against Champa, then against the Javanese kingdom of Singhasari, which led to its fall (1292) and the foundation of Majapahit (1293). The expedition was fruitless for the Mongols as they could not hold all fronts, so they chose to focus on the sensitive points of trade, specifically the Malay Straits (the expedition to Palembang in 1309). The dislocation of Srivijaya[88] paved the way for a new expansion of Javanese maritime power, which after a period of consolidation, passed into the hands of Majapahit around 1330.

This reconfiguration of merchant geopolitics modified the positioning of Brunei on three levels:

1. Brunei's commercial network expanded, especially through the development of indirect trade with Siam, attested by the abundance

---

[85] Ong Sum Ping in Low, "*Selesilah* (Book of Descent) of the Rajas of Bruni", p. 16; Ong Sum Peng in Sweeney, *Silsilah [B]* § 2.

[86] Low, ibid., p. 2; Sweeney, ibid., *Silsilah [B]* § 5. The official version kept by the Brunei authorities in this case is that of Sweeney's *Silsilah [A]*.

[87] These Javanese campaigns would last until the attack on the Singhasari by the Mongols in 1292; see Wolters, *The Fall of Śrīvijaya in Malay History*, p. 45 and Ferrand, *L'empire sumatranais de Çrivijaya*, p. 179.

[88] Wolters, ibid., ch. 5.

of ceramics from Sawankalok[89] on several land sites in Brunei and the presence of camphor, which the Siamese procured in Brunei or via Sumatran ports, in Siamese tributes to the Chinese court. The success of Brunei demonstrates its capacity to commercialise one of the most sought-after items in long-distance trade—camphor—for which it bartered with neighbouring populations living in the hinterland, as well as its capacity to maintain trade partnerships along the sea lanes leading to Manila through the Sulu Sea, following a pattern close to what Pasai used for pepper[90] in the same period.

2. Brunei thus occupied a dominant position in the junction linking the Chinese coasts to the Moluccas, at the nexus of a network of a dozen trading posts[91] including Sulu, Mindoro, Manila, "Butuan" (or Pudian, in the north of Mindanao), etc. It is not surprising that the Mongols made the line of demarcation between the eastern and western oceans pass along a Brunei/Karimata axis (southwest of Borneo).[92]
3. On that basis, Brunei increased contacts with Islam, notably via the port of Quanzhou, which included a good number of Muslims among its richest merchants.[93] To judge by Brunei's oldest (undated)[94] stele in Arabic, that of a "sultan, wise and just, protector and *conqueror* [...] Maharajah of Brunei", whose material (diabase), style and calligraphy indicate fabrication by a lapidary engraver of

[89] Tom and Barbara Harrisson, "Kota Batu in Brunei", p. 314 and pl. XIV; Matussin bin Omar and Dato P.M. Shariffuddin, "Distribution of Chinese and Siamese ceramics in Brunei", *BMJ* 4, 2 (1978): 59–65.

[90] Described in K. Hall, *Maritime Trade and State Development in Early Southeast Asia*, pp. 283ff.

[91] 元大德南海志 *Yuan Dade Nanhai zhi* [*Gazetteer of the South Sea compiled during the Dade period of the Yuan Dynasty*], cited by Wang Zhenping, "Reading Song-Ming records on Pre-colonial History of the Philippines", 東アヅア文化交渉研究空, *Higashi Ajia bunka kōshō kenkyū* [*Bulletin of the Institute for the Cultural Interaction Studies*] (2008): 249–60; Brunei is transcribed here as *Foni* 佛坭. Also Carrie C. Brown, "The Eastern Ocean in the Yung-lo Ta-tien", *BMJ* 4, 2 (1978): 46–58.

[92] Hsu Yun-ts'iao, "Notes relating to Admiral Cheng Ho's expeditions", *JMBRAS* 49, 1 (1976): 134–40.

[93] On the impact of Hanafite Chinese networks, see H.J. de Graaf, Th. Pigeaud and M.C. Ricklefs, eds., *Chinese Muslims in Java in the 15th and 16th centuries, the Malay Annals of Semarang and Ceribon* (Melbourne: Monash Papers on Southeast Asia 2, 1984), 221 p.

[94] Found in a graveyard containing other Muslim tombs, located at the centre of the old town.

Quanzhou in the first half of the 14th century,[95] the new religion penetrated palatine milieux. This first Islamisation of a portion of the elites seems confirmed *a posteriori* by the dated inscription on the tomb of the princess Zainab (c. 1457), which mentions her great-grandfather Muhammad Shah already bearing the title of sultan.[96] The same source as before (1578) states that after the Chinese Muslims appeared, Islam was passed on to the indigenous people by Arab preachers, who might have constructed the sumptuous mosque later discovered by the Spanish. This corroborates the data from the royal genealogy asserting that the third sultan, Sharif Ali, was an Arab from Taif.[97]

Playing the Double Game of Tribute and the Ming Dynasty (1370)

It was at this point that the evolution of the Chinese conjuncture modified once again the balance of forces in the *Nanhai* (southern seas): the withdrawal of the Mongols from Southeast Asia due to problems within the empire, enabled the ambitions of regional powers to come to the fore.[98] The destabilisation of the whole of Southeast Asia caused shock waves that deeply affected the very nature of the Bruneian entity on three levels.

---

[95] Chen Dasheng, "Une pierre tombale du début du XIVe s. retrouvée à Brunei", *Archipel* 42 (1991): 47–52.

[96] Stele 29 "daughter of sultan 'Abd al-Madjîd ibn Yûsuf ibn Muhammad Shâh al-Sultân", in Ludwik Kalus and Claude Guillot, "Les inscriptions funéraires islamiques de Brunei (2ème partie)", *BEFEO* 93 (2006): 150ff.

[97] Low, "*Selesilah* (Book of Descent) of the Rajas of Bruni", pp. 2, 16; and Sweeney, *Silsilah [A]* p. 11 (f. 2) and *B* (f. 5). The *Batu Tarsilah* adds that Sharif Ali is a descendant of Hassan, the grandson of the Prophet (Hugh Low, "Transcription and translation of a Historic Tablet", p. 22). For a biographical hypothesis of Sharif Ali, based on a comparison of Arab and Malay genealogies (Brunei, Sulu and Mindanao), see Jamil Al-Sufri (Pehin Dr. Awang Haji Mohd.), *Sultan Sharif Ali*, Tajuk kertas kerja, Seminar Sejarah Brunei (BSB, Jabatan Pusat Sejarah, 28–31 Ogos 1989), which connects the sultan to the sheriffs of Mecca (p. 10) but, unfortunately, without citing any source.

[98] *Barune* is mentioned in the *Nagarakertaga* as one of the 22 dependencies of Majapahit (which had a total of 68 tributaries) in Borneo. See Slametmuljana, *A Story of Majapahit* (Singapore: Singapore University Press, 1976), p. 139. This information is corroborated by the *Silsilah* (A. Sweeney, *Silsilah [B]*, f. 1) signalling that the first sultan, Awang [Kh]alak Betatar, was a vassal of the king of Majapahit "dita'lok oleh Betara Majapahit dan Pateh Gajah Mada".

Liberated from Mongol pressure, Majapahit was able to impose its suzerainty on the principal emporiums of the region in the years 1355–60. Attacked by the Javanese (of whom it obviously did not become a willing tributary and who ten years later made off with Singapura),[99] Brunei was forced to deliver an annual tribute including 40 *kati* of camphor[100] and perhaps areca nuts.[101] In return, the Javanese repelled an attack on Brunei by Sulu in 1368,[102] when one of its chiefs took advantage of the decline of the Yuan to try his luck. After these successive attacks, Limau Manis[103] lost its status as capital: Chinese sources show that it went from a capital protected by a wooden palisade (under the Song and the Yuan[104]) to a royal city guarded by a stone rampart at the start of the Ming Dynasty, which explained the toponym *Kota Batu*.[105] The change is also demonstrated by archaeological data: Limau Manis is by far the richest of all the sites excavated in Brunei, notably in Chinese shards and coins of the Song era (including Southern Song),[106] whereas

---

99 Brown, C.C. and R. Roolvink, *Sejarah Melayu 'Malay Annals'* (Kuala Lumpur: Oxford University Press, rep. 1976), ch. IV.

100 Wade, trans., *Southeast Asia in the Ming Shi-lu: An Open Access Resource*, http://epress.nus.edu.sg/msl/entry/2436; 明實錄 *Ming Shi-lu*, vol. 11, pp. 1127/28, http://epress.nus.edu.sg/msl/entry/612; and Ptak, Roderich, "Camphor in East and Southeast Asian Trade, c. 1500: A Synthesis of Portuguese and Asian Sources", in *Vasco da Gama and the Linking of Europe and Asia*, ed. Anthony Disney and Emily Booth (New Delhi: Oxford University Press, 2000), p. 151.

101 Hugh Low, "*Selesilah* (Book of Descent) of the Rajas of Bruni", *JMBRAS* 5 (June 1880): 1. This *Silsilah*—whose form goes back to the start of the 19th century—mentions areca nut and not camphor, which could be explained by the fact that camphor at the time had lost the commercial importance it had enjoyed under the Ming Dynasty while areca nut had become a major commodity.

102 Song Lian 宋濂, *Boniguo rugong ji* 勃尼國入貢記, in Kurz, *Boni in Chinese Sources*, pp. 27ff; Groeneveldt, *Notes on the Malay Archipelago and Malacca*, p. 103; and Wang Zhenping, "Reading Song-Ming records on Pre-colonial History of the Philippines".

103 Nearly 50,000 coins and shards of the Song era in Limau Manis (see above), 199 in Tanjung Batu (Matussin Omar, "A preliminary account of surface finds", 1973). Kota Batu has until now delivered only about 35,000 Ming coins and shards (Matussin Omar and Dato P.M. Shariffuddin, "Distribution of Chinese and Siamese ceramics in Brunei", *BMJ* 4, 2 [1978]: 62).

104 Kurz, *Boni in Chinese Sources*, p. 4 (*Taiping huanyuji* 太平環宇記) and p. 9 (Zhao Rugua 趙汝適, *Zhufanzhi* 諸蕃志).

105 *Kota* (*kuta* in Brunei Malay, cf. *Kamus Bahasa Melayu Brunei* [BSB, DPB, 2007], p. 173) means rampart or fortified place.

106 Except for a coin of the Tang era (Kai Yuan, 618–27).

Kota Batu contains mostly Ming ceramics.[107] This displacement of the capital was frequent in riverine Nusantarian societies, where people did not hesitate to migrate collectively, by flotillas of hundreds of boats.[108]

After their accession to power, the Ming emperors tried to retake control of their turbulent maritime southern margins by restricting trade with Southeast Asia to the sole framework of tribute,[109] and by sending emissaries to explain the new rules of the game to the former tributaries of the Song dynasty. As a token of its importance, Brunei received an imperial emissary starting in 1370, just after Majapahit (whose representatives witnessed the meeting),[110] the Chinese observer specifying that the kingdom was the same *Boni* as the one that had sent embassies in 977 and 1082. The following year (1371), Brunei sent tribute to Nanking; its reinsertion into Chinese suzerainty was notified in 1375 by its mention in the Imperial sacrifice for the spirits of mountains, lakes and seas. Due to its privileged linkage with Quanzhou, Brunei was now placed under the administrative dependency of Fujian. In three centuries (since the last embassy), the country had noticeably enriched itself, as the missives sent by the king to the Chinese ambassador, once written on fine bark strips, were now on gold leaf.[111]

However, the Ming interdictions were hardly respected—as attested by their being reiterated until 1397, and the fact that Ming embassies were occasionally attacked (notably by the Javanese in 1377)—and Brunei did not consider it necessary to send a delegation to Nanking. Plausibly, trade continued to be favourable, and private Southeast Asian or Arabo-Muslim traffic could get around the interdictions that affected Chinese junks. The advent of Yongle in 1403 radically modified the Chinese policy, however, since the war to support the foundation of the new dynasty, followed by Yongle's battles for succession, exhausted imperial

[107] Tom and Barbara Harrisson, "Kota Batu in Brunei (Introductory Report)", *SMJ* 7, 8 (new series), 23 (1956): 283–319; and for the excavation of the ramparts, Matussin Omar, "A Note on the Stone Wall and Earthen Causeway at Kota Batu", *BMJ* 5, 3 (1983): 27–38 + 9 pl.

[108] Wolters, *The Fall of Śrīvijaya in Malay History*, p. 12.

[109] Geoff Wade, *Ming China and Southeast Asia in the 15th Century: A Reappraisal* (Singapore: Asia Research Institute, Working Papers series no. 28, July 2004), p. 6.

[110] Song Lian 宋濂, "A Report about Boni Submitting Tribute", in Kurz, *Boni in Chinese Sources*, pp. 27ff.

[111] *Ming Shi-lu* 明實錄, vol. 3, p. 1264 (see an example of this gold leaf in Pg. Dr. Karim bin Pg. Haji Osman, *Sungai Limau Manis*, p. 147).

finances.[112] Yongle imposed a public monopoly on maritime trade and gave the Chinese the means for effective supervision with the creation of controllers in the Southern coastal provinces and the setting up of inns along the routes of tributaries' embassies. To demonstrate Chinese power, he also launched great expeditions[113] that were heavily armed (in particular with firearms)[114] toward the southern seas, under the high command of admiral Zheng He; the leaders of the squadron acquired commercial and military responsibilities and the crews were essentially composed of soldiers. The pivot of this Chinese strategy of controlling maritime routes was Malacca (founded c. 1400), whose commercial success rested largely on the Chinese fleet.

After the first passage of Zheng He[115] along its coasts (1405), *Boni* hastily sent an embassy to Nanking. To make the point that only the Ming had the authority to legitimise local powers, the Chinese quickly sent the sovereign of Brunei, without waiting for the embassy to return, two symbols of recognition by the Imperial chancellery—a seal and a certificate—and proceeded to establish the required tribute on an annual basis. After a second embassy in 1407, the king of *Boni*, his wife and his son arrived in Nanking in 1408 with a delegation of 150 persons; he died there a month later. Once the sovereign was buried according to imperial protocol and his son recognised as successor, Brunei was relieved by the Chinese of its obligations to Majapahit (which could refuse nothing to the Ming after experiencing its strike force the preceding year). At the request of the delegation, Yongle enfeoffed the mountain overlooking the capital as the "Mountain Which Will Ever Peacefully Protect the Country",[116] the same title as that granted in 1405 to the "western mountain" of Malacca.[117] The son of the dead sovereign, Xia Wang, was sent back to Brunei, flanked by a Chinese escort who

112 Wolters, *The Fall of Śrīvijaya in Malay History*, p. 156.

113 In July 1405, the Zhejiang shipyards were ordered to build 1,180 sea junks *(Ming Shi-lu*, vol. 10, p. 686).

114 Geoff Wade, *Zheng He Voyages: A Reassessment* (Singapore: ARI Working Paper no. 31, Asia Research Institute, October 2004), p. 9. See the cannons from the end of the 15th or start of the 16th found off Brunei in M. L'Hour, *La mémoire engloutie de Brunei: une aventure sous-marine*, vol. 2, pp. 153–4.

115 Wade, *Zheng He Voyages: A Reassessment*, p. 10 n. 51.

116 *Chang ning zhen guo de shan* 長寧鎮國之山 (Wade, trans., *Ming Shi-lu*, vol. 11, pp. 1133–6 [Yong-le: Year 6, Month 12, Day 4]).

117 "Protector mountain of the country", obviously the Bukit China [Chinese Hill] today.

stayed for almost two years. Brunei sent embassies quite regularly until 1421 (although contrary to the provisions of 1405, they were despatched only every other year), then a final embassy in 1426. As for the Chinese, they sent an emissary charged with gifts in 1411.

The years 1405–26 saw intense relations between Brunei and the Ming. Along with Malacca, which positioned itself symbolically as the heir of Srivijaya and lawful heir to the Funanese heirloom of the "Mountain Kings", in line with the *Sejarah Melayu*,[118] Brunei was the sole kingdom to have benefited (at its sovereign's demand) from the ennoblement of its tutelary mountain. This statutory parity was reaffirmed by the granting to the king of Brunei in 1408 the same funeral arrangements as those granted to the two "kings" of Sulu, who died in China under similar circumstances in 1417[119] and 1421, when these Sulu kings were classified in 1417 at the same rank as Malacca.[120] It is plausibly from these embassies that Brunei brought back a ceremonial weapon rare in Insulindia, the *changkah*,[121] a sort of two-pronged fork that was originally used for overturning the horses of aggressors along the Silk Road. And it is the Chinese who, according to the *Batu Tarsilah*, erected the stone ramparts of "Kota Batu" at the request of the third sultan, Sharif Ali.[122] This seems to be corroborated by the excavations undertaken at the site since 2010, where the foundations of a door whose quadrangular structure is reminiscent of the doors of Chinese towns have been unearthed.[123]

---

[118] The foundation of Malacca by a prince of Palembang, previously installed in Singapura (Wolters, *The Fall of Srivijaya*, p. 87).

[119] An embassy conducted jointly by the "three kings" of Sulu, with a suite of 340 persons (Wang Zhenping, "Reading Song-Ming Records of the Pre-colonial History of the Philippines", 東アジア文化交渉研究, 創刊号, Kansai University, *Bulletin of the Institute for the Cultural Interaction Studies* [March 2008]: 249–61).

[120] *Ming Shi-lu*, vol. 13, p. 2021.

[121] From the Malay *cangga[h]*, two-pronged spear used for catching fish in rivers (see Appendices 2, "Lexicon").

[122] Low, "*Selesilah* (Book of Descent) of the Rajas of Bruni", p. 22.

[123] In view of the rarity of stone buildings in Borneo, it is obviously not an ordinary dwelling that took advantage of such a defensive apparatus, especially given the dimensions of the blocks exhumed on the Kota Batu site (on average some 1–1.2 m long and 40–50 cm thick). Recent digs on the site have revealed what might constitute one of the doors of the city (see *Brunei Times*, 19 Oct. 2010). On the stone wall and the ditch of Kota Batu revealed by the excavations of Tom Harrisson in 1952, see Matussin Omar, "A note on the Stone Wall and Earthen Causeway at Kota Batu", *BMJ* 5, 3 (1983): 27–38 + 9 pl.

Figure 1. Walls of Kota Batu and Bases of the Columns
(Photo by author, 28 October 2010)

But when the pressure of the steppe imposed a shift in Chinese imperial policy, which translated into the displacement after 1421 of the capital to Peking and a halt to the great expeditions, Brunei again ceased to play the game of official exchanges. It interrupted its embassies after 1426,[124] and in doing so, distinguished itself from the principal merchant powers of Southeast Asia—Majapahit, Samudra-Pasai and Malacca—which maintained their embassies until the end of the 15th century. Chinese textual sources thus, unfortunately, ended, but archaeological data testify to a development of commerce throughout the 15th century, this time with new partners: Southeast Asians, Siamese and Tonkinese (whose ceramics partially took over from Chinese ceramics after the

[124] Even though the Ming launched a final expedition in 1433.

decline caused by the interdiction of private Chinese foreign trade by the Ming government)[125] and Indo-Muslims, as illustrated (for the latter) by the presence of a 1402 stele bearing both date and epitaph in Arabic and the entry of the toponym "Sea of Brunei" into Arab geographies in 1462.[126]

Islamisation of the Brunei Polity

Playing the Chinese card—which saw the Sino-Muslims gaining the largest share, notably in Zheng He's sphere of influence—then abandoning it for Malacca, which concretised under the reign of Mansur Shah (1445–58)[127] by the payment of tribute to the sultanate,[128] went hand-in-hand with a very gradual Islamisation of the Brunei elites.

Already in the 1371 embassy, the emissary of Brunei was a certain Yisimayi (probably a transcription of the Muslim name Ismail), and his sovereign was Mahemosha (Mahmud Shah),[129] the latter's name corresponding to the genealogy of the princess Zainab (see above). Moreover, *Boni* seems to have changed its writing,[130] adopting a script (at least temporarily) similar to the Mongol writing *huihu*,[131] which was created at the start of the 13th century and borrowed from Uighur, that is to say, it was derived (through Sogdian) from the Aramaic alphabet[132] and was visibly close to the Arabic alphabet. As these same Chinese sources attest to the spread of Buddhism among the population and to the non-respect of the Muslim food laws, it seems that the Islamisation of Brunei at this time was limited to just a section of the royal entourage.

---

[125] Matussin Omar and Dato P.M. Shariffuddin, "Distribution of Chinese and Siamese ceramic in Brunei", *BMJ* 4, 2 (1978): 59–66; P.-Y. Manguin, "Réseaux marchands et navires en mer de Chine méridionale", in *La mémoire engloutie de Brunei: une aventure sous-marine*, ed. M. L'Hour, pp. 7–17.

[126] G.R. Tibbets, *Arabic Texts on South-East Asia*, pp. 195, 198, 207, 255.

[127] H.J. de Graaf, *Geschiedenis van Indonesië* (La Haye, W. van Hoeve, 1949), p. 76.

[128] C.C. Brown and R. Roolvink, *Sejarah Melayu 'Malay Annals'*, 2nd ed. (Kuala Lumpur: Oxford University Press, 1976), p. 82.

[129] Kurz, *Boni in Chinese Sources*, p. 39, citing P. Pelliot.

[130] P.M. Shariffuddin and R. Nicholl, "A possible example of ancient Brunei script", *BMJ* 3, 3 (1973): 116–22.

[131] Ibid.

[132] Isaac Taylor, *History of the alphabet, Part 1. Semitic alphabets* (London: E. Arnold, 1899), pp. 307ff.

This hypothesis is reinforced by epigraphy: out of the 20 dated steles[133] found at the mouth of the Brunei River, 10[134] concern the period 1400–60. This is similar to Pasai in the second phase of its Islamisation half a century earlier: 11 dated steles over a period of 60 years (1350–1410),[135] although one of the steles bears a bilingual Sanskrit/Arabo-Malay epitaph (1418), another is in Arabic and 8 others in Arabo-Malay, whereas in Pasai epitaphs in Arabic are the norm. The Islam of Brunei therefore appears largely "indigenous Malay", which implies that after several centuries of contact via the southern Chinese, it took the mediation of Islamised Malays for the new religion to take root,[136] probably via Samudra-Pasai, considering the lag in the chronology.[137]

A re-reading of Chinese sources implies the adoption of Islam by a portion of the Brunei political elites in the first half of the 15th century. If the Chinese tomb of the "King of Boni" who died in Nanking in 1408 shows a "path of souls" conforming to traditional Chinese symbolism (which precedes Buddhism),[138] on the other hand, only sheep were sacrificed—a sufficiently unusual practice that required the breeding of sheep solely for this purpose in Nanking (sheep were more common in Northern China), a waste that Chinese sources would later deplore.[139] In other words, imperial symbolism accommodated Islamised funeral

[133] Out of 37 Muslim steles of the 15th and 16th centuries found in Brunei.

[134] Given the uncertainty about stele 14, which might be dated 1397 or 1494 (Ludwik Kalus and Claude Guillot, "Les inscriptions funéraires islamiques de Brunei [2ème partie]", *BEFEO* 93 (2006): 139–81).

[135] Claude Guillot and Ludwik Kalus, *Les monuments funéraires et l'histoire du Sultanat de Pasai à Sumatra [XIII–XVIe siècles]* (Paris: Cahiers d'Archipel 37, 2008), 402 p.

[136] According to the *Sya'ir Awang Simawn*, Islam was introduced by a certain Sarip Mupakih (Syarif Mufakih, meaning a jurist).

[137] A similar hypothesis was formulated by Daniel Perret about the Islamisation of Patani by means of either Pasai or Brunei. See "Tombes musulmanes anciennes et voies possible d'islamisation de la région de Patani", in *Études sur l'histoire du sultanat de Patani*, ed. D. Perret, Amara Srisuchat and Sombun Tanasuk (Paris: EFEO, 2004), pp. 164ff.

[138] See R. Nicholl, "The Tomb of Maharaja Karna of Brunei at Nanking", *BMJ* 5, 4 (1984): 35–45.

[139] By the end of several generations, the Chinese authorities found themselves with a flock of sheep they did not know what to do with (*Ming Shizong shilu*, vol. 79, pp. 2751–2).

meals, which are also evocative of Javanese *slametan*.[140] Moreover, at least two of the embassies from *Boni* that were not directed by the sovereign included enough Muslims for the administration to deliver "special rations" to them, that is, without pork (the only meat allowed in normal rations), one in either 1405, 1410 or 1417, the other in 1426.[141]

Given the privileged links between Brunei and Malacca (according to the *Sya'ir Awang Simawn*,[142] the father of Sultan Bolkiah, Damang Libar Daun, was the *juru Shahbandar* of Brunei, homonym of the regent of Palembang of the *Sejarah Melayu*,[143] who yielded power to the founder of Malacca[144] after he became his son-in-law, etc.), such an evolution was normal. The sovereign of Malacca adopted the Muslim religion during the 1410s,[145] approximately at the time when, if we refer to the official genealogy, a "princess of Johor"[146] married the first sultan of Brunei. The Islamisation of Malacca must be seen in the context of all the Malay

---

[140] This death can be compared with that of one of the Sulu kings, Ba-du-ge Ba-da-la [*Batara* = the king]. He died in 1417 in Dezhou and was buried under the same conditions, although his concubine and second son obtained the right to remain in Nanking to watch over the grave. The Empire allotted them grain, money and three Muslim families to serve them, which proves that the sovereign of at least one of the Sulu polities was already a Muslim at this date (*Ming Shi-lu*, vol. 117, pp. 8936–7).

[141] Carrie C. Brown, "Some Ming regulations on the provisions for tributary delegations", *BMJ* 1 (1974): 230–1.

[142] Maxwell, "Accessing the Epic Status of the Brunei Malay Sya'ir Awang Simawn", p. 14.

[143] The *Sejarah Melayu* states that the regent of Palembang, Damang Libar Daun, was the descendant of Raja Shulan, himself an offspring of the well-known hero Iskandar Zulkarnain (Brown and Roolvink, *Sejarah Melayu* [54–5], p. 13).

[144] The two epics evoke the union of a prince with the daughter of a king of the marine world: in the *Sya'ir Awang Simawn*, Sultan Muda Jalilul-Alam dives to the bottom of the sea, kills the king of the Nagas and marries the king's daughter; in the *Sejarah Melayu*, it is Raja Shulan, grandson of the Chola king Raja Chulan, himself a descendent of Alexander, who dives and marries the princess, but without slaying her father.

[145] See the mention of a king Iskandar in 1411 by Ming sources, Wang Gungwu, "The First three Rulers of Malacca", in *Southeast Asia–China Interactions, Reprint of Articles from the JMBRAS*, ed. Geoff Wade, p. 322.

[146] Low, "*Selesilah* (Book of Descent) of the Rajas of Bruni", p. 1. Johor was founded only after the fall of Malacca, so if the genealogy dates the foundation of the sultanate to a century earlier, it should be understood that Malacca is being referred to, especially since the *silsilah* was compiled at the start of the 19th century for purposes of legitimation, at a time when only Johor was counted.

states, which saw adherence to the new religion as a counterweight to the advance of the Siamese, who ended up controlling the whole Malay Peninsula around 1460. This Malay Islam received some Arab support, as incarnated by Syarif Mufakih, the propagator of Islam in Brunei according to the *Sya'ir Awang Simawn*, in addition to the third sultan Sharif Ali.[147]

However, Western sources appear to be in contradiction. Why, in contrast to epigraphic data, do the first Western sources date the adherence to Islam by the sovereign of Brunei to a century later (c. 1515)? A critical reading of the first testimony about *Bornei*, that of the Italian Ludovico de Varthema,[148] shows that he may have landed in Borneo around 1505, but certainly not Brunei, since he notes a distance of some 300 km between *Bornei* and the Moluccas, whereas the archipelago is separated from the Brunei Bay by more than 2,000 km; moreover, the latter toponym referred as well to the whole west coast of the island. With the lack of precision of Western nautical maps at the time, the distance might not be accurate, but it is hard to imagine that it could have been reduced to one-sixth of the actual distance! On the other hand, Varthema mentions trade in camphor,[149] of which Brunei was certainly the principal emporium, but the commodity was also sold in other ports of the island, notably in Sukadana and in the southwest of Sulawesi (in Makassar and in Bugis country).

In fact, the Captain-General of Malacca, Rui de Brito, who never went to Brunei, nuanced this assessment of the religious situation ten years later in 1514, specifying that "the king [of Borneo] is pagan but the merchants [are] Muslims". His contemporary, Tome Pires, in direct contact with the merchants because he was responsible for the spice trade in the Portuguese trading post, stated about the same time (1515) that only the principal city of Borneo, whose king had converted "not long ago", was inhabited by Muslims. The imprecision of dating in societies

---

[147] "Sarip Mupakih", in Maxwell, "Accessing the Epic Status of the Brunei Malay Sya'ir Awang Simawn", p. 15; for the stele (undated, name illegible) attributed to him, see L. Kalus and C. Guillot, "Les inscriptions funéraires islamiques de Brunei", p. 249.

[148] *The Itinerary of Ludovico de Varthema of Bologna from 1502 to 1508*, trans. by John W. Jones, with *A discourse on Varthema and his travels in Southern Asia* by Sir Richard Carnac Temple (London: The Argonaut Press, 1928), pp. lxxv, 8.

[149] One plausible explanation might be that he confused two successive landings, Buru in the south of the Moluccas (which corresponds better with the distance and duration of navigation) and Brunei where the source of camphor was located.

where most residents had access only to oral tradition, is understandable indeed. But the testimony of Rui de Brito about the religion of the Bruneians is undermined by one of the great dignitaries of the sultanate, who was literate and had witnessed as a child the coming of Pigafetta, the Venetian explorer who sailed with Magellan. Questioned by a Spaniard, he mentioned in 1578[150] the presence of a mosque "since three hundred years ago" and the existence of six Muslim kings of the same lineage who preceded the sultan Saiful Rijal.[151] The confusion could perhaps be explained by the existence of several anchorages in the very vast Brunei Bay, which remain to be identified. In any case, epigraphy and Chinese sources already resolve the contradiction raised by the sole Western sources on this religious issue.

---

[150] Carroll, "Francisco de Sande's invasion of Brunei in 1578", p. 51. The informant is the old "Raja of rajas" (the Maharaja di Raja himself, one of the principal dignitaries of the Court, the fourth of the Cheteria, cf. Sweeney, *Silsilah [A]*, p. 47, [f. 66]), who had been as a child the eyewitness of the visit of Pigafetta in 1521.

[151] Data perfectly in accord with that of the *Silsilah [A]* p. 12 (f. 2), written in 1735, reproduced in the *Silsilah [B]*, p. 54 (f. 6).

The Golden Age of Brunei (1500–78)

Unprecedented Prosperity

At the end of the 15th century, the withdrawal of the Ming navy from the China Sea, the erosion of Majapahit[152] and the decline of Champa, which had been suffering the growing encroachments of the Tonkinese since the seizure of its capital Vijaya in 1471, paved the way for a new political model hitherto confined to the north of Sumatra, the Straits of Malacca and Brunei: the Malay sultanate, which extended to the coastal regions of Java and the Moluccas (1480). This resulted in the first redistribution of the major commercial stakes. Thirty years later, the capture of Malacca by the Portuguese in 1511 again modified the game: the sultanate's traffic along the straits was partly taken over by Aceh (in the north, after the annexation of Pasai in 1524) and Johor (in the south); commerce along the Javanese coasts boomed to the point that new powers emerged in Banten (on the Sunda Strait) and in Demak (north coast of Java), which also benefited Brunei.

Judging by archaeological findings (Ming blue-and-white wares in Kota Batu), the wrecks discovered in 1997 off the coast[153] and abundant Iberian testimony, Brunei probably luxuriated in its apogee between the end of the 15th century and the end of the 16th. The city discovered by Magellan's companions in 1521 was indeed a flourishing one of some

152 The last inscription of Majapahit dates from 1486.

153 L'Hour, *La mémoire engloutie de Brunei: une aventure sous-marine.*

5,000 homes,[154] almost all built on the waterside except for the royal palace, which was built on land and protected by wooden ramparts whose imposing artillery of 62 cannons, famous throughout the Malay world,[155] was combined with a fleet of several hundred war pirogues. Frequented by merchants from all over the region,[156] its wealth was demonstrated by the refinement of dress and equipment used by the *shahbandar*[157] and the royal court (silks, brocades, richly ornamented daggers, crockery). In addition, the Sultan possessed two exceptionally large pearls, regalia apparently already mentioned by Zhao Rugua[158] at the start of the 13th century. The only power on the west coast of

[154] Among others, see Nicholl, *European Sources*, p. 14 n. 8; and Anthony Reid, *Southeast Asia in the Age of Commerce 1450–1680*, vol. 2, *Expansion and Crisis* (New Haven: Yale University Press, 1993), pp. 69–70. Pigafetta estimates the number of homes to be 25,000. Based on 4 to 6 persons per home, 25,000 homes corresponds to 100,000–150,000 inhabitants; so it seems that Pigafetta was mistaken and that there were 5,000 dwellings, not 25,000. This estimate of about 5,000 houses in 1522 was retrospectively corroborated by Carroll, "Francisco de Sande's invasion of Brunei in 1578", p. 54. An eyewitness mentions 5,000–6,000 houses at the time of the Spaniards' arrival, a quarter of a century later—assuming that Brunei did not suffer any kind of conflict that might have caused a drop in its demographics. In fact, in 1600, the total population of Southeast Asia was no more than 23 million and that of Borneo 670,000 inhabitants (Anthony Reid, *Southeast Asia in the Age of Commerce 1450–1680*, vol. 1, *The Lands below the Winds* [New Haven: Yale University Press, 1988], p. 14). If we apply the same demographic growth rate of 0.2% to the preceding century, Borneo would have had 573,000 inhabitants in 1522. If the Brunei River had 100,000–150,000 inhabitants, it would have been home to more than a quarter of the total population of the island, which is invalidated by the existence of ports such as Kutei, Banjermasin, Martapura, Sukadana, etc., not to mention the very geography of the site. To close the debate, the district of Brunei-Muara (which includes Bandar Seri Begawan and the historical site of Kota Batu, and the residential zone of Muara) had only 279,842 residents in 2011 (*Laporan Awal, Preliminary Report, Banci Penduduk dan Perumahan*, BSB, Jabatan Perangkaan, Jabatan Perancangan dan Kemajuan Ekonomi, Department of Statistics, Department of Economic Planning and Development, Jan. 2012, p. 32).

[155] Tom Harrisson, "Brunei Cannon: Their Role in Southeast Asia (1400–1900 A.D.)", *BMJ* 1, 1 (1969): 94–117; P.M. Shariffuddin, "Brunei Cannons", *BMJ* 1 (1969): 72–93; P.-Y. Manguin, "L'artillerie légère nousantarienne, à propos de six canons conservés dans les collections portugaises", *BEFEO* 32 (1976): 233–68.

[156] Goncalo Pereira, cited in Nicholl, *European Sources*, p. 29.

[157] Harbour master.

[158] These were placed in a sanctuary but had to be removed with the spread of Islam; Kurz, *Boni in Chinese Sources*, p. 14.

Borneo adhering to Islam, Brunei at the start of the 16th century had re-established suzerainty[159] over Sulu[160] (where it acquired huge pearls[161] and delegated a *pengiran*[162] who possessed houses in Brunei),[163] Mindoro[164] and Manila, thereby controlling the route leading from Brunei to Luzon. Brunei had more trouble establishing its tutelage over the island's southwest coast, especially the mouth of the Kapuas (Lawa), which gambled with the Javanese and so had to abandon Tanjung Pura to them.[165] And in the Brunei Bay itself, where the sultanate possessed four trading posts,[166] it had to counter recurrent attacks from a dissident and maverick anchorage that had not yet adhered to Islam and which tried to lay hands on the camphor networks[167] before disappearing in the next half-century.[168]

The prosperity of Brunei derived from its location at the intersection of four maritime routes used by a number of pirate bands that roamed over the region (Javanese, Malays, Chams, Acehnese, etc.), on top of what were purely merchant activities, with the same actors flitting from one business to another according to changing circumstances.

1. Two to four junks sailed each year between Brunei and Malacca, exchanging camphor, gold, rice, sago, wax, pearls,[169] etc., for Indian cotton fabrics, which were a common means of payment used in Insulindia, as well as glass beads that enabled them to negotiate with tribes from camphor-producing zones. Exonerated from customs

[159] Pigafetta, in Nicholl, *European Sources*, p. 13; and D.E. Brown, "Spanish accounts of their expeditions against Brunei in 1578–79", *BMJ* 3, 2 (1974): 180.
[160] Low, "*Selesilah* (Book of Descent) of the Rajas of Bruni", p. 2.
[161] The tribute brought by Sulu to the Ming regularly included pearls larger than a thumb.
[162] Member of the royal family. This subjugation was strengthened by matrimonial alliances since the Sultan of Sulu had married the sister of the Sultan of Brunei at the start of the 1630s; R. Nicholl, "The Letter of Bras Bayão", *BMJ* 5, 3 (1983): 51–60.
[163] Brown, "Spanish accounts of their expeditions against Brunei in 1578–79", p. 192.
[164] Carroll, "Francisco de Sande's invasion of Brunei in 1578", p. 52.
[165] Nicholl, "The letter of Bras Bayão".
[166] *Asia Portuguesa*, vol. II, p. 243 (1530), in Nicholl, *European Sources*, p. 29.
[167] Pigafetta, in Nicholl, *European Sources*, p. 11.
[168] A note in the old Milanese edition (J.F. Robertson, "Using Pigafetta's Journal", *BMJ* 3, 1 [1973]: 100–4) mentioned that some Portuguese missionaries had visited this specific mooring.
[169] Pigafetta and Albuquerque (1524), in Nicholl, *European Sources*, pp. 11, 23.

duties, they still had to give the usual presents to the *shahbandar*. These commercial links induced matrimonial alliances, mentioned in both Malay sources and the first Western accounts: a relative of Sultan Mahmud Shah (the penultimate sultan of Malacca) married a daughter of a Brunei raja,[170] and at the start of the 1510s, the *tumenggung* of Malacca,[171] whose ship was attacked by partisans of the dethroned sultan,[172] came from Brunei.[173] The two emporiums feuded from time to time—the *Hikayat Hang Tuah* evokes an attack on the Malacca fleet off the cape of Karawang (not far from Jakarta) by Adipati Solok,[174] the young son of the Brunei king. And despite the shock of the capture of Malacca by the Portuguese in 1511, Brunei maintained its commercial ties with the new masters.

2. Notwithstanding the Ming prohibitions, Brunei continued to be regularly frequented by ships from Southern China: the sultanate is mentioned in several route charts of the 15th and 16th centuries reprinted in the *Shun Feng Xiang Sun*,[175] but this time under the Hokkien toponym *Bun Lai*,[176] which specifically refers to the Brunei River, aside from the Toponym Muara (*Mao-hua-la*). Incidentally the *Shun Feng* confirms that *Bun Lai* is indeed located at *Boni*.
3. Apart from the sultanates of the Malay Peninsula, with which it exchanged delegations,[177] Brunei traded regularly with Siam (Ayutthaya

---

170 Brown and Roolvink, *Sejarah Melayu*, p. 119, *raja* referring here to a prince and not to the sovereign.

171 The Portuguese initially maintained the former commercial administration of the sultanate, with a *Bendahara* and a *Tumenggung*, but later modified its structure: the *Bendahara* was responsible for *Kelings* (mostly Indians from Coromandel), the *Tumenggong* for Malays (Paulo Jorge Sousa Pinto, "Purse and Sword; D. Henrique Bendahara and Portuguese Melaka in the late 16th century", *Santa Barbara Portuguese Studies* II [1995]: 75–93).

172 Brown and Roolvink, *Sejarah Melayu*, p. 173.

173 Rui de Brito (1514), in Nicholl, *European Sources*, p. 4 and Jorge Alvares (1514), in ibid., p. 5.

174 The title attests to Sulu being under the tutelage of Brunei; see Denys Lombard, *Le Carrefour javanais, essai d'histoire globale, II—Les réseaux asiatiques* (Paris: EHESS, 1990), p. 198.

175 *Shun Feng Xiang Sun* 順風相送 [*In the Company of Good Winds*], route chart written around 1630 and based on information from the 1430s (J.V. Mills, "Arab and Chinese Navigators in Malaysian Waters in about A.D. 1500", *JMBRAS* 47, 2 [1974]: 1–82).

176 汶萊, mand. Wen Lai.

177 Notably in Pahang, see Nicholl, *European Sources*, p. 33.

and Ligor),[178] Patani, Champa[179] and with the Burmese coasts.[180] Given the similarities between their Islamic funerary arts at the start of the 1530s, Brunei must also have had close connections with Aceh,[181] as attested to by the importation of steles.[182]

4. Finally, Brunei constituted a stop on the northern route leading from Malacca to Philippines (it controlled exchanges with Luzon)[183] and to the Moluccas; in addition to being half as long, this second itinerary towards the rarest spices avoided the Javanese ports, then prey to political turmoil. Thus cloves and nutmeg were available in Brunei from time to time.

The importance of Brunei is also demonstrated by the regular stops of Arab navigators who continued to include it on their route charts (c. 1511).[184]

The continuity between the lacustrian city discovered by Pigafetta and the polity mentioned by Ming sources is also confirmed *a posteriori*. The seals[185] decorated by a two-humped camel that were granted by the first Ming emperors to Southeast Asian sovereigns turned up in early 17th-century Chinese sources, which mention the use in marriage rites in Brunei of an animal seal (unspecified) given by Emperor Yongle,

---

[178] Ibid., p. 32.

[179] Ibid., p. 34.

[180] Fernão Mendes Pinto, *Pérégrination* (Paris: ELA La Différence, 1991), p. 504.

[181] Ludwik Kalus and Claude Guillot, "Quand le style funéraire de Brunei se retrouve à Aceh", *Archipel* 77 (2009): 57–68.

[182] Karim bin Pengiran Haji Osman, "A Report on archaeological excavation and exploration on Pulau Terendak and its surrounding area", *BMJ* 7, 4 (1992), p. 25 n. 60.

[183] Luis Felipe F.R. Thomaz, "Malaka au tournant du 16e siècle", in *Marchands et hommes d'affaires asiatiques dans l'océan Indien et la Mer de Chine 13e–20e siècles*, ed. Denys Lombard and Jean Aubin (Paris: EHESS, 1988), p. 38.

[184] J.V. Mills, "Arab and Chinese Navigators in Malaysian Waters in about A.D. 1500", *JMBRAS* 47, 2 (1974): 1–82, reprinted in Geoff Wade, ed., *Southeast Asia-China Interactions, Reprint of Articles from the JMBRAS* (Kuala Lumpur: MBRAS, 2007), pp. 409–88.

[185] *Dong xi Yang kao* 東西洋考 (book V) mentions that the golden seal given by Emperor Yongle to the king of Brunei was decorated with an animal (Groeneveldt, *Notes on the Malay Archipelago and Malacca*, pp. 101–2). The handle of this type of seal was decorated with a camel. The tradition endured under the Qing, since King Mongkut (1851–68) was offered two seals of the same type (see Annabel Teh Gallop, "Camels, Seals and the Early Tin Coinage of Brunei", *Archipel* 70 [2005]: 261–80).

impressed on the back of the newly-wed.[186] Its symbolic importance (linking the sultanate to the Chinese Emperor) was such that in the second half of the 17th century, though the practice of sending embassies to China was abandoned for long, coins hammered out by the sultanate still featured a Bactrian camel.[187]

The Spanish Raid

The sultanate's wealth meant that, in addition to its indigenous rivals, it found itself in direct competition with the Portuguese, who started taking the northern route of the Moluccas in 1527. If relations with Malacca were smooth at first (the Portuguese opened a factory in the sultanate around 1530), Brunei broke off relations in 1536, after repeated Lusitanian exactions upon the Moluccas. As the Spanish were now in the position to bankroll an Asian strategy, thanks to the exploitation of silver mines in Potosi (Peru) in 1530, the Spanish presence had to be reckoned with as well, increasing Western pressure. Brunei then played the card of the regional ascending powers: the Sultan sent his *orang laut* (Bajaus) to support the 1540 Acehnese expedition against Aru, alongside various mercenaries from the Indian Ocean (Turks, Malabars, Gujratis and so-called Abyssinians[188]). Four years after he had landed in Mindanao (1542), Villalobos also sent 250 ships to Demak (Java)—a big fleet in those times.[189] Finally, while Brunei cunningly tolerated the passage of Catholic missionaries along the west coast of Borneo in order not to

---

[186] Till today, the regalia of the Bolkiah include two gold lions bestowed by the Ming emperors, called *kuching mas* (gold cats). *Kuching mas* was also the name given to the smallest tin currency, linking these coins (hammered out by the Chinese) with the insignia of legitimation given by the Ming (A. Teh Gallop, ibid.). Moreover, they have been included into the sultan's and queen's personal standards (*Bendera dan Lagu Kebangsaan Brunei, The Brunei State Flag and National Anthem* [BSB, 1981] p. 12). The lions of the Bolkiah should also be compared to the older lion found in the Limbang treasure (Tom Harrisson, "Gold & Indian Influences in West Borneo", *JMBRAS* 22, 4 [Sept. 1949]: 62).

[187] This animal is emblematic of northern China, which in 1900 owned the world's prime stock of two-humped camels.

[188] Fernão Mendes Pinto, *Pérégrination* (Paris: La Différence, 1991), p. 99; also Nicholl, *European Sources*, p. 31. Since the Abyssinians *stricto sensu* had lost control of their maritime position, these so-called "Abyssinians" must have been Somalis or Socotranese.

[189] Pinto, ibid., pp. 590ff.

offend the Iberians, it promoted at the same time the propagation of Islam in the territories under its supervision,[190] from the Sulu archipelago to the mouth of the Sarawak River.

But the Spanish went beyond a few modest exploratory trips. Legazpí landed at the mouth of the Sulu Sea in Cebu, then Iloilo (1564), which triggered a first skirmish with the Bruneians at Bohol in March 1565, followed by a second, significantly larger one in 1569 near Cebu[191] (from which the Spaniards were expelled by the Portuguese the following year).[192] Worse, after an aborted attempt in 1570, Legazpí captured one of the most important dependencies of the sultanate the following year: Manila. A confrontation was now inevitable. After the failure of a first expedition in 1572 due to typhoons, then of a second one due to opposition by some chiefs of Luzon,[193] Brunei—which meanwhile had negotiated the neutrality of the Portuguese[194]—fomented a revolt in Manila (1574). But internal rivalries and procrastination by the Bruneians, aware of the risks they were running in their capital by sending a major part of their fleet[195] on a distant expedition, doomed the operation. A few months later, in December, one of the greatest pirate chiefs of Southern China settled in Pangasinan after pressure from the Ming and ransacked Manila.[196] Without seizing the opportunity to attack the Spanish, the sultanate relied on ideological subversion[197] by supporting

---

[190] Cesar A. Majul, *Muslims in the Philippines* (Quezon City: University of the Philippines Press, 1999), pp. 92ff.

[191] Twenty Bruneian and Sulu ships against nine Spanish ones.

[192] Graham Saunders, *A History of Brunei* (Kuala Lumpur: Oxford University Press, 2002), p. 52.

[193] Carroll, "Francisco de Sande's invasion of Brunei in 1578", p. 47.

[194] On 24 April 1578 the Spanish found a letter from the King of Portugal dated 7 March 1573 (Nicholl, *European Sources*, p. 55).

[195] Ten fighting galleys and 100 small boats setting off to attack Manila turned around after 30 km so as not to leave the sultanate exposed (testimony of 1578, quoted in Nicholl, ibid., p. 51).

[196] *Limahon, al. Lim Ah Hong al. Lim Ah Feng* (林阿風) mand. Lin A Feng, of Teochiu origin, assembled a band of Chinese and Japanese roaming the coasts in South China Sea. He left Pangasinan with 62 junks to attack Manila (see Geo Phillips, "Early Spanish trade with Chin Cheo [Chuan Chou]", *The China Review* 19 [1895]: 243–55).

[197] Islam was not only the vector of a religion, a linear time and a broad space from Eastern Asia up to the Mediterranean Sea, but also of a political and merchant ideology whose instruments were both material and cultural (see Denys Lombard, *Le carrefour javanais, essai d'histoire globale, II—Les réseaux asiatiques*, ch. III "Le stimulus islamique" [Paris: EHESS, 1990], pp. 131–206).

the propagation of Islam in the Philippine archipelago.[198] Admonished by a pretender to the Bruneian throne,[199] the Spanish sent a squadron in retaliation in 1578. Peace talks failed when the Spanish emissary was executed and they opened fire. After an artillery duel[200] in which the Hispanic cannons proved to have a longer range than the Bruneians (which were partly of Portuguese origin), the sultan gave the order to burn the town. This was scarcely respected since the Spaniards pillaged it without hindrance[201] and burned the mosque, whose ten doors they took to Manila[202]—a crime that was condemned by the Bishop of Manila himself ten years later.

The Spanish invaders discovered a flourishing emporium that traded mostly with China, Siam and Patani (the latter two supplying saltpetre),[203] but also with Pegu, the Malay Peninsula, Java—where it bought slaves who were resold to the Portuguese—and most ports of the archipelago as far away as the Moluccas. While continuing to take concubines among the local chiefs' daughters, notably among the Bajau, who sent yearly tributes of pearls and served as coastguards, the royal family was now allied by marriage with its Nusantarian equivalents, the Javanese and Malays (Sulu, Maguindanao, Ternate). If the sultanate failed to impose its suzerainty over the Sambas, on the southwest of the island,[204] which played the Javanese card (Japara), it nonetheless controlled the Sulu/Palawan axis (as far as the Calamian Islands to the north of

198 Nicholl, *European Sources*, pp. 39–40; 59; *Sya'ir Awang Simawn* part VII (Maxwell, "Accessing the Epic Status of the Brunei Malay Sya'ir Awang Simawn", p. 15).

199 Pengiran Buong Manis, al. Sri Lela (Low, *Silsilah*, p. 6; F. Delor Angeles, "Brunei and the Moro Wars", *BMJ* 1, 1 [1969]: 123).

200 There were 40 ships on the Spanish side, 50 on the other (Nicholl, *European Sources*, p. 61).

201 The Spanish took 17 galleys and 170 pieces of artillery, which the Bishop of Manila wanted to restore to Brunei as he felt that it had been unjustly attacked (Nicholl, "Myth and Legend in Brunei History", *BMJ* 6, 1 [1985]: 32–41).

202 These were reused in the fortress and churches (Carroll, "Francisco de Sande's invasion of Brunei in 1578", p. 52), probably in the oldest church of Manila, San Augustin, burned down in 1574 and rebuilt in 1583, and perhaps in the cathedral too, built originally of the same materials as the palace of the sultan of Brunei. The doors that did not perish in the frequent fires disappeared in the bombings of World War Two.

203 F. de Sande, *Relation of the Philippine Islands*, in Nicholl, *European Sources*, pp. 39ff.

204 Carroll, "Francisco de Sande's invasion of Brunei in 1578", p. 52.

Palawan) plus Mindoro and the northern coast of current Sabah as far as Kinabatangan. And with the lifting of commercial restrictions by the Ming in 1567, the bulk of Chinese trade had never been so important. The authorities thus applied the strategy used by Malay countries, which consisted of luring the traders of the richest trading posts (Chinese, Indian, Siamese, Japanese, etc.), holding them to ransom and raiding the neighbouring coasts.

Since the arrival of Pigafetta, Brunei continued to prosper. Possessing its own shipyards, the city seemed particularly well equipped: bamboo pipes carried water from the surrounding hills to well-constructed houses; it possessed a superb mosque with five floors, built in a dark wood resembling ebony wood (probably aloes wood)[205] that had alongside the *minbar* a stone block with gold Arabic calligraphy.[206] The palace, which had changed location since 1521, moving from water to land,[207] was as richly gilded as the mosque, and was solidly defended.[208]

However, the Spanish operation was a failure, for the king[209] and most of the population withdrew to the mountains and marshes, and the remainder left for Sarawak. Worse, the Spanish, who made hasty fortifications, fell ill with dysentery one after another. After 72 days of occupation, the squadron left for Manila. The Bruneians, who had recovered some of the artillery pieces of their adversaries but lacked munitions, which they intended to procure in Siam,[210] soon re-established themselves above Kota Batu and resumed their shipbuilding. The Spaniards sent a fleet to re-open negotiations with Brunei in 1579 but were unable even to meet the sovereign. Realising that they could not hold the

[205] Ibid., p. 36.
[206] And not, as stated by the notary Alfonso Bertran (Nicholl, *European Sources*, p. 46), ornamented with gilt figurines, which would hardly have been appropriate near the *minbar*. It was evidently a bas-relief for the consecration of the mosque and thus detested by the Spanish, who took it back to Manila and idiotically used it as a millstone in the docks (Carroll, "Francisco de Sande's invasion of Brunei in 1578", p. 67).
[207] Ibid., p. 52.
[208] Contrary to what is stated in *A Relation of the Philippines Islands* (c. 1586, Nicholl, ibid., p. 61), the palace and main buildings were built of wood, not stone. This is logical given the scarcity of the material and the nature of the habitat.
[209] He positioned himself with his galley in Pulau Chermin, beside Muara, Brunei's main port.
[210] Nicholl, *European Sources*, p. 84.

terrain,[211] they abandoned any desire to conquer Brunei, especially once they learned of the death of their protégé Pengiran Seri Lela.

Reconstruction and Resumed Expansion

Brunei was, however, under shock. The genealogy of the sultans, engraved on a gold plaque, disappeared in the confusion.[212] This opened a breach in the dynastic continuity, on which legitimacy was partly founded; the dissension within the royal family stirred up by the Spanish (1578, 1581, etc.) only aggravated matters. From 5,000–6,000 homes (25,000–36,000 inhabitants) in 1578,[213] Brunei town was left with only 200–300 homes in 1600 (a twentieth of its former population),[214] as its inhabitants re-settled in other places on the west coast, notably Lawas and Sarawak. Worse still, the attack occurred during a full restructuration of Insulindian equilibrium: the empire of Mataram was on its way to dominating a major part of Javanese territory except for Banten (West Java), and the Portuguese, who had just been expelled from one of the two most important emporiums of the Moluccas (Ternate) and were subject to incessant pressure from Aceh (supported by the Ottomans since 1564), were seeking a fresh strategy.

In addition to preventing a new attack by rebuilding the capital more upstream so it would be protected by the narrowness of the channel and by a bastion at Pulau Chermin, Brunei had no choice but to reinforce its ties with the Malay sultanates, in particular with the closest one, Patani, which was an interface with the prime power of the Indochinese Peninsula: Siam. While the sultanate still showed superficial goodwill towards the Spaniards, it tried in 1588 to foment a new insurrection in Manila with the help of its tributaries of Sulu and Mindanao and support from Japanese mercenaries. But the Spanish, who got wind of it, executed the principal conspirators in Manila[215] and exiled their

[211] There was no other place to settle than the Brunei River, which implied living alongside the sultan, whose subjects would be ungovernable by foreigners (Nicholl, ibid., pp. 78, 86–7).

[212] Carroll, "Berunai in the *Boxer Codex*": 4.

[213] Carroll, "Francisco de Sande's invasion of Brunei in 1578", p. 54.

[214] Van Noort, in Nicholl, *European Sources*, p. 99.

[215] Related to the reigning family of Brunei.

Figure 2. Ship of the Sultan of Brunei, Armed with Two Cannons in the Prow
(Olivier van Noort, *Description du pénible voyage faict entour de l'univers ou globe terrestre*, Amsterdam: C. Claesz., 1602, pl. XIV no. 2)

families to Mexico.[216] Brunei then expanded towards the south by taking control of Sambas,[217] given to the second son of the sultan of Brunei, Raja Tengah. Then, tired of war, it signed a treaty with the Spaniards in 1599. Trade between Manila and Brunei soon resumed: Bruneians brought camphor, magnificent palm nets, sago, slaves, ceramics and black terracotta jars, and they went away with Spanish wine, rice and cotton fabrics.[218]

216 The Spaniards were ruthless: they decapitated several nephews, sons and grandsons of Raja Suleiman, the last raja of Manila (Nicholl, *European Sources*, p. 92).

217 E.U. Kratz, "Silsilah raja-Raja Sambas as a source of history", *Archipel* 20 (1980): 255–67.

218 Antonio de Morga, *Successos de las Islas Filipinas*, trans. J.S. Cummings (Cambridge: Cambridge University Press and The Hakluyt Society, 1971), p. 309; Morga stayed in the Philippines from 1595–1603 as a magistrate.

NEW COMMERCIAL ROUTES AND INTERNAL RIVALRIES (1600–1905)

The Dutch Card and Its Failure

The Reign of Sultan Hassan

After the Spanish devastation, the "re-foundation" of the sultanate's institutions began, re-ordering social and political space, particularly since the commercial context had once again become favourable to Brunei. The deviation of a share of the Chinese trade towards Manila was now balanced by the success of the Japanese trade during the first two decades of the 17th century.[1] The opportunity was supplied by the irruption of a new Western player on the scene, present too in Japan and enemy of the Iberians: Holland. The first Dutch expedition (Van Noort, December 1600–January 1601) was aborted. The Dutch, whose company Vereenigde Oost-Indische Compagnie (VOC) was being set up,[2] distrusted their contact (a Chinese from Patani) and withdrew after ten days. Several months later, a strong personality, Sultan Hassan, ascended the Bruneian throne. To counter the Spanish threat, he resumed contact with the Dutch in Patani in 1604. Despite the communication delays, Bruneian advances were rewarded three years later (1609) by a letter from the *Staathouder*. Meanwhile, the VOC, whose sole objective was to secure its supply lines, especially with the Moluccas, had already expelled the Portuguese

[1] Iwai Hino and S. Durai Raja Singam, *Stray Notes on Nippon-Malaisian Historical Connections* (Kuala Lumpur: KL Museum, vol. 5, 1944), 164 p.
[2] Founded in 1602.

from Ambon (in 1605) and negotiated an agreement at Banda (1607). However, the company deliberately disobeyed its supervising authorities in 1609: it supported the revolt of Bruneian officials on the coastal band extending from Sambas (known for its diamantiferous potential) to Mukah, which proclaimed its allegiance to Johor,[3] and did not send the *Staathouder*'s missive to its addressee.

Brunei launched an expedition against Sambas but it had to turn back due to bad weather. This was, however, only a postponement. The Dutch, massacred in Sambas in January 1611 by partisans of Sultan Hassan, discovered too late that they had bet on the wrong player.[4] After ordering the execution of his opponents,[5] Sultan Hassan decided to consolidate the royal government, taking inspiration from the institutions set up in Aceh by Sultan Iskandar Muda,[6] whose efficacy was demonstrated by his capture of sensitive trading outposts west of Sumatra.[7] While the VOC in return raided Sambas, Hassan, who was able to regain control of Sulu in 1612 and delegate it (if we can trust information from Brunei and not from Sulu)[8] to one of his sons (Raja Bongsu)[9] as viceroy (*adipati*), now found himself in a stranglehold between the Spaniards and the dominant rivalling powers of the Malacca Strait, Aceh and Johor. Hassan took the side of Aceh, too distant to represent any threat. The calculation paid off, since Brunei found itself in 1615 on the winning side. But the calm was short-lived: Hassan's death around 1617[10] sparked off a new succession crisis, while the regional context continued to

---

[3] Showing that Brunei at the time was as important as Johor within the Malay world, E.U. Kratz, "*Yang tersurat dan yang tersirat*, Historicity and Historical Truth", *Archipel* 60 (2000): 22–44.

[4] L.C. van Dijk, "Dutch Relations with Borneo in the Seventeenth Century (I)", *BMJ* 5, 3 (1983): 61–80.

[5] Sweeney, *Silsilah [A]*, p. 20 (f. 16).

[6] Low, "Selesilah", p. 17; Low, "Batu Tarsilah", p. 22; Sweeney, *Silsilah [A]*, p. 12 (f. 3) and *Silsilah [B]*, p. 56 (f. 9).

[7] Denys Lombard, *Le sultanat d'Atjéh au temps d'Iskandar Muda, 1607–1636* (Paris: PEFEO, 1967), 297 p.

[8] C. Majul (*Muslims in the Philippines*, pp. 15, 421ff.) thought he was related to the royal family of Brunei, but there is no evidence that he was the son of Sultan Hassan.

[9] R. Nicholl, *Raja Bongsu of Sulu: A Brunei Hero in His Time* (Kuala Lumpur: MBRAS, monograph no. 19, 1991), 78 p.

[10] Hugh Low, ed. D.E. Brown, "Hugh Low on the History of Brunei", *BMJ* 1, 1 (1969): 147–55; R. Nicholl, "Some Problems of Brunei Chronology", *JSAS* 20, 2 (Sept. 1989): 187.

deteriorate. Due to growing pressure from the Spaniards, Sulu unleashed hostilities in 1627 by raiding the naval dockyard at Camarines[11] with the help of Bruneians subjects, notably the Bajaus; in retaliation the Spanish pillaged and destroyed the tombs of the last three sultans in Jolo. Afraid of being the next target, Brunei sent a first embassy to Batavia,[12] with no apparent result other than the arrival of a VOC ship in Brunei. The Portuguese secular partnership was losing momentum: even if it succeeded in reinstalling the sultan of Johor to his throne in 1629 after a crushing victory over Aceh,[13] it could not prevent Johor from allying with the VOC.

Spanish Manoeuvres

In the 1630s, the situation went from bad to worse, as conflict with Sulu regularly ravaged the north coasts of Borneo.[14] Brunei was forced to rely on the Bajaus (*orang laut*), who pillaged boats that passed within range and occasionally preyed along the Philippine coasts,[15] and to prepare a counter-offensive, presumed imminent in 1637.[16] The Spanish profited from the conflict to establish their pawns in the south: they built a fort at Zamboanga in 1635, took Maguindanao in 1637, then Sulu in January 1638,[17] whose sultan took refuge in Tawi-Tawi. Fearing that it would be the next target, Brunei sent an emissary to Batavia in May 1638,[18] who managed to extract a promise of support from the VOC although it remained vague, since the Iberians were seemingly unable to get a perennial foothold in southern Philippines. Faced with the revolt of the Chinese in Manila in 1639, all the more threatening because it echoed

---

[11] C. Majul, *Muslims in the Philippines,* p. 141.

[12] It left Batavia in June 1627; A. van der Chijs, ed., *Dagh Register gehouden in't Casteel Batavia 1627* [henceforth *DR*] (The Hague: M. Nijhoff), p. 317.

[13] Barbara Watson Andaya and Leonard Y. Andaya, *A History of Malaysia* (London: Macmillan, 1982), p. 61.

[14] C. Majul, *Muslims in the Philippines,* p. 198.

[15] The *Camucones* in Spanish sources (A.V. Horton, *Turun-temurun: A Dissection of Brunei Darussalam* [Bordesley: AVM Horton, 1998], p. 14).

[16] R. Nicholl, "Some problems of Brunei chronology", *JSAS* 20, 2 (September 1989): 188, quoting *The Philippines Islands*, ed. Emma Blair and James A. Robertson, vol. 21.

[17] Where they destroyed Korans and other precious Arab manuscripts (Majul, *Muslims in the Philippines*, p. 94).

[18] L.C. van Dijk, "Relations of the East Indian Company with Borneo (Brunei), the Sulu Archipelago, Mindanao, etc.", *BMJ* 5, 4 (1984): 25.

the troubles that augured the fall of the Ming dynasty in continental China, they had to abandon Maguindanao. As soon as the VOC, which profited from the decline of Aceh following the death of Iskandar Muda (1636) to strengthen its alliance with Johor in 1639,[19] took Malacca in January 1641,[20] the company renewed its support for Brunei, which feared the coming intrusion of a Spanish fleet of 100 ships and urgently demanded munitions.[21] As the sultan had just escaped an attack fomented by a Portuguese from Cambodia,[22] the sultanate now sent a delegation to Batavia each year.[23] Sulu, which had regained the support of Brunei in 1642, followed with two embassies (1642 and 1644)[24] and obtained from the VOC the sending of two ships to Jolo, which failed initially to destroy the Spanish fort but succeeded in 1646. The Spanish signed peace treaties with Maguindanao (1645) and Sulu (1646),[25] then withdrew their troops from southern Philippines (keeping only Zamboanga), in order to defend Manila from a possible attack by the merchant-pirates and Ming loyalists of Zheng Chenggong.[26] Brunei then mounted an operation

[19] L. Andaya, *The Kingdom of Johor 1641–1728* (Kuala Lumpur: Oxford University Press, 1975), pp. 24–7, 56–7.

[20] On the taking of Malacca by the VOC, see A. Gerring, *De verovering van de stad Malacca (thans Singapore genaamd) door de Oost-Indische Compagnie in het jaar 1641, overgenomen uit het dagh-register van het Casteel Batavia* (Soekaboemi, Tan Soeij Bing, 1927), 36 p. The Dutch on this occasion offered a delicate present to the Sultan of Brunei's envoy: 5 *picul* [see glossary in Annex II] of sulphur, as much saltpetre, 100 *catties* of Dutch powder and 220 cannon balls.

[21] Brunei sent an ambassador to Batavia along with 60 other men on a boat loaded with camphor and slaves; the sultan demanded saltpetre and sulphur, gunpowder and cannon balls, and offered the governor a significant present: 3 *bezoars*, one *catty* of camphor, a *picul* of wax and two slaves (*DR* 1641, 21–22 April, p. 268).

[22] Fernando de Lima Pacheco, who exported Cambodian rice to Brunei, tried to poison the sultan and his principal dignitaries. He was executed and his slaves were resold by Bruneians—who did not lose their way—to Batavia [L.C. van Dijk, "Relations of the East Indian Company with Borneo (Brunei)", p. 26].

[23] *DR* 1644, p. 70.

[24] The emissary was described as Pengiran "Silikala" (the Dutch transcription of his title *Siri Lela*), grandson of the *Bendahara* of Sulu (*DR* 1644, p. 46).

[25] Moshe Yegar, *Between integration and secession, the Muslim communities of Southern Philippines, Southern Thailand, and Western Burma/Myanmar* (Lanham: Rowman & Littlefield, 2002), p. 202.

[26] After the capture of the leader of the Ming loyalists merchant-pirates, Zheng Zhilong, held hostage in Peking in 1646, his son Zheng Chenggong (aka. Koxinga in Western sources), supported by the majority of the clan, took over the paternal commitments: he supported the Ming pretenders, who had taken refuge in South China, which led to a resumption of piracy against the upholders of the Qing order.

of 250 ships and 5,000 men against the Spaniards in 1647, but failed to reach Manila.[27]

In retaliation, as soon as the Zheng menace was gone (1649), the Spanish took the lead, not by directly attacking the heart of the sultanate but by raiding the coasts of north Borneo under its control.[28] Brunei interrupted its embassies to Batavia as significant internal difficulties had arisen. After the assassination of Sultan Muhammad Ali by the *Bendahara*, the monarchy split into two rival branches.[29] One of the pretenders, ex-*Bendahara* Abdul Mubin,[30] was installed in Pulau Chermin while the other, Muhyiddin, in the former capital, which drove away a good portion of the foreign traders, starting with the Chinese. The intervention of Sulu (after the retirement of Raja Bongsu around 1649) on the side of Muhyiddin (if we follow Brunei's version of the story)[31] ended with the abandonment of Bruneian privileges on part of the northern coast of Borneo, normally held by the members of the royal family (called *pulau raja*) who benefited from their kinship with the Bajaus through the maternal line.[32] Abdul Mubin destroyed all the regalia, sending them into the bay with a cannon shot. He was ultimately executed. The Sulu archipelago then left the orbit of Brunei.

Brunei's position became more fragile as a series of new polities appeared in the northeast of Borneo, of which the most important was Bulungan, founded by a Brunei aristocrat c. 1650.[33] It was not until 1654

[27] van Dijk, "Relations of the East Indian Company with Borneo (Brunei)", p. 30.
[28] Nicholl, *European Sources*, p. 106.
[29] See an exact dating of the event in Nicholl, "Some Problems of Brunei Chronology", *JSAS* 20, 2 (September 1989): 175–95; C. Majul, *Muslims in the Philippines*, p. 199 gives the date 1662 for the start of the civil war between the two pretenders.
[30] He was assassinated with all his sons, except for the last two. At first Abdul Mubin ascended the throne and named Muhyddin *Bendahara*; the latter pushed him to settle in Pulau Chermin for security reasons, then seized power in the capital and proclaimed himself sultan (D.E. Brown, "Hugh Low on the history of Brunei", *BMJ* 1 [1969]: 151–3).
[31] See Brunei's *Silsilah*. The Sulu version is slightly different: both parties bid for the support of the Sulu fleet when it arrived. Sultan Muhyiddin offered the countries north of the Kimanis river (*tulin*, i.e. personal property of its rival Abdul Mubin) and Abdul Mubin, the land west of the Brunei River. The Sulunese choose Muhyiddin's offer, as it was closer to their own land (D.E. Brown, "Hugh Low on the history of Brunei", *BMJ* 1 [1969]: 162–3).
[32] Low, "*Selesilah*", p. 11.
[33] Bernard Sellato, *Forest, Resources and People in Bulungan: Elements for a History of Settlement, Trade and Social Dynamics in Borneo 1880–2000* (Jakarta: Center for International Forestry Research, 2001), pp. 17ff.

that Muhyiddin,[34] who had re-established his authority in Serudong[35] (north of current Sabah) while maintaining control south of Palawan, asked again for Dutch help against the Spanish. His request was refused due to the Treaty of Westphalia;[36] the embassy of 1655 was similarly turned away.

However, Brunei did manage to reinstate its tutelage over Sambas while reconstructing its commercial network upset by the civil war. According to the ceramics and coins found in Kota Batu, the Chinese were very active, alongside various commercial ethnic groups and Westerners. Among the latter were the *Vrijburghers* ("free merchants" operating outside the VOC), who exchanged opium procured in Bengal and Indian cotton fabrics (one of the commodities most in demand in Insulindia) for gold.[37] Brunei regularly imported iron, new or used, to feed its forges.

With Spain completing its withdrawal from the South Philippines in 1663 (abandoning Zamboanga because of the Zheng threat, the latter having just expelled the VOC from Taiwan), Brunei tried again to play the Dutch card. It despatched a first embassy to Malacca in June 1663, which left two months later with a trading licence, despite a lack of interest from the VOC due to the modesty of the traffic, and renewed the operation in 1664. In 1666, it accelerated the process by sending a delegation directly to Batavia to negotiate passports for Siam and Patani. This delegation included a missive from the sultan of Sulu,[38] thus proving the re-establishment of positive relations between the two kingdoms. While the permits were granted, abuses were unfortunately so frequent that the Dutch governor demanded in 1667 the repayment or restitution of merchandise owed for seven years to a Malay resident from Batavia by one of the sultan's sons.[39]

---

[34] According to the version of the *Silsilah* translated by H. Low ("*Selesilah*", p. 12), Abdul Mubin, once defeated, ordered the destruction of all the regalia (including the insignia given by the Chinese to the king of *Boni*) and sent the crown of Brunei into the bay with a cannon shot.

[35] Also confirmed by Spanish sources (Nicholl, "Relations between Brunei and Manila A.D. 1682–1690", *BMJ* 4, 1 [1977]: 131).

[36] The Treaty of Westphalia (1648) put an end to the Thirty Years' War and recognised the independence of the Netherlands.

[37] van Dijk, "Relations of the East Indian Company with Borneo (Brunei)", p. 30.

[38] Written in Spanish, although it could have been written in Malay, since the VOC had many interpreters in Batavia (*DR* 1666, pp. 91–4).

[39] Pengiran Adil (*DR* 1667, p. 316).

Competition from Emporiums in South Borneo

The political situation seemed to deteriorate in Brunei once again after the death of Muhyiddin (c. 1671),[40] judging by the decline in material conditions for foreign trade, which was penalised by increasing exactions from the officials, whose practices included putting creditors in jail. The new sultan tried in 1673 to revive relations with the VOC by sending back to Batavia three merchants who had been held in Brunei for the last two years. As a preamble to any agreement, the Company required the normalisation of trade rights and detained the Bruneian emissaries sent to Batavia until the sultan had settled the debts of his subjects[41]—although this did not prevent a boat from leaving for Brunei in the middle of talks.[42] The contention seemed to be resolved in 1675, as exchanges between Batavia and Brunei resumed and were maintained—even on a very modest scale—until the end of the 1670s, when Brunei once again demanded the support of the VOC in a letter sent to Malacca (in 1679).[43]

Brunei was challenged by emporiums from south Borneo (Banjermasin and Sukadana) and by the rise of new actors, most of them Bugis, at Pasir and Berau, on the east coast of the island. Since the Dutch conquest of the sultanate of Goa-Makassar (1669), the rivalries between the various principalities southwest of Sulawesi, as well as the rise of regional commerce, had pushed the Bugis to relocate their power centres.[44]

The Dutch card having proven disappointing, Brunei reopened negotiations with Spain in 1682, hoping to resume trade by attracting the Chinese through Manila. The Spanish sent an embassy to Brunei in 1685,[45] generating in its wake a new series of historical sources revealing

---

[40] Nicholl, "Some Problems of Brunei Chronology", p. 190.

[41] *DR* 1673, 8–10 July (pp. 186–8) and 4 Sept. (pp. 248–50), the Dutch sources not mentioning the name of the sultan.

[42] *DR* 1673, p. 244.

[43] Letter from Pengiran Di Gadong, van Dijk, "Relations of the East Indian Company with Borneo (Brunei)", p. 31.

[44] Watson Andaya and Andaya, *A History of Malaysia*, p. 72.

[45] The sultan mentioned by the Spanish sources (Muhammad Aliuddin, who, according to Brunei official historiography, should have reigned from 1730–37, cf. Saunders, *A History of Brunei*, p. 43) was ready to redeem the captives raided along the Philippine coasts for seven times less than the usual price: 50 pesos per capita as opposed to 350 (R. Nicholl, "Relations between Brunei and Manila AD 1682–1690", *BMJ* 4, 1 [1977]: 144).

that a little over a century after the destruction of its capital, the sultanate had rebuilt its political apparatus[46] and had largely recovered its prosperity. The king gave his orders by the mediation of the *Bendahara*, who served as prime minister; justice was dealt with by the Tumenggong; finances and storage by the Di Gadong, who kept accounts of the tribute paid by the various holders of riverine privileges. The supervision of weaponry was judiciously divided between two officials: the *Bendahara* held the stocks of saltpetre and sulphur necessary for making gunpowder; the Panglima, who commanded the fleet, was in charge of its fabrication.[47] It was capable of putting 8,000 armed men[48] along the Spanish ambassador's way; supposing that about one-third of male adults was thus mobilised, the capital—elsewhere described as densely populated—would have contained at least some 60,000–70,000 persons. Apart from the one resource that had made its reputation, camphor, the kingdom also produced pepper (in Mukah and Tuaran),[49] wax, pearls and diamonds, by the intermediary of non-Malay, coastal (Bajau and Bisayah) and hill tribes. The latter remained particularly bellicose, to the point that the Bruneians only went to the hills under escort and highly armed. The principal commercial partners of the sultanate—apart from the Chinese—were Siam (goods were weighed in Siamese *cattys*)[50] and Patani. Trade practices somehow improved, since Brunei obtained an agreement with the VOC few years later in 1688.

[46] However, the Spanish sources do not mention the *Pemancha*, whom the emissaries must not have met, unless the office was vacant at the time.

[47] The capital was built on water, except for the palace, which was built on land and strongly defended, and whence the king never left.

[48] Nicholl, "Relations between Brunei and Manila", p. 166.

[49] Ibid., p. 157.

[50] *DR* 1673, p. 187. 1 Siamese *catty* = 1/2 Chinese *catty*, or about 300 grams (Sir John Bowring, *The Kingdom and People of Siam*, vol. 1 [London: John W. Parker & Son, 1857], p. 259).

The Double Gap in the 18th Century

The Silence of Sources

The calm was short-lived. The death in 1690 of Sultan Muhammad Aliuddin (as the Spanish sources refer to him,[51] whereas his name is absent from both the *Silsilah* and the *Batu Tarsilah*) and the fact that his successor was underaged unleashed a new cycle of civil war, as evidenced (by default) by the silence of Western sources in the following decade. The conflict again emptied the capital of a large part of its population, which included no more than 2,000–3,000 houses (10,000–20,000 people)[52] at the start of the 18th century. The political situation seemed somewhat more stable at the turn of the century, with the sultanate developing the opium trade in 1704[53] and exporting pepper at the start of the 1710s.[54] In addition, it resumed diplomatic activity, sending embassies to Jambi in 1704, to Batavia in 1712, to Palembang (1714[55] and 1718[56]) and three years later (1721)[57] to Malacca.

[51] Nicholl, "Relations between Brunei and Manila", p. 173. On the other hand, Sultan Muhammad Aliuddin is not mentioned in Sweeney, *Silsilah [A]*, p. 13, which does mention instead a Sultan Muhiuddin.
[52] On the basis of five to six persons per home; François Valentyn, "A description of Borneo and our Trade There", *Oud en Nieuw Oost Indies* (Dordrecht: Joannes van Braam, 1726), Book 3, Chs. 1–3, translated in *BMJ* 4, 2 (1978): 76.
[53] Willem P. Coolhaas et al., eds., *Generale missiven van Gouverneurs-generaal en Raden aan Heren XVII der Verenigde Oostindische Compagnie*, 26 February 1704, vol. VI, p. 281.
[54] Cf. *Generale missiven*, vol. VII, p. 174.
[55] Ibid.
[56] Carrying a letter from the "viceroy"—the *Bendahara* Sri Maharaja Parameswara (*Generale Missiven*, vol. VII, p. 398, August 1713).
[57] Ibid., p. 598.

Then Brunei disappeared once more from Western sources (at least published ones,[58] there might be mentions in unpublished Dutch and Iberian documents) for more than half a century. This, combined with the hiatus of 70 years in Low's genealogies, from the 17th sultan (based on the treaty of 1685 and if the Spanish transcription in the name of the sovereign is valid) to the 18th sultan[59] (who reigned in 1762 and died in 1795), attests to recurrent crises. Given the political system in Brunei, where the major part of the "useful" territory—the rivers and deltas—was divided into domains endowed to officials (sultan, *kerajaan*; viziers, *kuripan*) or granted by hereditary positions (in princely estates or *tulin*), each crisis further destroyed the territorial linkage among the various estuaries that composed the sultanate.

Brunei between Sulu and the Bugis

Worse, these internal conflicts echoed two kinds of external pressure emanating from the Tausug of Sulu and the Bugis of Sulawesi, which progressively squeezed Brunei.

First, the coastal north of Borneo that Muhyiddin had ceded to the sultan of Sulu in exchange for his support against the usurper Abdul Mubin managed to escape Brunei's tutelage at the beginning of the 18th century.[60] Yet Sulu was unable to exercise any real control since it was forced to lead several expeditions against Tirun (also called Tidung)[61] starting from the late 1710s.[62] The same was true of South Palawan, whose sovereignty was apparently ceded by the Bruneians to the sultan of Sulu at the end of the 17th century, who in turn offered it unsuccessfully to Spain in 1705. Hence the Bajau, who had therefore guarded

[58] For the Dutch sources, *Generale missiven*, vol. IX *1730–1736*, vol. X *1737–43*, vol. XI *1743–1750*, vol. XII *1750–1755*, vol. XIII *1756–1761*, La Haye, 1985–2007.

[59] Low, "*Selesilah*", p. 19 and Sweeney, *Silsilah [A]*, p. 12.

[60] Based on the counting of generations in A. Dalrymple, "Essay toward an account of Sulu", in *Oriental Repertory* (London: G. Bigg, 1793), pp. 525–31.

[61] Located on the north-eastern coast of Borneo, Tidung/Tirun (Seyasap) came about in the middle of the 17th century after the coagulation of coastal tribes and foreign merchants, some of whom (the Tausug of Sulu and Bugis) were bearers of a more advanced political model. The same was true of a second polity named Tidung, Tidung Sembakung, first situated at Pulau Mandu, whose inhabitants then settled in Pagar (Sellato, *Forest, Resources and People in Bulungan*, pp. 19ff).

[62] Majul, *Muslims in the Philippines*, p. 200.

the coasts of Brunei, were left to their own devices, and some clans re-pledged allegiance to Sulu.[63] Thus at the beginning of the 1760s Sulu assumed sovereignty of four districts in current Sabah: Marudu, Maguindora, Tirun and Kinabalu (the latter separated from Brunei by the Kimanis).[64] Brunei refused to acknowledge the claims of Sulu over these four districts, which had become uncontrollable. As the sultan still held some personal possessions (*tulin*) in Palawan in 1778,[65] skirmishes between both sultanates became more and more frequent.

Second, Brunei had to thwart the push of the Bugis. Not only did they settle permanently on the nodal points of the intra-Insulindian trade, they also profited from the crumbling of local political powers, who were subject to growing pressure and competition from Westerners, to grasp political command. The Bugis served as "palace administrators" in Johor (Riau) starting from 1721; founded a new dynasty in Aceh (1727); established an independent sultanate in Selangor; and even laid siege to Malacca twice (1756–57 and 1784). In Borneo, they settled in Pasir on the east coast, then the gold and diamond-trading regions of Kutai, Samarinda, Pontianak,[66] etc. Although they were ignored by the various *Silsilah* of Brunei, save for a few epigraphic traces, their influence is attested to by three kinds of sources: the *Sya'ir Awang Simawn*, which repeatedly mentions conflicts opposing Brunei and the Bugis in north

---

[63] D.E. Brown, "Brunei and the Bajau", *BRB* 3, 2 (1971): 57. The Bajaus' link with the sultan of Brunei is similar to that of the *orang laut* of Riau with Johor: they ensured supervision of the coasts northwest of Borneo in the sultan's name; in exchange, they paid themselves "in kind", by plundering passing ships (see Leonard Andaya, *Leaves of the Same Tree: Trade and Ethnicity in the Straits of Melaka* [Cambridge History of Early Modern Southeast Asia, 2008], Ch. 6, pp. 173–201). Better still, the Bajau were matrimonially allied with the *Temenggong*, just like how in Malacca and Johor, the *orang laut* were allied with the *Laksamana* (p. 186, referring to *Hikayat Hang Tuah*), then after the end of the 18th century (in Johor) to the *Temenggong*.

[64] Also called Papal; Dalrymple, "Essay toward an account of Sulu".

[65] F.W. Douglas, "Notes on the Historical Geography of Malaya and Sidelights on the Malay Annals", in *The Study of Ancient Times in the Malay Peninsula and Straits of Malacca*, ed. Roland Braddell (Kuala Lumpur: MBRAS, 1980), p. 474, mentions having found in Singapore in 1913 a document from 1778 signed and sealed by the sultan of Sulu attesting that the *tulin* of Palawan was the property of the sultan of Brunei.

[66] James Warren, *The Sulu Zone 1768–1898: The Dynamics of External Trade, Slavery, and Ethnicity in the Transformation of a Southeast Asian Maritime State* (Singapore: Singapore University Press, 1981), pp. 10ff.

Borneo;[67] the *Tuhfat al-Nafis*;[68] and finally by the British. Dalrymple signals in 1768 that Brunei had been in a state of civil war for several years and that the Bugis exercised considerable influence;[69] Thomas Forrest mentions a Bugis pirogue displaying the British flag in February 1776 and employed three Bugis caulkers for his own ship.[70] On top of various written testimonies, many Bugis terms are found in the Malay dialect of Brunei.[71]

Thoroughly weakened, Brunei was attacked by Sulu in 1771. To gain external support, Sultan Omar Ali Saifuddin I signed in June 1774 a treaty with the promising newcomers—the British—who were in search of a warehouse on the route to Canton and who obtained exclusive rights to the pepper trade in exchange for their military help.[72] The British had been particularly successful, taking Manila in 1762, and while they abandoned it in 1764, they also signed a treaty with Sulu (whose sovereign they had liberated from the Spanish) that granted them Balambangan, where they established themselves in 1770. The British soon opened an outlet in Brunei, and when Sulu attacked Balambangan in 1775, its leaders took refuge in Labuan.[73] But the financial abyss of Balambangan (and through it, the loss of the East India Company as a whole) was such that, despite the offer of Labuan, the British left Brunei in 1777.

A Loss of Substance

During this troubled period, Brunei nevertheless remained well integrated in regional commerce: the sultanate continued trading with Western

[67] In Utay, Papan, Sandungan, Kuran, etc. (Maxwell, "Accessing the Epic Status of the Brunei Malay Sya'ir Awang Simawn", 2006: part II: 26–9, 39).
[68] It mentions the alliance between Utin Nawang and the *pangeran* Abd al-Ghafur, raja (and not sultan) of Brunei at the time of the foundation of Pontianak (V. Matheson and B. Watson Andaya, eds., *The Precious Gift [Tuhfat al-Nafis], translated from Raja Ali Haji Ibn Ahmad* [Kuala Lumpur: Oxford University Press, 1982], p. 29).
[69] Quoted in Saunders, *A History of Brunei*, p. 65.
[70] Thomas Forrest, *Voyage aux Moluques et à la Nouvelle Guinée fait sur la galère le Tartare en 1774, 1775 & 1776 par ordre de la Compagnie Angloise* (Paris, 1780), pp. 413–4.
[71] Interview with Mariam Ali, Universiti Brunei Darussalam (UBD), November 2010.
[72] J. Warren, *The Sulu Zone 1768–1898*, p. 77.
[73] They wanted to force the cousin of the sultan of Sulu to discharge his liabilities (Johannes Willi, "Early Relations of England with Borneo to 1805", PhD dissertation, Berne, Langesalza, 1922, p. 110).

countries—with the Dutch via Malacca, and the Portuguese via Macao. Given their presence in Sulu, at least a dozen Bugis ships should have stopped by each year. Chinese junks (four to seven a year from Amoy[74] and one or two from Macao)[75] that exported ceramics[76] and loaded pepper, camphor, birds' nests, etc., also anchored in Brunei throughout the years 1760–90.[77] Since these products all originated in the sultanate's hinterland, and particularly in today's Sabah, this Chinese presence shows that even if Sulu had seized a section of the supply channels for North Borneo to nurture its trade to China, supported by the resumption of tribute sending after three centuries of interruption,[78] Brunei still preserved links with its traditional suppliers. As a matter of fact, junks of 500–600 tonnes were still constructed on the Brunei River by Chinese naval carpenters.[79] And daily trade in the sultanate's capital remained very lively, with thousands of small boats stretched almost a dozen kilometres along the river.[80]

However, the dissensions within the monarchy ended up reducing the power of the sultan to a largely symbolic suzerainty beyond the Brunei Bay, giving rise to two opposing movements, material and cultural. Starting out with some 15,000 inhabitants at the start of the 19th century, the capital's demographic growth was slowing down. Not only had its population stagnated within a century, half of these residents were now Chinese, either businessmen or pepper growers.[81] The "Malays" of the Brunei River had emigrated to the north of Borneo or to

---

[74] "… of five or six hundred tonnes each" (Forrest, *Voyages aux Moluques et à la Nouvelle Guinée*, pp. 431, 434).

[75] Pierre-Yves Manguin, "Brunei Trade with Macao at the Turn of the 19th Century, à propos of a 1819 letter from Sultan Khan Zul Alam", *BMJ* 6, 3 (1987): 16–25.

[76] Jim Hendrick, "Ceramics found at Sinaut agricultural training centre", *BMJ* 7, 3 (1991): 1–9.

[77] Alexander Dalrymple, *HEIC MS Borneo Factory Records*, p. 495, quoted by R. Nicholl, "Some problems of Brunei chronology", *JSAS* 20, 2 (September 1989): 192; Forrest, *Voyage aux Moluques et à la Nouvelle Guinée*, pp. 432ff.

[78] In 1725 (Majul, *Muslims in the Philippines*, pp. 300ff).

[79] *Singapore Chronicle*, December 1824, citing John Jesse, British resident in Brunei (1775), in "Borneo Proper", *Notices of the Indian Archipelago, and adjacent countries: being a collection of papers relating to Borneo…*, ed. J.H. Moor, 1837, pp. 1–4.

[80] A distance similar to that between "London and Westminster bridges" (Forrest, *Voyages aux Moluques et à la Nouvelle Guinée*, p. 433).

[81] J. Willi, *Early Relations of England with Borneo to 1805*, p. 102, citing J. Hunt's report.

Sarawak,[82] revealing the political dysfunction of a society that once hosted hundreds of ships.

The government tried to remedy the social haemorrhage by a cultural reconstruction of the political apparatus at the top, which had suffered several crises of succession. While the royal *Silsilah* had not been put down in writing since its destruction in 1578, the document was transcribed for the first time by Datu Imam Ya'akub around 1735.[83] Seventy-five years later in 1807,[84] in order to quell contestation, it was engraved on the *Batu Tarsilah*, near the grave of the sovereign who had ordered its writing (Muhammad Tajuddin). In the same period, the Brunei myth of foundation was formalised in the *Sya'ir Awang Simawn*, modelled on great royal epics such as the *Sejarah Melayu* or the *Hikayat Banjar*: none of the episodes related in Brunei's epic occurred later than the second half of the 18th century.

---

[82] See especially the story of Pg. Mohammad Ali, from the royal family of Brunei, settling in Oya, in the Batang delta (Heidi Munan, *Thrills and Treasures of Historical Landmarks, Sarawak* [Kuala Lumpur: Marshall Cavendish, 2007], p. 22).

[83] Sweeney, *Silsilah [A]*, p. 46. Ya'akub held the genealogy from sultans Muhyiddin and Kamaluddin.

[84] Sweeney, P.L. Amin, "Batu Tarsilah, A Short Comment", *JMBRAS* 56, 2 (1974): 151–2.

Playing the British Card and Its Avatars (1803–1905)

Redistribution of the Insulindian Cards

As the bankruptcy of the VOC (1799) and the Napoleonic Wars reshuffled the Insulindian cards among the Western powers to the benefit of the British, Brunei tried in vain to revive relations with the Spanish by sending an embassy to Manila in 1802. Spain, however, favoured Sulu, with its soaring trade and greater capacity to stir things up.

As soon as the British came back to Balambangan in 1803—with instructions to remain neutral in the conflict opposing Sulu and Brunei, with the latter trying to recover north Borneo, even assassinating Sulu's emissary—Muhammad Tajuddin offered them the chance of settling in Brunei. But the British abandoned their factory in 1805 and the sultan died two years later. Sulu now had a free hand to take control of the riverine Sabah trade. The Tausug leaders took over several loading docks for merchandise collected by the hill tribes, and its dignitaries[85] cunningly financed ongoing raids by the Iranun and Balangingi on other parts of the coast.[86] The dangers of maritime traffic became such that the medium-distance trade of Brunei collapsed, deserted by the Chinese junks at the end of the 1800s.[87] The sultanate still managed to maintain

[85] *Singapore Chronicle*, December 1824, citing John Jesse, resident in Brunei (1775), in "Borneo Proper", *Notices of the Indian Archipelago, and adjacent countries: being a collection of papers relating to Borneo*..., pp. 1–4.

[86] Warren, *The Sulu Zone 1768–1898*, p. 78.

[87] J. Hunt, "Sketch of Borneo, or Pulo Kalamantan", in Sir Henry Keppel, *The Expedition to Borneo of H.M.S. Dido for the suppression of piracy*..., Vol. II, Appendix II, p. xxi.

and even re-establish a semblance of influence over a good portion of today's Sabah. In 1812—judging from the Hunt Report[88]—the so-called "Kimanis province" (which had been offered to the British by Sulu 40 years earlier) continued to export its products via the port of Brunei. The same was true of Bankaka, on the west bank of the Marudu Bay, even closer to Jolo. In one way or another,*orang kaya* of both regions managed to re-open lines with Brunei. And the sultanate remained sufficiently prized by the Muslim world for a Brunei house to be opened in Mecca in 1807.[89]

When in 1811 the British assumed control of Java and were confronted with additional problems relating to maritime security, they engaged in a struggle against the presumed nexus of piracy: Sambas, where Pangeran Anom, a charismatic Chinese half-breed, partnered Iranun bands and Bruneians (from the Brunei River, which had become a bandits' lair,[90] and from Sarawak) to prey upon the traffic of Chinese junks at Banjermasin and Pontianak, in addition to occasional Western ships.[91] After two British interventions in Sambas in 1812 and 1813, the sultan of Brunei, Muhammad Kanzul Alam, prudently refused the advances of their Dutch competitors, who sent emissaries twice, first via Sambas (1822) and then directly (1823). But the death of the sultan around 1824 resulted in yet another succession crisis, resolved by the execution of one of the pretenders, Raja Api,[92] and the accession of his rival, Omar Ali Saifuddin II.

---

88 Hunt, ibid., pp. lviii–lix.

89 Dr lik Arifin Mansurnoor, "Islamic Education, State and Society in Brunei Darussalam: An Intellectual History of the Ulama World (1903–1974)", *The International Seminar on Islamic Studies in the ASEAN Region: History, Approaches and Future Trends*, 25–28 June 1998, Prince of Songhkla University, Pattani Campus.

90 Leigh Wright, "Brunei, an historical relic", *Journal of the Royal Asiatic Society Hong Kong Branch* 17 (1977): 18, citing chart routes by James Horsburgh (1811).

91 The *Commerce* ran aground and was boarded by a mixed band from Sambas/Sarawak, and its captain and 45 crews members were sold as slaves in Brunei (Andrew Smith, "An 'arch-villain' to be rehabilitated? Mixed perceptions of Pangeran Anom of Sambas in the early nineteenth century; with an appendix on John Hunt", *BRB* [annual, 2007]: 101–17). When he became sultan in 1815, Pangeran Anom asked the Dutch to return to Sambas in 1818.

92 "Raja Api" ("Fire King"), so called either because of his bad temper or an epithet that evoked the "Fire King" and "Water King" among the Jorai, also from Austronesian stock, see Jacques Dournes, "Modèle structural et réalité ethnographique [à propos du 'Triangle culinaire]", *L'Homme* 9, 1 (1969): 42–8. Son of Muhammad Kanzul Alam, Api appeared in the official genealogy under the name Sultan Muhammad

The new sultan seized the opportunity afforded by an 1824 treaty that stabilised the positions of the two most important colonial powers in the zone, the United Kingdom and the Netherlands, to send an embassy to Singapore, accompanied by 119 boats (*perahu*),[93] that carried, in addition to traditional goods, a kind of ore (a product of Sarawak for a long time) for which the West had recently discovered new applications: antimony.[94] Since there was now renewed interest on the part of the Dutch, whose tutelage over the neighbouring sultanate of Sambas was confirmed by the 1824 treaty, he named Pengiran Indera Mahkota Mohamed Salleh as governor in 1827. Pengiran Indera Mahkota Mohamed Salleh had received a Western education in Batavia[95] and was related to the reigning family of Sambas who founded Kuching and controlled the antimony mines.

A Tenacious Predator: James Brooke

In a society where privileges meant that authority was inseparable from wealth gained from trade (which alone was enough to attract a clientele), the drop in revenue that began in Brunei at the start of the 19th century —medium-distance trade with China had disappeared when piracy declined due to Western pressure—exacerbated internal tensions among the ruling elites. The supremacy of the sultan over the princely estates,

Alam (1826–28), but the genealogy established by Low in 1875, as well as the documents of his contemporary James Brooke used by D.E. Brown (*Brunei: The Structure and History of a Bornean Malay Sultanate* [Brunei: Brunei Museum, 1970], pp. 146ff), imply that in 1822 he was strangled on the demand of his twin sister, widow of Sultan Md. Jemalul Alam (1792–93), who had died prematurely (an execution corroborated by Malay sources). The future Omar Ali Saifuddin II was prevented from ascending the throne because of his young age, on top of a physical deformity (an extra thumb on his right hand), and so was replaced by his maternal grandfather and paternal grand-uncle, Muhammad Kanzul Alam, which explains the ambitions of Raja Api. But tensions were such that Muhammad Kanzul Alam was never crowned, and neither was Omar Ali Saifuddin II.

93 According to J. Crawfurd, cited by Nicholas Tarling, *Britain, the Brookes & Brunei* (Kuala Lumpur: Oxford University Press, "Oxford in Asia", 1971), p. 32. The *Singapore Chronicle*, less well-informed, mentions 40 boats (December 1824, in *Notices of the Indian Archipelago*, ed. J.H. Moor, 1837, pp. 1–4).

94 It was used as an emetic and also combined with lead to make projectiles.

95 Matassim Hj. Jibah, "Pengiran Indera Mahkota Shabandar Mohammad Salleh and James Brooke in the History of Brunei", *BMJ* 4, 3 (1979): 38–51.

in particular those passed on through inheritance (*tulin*), became increasingly tenuous, and the growth in the number of *pengiran* made it difficult to exercise authority traditionally founded on the control of people rather than of land.[96] The Armenians of Singapore jumped into the antimony trade in 1834,[97] and the opening of the Sarawak mines sharpened the rivalries between two court factions, in the persons of its governor, Pengiran Indera Mahkota Mohamed Salleh, and an itinerant emissary of the sultan, Pengiran Muda Hashim, wazir and brother of Raja Api, who went around in 1837 to inspect, that is, to put pressure on his riverine estates in Sarawak. As the exploitation of local populations was outstripping customary norms, both men were confronted with a small-scale rebellion that lasted several years but which did not threaten Kuching.

It was at this very moment in 1839 that an English adventurer, James Brooke, burst onto the scene. Born in Benares in 1803 of a father who served as a military officer for the East India Company during the first Anglo-Burmese war, Brooke had travelled in Malay and Southern-Chinese waters for several years. Endowed with not inconsiderable means (he had used his paternal inheritance to acquire a schooner) and knowledgeable about the zone, Brooke was mandated by Singapore traders to get in touch in as cheaply a way as possible with Pengiran Muda Hashim. After returning to Singapore, he went back to Sarawak in August 1840 as he had seen opportunities to boast about to his partners. Pengiran Muda Hashim coveted the throne of Brunei and asked Brooke for his help against the rebellion. Brooke agreed on two conditions: amnesty for those responsible for the revolt (so that he could set up a network of these Malay and tribal people obligated to him) and his appointment to the post of governor of a territory of modest dimensions: the mouths of the Sarawak, Sadong, Lundu and Samarahan rivers.

Once the rebellion squashed, however, Pengiran Muda Hashim, deprived of any power of appointment (which was the sole authority of the sultan) wavered and underhandedly incited new troubles. After months of talks, Brooke, who had prudently chartered a second ship from Singapore as backup, took the office by force. But his appointment had yet to be ratified by the sultan. In July 1842, he went to Brunei, where

---

[96] Colin Crisswell, "Some historical aspects of local & sovereign rights in Nineteenth Century Brunei", *Journal of Oriental Studies* 10, 1 (1972): 52.

[97] G.W. Earl, *The Western Seas* (London: Allen & Co., 1837), pp. 317–8.

Omar Ali Saifuddin II[98] had unfortunately captured the cargos and crew of two British ships foundering off its coasts. Brooke took charge of the affair, informed the East India Company, and had a ship despatched to point its cannons at the palace. Under these circumstances, Sultan Saifuddin ratified his appointment, although he also absolved him of all tribute, thus signifying a different status for him than the other holders of *kuripan*. Brooke was legally enthroned upon his return to Kuching. While making known to the East India Company his wish to transfer Sarawak to the British Crown, Brooke again brandished the threat of piracy (and his desire to fight against slavery) in 1843 to ensure support in Singapore for the two British vessels.

He then scored two coups: first, bringing Pengiran Muda Hashim and his brother back to Brunei in 1844, thus preventing any attempt of subversion on his territory; and second, providing military support for Hashim against his rival, Pengiran Yusuf, the latter being linked to the Iranun piracy networks[99] and father-in-law of one of the sultan's sons,[100] so as to possess an ally at the palace.

Once more the threat of cannons overcame Brunei's hesitations, and Pengiran Yusuf was relieved of his office in favour of Pengiran Muda Hashim. Brooke even obtained the right to designate his successor in Sarawak. Since the steam navigation era had arrived and the Western powers were greedy for coal, he informed the British of its abundance in Labuan and the perspicacity of establishing a British presence there.[101]

Far from being totally decrepit, the capital of Brunei had 30,000–40,000 inhabitants[102]—at least twice the number as it had at the start of the 19th century—originating from all the ethnic groups of the region. The sultan's court and palace seemed noticeably more modest than at the end of the 16th century, but they maintained their proud allure; even if locals no longer saw Chinese junks, the river continued to be frequented by a multitude of *perahu*. On the other hand, the commercial rupture

---

[98] The sultan spoke a few words in Spanish to him (S. Baring-Gould and C.A. Bampfylde, *A History of Sarawak under its Two White Rajahs 1839–1908*, 2nd ed. [Kuala Lumpur: Synergy Media, 2007], p. 93).

[99] D.E. Brown, *Brunei: the structure and history of a Bornean Malay Sultanate*, p. 149.

[100] See the story from an eyewitness in Frank S. Marryat, *Borneo and the Indian Archipelago: Drawings, Costumes and Scenery* (London: Longman, Brown, Green & Longmans, 1847), pp. 108ff.

[101] In addition to Muara and Pulau Chermin.

[102] Marryat, *Borneo and the Indian Archipelago*, p. 106.

Figure 3. Brunei in the Time of James Brooke: The River (top) and the Court of the Sultan (bottom)

(Frank S. Marryat, *Borneo and the Indian Archipelago: Drawings, costumes and scenery*, London: Longman, Brown, Green & Longmans, 1848, pp. 106, 109)

with China, the main supplier of second-hand iron and copper alloys, and a major importer of silver, had entailed the involution of trade, increasing the price of non-precious metals and nearly causing the abandonment of the indigenous currency in the first half of the 19th century. The only means of payment manufactured locally had become unstamped round and rectangular iron coins,[103] and for larger transactions, miniature cannons of bronze, which were still in use at the turn of the following century.[104]

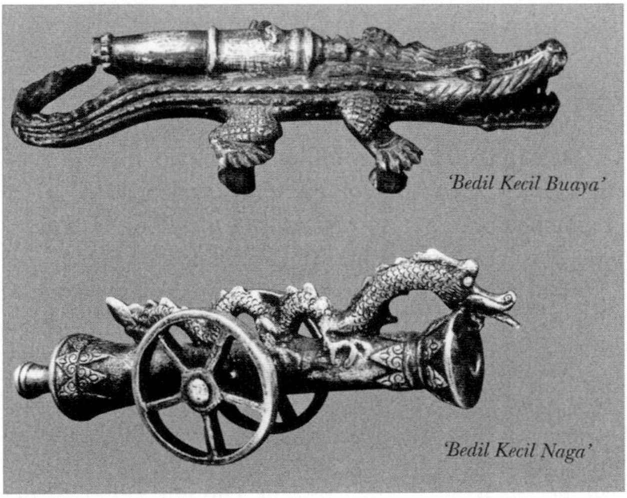

Figure 4. Miniature Cannons
(The Brunei Museum, *40th Anniversary of the Brunei Museum Department 1965–2005*, p. 50)

The arrival in 1845 of the Americans, who offered the sultanate a commercial treaty in exchange for coal rights,[105] further improved

[103] Ibid., p. 113; iron rectangles are reproduced in J.A. Davidson, "Brunei Coinage", *BMJ* 4, 1 (1977): 56, and in Rozan Yunus, *The Golden Warisan Brunei Darussalam*, BSB, 2009, vol. 1, p. 105. On Brunei currency, see William L.S.L. Barrett, *Brunei and Nusantara: History in Coinage* (BSB, Pusat Sejarah Brunei, 1988), 273 p.
[104] W.H. Treacher, *British Borneo, Sketches of Brunei, Sarawak, Labuan, and North Borneo*, Singapore, rep. *JSSBRAS*, 1891: 30; their size varied from 10–20 cm (Rozan Yunus, ibid., p. 89). When an *orang kaya* died, his tributaries had to pay a contribution of one cannon to the burial costs; the payment of a cannon (sometimes of a large size) might also be a criminal fine.
[105] Saunders, *A History of Brunei*, p. 79.

Brooke's position. His success earned him the post of special agent to the sultan, particularly since he announced a plan to "reform" Brunei to render it more in line with British ways. To overcome adversaries who had wide popular support, Brooke pushed for the eight ships dispatched by the Admiralty to be used against the pirates of the north coasts of Borneo and attack the homes of Yusuf, who would finally be executed by order of the sultan in Kimanis.

However, the triumph of Hashim's pro-British faction was short-lived. He was assassinated along with his brother Pg. Badruddin, Pg. Tajuddin and their families at the end of 1845 by a band led by Haji Saman (who supported the faction of Pg. Yusuf and his son-in-law Pengiran Anak Hashim[106]), probably with the sultan's agreement. Brooke organised a retaliation expedition in 1846, destroying the small forts upstream of Brunei town and forcing the sultan on the run to return to the capital. The sultan was obliged to confirm Brooke's rights and offer him exclusivity on coal from Mengkabong to Tanjung Baram.[107] The sultan humbly apologised to the British and, like his predecessors, offered the island of Labuan; this time the British accepted it. The accord was formalised by a first treaty in December 1846, followed by a second in May 1847,[108] of which Article 10 forbade Brunei any cession of territories without the formal agreement of the British government, which constituted the first encroachment to its sovereignty—and revealed a glimmer of foreign interest in its territorial integrity. The British reluctantly named James Brooke governor of Labuan and consul-general in Brunei and the other principalities of Borneo. Meanwhile the Americans, who were more actively interested in the Pacific now that they had reached California, returned to the charge in 1850 and signed their own treaty with the sultanate.

[106] Haji Saman, from Kampong Saba ("upstream village") hid the young Pengiran Anak Hashim when he was sought by allies of the British (Brown, *Brunei: The structure and history of a Bornean Malay Sultanate*, p. 54). See the (obviously partisan) narration of events in "British authorities in Borneo: forcing the Brunei River, the capture of forts and the town of Borneo (Bruni) and the complete success of British policy", *The Chinese Repository* (Canton), 19 Aug. 1846.

[107] Tarling, *Britain, the Brookes & Brunei*, p. 66.

[108] It was then that Pg. Indera Mahkota Shahbandar Mohamed Salleh composed the *Sya'ir Rakis*.

But the tide was turning. Brooke's presence played against British private interests in raw materials and he had to respond to accusations in London, then Singapore, before the House of Commons, brought against him by his detractors (who had been informed by the sultan). He was blamed in particular for his expedition against the Dayak pirates of Saribas and Skrang, which were under the nominal control of Brunei. In Brunei, where strong religious disputes bearing on the perception of God in Islam had been going on for a dozen years,[109] and where rivalries within the royal family were legion, the death of Omar Ali Saifuddin II opened a new succession crisis that resulted in the accession of an outsider, Abdul Mumin, who named as *shahbandar* one of the fiercest opponents of Brooke, the former governor of Sarawak, Pg. Indera Mahkota Mohamed Salleh. Yet, given the state of his finances, Abdul Mumin had no choice but to grant Brooke a new parcel of territory in 1853 (the mouths of the Batang, the Skrang, the Saribas and the Rajang), in exchange for rent and half the eventual profits. At the same time, the Bruneians took advantage of Brooke's resignation as consul-general and governor of Labuan[110] (although he had been acquitted, he came out weakened from the enquiry into his affairs). With assistance from the former governor of Sarikei (on the Rajang), the Bruneian clans opposed to Brooke attempted a series of coups with the support of Chinese secret

---

[109] Spenser St. John, *Life in the Forest of the Far East*, Vol. II (London: Smith, Elder & Co., 1862), pp. 258–9, states that the debate was over the existence or not of a "personality of God". The dispute was animated by pilgrims returning from the Hajj and instrumentalised by various clans of the royal family. The troublesome imam, Hj. Muhammad, who had made the trip to Mecca several times in the 1840s, had erected a mosque that competed with the main mosque along the Kedayan River, in the Temenggong kampung (St. John, ibid., and Brown, *Brunei: The structure and history of a Bornean Malay Sultanate*, pp. 45, 47). He died c. 1858 in Brunei (St. John, ibid., p. 256). In the light of the politico-religious situation in the Arab Peninsula (the Wahhabites had taken Mecca and Medina in 1803–05, which were reconquered by Muhammad Ali in 1813 in the name of the Ottomans) and information relating to the doctrine of Hj. Muhammad, who recalled the positions of Muhammad ibn 'Abd al-Wahhab on the need to interpret literally the *tawhid* (proclamation of the unity of God), a Wahhabite doctrinal current might well have existed in Brunei in this decade. Among the Minangkabau of West Sumatra, it led to the Padri wars (1821–37), the Padri being religious teachers influenced by the Wahhabi doctrine during their sojourn in Mecca. Brunei's ties with the Minangkabau were long-standing as one of the two royal *nobat* was said to be of *minang* origin.

[110] Ratified by the British authorities at the end of 1855.

societies:[111] they covertly supported the revolt of the Chinese miners of Bau in 1857—which failed due to help from the Dutch and some Malays of Sarawak—then organised occasional attacks on Sarawak in 1859 and an attempt to overthrow the Rajah in 1860. In addition, Brunei opposed Brooke on the question of Mukah, the centre of sago trade that was dominated by merchants of the sultanate until their eviction by Sarawak. On the pretext that one of the initiators of the plot had taken refuge there, the Brooke party attacked Mukah. To their great surprise, they were quickly threatened with reprisal from an East India Company ship, at the request of the governor of Labuan, who based his position on the British refusal to recognise the independence of Sarawak at the end of 1859,[112] and who deplored the competition between Sarawak and Labuan. But as the governor was finally disavowed by his tutelary authorities and as the Royal Navy supported the Brooke side, Brunei once again had to forsake land in August 1861 in return for rent; this time, however, it was a significant portion of its territory—the coastal and riverfront strip that extended from north of Sibu to Kidurong, including Mukah, Bintulu, etc.

The situation was all the more critical for the sultanate because the British were not playing above board: they were careful not to put pressure on the concessionaire of the coal mines of Muara, the China Steamship and Labuan Coal Company, to pay back its debts. Abdul Mumin gave the first American Consul, Moses, who had settled in 1865, a vast concession around the Kimanis, whose rights would soon be transferred to the American Trading Company of Borneo through the intermediary of its director, Joseph Torrey. But it held on for barely a year; desperate, the consul simulated an attack on his consulate before being relieved of his functions.[113] Two years later in 1868, the United States closed the consulate.

---

[111] Brooke had tackled head-on the *kongsi* 公司 (societies, Chinese autonomous communities operating in the mining sector) of Sarawak where the *Tian di hui* 天地會 (Heaven and Earth Society) had a strong presence; tensions were exacerbated by the breaking out of the second Sino-British war in 1856 (see Colin N. Crisswell, *Rajah Charles Brooke, monarch of all, he surveyed* [Kuala Lumpur: Oxford University Press, 1978], Ch. 3, pp. 41ff; S. Baring-Gould and C.A. Bampfylde, *A History of Sarawak under its Two White Rajahs 1839–1908*, ch. 6).

[112] Tarling, *Britain, the Brookes & Brunei*, p. 141. The British opened a consulate in Kuching in 1863, but without fully recognising the country's independence and Brooke's full sovereignty (ibid., p. 152).

[113] See H.G. Keith, *The United States Consul and the Yankee Raja*, BSB, Museum Monograph no. 4 (1980), 256 p.

The Noose Tightens

Brunei found itself with no other choice but to make a rapprochement with the British in order to escape the rapacity of the Brooke dynasty, especially since the second rajah Charles, who formally acceded to power in 1868 but who had been in command since 1863, proved even harder to manipulate than his uncle James.

Dutch interest in Borneo grew when the Spanish increased pressure on Sulu. Joseph Torrey ceded for a good price his rights over North Borneo to the Austrian consul in Hong Kong, Baron van Overbeck, who hoped to interest Austria in the operation. After a visit to Brunei in June 1875 to confirm the validity of the offer, and noting the lack of interest from the Austro-Hungarians, Overbeck associated with Alfred Dent[114] to enlarge his financial base. Returning to Brunei in December 1877, he obtained from the sultan[115] the cession of territories running from the Kimanis to the Sebuku, in return for a rent of SS $12,000 (in silver dollars)[116] for himself and of another SS $3,000 for the *Temenggong*. As a precaution, Overbeck negotiated for a second time in January 1878 a transfer of sovereignty from Pandasan west to the Sebuku,[117] from the sultan of Sulu, but for only SS $5,000 in rent. These amounts reveal the de facto rights of Brunei and Sulu over the territories involved, on a ratio of 2.5 to 1. Overbeck later withdrew from the operation to the benefit of his associate. Once implemented, the deal revealed that Brunei barely exercised any control over the territories rented at such a high price: confrontations were incessant after a growing number of Illanun and Bajau settled in North and West Sabah.[118] The rents were sharply reduced

[114] His former employer, a trader from Hong Kong specialising in opium, among other commodities.

[115] The sultan gave him the title of Maharajah of Sabah. On the conditions of the cession, see M.L. Delavaud, lawyer at the Paris High Court, *Études des colonies espagnoles—Bornéo* (Toulouse, Imprimerie et fonderie générale du Sud-ouest, 1884), 25 p.

[116] Dollars of standard silver (24.44 g of pure silver) from the United Kingdom, Japan, or the United States (after the British closed the Hong Kong mint in 1868).

[117] Sulu was present in Sebuku, unlike Brunei (I.D. Black, "The Ending of Brunei Rule in Sabah 1878–1902", *JMBRAS* 41, 2 [1968]: 176–92).

[118] See the map in D.S. Ranjit Singh, "Brunei and the Hinterland of Sabah: Commercial and Economic Relations with Special References to the Second Half of the Nineteenth Century", in *The Southeast Asian Port and Polity: Rise and Demise*, ed. J. Kathirithamby-Wells and John Villiers (Singapore: Singapore University Press, 1990), pp. 231–45.

in 1880 (SS $5,000 for the Sultan, SS $2,500 for the *Temenggong*); after obtaining the British licence, the British North Borneo Chartered Company was created at the end of 1881.

But as these land leases did not suffice to ensure the survival of dignitaries, Abdul Mumin no longer filled all the posts and granted an increasing number of licences to the Chinese of Labuan,[119] while he and the *pengiran* put even more financial pressure on the few territories remaining under their direct control. The result was a growing rebellion, notably along the Baram, where the Kayan repulsed a punitive expedition from Brunei in 1870. The neglect attracted predators and Charles Brooke claimed Baram in 1872, then campaigned for Brunei to be placed under his tutelage or made a British protectorate. Britain was initially opposed to the annexation of Baram, but after the replacement of the consul-general (whose function was now combined with that of governor of Labuan), they conceded and the cession of North Borneo created a precedent for the application of Article 10 of the 1847 treaty. Charles Brooke then deducted from the annual rent paid to the sultan the debts incurred by his subjects to the Sarawak merchants, thus reducing the rent by a third.[120] Unable to make the *pengiran* settle their accounts, Abdul Mumin agreed to the transfer of Baram to Sarawak in 1882, in exchange for additional rent for himself and the *Temenggong*.

Given the advanced age of the sultan (now nearing 100 years old), what remained of the territory was now sold off to the highest bidder: Muara coal was assigned to a Briton in 1882; a portion north of the Brunei Bay was sold to a Chinese in 1883. The noose tightened with the nomination of the governor of the North Borneo Company (NBC) as consul-general in Brunei. Meanwhile a violent rebellion broke out in Limbang, which was over-exploited by Temenggong Hashim as *kuripan*, directly threatening the capital. Against the backdrop of the rivalry between the *Temenggong* party (steered by Charles Brooke) and their opponents, under the *Bendahara*[121] and *Di Gadong* (the two sons of Pengiran

[119] Nicholas Tarling, "The Entrepot at Labuan and the Chinese", in *Studies in the Social History of China and Southeast Asia: Essays in Memory of Victor Purcell (26 January 1896–2 January 1965)*, ed. J. Ch'en and N. Tarling (Cambridge: Cambridge University Press, 1970), pp. vii, 365–74.

[120] Saunders, *A History of Brunei*, p. 89.

[121] In addition, the *Bendahara* had married a daughter of the *Temenggong* (Sir Reginal E. Stubbs, "Two Colonial Office Memoranda on the History of Brunei", *JMBRAS* 41, 2, no. 214 [Dec. 1968]: 91).

Tajuddin, who was assassinated at the end of 1845 on the order of the future Temenggong Hashim), the sultan asked for British mediation. Treacher (in other words, the NBC), who had loaned SS $15,000 to the *Di Gadong* because he held the two most important regalia (the seal and the kris), successfully negotiated with Limbang, but when he discovered that behind his back the sultan was pushing the Murut of Trusan to attack the rebels, he sailed on a war ship to Brunei. Despite the machinations of Charles Brooke,[122] North Borneo took back Padas Klias, Tuaran and Putatan in 1884, but without the *Temenggong* getting any remuneration. The same year, the revenue of the Pandasan River was ceded to Brooke's agent in Brunei, A.H. Everett. Passing through Brunei to settle promised rents, the representative of Sarawak seized the assassination of several of his countrymen by the Murut of Trusan as a pretext to deal out two strikes: he demanded the cession of both Trusan and Limbang, proposed a total of SS $9,500 to the *Temenggong* (who had just been appointed regent) and threatened to suspend the payments for two years if he was refused.

While the territorial status of Trusan was simple (*tulin* of the *Temenggong*), the same was not true of Limbang where various land rights overlapped.[123] Kawang was then ceded to North Borneo in 1885.[124] In a desperate turnaround, the sultan persuaded the *pengiran* (except for the *Pemancha*) to take an oath[125] not to abandon any more of Brunei's territory. Upon his death a few weeks later, the *Temenggong* succeeded him under the name Hashim Jamilul Alam. He granted the cession of

---

[122] C. Brooke sent a Sarawak *pengiran* to create havoc in Padas-Klias but he was expelled. He sent a second one who managed to unleash troubles that would cause the death of two Europeans, among others (K.G. Tregonning, "The Partition of Brunei", *Journal of Tropical Geography* 11 [1958]: 86).

[123] It was probably partly the *tulin* of the *Temenggong* and partly that of Sultan Abdul Momin, who would have given his rights to the two princes destined to become *Bendahara* and *Di Gadong* after his death (R. Haller-Trost, *The Brunei-Malaysia dispute over territorial and maritime claims in International law*, Vol. 1, no. 3 [Durham: IBRU, 1994], p. 11).

[124] Against a backdrop of land litigation: Pg. Jahir furnished written proof that the territory was indeed his *tulin*, but Pg. Raup contested the ownership for the settlement of his Bajaus on the land. Pg. Raup then pushed the Bajaus to revolt. When Hashim accessed the throne, he confirmed the rights of Pg. Jahir (Crisswell, "Some historical aspects of local & sovereign rights in Nineteenth Century Brunei", p. 53).

[125] Stubbs, "Two Colonial Office Memoranda on the History of Brunei", p. 93.

Trusan, re-negotiated that of Padas,[126] but refused to sell Limbang, as it was the prime source of food supplies for the sultanate. In 1887, he asked Queen Victoria to forbid any additional abandonment of land as per the 1847 treaty. Nevertheless the *tulin* of Padas Damit was ceded to North Borneo in 1888, since the sultan did not control private property belonging to the *pengiran*. After the creation of an enquiry commission led by an expert on the Malay world, the governor of the Straits Settlements Sir Frederick Weld, who discovered the firmness of the sultan's position (he had prudently left vacant the post of *Temenggong* to prevent further challenging of its authority) and took into consideration his demand for the creation of a residency similar to those implemented in the princely Malay States, London chose a half-measure: Sarawak, North Borneo and Brunei became British protectorates in September 1888, but were not granted a residency. And Article III of the 1888 treaty included Sarawak and North Borneo in the list of territories with which Brunei could only negotiate through the agency of Britain; in case of litigation, it would be Her Majesty's government that decided.[127]

Yet the game was not over, since the British were now favourable to a partition of the sultanate. They did not oppose the forced annexation of Limbang in March 1890 by Charles Brooke, who claimed that the "local chiefs" (actually mostly of the Bisayah and not the other ethnic groups)[128] had brandished the flag of Sarawak in the presence of the raja's representatives (which obviously throws doubt on the spontaneity of their demonstration). And they entrusted the management of Labuan (whose governor had hitherto been the consul-general for Borneo) to North Borneo in 1890.[129] Despite the extension until 1895—on British advice—of the ultimatum made by Charles Brooke in order to legalise

[126] Also the cause of litigation between the Shahbandar and the sultan.

[127] The text of the "Agreement between Her Majesty's Government and the Sultan of Brunei for the establishment of a British protectorate over the State of Brunei" is in Khoo Kay Kim, ed., *Sabah: History and Society* (Kuala Lumpur: Malaysian Historical Society, 1981), pp. 31–2.

[128] Saunders, *A History of Brunei*, p. 93; to increase the pressure, the sultan was offered SS $6,000, to be deposited in a bank account for him over a period of three years, but to no avail (Crisswell, "Some historical aspects of local & sovereign rights in Nineteenth Century Brunei", p. 57).

[129] The governor of the Straits Settlements then became consul-general for Borneo; a consul for Brunei and Sarawak was placed in Labuan (Stubbs, "Two Colonial Office Memoranda on the History of Brunei", p. 86).

the operation, the sultan held firm, though without obtaining justice. The loss without compensation of income from Limbang and the deviation of its sago trade to Sarawak depleting the sultanate's treasury even more, Charles Brooke could once again intensify the pressure. While he had already bought out the mining licence for the coal of Muara in 1888, ten years later he grabbed those of Pulau Berembang, although it had been ceded by one of the sultan's sons-in-law to a Singapore merchant. And in 1903, he repurchased 1,418 hectares of land in Kota Batu from the heirs of a former British consul agent.[130] The raja of Sarawak thus privately controlled a strategic portion of both banks of the Brunei River, as well as its mouth at Muara. The North Borneo Company acted in a similar fashion. The troubles that broke out in 1896 in the wake of the revolt of Mat Salleh on the Inamam and Mengkabong rivers and a series of other water courses,[131] allowed it to obtain river rights without too much difficulty in 1898—a threat to suspend the income paid to Bruneian "authorities" was enough. Then it was Sipitang and Lawas (1901), followed in 1904 by the portion of land between Lawas and Trusan, but the company finally abandoned Lawas to Sarawak at the end of 1904.[132]

Fuelled by a rise in all six taxes[133] and by epidemics (cholera in 1902 and smallpox in 1904), revolts multiplied after 1898 in areas surrounding the Brunei River, at Tutong, Belait,[134] as well as Limau Manis,

---

[130] Inche Mohammad, who died in 1890.

[131] Menggatal, Gantisan, Api-Api, Membakut (the latter, *tulin* of the *Pemancha*).

[132] The cession of Lawas was particularly complex. The sultan ceded his sovereignty rights over Lawas to the NBC for the modest sum of SS $600; Pg. Bakar, his *tulin* rights for SS $900; only negotiations with the Lawas chief, Abu Bakar, who lived on the spot, remained to be undertaken. The Foreign Office settled the case, finally recognising Abu Bakar as sole legitimate owner (Crisswell, "Some historical aspects of local & sovereign rights in Nineteenth Century Brunei", p. 59). The latter then gave management of his rights to a Briton working for the NBC. After the death of Abu Bakar in October 1904, his rights were transferred to the Brookes by the governor of the NBC, who was in need of funds.

[133] These were: (1) poll tax; (2) commercial tax; (3) "submission" tax (these three taxes were on an annual basis); (4) tax "for washing feet" (when the titular Pengiran went upriver); (5) right to anchor (when he went back downriver); (6) contribution to the expenses caused by all the important events occurring in the Pengiran's family (P. Leys, "Observations on the Brunei Political System, 1883–1885", *JMBRAS* 41, 2 [1968]: 126).

[134] The Colonial Office had envisaged in 1897–98 exchanging Limbang for Tutong and Belait, thus solving the conflict between Sarawak and Brunei (B.A. Hussainmiya, *Brunei Revival of 1906: A Popular History* [BSB: Brunei Press, 2006], p. 48).

which was looking all the more toward Sarawak where the poll tax was much lower. British Consul Hewett negotiated for the shift of three districts to the supervision of Sarawak but failed. Not only did Hashim Jamilul Alam refuse (in 1902), he also obtained the support of the governor of North Borneo for a residency. It was high time: in 60 years, Brunei had lost some 18 riverside districts to Sarawak and more than 30 to North Borneo. With the four rivers that remained under its possession, its "useful" territory had been reduced to one-eighth of its original[135] and financially, the sultanate was bankrupt.

But the wheels turned. Petroleum was discovered in 1903 in Berembang—in Charles Brooke's coal mine. The sultan also attempted to make contact with the Ottoman Empire.[136] The debate over the future of the sultanate resumed; the consul-general, considered too favourable to Sarawak, was recalled. To determine its position, London, which was beginning to worry that Brunei might seek other protectors, mandated Malcolm McArthur, a British civil servant in the Federated Malay States, to conduct an inquiry in 1904. McArthur's diagnosis was as follows: (1) beyond the exercise of taxation rights, no government in the Western sense of the term existed in Brunei; most government duties were not carried out;[137] (2) although the sultan was emptied out financially, the sultanate was not totally void of commercial potential; (3) most of local heads[138] were opposed to attachment to Sarawak, whose government was in fact more autocratic than admirable; (4) given the mediocre management by the North Borneo Company since 1890, the Crown should reassume the administration of Labuan and return it to Brunei; (5) on that basis, the establishment of a British residency in Brunei would be profitable to both parties.

---

[135] A.V.H. Horton, *The British Residency in Brunei, 1906–1959* (Hull: University of Hull, Centre for Southeast Asian Studies, Occasional Papers no. 6, 1984), p. 5.

[136] Hussainmiya, *Brunei Revival of 1906: A Popular History*, p. xi. The letter was actually intercepted by the British (Tarling, *Britain, the Brookes & Brunei*, p. 498). In the framework of a pan-Islamic foreign policy, Sultan Abdul Hamid had created an official publisher in Mecca in 1884, which published in Arabic, as well as Malay and other languages (Arifin Mansurnoor, "Islamic Education, State and Society in Brunei Darussalam: An Intellectual History of the Ulama World [1903–1974]", 1998).

[137] Those presumed to be guilty or convicted were in the habit of fleeing to Sarawak and coming back brandishing the Brookes flag—knowing that the number of offences was quite low (Hussainmiya, *Brunei Revival of 1906: A Popular History*, p. 41).

[138] Most of the local leaders were not among the 26 who had signed a petition demanding the attachment of Brunei to Sarawak (Saunders, *A History of Brunei*, p. 109).

The least that can be said is that up to that point, Brunei had not benefited from a British protectorate; it had in fact worked to its detriment! Petroleum was not considered to be pertinent then. Negotiated by McArthur, who meanwhile had been appointed consul, the new treaty was signed in January 1906. In compensation for abandoning its sovereign rights, the Sultan received SS $12,000 in annual indemnity and the two wazirs got half that sum; their *tulin* were also transferred to the new government.

FROM RESIDENCY TO INDEPENDENCE (1906–84)

In 1906 the management of Brunei was entrusted to a State Council presided by the sultan. In addition to the two wazirs, the Council included two *cheteriya*, three *menteri*,[1] the foremost religious dignitary,[2] the Resident installed in Labuan (administered jointly with Brunei from 1906) and an Assistant Resident (both British) who lived in Brunei.[3] Henceforth all advice by the Resident had to be "acted upon on all questions in Brunei, other than those affecting the Mohammedan religion".[4] Unlike the other Malay princely states, and armed with the precedent of control over tax matters, the Resident was vested with the authority to deal with issues arising from *adat*, Malay custom. The British government also received the mandate to "ensure the due succession to the Sultanate of Brunei".[5] All measures were enacted in the name of the sultan.

---

[1] *Cheteriya*: *Pengiran Shahbandar* and *Pengiran Kirma Indra*; *menteri*: *Perdana Menteri, O.K. Laksamana* and one *jawatan* (government officer), named Abu Bakar in 1907. Its composition varied over time (Hussainmiya and Tarling, *Brunei: Traditions of Monarchic Culture and History, R.H. Hickling's Memorandum upon Brunei Constitutional History and Practice* [BSB: Yayasan Sultan Haji Hassanal Bolkiah, 2011], p. 80).

[2] *Tuan Imam*, Horton, *Report on Brunei in 1904 by M.S.H. McArthur, introduced and annotated* (Athens: Ohio University Centre for International Studies, 1987), p. 65.

[3] A.V.M. Horton, *The British Residency in Brunei, 1906–1959* (Hull: University of Hull, Centre for Southeast Asian Studies, 1984), p. 12.

[4] "British-Brunei [Protectorate] Document, 3 December 1905", trans. B.A. Hussainmiya, *Sultan Omar Ali Saifuddin II and Britain* (Singapore: Oxford University Press, 1995), p. 394.

[5] Ibid.

Establishment of "Modern" Government and Administration (1906–41)

Under the supervision of the British High Commissioner in Singapore, McArthur became the first resident (1906–08). He objected when Charles Brooke (who bought the *Bendahara*'s support) requested to exchange Temburong for his rights in Muara. McArthur asked the British government to force the restitution of Limbang, whose annexation, far from benefiting Brunei as the rajah claimed, was severely prejudicial. Sir Charles refused in turn to limit the border between Sarawak and Brunei and raised a petition of 30 signatories from Kampung Ayer, demanding reattachment to Sarawak.[6] The death of Sultan Hashim in May 1906 further complicated matters, for his successor Muhammad Jamalul Alam II, a minor manipulated by the old *Bendahara*, signed a petition demanding the modification of five points of the 1905 treaty: (1) authority of customary magistrates over religious questions; (2) prior accord of the sultan and the State Council for the initiation of any procedures against persons of high rank; (3) government help in finding runaway slaves; (4) the Brunei national flag (created in 1906)[7] on official buildings; and

[6] Hussainmiya, *Brunei Revival of 1906: A Popular History*, p. 60.

[7] The first state flag added to the personal standard of the sultan (which was yellow and already existed in 1841) two diagonal bands evoking the colours of the individual standards of the two wazirs whose status had been maintained under Sultan Hashim and who were co-signatories of the treaty of January 1906: white for the *Bendahara* and black for the *Pemancha* (*Bendera dan Lagu Kebangsaan Brunei, The Brunei State Flag and National Anthem* [BSB: Muzium Brunei, 1981], 16 p). In 1959 the state crest was added. This traditionally comprised a pole (*alam besar*), a circular ornament

(5) the maintenance and inalienability of customs and laws in force in Brunei. While firmly reminding the sultan that the very purpose of the treaty was to reform the obsolete laws and customs of the Bruneian state, McArthur granted the first and fourth requests. Charles Brooke and the *Bendahara* presented a third petition in 1907, demanding that Brunei be incorporated into Sarawak;[8] the British authorities were scarcely inclined to undo a process they had begun more than 20 years before and turned down the petition. The most difficult task was instead how to provide the sultanate with the instruments (administrative, financial and socio-economic) of a state such as Westerners expected.

The Creation of a Modern State

An embryonic administration was set up in 1906 in the three most important domains: justice (with the collation of a first series of texts establishing the bases of Islamic family law); the police (who were also in charge of firefighting); and taxes (customs duties and poll tax, with the latter placed under the responsibility of a treasurer of Chinese origin). In parallel, Brunei was provided with the necessary infrastructure: quays, customs posts, a prison, treasury and courts (in 1908). The Resident presided over the high court of Brunei; four other bodies intervened at lower levels: courts of the first class, second class, indigenous magistrates, and the religious courts of the *kadis*, with the latter limited to family law and religion.[9] "Malay (that is, indigenous) magistrates" recruited in Malaya or Sarawak[10] took charge of district courts established on the basis of the four river systems that now constituted the territory of the

---

below the pole with a flat part and a jagged part (*nanglong*), two "wings" (*sayap puja*), a pole (*champaka*) and five steps (*kedudukan*). Composed of five parts representing the five highest state dignitaries since Sultan Hassan (Abdul Latif Haji Ibrahim, *Sejarah rengkas panji² negeri Brunei, A Short History of the Brunei State Crest* [BSB: Muzium Brunei, 1972], 25 p), the crest was reduced to three (the sultan and his two wazirs) by Sultan Ahmad Tajuddin (1924–50).

[8] Most of the 27 signatories were minor dignitaries; Charles Brooke's agent in London, deputy Sir Edward Sassoon, made himself look ridiculous by presenting Brunei as part of Malaya (Saunders, *History of Brunei*, p. 109).

[9] Azrinah Binti Haji Abdul Rahman, *Legal System in Brunei Darussalam after the Signing of the Supplementary Agreement 1905/1906 between Brunei and Great Britain* (BSB: Working Paper for National Day Seminar, 2006), pp. 6–11.

[10] Their nomination was the responsibility of the Resident alone (Horton, *The British Residency in Brunei, 1906–1959*, p. 18).

sultanate. The Supreme Court of the Straits Settlements (in Singapore) served as an appeal court; the Privy Council (in London) as the Court of Appeal.[11] To prevent corruption, police officers came from the elite corps of the Indian Army (Sikhs and Pathans). Once these emergency measures had been implemented, the Bruneian members of the State Council, particularly the religious leaders, asked the Resident to confirm the Muslim dimension of the state. Following decrees of application relating to the Islamic family law of 1908, two more fundamental laws were quickly set: the Muslim code of 1912 and the marriage law of 1913 (the latter on the initiative of the resident),[12] which were accompanied by the formalisation of religious courts (under the authority of a *kadi* and a vice-*kadi*) in charge of family law.

The British presence was strengthened by the installation of the Resident in Brunei, whose administration was again separated from that of Labuan in 1914. This was accompanied by the suppression of the post of Assistant Resident. The fortuitous assassination of Resident E.B. Maundrell[13] by a Sikh policeman in 1916 resulted in the creation of a Malay police force in 1921 with 39 members.[14] Muhammad Jamalul Alam II died prematurely in 1924 and the minority of his successor, Ahmad Tajuddin, led to a new regency period (1924–31) that increased the Resident's power. The number of Malay representatives on the State Council rose to 25, then slumped back to 10 in 1927. Four series of provisions completed Muslim law in 1924. Administration was improved at the start of the 1930s. Departments of forest and agriculture were created to support the establishment of forest reserves and agricultural stations charged with promoting rice field irrigation and new technologies. The Resident also appointed "governmental" *penghulu* and acknowledged *ketua kampung* (village leaders) in the rice-growing districts. The Assistant Resident position was re-established and was charged with the petroleum zones of Belait (1931). At the same time, the preponderance of indigenous civil servants grew: Malay magistrates were promoted

---

[11] A.V.H. Horton, "British Administration in Brunei 1906–1959", *Modern Asian Studies* 20, 2 (1986): 364.

[12] He was inspired by that of Negri Sembilan (Arifin Mansurnoor, "Socioreligious Changes in Brunei during the British Residency").

[13] On this affair, see A.V.H. Horton, "The British Resident Murdered (Ernest Maundrell and Brunei 1915–1916)", *Sarawak Gazette* CXV, 1506 (December 1988): 14–20.

[14] Eighty-five members by the end of the 1930s.

to district officers in 1932, and in 1935 the prime post for an indigenous "high" civil servant, the Resident's secretary, was created at last. In order to control the Islamic courts through their integration in territorial administration, district officers were appointed to the post of vice-*kadi* in the three "rural" districts in 1938, and the Resident's secretary to vice-*kadi* of the capital; a post of chief *kadi* (member by right of the State Council) was created in 1939.[15]

In 1941, hopes that the thorny question of Limbang would finally be resolved arose when the rajah's private secretary Gerard MacBryan[16] (who had converted to Islam) attempted on the occasion of the centenary of the Brookes to negotiate Limbang's integration into Sarawak in exchange for an indemnity of SS $20,000 to the sultan, combined with SS $1,000 in annual rent, plus a total of SS $60,000 in indemnities and SS $6,000 in rent to the *pengirans* dispossessed of their *tulin* and SS $4,000 in income to the descendants of Pengiran Muda Hashim. This hope was quickly dashed by the British authorities who held Charles Vyner Brooke (Charles Brooke's nephew) in low esteem and considered his advisor to be a crank.

Finances and Public Services

Given the prevailing land system in Brunei and the confusion over *tulin*, land restructuring had to precede any financial reform that aimed to provide the state with regular income. Even though the sultan and the two wazirs had theoretically abandoned any privilege (*kerajaan* and *kuripan*) accorded by their offices with the 1906 treaty, the question of *tulin* remained unresolved. The first land code (1907) met with widespread opposition, and a second was prepared and promulgated in 1909, which made the land the property of the state (with the exception of land pertaining to property titles in good and due form).[17] The young sultan,

---

[15] Arifin Mansurnoor, "Islamic Education, State and Society in Brunei Darussalam".

[16] On MacBryan, see Bob Reece, *Masa Jepun: Sarawak under the Japanese, 1941–1945* (Kuching: Sarawak Literary Society, 1998), p. 2.

[17] The cession of state land property was at first agreed to for cultivation purposes, except otherwise specifically mentioned, and applied only to the surface and not to the underground; the government could take back and reattribute abandoned lands (Lim Hooi Siang, "Land Policy and Development: Case of Brunei Darusssalam", paper presented at the *ASCP-AESOP Joint International Congress*, Toronto [25–28 July 1996]).

manipulated by the *Bendahara*, claimed *all* land property. The threat of arms, as well as a diminution in his annual rent and even his possible deposition (in 1910) had to be brandished before he began to adhere to the new provisions.[18] The operation began with an inventory of the *tulin*, of which administrative and taxation rights were gradually bought between 1907 and 1911, in exchange for capital or annual rent.

On top of this princely vacillation came a near-rebellion of the Kedayan, who considered the hinterland as their own and refused any obligation other than the poll tax. After forceful negotiations, the latter accepted to cede their rights in exchange for 15 acres (6 hectares) to be exploited individually (for SS $2 in annual rent), or else a right to collective usage that would ensure the village's subsistence, combined with an exemption from the poll tax (the issue was only wholly solved in 1919). Meanwhile, relations with the young sultan improved; he recuperated his emoluments, obtained recognition of his ownership of land around the royal palaces and that of the two wazirs, and secured supplementary credits. As a sign of the restoration of consensus, he was appointed CMG[19] in 1914. Crowned (and knighted) in 1920, he went on an official visit to Singapore two years later, where he met the heir to the British crown.

Thus the government slowly bought back the concessions previously granted by Bruneian officials, restoring to the acquirers the sums they had spent (after the deduction of a pro rata corresponding to the number of years of ownership), as well as the rights granted by Sarawak and North Borneo to Bruneians in compensation for prior concessions (the last buy-backs took place in 1950). These were financed by loans from the Federated Malay State between 1906 and 1911, totalling SS $439,750.[20]

Since the rent paid to the sultan and two wazirs absorbed almost half of public receipts, the Resident (who took the place of prime minister and minister of justice, and whose emoluments were graciously paid by the Colonial Office until 1927)[21] tried to get extra financial resources by all means: he instituted customs duties and issued postage stamps

[18] B.A. Hussainmiya, *Sultan Omar Ali Saifuddin III and Britain, the making of Brunei Darussalam* (Kuala Lumpur: Oxford University Press, 1995), p. 18.
[19] Companion of the Most Distinguished Order of Saint Michael and Saint George.
[20] US $169,134 (US $1 = Straits Settlements [SS] $2.6), see Appendix I.
[21] Horton, *The British Residency in Brunei, 1906–1959*, p. 86 (table A, note B).

(1906), leased tobacco, opium, and gambling rights[22] (1907) and rented terrains to foreign planters. But returns were not immediate: the tax farmer who held the three monopolies was unable to honour his engagements after a year, so opium (like alcohol) was transformed into a public monopoly and the other two were abandoned. The financial difficulties were such that in 1917, Resident G.E. Cator requested to exchange with Sarawak the remote and unproductive district of Belait for the districts of Trusan and Lawas. It took all of McArthur's influence to convince the British High Commissioner (and it was even harder to persuade the Colonial Office) to decline the proposition. The modesty of its resources did not allow Brunei to start reimbursing its debt until after 1920; in 1928, almost four-fifths remained to be paid back.

Establishing the First Public Services

In the realm of public services, everything remained to be constructed. In 1905, education was limited to a few courses dispensed by religious leaders in prayer rooms (*balai*) or at their homes.[23] Two primary schools, one Chinese and the other Malay, opened in 1912 and 1914, but further education had to be pursued at the British college of Labuan. On the eve of World War Two, Brunei had 24 free Malay primary schools, 5 fee-paying Chinese schools[24] and 2 Catholic schools, one of which was attended by the sultan's sons; there was still no secondary establishment reserved for girls. The same was true of the health system:[25] while dispensaries and vaccination were rapidly introduced, Western medicine was only accessible in Labuan. Starting in 1919,[26] a doctor from Labuan made regular visits to the city of Brunei and itinerant nurses served the rural areas.[27] In 1929 a hospital was built and a practitioner trained in

[22] Charles Brooke had opened a gambling hall in Muara, which caused many Malays to fall into debt. McArthur took action and it was finally closed in 1924 (Hussainmiya, *Brunei revival of 1906: A popular history*, p. 48).
[23] Arifin Mansurnoor, "Socioreligious Changes in Brunei during the British Residency".
[24] Two Chinese schools were opened in Kuala Belait in 1931 and 1937 and one in Seria in 1938 (A.V.M. Horton, *Turun-temurun: A Dissection of Brunei Darussalam* [Bordesley: A.V.M. Horton, 2nd ed. 1998], p. 63).
[25] Entrusted to the postal director.
[26] The sultan and the royal family had themselves vaccinated en masse the same year.
[27] *Report for 1919 on the State of Brunei*, Federated Malay States (Kuala Lumpur, 1920), p. 6.

Western medicine was appointed to the newly created post of public doctor. Henceforth plantations were obliged to carry medical equipment. Yet the infant mortality rate remained quite high at the end of the 1930s (20% each year).[28] Financial penury was such that the development of economic infrastructure lagged behind: the telegraph was only installed in 1921 and water supplied to the capital (by a dam) in 1926. Municipal services were created in the capital in 1921, then in Belait and Tutong in 1929.

Economic Development

In 1906, the Bruneian economy had scarcely any taxable surplus since subsistence agriculture, essentially the cultivation of rice on slash-and-burn fields by the Kedayan, was the prime sector of economic activity. With SS $300,000 worth of exports in 1906, the Residency had less than SS $52,000 in budgetary revenue in 1907.[29] To increase returns and get the population settled down, the government introduced irrigated rice cultivation and from 1908, rubber, with five plantations[30] and tens of small exploitations. Penalised by the slowness of tax reform, the cultivation of hevea was struck by the rubber crisis at the start of the 1920s; once rubber became the prime export product, it ran up against the lack of manpower, which had to be imported from the Indian sub-continent. The introduction of other commercial crops—tea, coffee, cotton and Philippine hemp—turned out to be failures. In addition, there was the exploitation of forest products, of which the most important was *jelutong*, a gum used in the fabrication of linoleum. Fishing by the Malays barely covered local needs. In short, at the end of the 1930s, Brunei produced only a third of its own food (in good years), and its rubber production was small in comparison to its prime regional competitor, Malaya.

Industry was virtually non-existent. In 1906, Brunei had only one modern factory (created in 1900), which produced a natural khaki dye based on catechu,[31] and it had to import all other primary materials

---

[28] Horton, *The British Residency in Brunei*, p. 31.
[29] Ibid., p. 77.
[30] Two plantations in Brunei district and three in Temburong, of which one closed in 1912.
[31] *Acacia catechu*, or cutch.

from Sarawak as of 1904. The only craft that might constitute the kernel of any future manufacturing development was bronze and metalwork, represented in the capital by about 100 bronze and silver smiths, who were grouped into guilds. The weaving of cotton (or silk on occasion) was also widespread, as well as basketry, a speciality in which the sultanate excelled. But modernisation played against these traditional activities: Bruneian textiles crumbled in the face of cheap Japanese imports in the 1930s; basketwork and metalwork were relegated to the rank of artisanship for tourists, few in number at the start. The production of coal (controlled by the Brookes), which had taken over camphor as the principal export commodity, was likewise abandoned in 1924.

Only petroleum was left. While prospect increased between 1906 and 1922, it was without great success.[32] A first advance was achieved in 1923 when the British Malayan Petroleum Company (BMPC), belonging to Shell, bought the rights of the British Borneo Petroleum Syndicate, which was on the verge of bankruptcy, in exchange for royalties of a shilling per tonne. Then in 1929 petroleum was drilled up in Seria, and exploitation began three years later in 1932. The government earned two shillings per tonne, with the possibility of exchanging the royalty for 10% of production. In the absence of any estimate of the reserves, petroleum income was allotted for other purposes than current expenditure.

The oil fields were located at the mouth of the Belait, a sparsely populated district in the extreme west of the sultanate, whose communication links with the capital were cut off four months each year during the monsoon. Thus BMPC had to create its own infrastructure and recruit labour from all over Southeast Asia and the Indian subcontinent. The town of Belait quickly became a state within a state, with its own institutions (police, courts, health services, road maintenance), and where the company took charge of the well-being of its employees. Thus were erected, on a reduced scale, the bases of a "Shellfare State".

Overview of the British Residency, 1906–41

After more than three decades, an evaluation of the British Residency, endowed with few human resources (there were only five European

[32] Standard Oil, Kuhara (the current Nippon Mining Company) and D'Arcy (BP), folded their tents.

officials in 1932),[33] would lead to the following economic and political assessment:

- Brunei found itself the third producer of oil in the Commonwealth by 1935; foreign debt, more than triple the state revenue in 1914, was fully reimbursed by 1936. But while petroleum flowed abundantly, supplying 73% of public receipts in the 1930s, the budgetary surpluses that it generated were capitalised. The government favoured infrastructure (30% of the budget) over social spending (10%), and the gaps in the educational system (24 public primary schools providing very rudimentary education) seriously hampered the capacity of the sultanate to take charge in the medium term, especially since poverty remained high in rural areas.
- Brunei possessed an administrative apparatus and laws to govern the population. The sovereign, who trained for a year (1932) in the United Kingdom and had married the daughter of the sultan of Selangor[34]—attesting to his reintegration among the Malay political elites—was better able to confront the British administration, notably on financial matters, than his predecessor. But he had little success at the start since the Resident (whose services had a bigger budget than his until 1940) threw his weight and saw to it that no foreign sovereign attended his coronation in 1940.[35] Even though its establishment had been painful, the centralisation of administration and of religion around the nominal leader, the sultan, conferred on him a growing influence over the people, which on the eve of World War Two, noticeably outstripped a purely symbolic function. On the other hand, the traditional foundations of Bruneian society—its pronounced social stratification and the endogamy of its ruling class—had scarcely changed.[36]
- The paradox was that, under cover of an economic and political dispossession of the elites, the British Residency had not only consolidated its position internally, but had undertaken to give the sultanate a strategic financial lever. Moreover, it had reinforced the Islamic dimension of Bruneian society. On the other hand, in social matters,

[33] Horton, *Turun-temurun: A Dissection of Brunei Darussalam*, p. 20.
[34] Hussainmiya, *Sultan Omar Ali Saifuddin III and Britain*, p. 47.
[35] The sultan announced—despite British harassment—a generous contribution of SS $100,000 of public funds for the war effort (Hussainmiya, ibid., p. 48).
[36] Hussainmiya, *Brunei revival of 1906: A popular history*, p. 65.

Brunei appeared to lag behind Sarawak and North Borneo, although these countries were much less endowed with natural resources. What made the consensus even more fragile was that all the officials working in the sultanate had been trained abroad. At the end of the 1930s the result was the foundation of several nationalist movements inspired by those of Malaya, by educated young people in the entourage of *Pengiran Muda Tengah* (the crown prince and future Sultan Omar Ali Saifuddin), such as the *Persatuan Melayu Brunei*[37] (over which he presided several months), the *Sahabat Pena* (Pen Club), directed by Pengiran Pemancha Pengiran Anak Mohammed Yasin, and the *Persekutuan Guru^2 Melayu Brunei* (BMTA, in 1939).[38]

[37] Union of Malays of Brunei.

[38] Brunei Malay Teachers Association.

The Japanese Interlude and the End of the Residency (1942–59)

The Japanese Interlude

On the eve of the conflict with Japan, the British took precautions: they covered the oil wells with concrete and destroyed petroleum equipment since they had renounced defending Brunei. On 16 December 1941, 10,000 Japanese soldiers landed at Kuala Belait, then took the rest of the country. The Japanese kept the sultan in his functions and herded the British into camps; then they made Brunei one of the five prefectures in the north of Borneo and named as its head the former secretary of the resident, Inche Ibrahim—under the control, of course, of a Japanese governor. To sustain the war effort, they dug nine new wells in Seria, reopened the coalmine of Muara, and boosted the production of foodstuffs and khaki dye. Based on their practice in Burma and other Western possessions, they selected the most brilliant of the young nationalists aged 20 to 30 (for the most part from the SITC of Perak) for training abroad: Shaikh Azahari was thus sent to the Netherlands Indies and Pengiran Mohammed Yusuf to Japan.[39] For purposes of administering the conquered peoples, they set up the teaching of Malay in *rumi* (Latin characters), previously taught in Jawi,[40] and developed a press in Malay.

[39] Hussainmiya, *Sultan Omar Ali Saifuddin III and Britain*, p. 95.

[40] Geoffrey Gunn, *Language, Power and Ideology in Brunei Darussalam* (Athens: Ohio University Center for International Studies, Southeast Asia series no. 99, 1997), pp. 99ff. Thus it was the transliteration of the Japanese and not that of Wilkinson, which would serve as the basis for the teaching of Malay after the war in Brunei and in the Peninsula.

Initially not very severe, Japanese tutelage hardened when the war took an unfavourable turn for them in 1943: some Malay leaders were arrested and tortured, pushing others to take flight, and above all, Brunei reached the end of its reserves of consumption staples put aside by the British. Under the impact of scarcity, the inhabitants deserted the capital to forage in the forest. Thanks to American logistic support, Australian troops landed in June 1945 and took Brunei in a few days, bringing back British Military Administration (BMA) in their lorries.

The material destruction was considerable: the Japanese had set fire to the oil wells; the Allies had bombarded the capital for three days before occupying it and had destroyed almost all the buildings (including the Royal Palace[41] but sparing Kampung Ayer). In short, the entire modern infrastructure would have to be reconstructed.

Back on Track

Due to uncertainty about the future of British possessions in Borneo, reconstruction was dragged out. Highly critical of the Brooke administration and of the North Borneo Company, the Colonial Office envisaged the independence of their territories and thus of Brunei; the possibility of an eventual federation with Malaysia had been pending since 1943, just as the restitution of North Borneo to Brunei at one time (1944). But on the ground, the urgency lay elsewhere: the wells remained on fire until September 1945, and food distribution was made difficult by the lack of ships and the state of the roads. But the British Military Administration (BMA) had the wisdom to avoid any witch-hunt (even if it did imprison a few Bruneians for six months for collaboration), which allowed society to recover calmly with the goodwill and local expertise, mostly Malay and Chinese. Schools reopened (the sultanate counted 18 at the end of 1945) and police and customs were restored.[42]

Not until the failure of British negotiations with the sultans of the Peninsula, the departure of Australian troops and the arrival of Indian

---

[41] The regalia and jewels contained in the palace were also destroyed. The sultan demanded SS $64,630 in indemnity; after fierce bargaining, he would receive two-thirds of the amount (SS $40,000).

[42] On this whole period, see the testimony of T.S. Monks, *Brunei Days* (Lewes: Book Guild, 1992), 193 p. A scrupulous and efficient Chinaman, Chong Thau Fah, took charge of the treasury; Pengiran Mohammed bin Pg. Piut, future *Pg. Kerma Indera*, looked after the general secretariat (pp. 85ff).

troops of the Southeast Asia Command in January 1946 did operations accelerate. The resumption of production combined with daily shortages (the rice harvest of 1945–46 was only half the normal output) entrained a strike of Chinese workers in the oil sector in mid-1946, which was rapidly quelled by their firing and the hiring of other immigrants. In July 1946 civil administration was finally re-established, which quickly triggered urban renewal plans for the capital (1947), then for Kuala Belait (1949) and Seria (1950). When the two great British colonial banks, the Hong Kong and Shanghai Bank and the Standard Chartered Bank, were thrown out of continental China, they each opened a branch in Brunei, which thus came to possess for the first time the embryo of a banking system.

In the absence of any renegotiation of the 1906 treaty, Brunei was once again managed by a British Resident, except that the ceding of Sarawak[43] and North Borneo[44] to the British Crown unleashed a rapprochement among the administrations of the three territories, formalised in 1948 by the administrative fusion of Brunei and Sarawak, and by making the high commissioner the governor of Sarawak. The governors would meet every six months, share administrative services with respect to manpower (1947), justice (1951) and health, and cooperate on customs, police and maritime transport.

The Bruneians were strongly opposed to any de facto transformation into a sixth division of Sarawak, particularly since they had no desire to share their newfound oil wealth, and so the new configuration fuelled the resurgence of the nationalist agitation prevailing at the end of the 1930s, within half a dozen movements close to the palace. This included the *Barisan Pemuda* (BARIP), founded in May 1946[45] under the sultan's patronage, presided by Hj. Mohammed Salleh, who sent the high commissioner a petition for the independence of Brunei; the MUTU[46] in May 1947, which was housed with the *Pemancha*;[47] and the Brunei Malay

[43] Ceded to the British Crown by Rajah Vyner Brooke in July 1946. On the context, see Steven Runciman, *The White Rajahs* (Cambridge University Press, reprinted Kuala Lumpur: Malaysian Heritage, 2007), pp. 340ff.

[44] When North Borneo was ceded to the British Crown in July 1946, the British attached Labuan to it.

[45] According to Horton, *The British Residency in Brunei*, p. 53, it was founded in 1938, then refounded in 1946.

[46] *Persekutuan Murid Tua Melayu Brunei* (Association of former Malay students).

[47] Future father-in-law of the current reigning sultan, Hassanal Bolkiah, and of his brother Prince Mohamed.

Women's Association, which at the end of the 1940s gathered women interested in education, including several wives of dignitaries.[48] In 1946, Bruneians demanded out of the blue the authority of the State Council to recruit high-ranking officials (apart from the religious domain), an increased involvement in the management of their country, and for educated Malay candidates to be considered for administrative jobs, hitherto dominated by Anglophone Chinese—all of which implied the creation of secondary education in English in Brunei. To calm things down, the salaries of religious officials were adjusted upward. At the start of 1947, the BARIP, which wanted to proclaim publicly the pre-eminence of Malays, imposed (by threat) the closing of Chinese shops during the funeral of the sultan's mother. Named *Bendahara* in 1947, Omar Ali Saifuddin obtained in January 1948 the creation of a Bureau of Religious Affairs (*Penasehat^2 Juma'ah Shari'ah*, 19 members) to administer Islamic law and serve as an appeals jurisdiction. Population growth, due to the resumption of immigration induced by the resurgence of oil exploitation, led to the creation of an Islamic court in Belait in August 1950.[49]

Education, on the other hand, continued to lag behind. It was only in 1949 that a qualified head of education was recruited, and in 1951 that the first English-language public secondary school was opened in Brunei City and endowed with a scholarship system.

Accession of Omar Ali Saifuddin III and the Acceleration of Modernisation

After an interim during which MacBryan,[50] who had returned to Brunei at the start of 1950, had become close to Sultan Ahmad Tajuddin and pushed him to designate his eldest daughter Tuanku Ishani (Ehsan)[51] as successor, the sultan died prematurely in Singapore in 1950. Around the same time the creation of a state gathering Sarawak, Brunei and North

[48] It selected the first women sent to the *Malay Women's Teachers' Training College* in Malacca.

[49] The head of the district thus lost his office as vice-*kadi*.

[50] Gerard MacBryan, recalling the precedent set by the second sultan Ahmad, became a *haji*, and moreover, being psychologically unstable with episodes of delirium, saw himself marrying the sultan's eldest daughter and claiming the crown (Bob Reece, *The White Rajahs of Sarawak: A Borneo Dynasty* [Singapore: Archipelago Press, 2004], p. 124).

[51] The daughter of his first wife, a princess of Selangor, and herself once the wife of a prince of Selangor.

Borneo was being proposed (both proposals were rejected by the British, who did not wish to unleash a new cycle of succession crises). His brother Omar Ali Saifuddin III, endowed at the right time with several male heirs, succeeded him with the consent of the British, who quickly expelled MacBryan. Crowned amid great pomp in 1951, his remuneration doubled in comparison to his predecessor's, the new sultan made an official visit to the United Kingdom in 1952 and was knighted in 1953.

But behind the scenes of this upturn in relations with London, the sultan (the first Bruneian sovereign educated abroad) did not cease trying to gain the upper hand over the British economically and politically.[52] He played on the fact that (1) Bruneians henceforth formed the majority in the State Council, which decided on all matters; and (2) oil income gave them the means to self-finance their modernisation while the United Kingdom was in a complete slump.

On the socio-economic front, Omar Ali Saifuddin negotiated at the start of his accession an increase in corporate taxes, which rose from 10% to 20%, then to 30% in 1953. To the M $1.2 million (or US $0.39 million)[53] allotted to Brunei for war damages, were added oil revenues, which increased from M $1 million in 1946 to M $100 million (= US $32.6 million) in 1952—a surge augmented by a devaluation of the pound sterling by 30% on 19 September 1949.

A five-year plan (M $100 million) was implemented in 1953: infrastructure received 80% of the budget and social programmes 20%. Expenditure on education increased twenty-fold between 1952 and 1958, with the goal of generalising primary education to girls. After the opening of a first public secondary school in the capital in 1951, then a second one in Kuala Belait the following year, Malay primary education (made more attractive with the integration of a medical checkup) became free; school curricula remained oriented to the acquisition of traditional practical knowledge. In July 1954 the Sultan Omar Ali Saifuddin College was inaugurated; in 1957, Raja Isteri's School for Girls. The eight Chinese schools benefited from a subsidy of half their operating costs, while professional training aimed at the petrol sector was started in Seria.

---

[52] For example, on the issue of financing his pilgrimage to Mecca in 1951.

[53] Since 1939 (excluding the Japanese Occupation period), the Malayan dollar (M $) replaced the Straits Settlements dollar on the basis of M $1 = SS $1= 1 shilling 4 pence = US $0.32 (Shakila Yakob, *The United States and the Malaysian Economy* [New York: Routledge, 2008], p. xix).

Qualified teachers were initially recruited from the United Kingdom and Malaya, before a teacher training college was created in 1956. The best students received scholarships to continue their higher education abroad. Brunei laid the bases for a welfare state, with the establishment of a pension system and the extension of health coverage to the whole country: the capital and Kuala Belait (which possessed a hospital financed by the BMPC) were endowed with public hospitals, while dispensaries were created in most of the other small towns and nurses toured (by helicopter on occasion) the more remote villages. Water treatment was set up in the capital in 1956, then extended to Belait-Seria.

The government supported rice growing with irrigation and mechanisation, as well as small rubber producers, without great success at the start. The vicissitudes of other "jewels" of the modern economy—the catetchu factory (abandoned in 1952) and the Island Trading Company (finally closed in 1957 after struggling along)—and more generally, the absence of a deepwater port and the disaffection of the Malays for salaried jobs in business, continued to hamper the development of a manufacturing sector.

The sultan undertook a parallel renewal of politics with the application of a new concept, *Melayu Islam Beraja* or MIB, which defined Malayness on the dual basis of religion (Islam) and the political system (the monarchy):[54]

- In the name of the Islamic dimension of society and parallel with the reorganisation of civil jurisdictions[55] imposed by the transformation in 1946 of the protectorates of Sarawak and North Borneo into colonies of the British Crown, the sultan reorganised the primary and appeal religious courts in 1951. Henceforth appeals were made "to the Sultan and his Religious Council". In September of the same year, and for the first time since Sultan Haji Muhammad Ali (17th century), the reigning sovereign performed the hajj.[56] Between 1952

[54] His approach was reminiscent of that of Siam's King Vajiravudh (1910–25), who based the Siamese nation on the indissolubility of the triad "Nation, Religion, King" (David K. Wyatt, *Thailand: A Short History* [Yale: Yale University Press, 1984], p. 229), except that here it was not the nation that was being defined but the identity of its promoters, the Malays of Brunei.

[55] Creation of the Supreme Court of Borneo with jurisdiction over the three British territories.

[56] Horton, *Turun-temurun: A Dissection of Brunei Darussalam*, p. 60.

and 1955, the share of the budget for religious affairs quadrupled.[57] This was followed by the creation of a series of new bodies dedicated to religious affairs: the Consultative Religious Council (including some members of the Bureau of Religious Affairs), Department of Religion, Customs and Social Welfare[58] (July 1954, which served as the executive of the preceding body), and Religious Council (1956).[59] In 1955, the Islamic legal code was revised by the promulgation of a series of laws[60] that abrogated the preceding ones and disengaged religious administration from the hold of the British, by separating the jurisdictions relating to British common law from the Islamic courts.[61] The sultan also reorganised the propagation of the faith: Muslim teaching was reformed in 1955,[62] seven Muslim schools were opened in 1956 and an information section was created in 1958. To assert the Islamic dimension of society, the sultan asked the State Council to stop subsidies to Christian schools, which he finally obtained in 1959, after thwarting a last-ditch attempt to counter the move by the High Commissioner. The sultan thus gained wide support from the Malay teachers of the BMTA.

- The sultan also revived monarchical symbols: he took to composing *sya'ir*, a traditional poetic form,[63] and had the oral palatine customs

[57] Arifin Mansurnoor, "Socioreligious Changes in Brunei during the British Residency".

[58] The department would be divided into three in 1961.

[59] *Majlis Masyarakat Sharyiah*; *Majlis Ugama Islam dan Adat Istiadat Negeri.*

[60] Giving every district its Islamic courts.

[61] Azrinah Binti Haji Abdul Rahman, "Legal System in Brunei Darussalam after the Signing of the Supplementary Agreement 1905/1906 between Brunei and Great Britain", p. 11.

[62] Invited to evaluate religious instruction in Brunei, two *ustadz* from Johor noted that most of the students were unable to pronounce the *shahada* and were ignorant of the five pillars of Islam; and that villagers could not perform religious duties toward the deceased correctly (Arifin Mansurnoor, "Socioreligious Changes in Brunei during the British Residency").

[63] This royal practice of using poetry to legitimise royal power can be compared with the many re-writings of the *Rāmāyaṇa* in the Peninsula: in Cambodia, the *Rāmakerti* was reconceptualised in the 16th and 17th centuries to be a mirror of the Prince (Saveros Pou and Grégory Mikaelian, *Ramakerti I "la Gloire de Rama"* [Paris: L'Harmattan, 2007], p. 26; Grégory Mikaelian, "La gloire du prince charmant: de la reconfiguration des pratiques discursives du pouvoir dans le royaume khmer du XVIIᵉ siècle", *Péninsule* 56 [2008 (1)]: 51–70). In Siam, at the end of the 18th century, Rama I, founder of the Chakri dynasty, directed the verse re-writing of the Siamese *Rāmāyaṇa*, the *Ramakien*, in 1798 (Prince Chula Chakrabongse, *Lords of Life* [London: Alvin Redman, 1960], p. 94).

put down in writing (1958).[64] This enthronement of Malay royal culture was played up in ostentatious Muslim festivals, of which the most important throughout the ages was Hari Raya at the end of Ramadan, jointly celebrating Islam and the monarchy.

But after the British reopened the debate on the country's status in 1948, and when Indonesian independence was recognised in 1950, tensions grew within the most educated Malay circles. They crystallised around an emblematic figure, Shaikh Azahari, hero of the war of Indonesian independence, who came back from Jakarta at the end of 1952. An underground figure converted, it seems, to republican ideas, he was linked by lineage to the summit of the Brunei establishment.[65] At the start of 1953 Omar Ali Saifuddin III expressed his desire to establish a constitution.[66] He named a consultative committee comprising seven members of various social origins. After visiting districts and meeting the people, the committee recommended a constitution resembling that of Johor, of which one of the key points was the replacement of the Resident by a *Menteri besar*. The future constitution became a point of contention with the British; the Colonial Office and the high commissioners were also far from agreeing among themselves. Adept at revolutionary warfare, Azahari profited from dissension to get himself imprisoned in 1953[67] and win sympathy, including within police ranks. The sultan counter-attacked by creating consultative district councils in September 1954, whose members he personally appointed (after nominations), and which would delegate observers to the State Council. The State Council, increasingly critical of the Resident's actions, formalised at the start of 1956 a plan to create district and municipal councils with budgetary and administrative autonomy. Meanwhile Azahari, who founded the first political party of Brunei, the PRB (Brunei People's Party),[68] in January 1956, denounced the non-representative nature of the councils and the absence of free speech.

---

[64] Pg. Mohammed Yusuf, "Adat Istiadat Diraja Brunei Darus-salam", *BMJ* 3, 3 (1975): 43. A first measure had been taken at the end of the first half of the 18th century with the writing down of the royal geneaology (*Silsilah*) (see above).

[65] His mother was the sister of the *Temenggong* and his father was Arab-Malay.

[66] Hussainmiya and Tarling, *Brunei: Traditions of Monarchic Culture and History, R.H. Hickling's Memorandum*, pp. 81ff.

[67] He asked for a licence for a film production company, knowing very well that his request was bound to be rejected as it fulfilled none of the required conditions, then organised a violent demonstration in front of the resident's office.

[68] Azahari was the only leader to have received higher education.

In face of the widespread contestation provoked by the finalisation of Malaya's independence, the sultan went on the offensive in March 1956. He refused any plan for federation, thus cutting the ground from under the feet of the British. He announced the holding of elections to the district councils and promised that they would be held by secret ballot. He also launched an "official newspaper" distributed free by the palace, *Pelita Brunei*, so as to have direct control over public opinion. Undeterred, the PRB, with its 16,000 members (constituting three-quarters of all male adults and almost the entire labouring class), mounted an offensive at the start of 1957 with three demands: (1) election of three-quarters of the members of the State Council; (2) creation of a Federation of Kalimantan Utara [North Borneo] under Brunei's leadership; (3) fixing a date for independence. To prepare for the future status of the country, the sultan went to London in September 1957 and was shrewd enough to ask the British to receive the PRB delegation, which was hoping to conduct its own talks.[69] But the results were disappointing: the secretary of state refused the appointment of a *menteri besar* and two other Malay ministers, as well as the abrogation of the reserve powers of the high commissioner. Azahari, whose mission had failed, called for the boycott of elections to the district councils, which were then annulled by the sultan.

The sultan turned to Kuala Lumpur. The sovereigns and political authorities of the Federation were invited in 1958 to the inauguration of the sumptuous Omar Ali Saifuddin Mosque (before which he placed the royal barge made of marble,[70] emblematic of most of Southeast Asian kingship), and Malaya was granted a loan of 100 million ringgit. The sultan paid an official visit to Malaya in July 1959 and the King of Malaya returned his visit. Relations were now sufficiently positive that, foreseeing the replacement of the British by Malays of Malaya, he rejected the officials delegated by Sarawak. Another sign of the closer ties with Kuala Lumpur was the opening of a first Malay bank (Malayan Banking) in 1960.

Since the State Council, propelled by representatives of the district consultative councils, was constantly introducing amendments to the planned constitution, a second series of talks opened in London from March–April 1959. The constitution planned had nothing to do with the

[69] Hussainmiya, *Sultan Omar Ali Saifuddin III and Britain*, p. 183.
[70] The last one was destroyed during World War Two.

one negotiated in London two years earlier, save the clause (as in 1905) allowing the British High Commissioner (who replaced the Resident) to retain his right to be consulted on all decisions except those relating to religion and custom. On this basis, in September 1959 a new treaty was signed with the United Kingdom. Brunei recovered its political autonomy—which ruptured its administrative relations with Sarawak—and the British were left with control over only security and foreign relations. The first constitution, whose painful midwifery inspired the royal *Sya'ir Perlembagaan Brunei* [*Poem on the institutionalisation of Brunei*], was proclaimed on 19 September 1959. Two councils, one executive (14 members, 7 by right and 7 appointed) and one legislative, were set up. There was nothing really democratic in the new legislative formula: with 16 members elected by districts, 8 members by right, and 9 members appointed by the sultan (6 officials and 3 other personalities), the majority of members in the legislative council were non-elected. Moreover, allocations to members of the sultan's civil list were paid from the Consolidated Fund (the equivalent of the Treasury) and thus escaped any annual public debate,[71] and recruitment for public service was the sole purview of the Commission of Public Services. In addition, the sultan had a private council of three "royal" advisors (religion,[72] succession and regency).

Overview of the Postwar Residency from 1946–59

Thanks to the explosion in oil income, Brunei had become a relatively rich country in Southeast Asian terms and its production no longer relied on the traditional sectors of agriculture, fishing and crafts, but on hydrocarbons. It had also embarked on the path of social progress by instituting five-year plans starting in 1954.[73] With a budget of M $4 million per year assigned to education, 90% of boys and 37% of girls of school age were attending school by the end of the 1950s. The sultanate had 52 Malay primary schools, 3 secondary government schools, 8 British religious schools, and 8 Chinese schools. Paludism had been virtually eradicated and the mortality rate had fallen by almost half. More than 90% of the lodgings in Belait-Seria and the city of Brunei had electricity

[71] Hussainmiya, *Sultan Omar Ali Saifuddin III and Britain*, p. 201.

[72] The Department of Religious Affairs was separated from that of Customs and Social Welfare.

[73] Mark Cleary and Shuang Yann Wong, *Oil, Economic Development and Diversification of Brunei Darussalam* (New York: St. Martin's, 1994), p. 69.

and running water. The country was now served by two airports, in the capital and in Seria.

Yet education remained mediocre in quality, with overflowing classes at the primary level, limited access to secondary schools and a lack of professional training for teachers. And since 52% of those over ten years old were still illiterate in 1960,[74] most of the posts of responsibility continued to be held by Westerners and technical jobs by Asians who were not *bumiputera*.[75]

Political power was increasingly concentrated in the sultan's hands. In addition to religious affairs, he controlled the executive without any real countervailing powers; the British High Commissioner had less weight and the PRB (which was not invited to the 1959 talks in London) was marginalised. The upshot was that in the years since the launch of the first "Inter-territorial Conference" gathering the executive heads of the three British territories in Borneo of 1953, the future of Sarawak and North Borneo remained unresolved. This opened the way to all kinds of enterprises of external seduction that would make Brunei more fragile.

---

[74] *Ranchangan Kemajuan Negara 1975–1979* [*The National Development Plan 1975–1979*], 1980, p. 37.

[75] Literally "sons of the earth", in other words, autochthones, a term reserved in Malaysia for the Melayu, then by extension after 1963 for other ethnic groups indigenous to Malaysia; used on occasion in Brunei by Bruneians to refer to Bruneians of "Malay" ethnicity—a reminder of the primacy of blood rights over residential rights with respect to citizenship.

From Internal Autonomy to Independence (1984)

The 1962 Crisis and Its Consequences

Azahari invited the secretary-general of the Sarawak United Peoples Party (SUPP) and representatives of the PAS (Parti Islam Se-Malaysia), and the Partai Rakyat of Malaysia and Singapore to the 3rd Congress of the PRB in February 1960, where he launched the idea of cooperation among the SUPP, the PRB and other political leaders of North Borneo and discussion on a possible federation of North Borneo. The revival of the PRB was accompanied and nurtured by the development of workers unions, and the Brunei United Labour Front (BULF)[76] was founded in June 1960. The PRB's proposal was discussed at the SUPP congress in June 1960[77] in the presence of Azahari, who hoped to secure for Brunei a determining role in the new state. In December, the Legislative Council passed a resolution setting the independence of Brunei for 29 September 1965. A competing project that had the support of the British and which was mentioned in London by Tunku Abdul Rahman in June 1960 was to enlarge the Malay Federation. The sultan, who had limited the participation of Brunei to meetings dealing with future regional cooperation (while signing a monetary accord with Malaya and the British territories of Borneo),[78] was incorrectly presumed to be favourable, since he had

[76] *Barisan Buruh Bersatu Brunei.*

[77] Mohamad Yusop, "The Malaysia Plan and the First Brunei Elections, 1962", *JMBRAS* 71, 1 (1998): 59.

[78] See Peter J. Drake, *Currency, Credit and Commerce: Early Development in Southeast Asia* (London: Ashgate, 2004), pp. 143ff.

sent his sons to pursue their secondary studies in Malaya in the fall of 1960 and had even constructed a secondary residence there.[79]

Preparations for the first Bruneian elections (planned for August 1961) took place in this context, raising the question of citizenship. A draft law in September 1960 called for granting citizenship by right to "indigenous races", while other potential electors would have to show proof of 20 years of residence over the last quarter century and take an exam in Malay. The PRB quickly demanded the inclusion of Dayaks/Ibans among the so-called "indigenous races" and a reduction in the residency requirement from 20 to 10 years. Then it seized upon the inflow of employees recruited in Malaya to denounce the "neo-colonialism" of Kuala Lumpur, harassing on some occasion its nationals so they ended up going back en masse.[80] The leaders of the PRB went on trips to meet left-wing opposition parties in Singapore, Indonesia and Sarawak. In reaction, Brunei created the beginnings of an army in May 1961.

In May 1961 while in Singapore, Tunku Abdul Rahman committed the error of proposing, without prior consultation, an enlargement of the Malay Federation to include the three territories of Borneo—an offer that was received with only moderate enthusiasm in Sarawak and North Borneo and even more poorly in Brunei. The PRB took advantage of the situation to organise the first joint demonstration with the BULF[81] in June to demand elections, then formed a united front that also included North Borneo in the person of the director of the *North Borneo and Sabah Times*, Donald Stephens.[82] In August, the Bruneian government promulgated a nationality law that went into force on 1 January 1962, but delays in preparation caused the elections to be postponed again for a year. Tensions escalated: a second demonstration twice as large as the preceding one took place and a petition demanding pell-mell elections on the initial date, defence of the privileges of the *bumiputera*, the

[79] Persuaded that Brunei would be attached to the Malaysian Federation, the Malay government even constructed a palace in Kuala Lumpur intended for the sultan of Brunei, similar to those built for the nine sultans of the Peninsula. Since it was not used as such, the building was later assigned for other ceremonial tasks.

[80] The two brothers of Azahari mistreated a forest employee (Mohamad Yusop, "The Malaysia Plan and the First Brunei Elections, 1962": 256).

[81] Presided over by a Chinese, Ong Kee Hui.

[82] Mohamad Yusop, "The Malaysia Plan and the First Brunei Elections, 1962": 62.

softening of security, social measures, and a re-examination of the position of Brunei Shell was submitted. Azahari went to Jesselton (Kota Kinabalu) to meet the leaders of the two political parties of Sarawak and North Borneo and to shape a united front in support of a Borneo Federation. On their side, the British held negotiations with the Tunku on the integration of Sarawak and North Borneo into a federated Malaysian state.

On 5 December 1961, the sultan declared, seemingly on principle but really only after six months of pressure, that he was interested in Kuala Lumpur's proposal. Encouraged by the British, who wished to disengage from the region, Brunei participated in the second Malaysia Solidarity Consultative Committee (MSCC), presided over by D. Stephens, who thus broke with the PRB. In January 1962, the sultan designated an inquiry commission[83] into the admissibility of the Malaysian proposal. This commission was composed solely of local figures, including Azahari, whom the sultan also named to the Legislative Council out of prudence. Although the Commission's public hearings revealed the breadth of opposition to Malaysia and of support for the Borneo Federation plan, the sultan chose to ignore its conclusions: he sent observers to MSCC talks in Singapore in February 1962, then signed a memorandum accepting in principle integration into Malaysia. Azahari counter-attacked in April by asking the Legislative Council for a motion requiring the recognition of the historic sovereignty of Brunei over the whole west of Borneo; the Council refused and he resigned.

Nevertheless, the sultan announced his acceptance of the Malaysian proposal to the Legislative Council in July 1962—on condition that measures to protect the interests of the sultanate be included. Azahari then embarked on an electoral campaign demanding the outright rejection of the Malaysian offer, plus independence in 1963 and membership in a Federation of North Borneo. In parallel, he built a clandestine army of Kalimantan Utara, which united the most extreme Bruneians and some natives of Limbang and Lawas. Despite a profusion of small parties and a voting participation rate of 90%[84] in the elections of August 1962, the PRB won the totality of seats in all the district councils but one

[83] The Cobbold Commission performed for the British the same inquiry in Sarawak and North Borneo.

[84] Azahari, who did not have Bruneian citizenship because he was born in Labuan to a foreign father, was not eligible to vote.

(whose winner soon joined the party). Azahari now pulled out all the stops and demanded constitutional reform. In September 1962, he was received by the sultan (whom he tried to trick by feigning support for the fusion plan)[85] and made several trips to Kuala Lumpur, where he was courted for his support in exchange for power in Brunei. In response, the sultan adjourned the inaugural session of the Legislative Council thrice and tried to mobilise consensus by asking for the handover of Limbang.

These dilatory manœuvres won Azahari three sources of external support: the Philippines promised to abandon any claim over North Borneo, Indonesia affirmed its opposition to "Greater Malaysia" and the Communists of the region decried a neo-colonialist plot. The Tunku warned the sultan and the British of an imminent uprising. Unfortunately, the Bruneian executive had never been so weak, with a Bruneian *menteri besar*, a Malayan secretary of state for the interior and a British chief of police who could not get along with each other. When the Legislative Council refused to inscribe its motions into the inaugural session set for December, the PRB (in the absence of Azahari, who had left to recruit militants in Manila) proclaimed on 8 December 1962 the independence of the unitary state of North Kalimantan and coordinated a series of attacks on police stations in the three states. The next day,[86] the sultan explained on the radio that the rebellion did not have his approval. In conformity with the 1959 treaty, Gurkhas[87] quickly

[85] It was only after the failure of the rebellion that Azahari, to cover himself, claimed that the sultan had agreed to the plan for the Federation of Kalimantan Utara. This was denied by an eyewitness, the future *Pehin* Jamil al-Sufri, at the time Jamil Umar (Hussainmiya, *Sultan Omar Ali Saifuddin III and Britain*, p. 307). On British assessment of the real or presumed ambivalence of the sultan, see the official despatch from High Commissioner Sir Dennis White (Horton, *Turun-temurun: A Dissection of Brunei Darussalam*, pp. 30–1).

[86] The High Commissioner was away in England at that time and there was chaos on the British side. Someone (whose identity remains unknown) gave the order to all Europeans to evacuate Brunei and the administration was completely disorganised.

[87] *Gurkha(s)* is the usual spelling in Brunei. The rebellion caught the British troops by surprise, especially since the 1959 agreements did not provide for any security coordination in the three territories of northern Borneo; moreover, the leaders of the British high command were away. The fortuitous presence of a police detachment from North Borneo did allow the British to take immediate control of the airport, so they were able to bring troops by helicopter to Seria and take the city, then Kuala Belait. A considerable military presence was then installed in Brunei and its environs: five units of Gurkha infantry were sent to clean Sarawak of rebels and to prevent

"cleaned up" the capital, Kuala Belait and Seria. After particularly fierce resistance in Limbang, the rebellion was quelled on 20 December. Omar Ali Saifuddin suspended the constitution, dissolved the executive, legislative and district councils, banned political parties, proclaimed a state of emergency and named an emergency council of 14 members (including the High Commissioner). Under British monitoring, the treatment of opponents was lenient: they recovered their positions several months later after swearing allegiance to the sovereign; the government even took charge of subsistence for the families of the toughest rebels who remained in prison.

But entire areas of the administration of key sectors (public works, shipping) had tottered in the rebellion, revealing the fragility of the political edifice. With British help, the sultan methodically filled the gaps in the state apparatus for security and the armed forces, accepting the arrival of 150 Malayan police officers sent to protect their compatriots. To restore consensus, he strengthened social protection, stimulated economic development and even let some small political parties flourish on the ruins of the PRB. However, the sultan and his entourage had lost any confidence in democracy; the constitution, amended in May 1963, was stripped of anything that might have been the premises of liberalisation. The Legislative Council grew from 33 to 35 members (6 by right, 29 appointed),[88] and the Executive Council—with the addition of an assistant *menteri besar* post—dropped from 16 to 12 members (8 by right and 4 appointed), the sole concession to "modernity" being the suppression of seats reserved for wazirs on both councils. Relations between the United Kingdom and Brunei would henceforth be managed by the Secretary of State for Commonwealth Relations and no longer by the Colonial Office. The price to pay was not negligible. The Bruneian authorities now faced pressure from those who had saved them from disaster in two areas: the evolution of institutions toward something more acceptable to British public opinion and possible integration into Malaysia. The goals of the second development plan (1962–66) were dropped.

---

them from leaving for Indonesia, supported by 4,000 "Dayaks" and other backup troops from Tom Harrisson (a former special forces officer during the Pacific war who had mounted operations against the Japanese in Borneo, and who was at the time the curator of the Sarawak Museum), plus support from a dozen ships and airplanes (Hussainmiya, *Sultan Omar Ali Saifuddin III and Britain*, pp. 300ff).

[88] Ten officials and 19 other personages.

Failure of the Malaysian Option

Even though the negotiations of September 1962 had failed to convince Brunei of the urgency of joining the Malaysian Federation, the insurrection and especially London's insistence pushed the sultan to take an interest in the offer from Kuala Lumpur. While the first talks of February 1963 were vague, those in June covered four major points of discord: the cessation after ten years of Brunei's oil revenues to the federal government, the financial contribution of the sultanate, taxation on new hydrocarbon fields (especially since new fields had just been discovered offshore of Seria[89]), and the order of precedence among the sultans (the sultan of Brunei, the last potential adherent to the Federation, refused to be placed by protocol after the nine sultans of the Malay Peninsula). There was an impasse. After two more discussions, this time conducted at the highest level between the sultan and Tunku Abdul Rahman, the Malayan government issued Brunei an ultimatum. When the 48 hours had passed, the sultan left Kuala Lumpur on 21 June.[90] He rejected the mediation of the British General Commissioner for Southeast Asia. The context was now in his favour: the communist Chinese insurrection in Sarawak (on top of the remains of the communist insurrection in the Malay Peninsula) and the "confrontational" pro-Chinese policy of Sukarno's Indonesia conferred on Brunei a strategic dimension. As foreseen, the elections in Sarawak and Sabah revealed a majority in favour of Malaysia: the two territories proclaimed their independence on 31 August 1963, then joined the Malaysian federation in concert with Singapore.[91]

The inauguration of a second Malaysian bank, the United Malaysian Banking Corporation, in Brunei in 1963 spelled the end of neighbourly relations with Malaysia. The fixing of land borders and the imposition of customs posts in October 1963 aroused strong protests in Limbang and Lawas. At the start of 1964, Malaysia recalled hundreds of officials

---

[89] South West Ampa Field.

[90] According to Tunku Abdul Rahman, the sultan had asked (among other things) to become the next king of the Federation (*Star*, 19 October 1981), which was expressly denied by the *Begawan* in his response to the same newspaper (ibid., 7 November 1981), articles quoted by Pushpa Thambipillai, "Brunei in ASEAN: The Viable Choice?", *SAA 1982*: 107.

[91] This resulted in the creation of a supreme court in Brunei in 1963, followed by the recruitment of judges from Hong Kong in 1964.

sent to Brunei, then abolished places reserved for Bruneians in various Malaysian teacher-training centres (they were replaced by British or Singaporeans). After an ultimatum from the Sarawak authorities, some 100 boats quit Rangau for Brunei in September 1964. The tide was reversed when Malaysia expelled Singapore in August 1965, which permitted a rapprochement between the two wealthiest states in Southeast Asia.

Institutional Evolution

Once the Malaysian option had been discarded, the nationality code was redefined: the law of August 1964 made it obligatory to possess an identity card, with the corollary of a resident register. With the prospect of an eventual rupture of financial ties to Malaysia, a first Bruneian bank, the National Bank of Brunei, was created at the end of 1964 by the royal family, which held 70% of the capital, in partnership with the Sino-Malaysian Khoo Teck Puat, who held a 30% share. With the agreement of London, the government announced new constitutional amendments, ratified by a vote of the Legislative Council: direct elections for 10 of the 21 seats on the Council;[92] and reduction of the executive council to 11 members (6 ministers by right, 4 designated by the Legislative Council and the British High Commissioner). But the defeat of the parties by independent candidates in the elections of March 1965 made it difficult to form any "parliamentary" majority, although in London the new Labour government, having promised to withdraw from "East of Suez", pushed for democratisation.

The sultan then began a rapprochement with Malaysia in April 1965 by refusing to support the Philippine claim to Sabah. He went to London to negotiate the evolution of Bruneian institutions in April and May. After forceful discussions, he accepted the principle of a doubling of the number of elected posts and the gradual diminution of the appointed members of the Legislative Council—all consigned to a "white paper". Returning to Brunei, he appointed two vice-ministers among the elected members of the Legislative Council, and two others as representatives of the Chinese and Dusun communities. Far from calming things, this measure stirred up the political scene: Abdul Latif bin Hamid[93] tried

[92] The 11 other seats were split between 6 members by right and 5 named by the Sultan.

[93] He had just returned from the UK after five years of studies.

to federate the independents under the banner of the Barisan Rakyat Brunei[94] (BARA) and Pg. Hj. Ali,[95] ex-vice *menteri besar*, founded the Partai Kemajuan Rakyat[96] (PAKAR). The announcement of the British withdrawal from "East of Suez" at the start of 1966 accentuated the political vulnerability of the sultanate and so Brunei acquired a very rudimentary navy[97] and two helicopters. The elected members of the Legislative Council passed a motion demanding that foreign officials be flanked by local assistants within three years. In August 1966, the two political parties merged to create the Barisan Kemerdekaan Rakyat (BAKER),[98] which demanded immediate independence and sent a memorandum to the High Commissioner demanding application of the April 1965 accords. While London manifested some interest in February 1967, the Bruneian government equivocated: it explained in May 1967 that the white paper was a simple declaration of intent. Given the risk of abrogating the 1959 accords on security, the sultan went to London to avert full independence.[99] Applying the same precautionary principle, when the Singapore dollar separated from the Malaysian ringgit in June 1967, Brunei chose to preserve its currency's alignment with that of the city-state, where most of its financial accounts were managed, requesting for a currency board in order to guarantee parity between the two currencies.[100]

Small Steps toward Independence

As the British stepped up the pressure for democracy and named a commissioner who was not to the sovereign's taste, the latter disengaged by abdicating in favour of his oldest son on 4 October 1967: the new sultan was not bound by the commitments of his father (now titled *Paduka Seri Begawan*)[101] toward institutional change. In the absence of

[94] Brunei People's Front.
[95] A teacher known for his nationalism who was close to Pengiran Yusuf.
[96] Development People Party.
[97] A few motorboats for the use of the land army.
[98] People's Independence Front.
[99] An identical approach to that of most of the Arabian Gulf emirates.
[100] A currency board limited the central monetary creation to net reserves and banned the central bank from refinancing both the government and the commercial banks.
[101] His Highness [*Paduka*] the Respected [*Sri*] Blessed One [in the religious sense of the term, *Begawan*].

parliamentary democracy, the 1968 elections to the district councils roused only mild enthusiasm: winning just 30% of the seats, the BAKER party failed to unseat the independent candidates. Three of its leaders quit in September 1969, and with BAKER now reduced to a rump, elections to the Legislative Council were abolished in 1970 and the Council was replaced by a wholly appointed assembly. In 1972, elections to the district councils were annulled. Henceforth, there existed no counter-power to the Sultan.

The young sultan (aged 21 at his accession) pursued his father's policy towards Malaysia. To thwart Malaysian propaganda, the Palace published the private letters exchanged between the *Tunku* and the *Begawan* (September 1968). By the same token, after a schism in the Malaysia-Singapore Airlines, Brunei granted landing rights to Singapore Airlines and not to Malaysian Airlines. Despite the growing number of visits by British leaders in early 1969 to explain the implications of their withdrawal, Brunei persisted in its refusal to join Malaysia. On 29 September 1970, during the ceremonies marking the name change of Brunei Town to Bandar Seri Begawan, the *Begawan* recalled—to the regret of the British and some of the officials—that Limbang belonged to the sultanate. After the return to power of the Conservatives in June 1970, followed by talks in London and a study visit to Brunei, an amendment to the 1959 treaty restored full internal autonomy to the sultanate in November 1971: the High Commissioner lost all political and administrative responsibility and therefore his emoluments were now paid by the British. To constrain the United Kingdom to maintaining a battalion of Gurkhas, Brunei also abstained from participation in the defence agreement among the "five powers" (signed in December 1971),[102] designed to preserve the Commonwealth's interests in the region. Brunei, which had just bought two patrol boats, preserved some diplomatic and military protection administered by the Council for Defence. Although the amendment did not mention it, separate documents called for maintaining a Gurkha regiment, under British command but paid for by the sultanate. This new *modus vivendi* was strengthened by the visit of Queen Elizabeth II in 1972. The only shadow was the intransigence of Malaysia, which welcomed PRB leaders after their incredible escape from the camp of Berakas (whose director was Malaysian) in 1973. Now the main administrative posts were given to Bruneians.

[102] Australia, New Zealand, Malaysia, Singapore and the United Kingdom.

The return of a Labour government in October 1974 after four years of Conservative administration was an unfavourable turning point for Brunei, which was obliged to revise the terms of the 1971 agreement when Malaysia mounted the pressure by fomenting agitation in Limbang. However, the conjuncture soon turned to its advantage: the annexation of East Timor by Indonesia (1975)—discretely approved by Kuala Lumpur and tolerated by the West despite Portugal's opposition—was a reminder that nobody was safe from predators. The authorities acted accordingly and transformed the police special forces into a secret service.[103] After the *Begawan* visited London in March 1975, the British ceased as of November to support motions demanding free elections under UN supervision, which had been put before the United Nation by the PRB via Malaysia. As a matter of fact, London, which was looking after the sultanate's sterling reserves, found this to its advantage during the apogee of the oil crisis. A resolution demanding general elections was adopted by all the ASEAN countries except for Singapore;[104] the *Begawan* went to Limbang to mount a petition demanding its reattachment to Brunei, to which Sarawak responded with a counter-petition. The sultan also adopted in 1976 a corps of some 900 former Gurkhas as an all-purpose personal bodyguard.[105] With the accession to power of Hussein Onn in January 1976, Malaysia gradually let go of the PRB, due in part to British pressure, and in 1977 stopped presenting UN motions demanding independence from the British and elections from Brunei.[106] Moreover, while the reigning sultan expressed a desire to improve relations with his neighbours at the end of 1976, a few months later he finalised separation among the subsidiaries of Shell in Brunei, Sarawak and Sabah, by closing the oil pipeline that linked them.

After a visit by Sarawak and Sabah authorities to Brunei, Malaysia confirmed its change of position during a bilateral meeting with President Suharto at Labuan in May 1978, where the two countries declared that they were favourable to the entry of Brunei into ASEAN. Informal

---

[103] A.J. Crosbie, "Brunei in transition", *SAA 1981*: 89.

[104] Saunders, *History of Brunei*, p. 164.

[105] The Ghurkha Reserve Unit (Abu Bakar Hamzah, "Brunei Darussalam, continuity and tradition", *SAA 1989*: 99). According to some sources, they were in charge of distributing munitions to the regular troops (Horton, *Turun-temurun: A Dissection of Brunei Darussalam*, p. 135, citing *The Economist*, 10 October 1992, p. 84).

[106] The last one (dated 1976) was voted in November 1977 (Pushpa Thambipillai, "Brunei in ASEAN: The Viable Choice?", *SAA 1982*: 108); Singapore chose to abstain.

meetings with Bruneian authorities in London ensued. The presence of a Gurkha regiment in Seria (even financed by Brunei) now seemed less imperative, and whether to maintain it or not came back onto the agenda in March 1978. Nonetheless, this did not interrupt progress towards independence: a joint declaration (June 1978) set a deadline of 31 December 1983, and a treaty of friendship and cooperation with the United Kingdom (7 January 1979) laid down the details. A "permanent resident" status would be granted to long-standing residents,[107] which was the condition set by the British for the maintenance of British military cooperation[108] and judicial assistance.[109] The sultanate reinforced its ties with Singapore:[110] two visits by Lee Kuan Yew in 1979 preceded the organisation of a first joint naval exercise,[111] followed by an official visit by the sultan in January 1980. The appeasement of regional tensions paved the way for Brunei's future admission into ASEAN: in April 1981, the sultan visited Indonesia, and Brunei was invited to the Association's ministerial conference on foreign affairs in Manila in June. A few months later in September, President Marcos abandoned Philippines claims on Sabah. The King of Malaysia (Sultan of Pahang) attended a polo tournament in Brunei in early 1983, followed by a delegation from the Religious Council of the state of Pahang. Despite continuing friction with London on security matters, an agreement confirming the maintenance of the Gurkha regiment in Seria was finally signed in September 1983 with Margaret Thatcher's Tory government (in power since May 1979), with the presence of Shell more or less in the balance.[112]

The approach of independence signalled an assertion of identity values in the course of the 1970s: cultural to begin with, with the cessation of subsidies to Chinese schools (1970),[113] the publication of bilingual annual reports starting in 1974, and debate on the language used for secondary education, which provoked a surge of popular nationalism

[107] Crosbie, "Brunei in transition", *SAA 1981*: 76.
[108] The information services were dissolved in November 1979.
[109] It is noteworthy that Hong Kong would continue to supply judges to the High Court and the Court of Appeal.
[110] The Singapore Army (a battalion of infantry or artillery) trained each year in Brunei.
[111] Tilak Doshi, "Brunei, the Steady State", *SAA 1991*: 78.
[112] Roger Kershaw, "Illuminating the Path to Independence: Political Themes in *Pelita Brunei* in 1983", *SAA 1984*: 72.
[113] Crosbie, "Brunei in transition": 87.

during the national mourning decreed upon the death of Sultan Hassanal Bolkiah's mother in 1979.[114] An assertion of religious values followed, with the appointment of Pehin Dato Abdul Aziz to the post of *menteri besar* in October 1981,[115] which triggered an accelerated Islamisation of the regime. This resulted in the creation of a department of religious affairs and Muslim schools; the application of Muslim behavioural norms (ban on alcohol, wearing of the veil in schools, etc.). This identity politics spilled over to the question of property: since 1979, any acquisition (or long lease) of land by an individual—even a Bruneian—or an entity was subject to the sultan's approval.[116] The authorisation to transfer land property was not a right but was ruled case by case by the relevant authorities under the supervision of the Ministry of Development; unofficially, and with some notorious exceptions to the rule, the Chinese could not purchase estates larger than two hectares, although property rights previously acquired were respected.

But what played against political agitation even more than the eradication of the emblematic tools of democracy or the instrumentalisation of Bruneian specificity was economic prosperity. A sign of the times was that Citibank opened a subsidiary in Brunei in 1971. The timing was good: between 1970 and 1980, Brunei's oil production increased by 75% while oil prices increased eleven-fold.[117] By the end of the decade, hydrocarbons generated 78% of the GDP, and oil exports (which had multiplied by 34 times[118] in current dollars during the decade) contributed to a current account balance surplus of almost B $5 billion. Given Brunei's socio-economic dimensions, the surplus was such that the Ministry of Finance created a planning department in May 1973. Its participation in Brunei Shell[119] rose from 25% in 1973 to 50% in 1975, and its share in Brunei LNG rose from 10% in 1972 to 33% in 1977.[120] To promote new sectors of activity, an Economic Development Bureau (EDB), conceived on the Singapore model, was created in January 1976.[121]

---

[114] Paduka Sri Seri Begawan, in 1979 (Crosbie, ibid.: 88).
[115] Horton, *Turun-temurun: A Dissection of Brunei Darussalam*, p. 169.
[116] Crosbie, "Brunei in transition": 86.
[117] From US $3.39 per barrel in 1970 to $37.42 in 1980, "Historical Crude Oil Prices (Table)", 15 July 2009, http://www.inflationdata.com/inflation/Inflation_Rate/Historical_Oil_Prices_Table.asp.
[118] *Brunei Statistical Yearbook 1976/77*, p. 51 and ibid., *1986*, p. 52.
[119] Horton, *Turun-temurun: A Dissection of Brunei Darussalam*, p. 32.
[120] Timothy Teck Mong Ong, "Modern Brunei, some important issues", *SAA 1983*: 78.
[121] *State of Brunei Annual Report 1976* (BSB, 1977), p. 335.

When the upward tendency in oil prices was reversed at the start of the 1980s, gas took over. This manna resulted in the creation in July 1980 of a second Bruneian bank, the Island Development Bank,[122] and an investment fund in December 1982, QAF Holdings, which gathered various princely financial assets and was introduced into the Singapore stock market in 1984. It became necessary to diversify the sultanate's investments abroad, hitherto placed in pounds sterling: thus in July 1983 a sovereign fund was created, the Brunei Investment Agency (BIA),[123] whose assets were estimated at some B $10 billion[124] (US $4.7 billion), and which relied on the services of four securities firms, two American and two Japanese.[125]

After a nine-year hiatus due to political uncertainties, Brunei could go ahead with two more five-year plans (1975–84), which for the first time prioritised social issues (36.6% and 28.2% of the budget in the third and fourth plans respectively), followed closely by communications (33.6% and 23.3%) and other infrastructures (20.3% and 14.3%); the fourth plan added the construction of public buildings (16.4%) and security (15.5%).[126] Sewerage was installed in the main cities; the hospital system was modernised[127] and full coverage of health costs was extended to nationals;[128] and education was boosted by the opening of public secondary classes and the sending of a growing number of scholarship students abroad, plus the continuing education of local workers. Amenities increased alongside the inauguration of television (1975), such as the building of an international airport, a deepwater port at Muara and an oil terminal at Seria; the purchase of an airline company (March 1980); extension of the road and telephone networks; and acquisition of up-to-date military materiel. A programme to re-house the population (aimed

[122] On the basis of a partnership between the Philippine E. Zobel de Ayala, the royal family and the Japanese Dai Ichi Kangyo (Cleary and Wong, *Oil, Economic Development and Diversification of Brunei Darussalam*, p. 114).

[123] BIA opened offices in London and New York (Cleary and Wong, ibid., p. 115).

[124] Sharon Siddique, "Negara Brunei Darussalam: 'A New Nation but an Ancient Country'", *SAA 1985*: 103.

[125] Morgan Guarantee Trust, Citibank, Nomura and Daiwa Securities.

[126] Cleary and Wong, *Oil, Economic Development and Diversification of Brunei Darussalam*, p. 84.

[127] Construction of a big hospital at Kiulap in the suburbs of the capital in 1979; opening of dispensaries.

[128] Itinerant doctors regularly visit remote regions, while the medical fees applied to foreigners remain very moderate.

essentially at Kampung Ayer) in modern residences was launched in 1980. The development of public employment beyond the simple indigenisation of white-collar workers, through the gradual promotion of Malaysians to official posts and the opening of jobs to qualified Bruneians brought about social peace at last. The erection of the sumptuous and monumental Nurul Iman (Light of Faith) palace symbolised Brunei's renaissance: when independence was proclaimed on 1 January 1984,[129] the sultanate proudly assumed its traditional denomination of Brunei *Darussalam*. The presentation by the monarch of a new government with all the ministries necessary for the exercise of full sovereignty closed the book on 80 years of British monitoring.

[129] The official celebration of Independence (in the presence of foreigners) would take place on 23 February 1984, and this was the date retained for the national holiday.

III

INDEPENDENCE AND AFTER, 1984–2014

POLITICAL INDEPENDENCE

The independence of Brunei Darussalam took place under apparently favourable auspices: the political situation had been stable for two decades and the petroleum manna made it one of the richest nations in East Asia (after Japan and Singapore). There was only one shadow: 82% of the local workforce had no training.[1] Thus to the two policy priorities that emerged after the 1962 crisis—maintaining domestic stability and pursuing development compatible with local conditions—was added a third: establishing a foreign policy that could compensate for the sultanate's territorial and demographic exiguity, thus strengthening the security ensured by the military presence of the former colonial power. These major orientations would be combined in contrasting ways during the following three decades, in what can be described as three phases: the first (1984–89) maintained most of the previous orientations; the second (1990–99) multiplied socio-economic transformations; the third (2000–14), following the failure of an accelerated diversification of production, was inversely more prudent.

[1] Cleary and Wong, *Oil, Economic Development and Diversification of Brunei Darussalam*, p. 117.

Well-tempered Modernisation, 1984–89

Mastering Internal Tensions

The first six years of the postcolonial era were marked by increased political control by the reigning sultan.[2] The tone was set by the independence ceremony: the inaugural speech promoted the concept of *Melayu Islam Beraja* (MIB), formulated by the *Begawan* in 1950, to the rank of official ideology, echoing the instauration of the *Rukunegara* in neighbouring Malaysia in 1970.[3] A committee for the diffusion of MIB was set up a year later to create pedagogic materials for schools when teaching became officially bilingual[4] and the English and Malay curricula were merged.[5] The Legislative Council, whose members had been nominated since 1970, was suppressed in February 1984. Four months after the Brunei National Democratic Party (BNDP) was founded in May 1985, government officers—48% of the active population and the quasi-totality of nationals in the workforce—were forbidden from being members. Emptied of its substance, the party evolved at the end of 1985 into a

[2] This did not prevent the creation of a Ministry of Culture, Youth and Sports in January 1984, entrusted to Prince Jefri.

[3] After the 1969 ethnic troubles, Malaysia adopted on 31 August 1970 a national ideology, the *Rukunegara*, based on five principles: (1) Belief in God, (2) Loyalty to the King and country, (3) Respect for the Constitution, (4) Rule of law and (5) Good conduct and morality (Watson Andaya and Leonard Andaya, *A History of Malaysia*, p. 281). Unlike in Indonesia and Brunei, it was very partially implemented.

[4] Bilingualism (*dwibahasa*) was seen as a means to strengthen national unity based on MIB (Horton, *Turun-temurun: A Dissection of Brunei Darussalam*, p. 66).

[5] Science, economics and mathematics were taught in English.

new body, the Brunei National United Party (BNUP).[6] Nonetheless, its membership remained derisory: after two years of existence, it had only 60 dues-paying members. The arrest of the BNDP leaders put an end to its activity in January 1988;[7] the president of the BNUP resigned in May of the same year. To diversify information channels (which remained tightly controlled), the government created an additional journal: *Pusaka*.[8]

The pressure exerted on civil institutions was due essentially to growing tensions at the very heart of the monarchy, sparked by the *Begawan*'s attempt in May 1985 to use religion to regain partial control of the state apparatus: he ordered mosques to refer to him by the titles of Sultan and *Yang Di-Pertuan*, normally reserved for the reigning sovereign.[9] The sultan retaliated by banning the broadcast of religious services by Bruneian radio and television (RTB), and made the police pledge an oath of loyalty (15 May) to counter possible army support for the *Begawan*, at the time Minister of Defence. To remind everyone that he was still in command, the sultan freed several political prisoners who had been held since 1962 in August, despite his father's objections. Finally, he modified the composition of the Council of Succession to better protect the rights of his eldest son. The crisis within the royal family ended in late 1985: upon his return from London, the *Begawan* received from the sultan a helicopter furnished with all the medical equipment necessary for his health, and reminded everyone that there was a sole sovereign in Brunei. The *Begawan*'s death on 7 September 1986 further strengthened the sultan's powers. He now assumed direct charge of the Ministry of Defence, placed one of his liege-men, Pehin Haji Isa, at the head of the Ministry of the Interior[10] and entrusted finance to Prince Jefri, with Prince Mohamed keeping the foreign affairs

[6] Brunei People's Party, Partai Perpaduan Kebangsaan Brunei (PPKB).
[7] Latif Chuchu demanded the lifting of the state of emergency, the sultan's resignation as prime minister and the organisation of general elections; worse, he even threatened to raise the question of human rights before the United Nations' ad hoc commission. Thirty-four political detainees would be released two years later, on the occasion of the sovereign's birthday in July 1988.
[8] *Pusaka* was edited by one of the intellectuals closest to the Palace, Pehin Mohd. Jamil Al-Sufri, also director of the Pusat Sejarah (Historical Centre).
[9] Saunders, *A History of Brunei*, p. 184.
[10] Born c. 1936, jurist by training, he kept this post until 2005.

portfolio. On 20 October, a *titah* (rescript)[11] forbade any evolution of institutions.[12]

On the religious front, the situation seemed more delicate. To counter the rise in fundamentalism and the manipulation of religion, the sultan see-sawed between the "neo-traditionalists", who followed Malaysian Prime Minister Mahathir's model of promoting Middle Eastern religious codes previously largely unknown in the Malay world, and the "modernists", who supported more Westernised practices. Thus MIB courses were organised for teachers at the end of 1984,[13] and the press, videos, radio and television broadcasts were heavily censored. In January 1985, Brunei opened an Islamic Propagation Centre,[14] and four years later an Institute for Islamic Studies (IIS) designed to oversee the training of clerics. To signal the adhesion of elites to Islamic orthodoxy, the statutes of the Universiti Brunei Darussalam, inaugurated with great pomp in October 1985, required Malay students to respect a new dress code. The sultan responded a month later by refusing to participate in the procession of the Maulud,[15] after the Brunei clerics modified its traditional ordering by separating the sexes.[16] Along the same lines, he ordered female presenters on RTB to remove their veils (*tudung*). After the *Begawan*'s death, a Ministry of Religious Affairs was created during the government reshuffle at the end of 1986. And like his father 36 years earlier, the sultan (along with Prince Mohamed) performed the hajj in 1987.

Financial Uncertainty and the First Diversification

Economic management proved less sensitive than politics during the years 1984–89. On the eve of independence, hydrocarbons provided 70.6% of Brunei's GDP; commerce, 10%; administration, 7.4%; and

[11] *Titah*, literally "order", is translated here as *rescript*, which better corresponds to Bruneian usage (see Appendix II, "Lexicon").

[12] Abu Bakar Hamzah, "Brunei Darussalam, continuity and tradition", *SAA 1989*: 92.

[13] Sharon Siddique, "Negara Brunei Darussalam: 'A New Nation but an Ancient Country'", *SAA 1985*: 101.

[14] *Pusat Dakwah Islamiah* (PDI), inaugurated by the sovereign in December 1985.

[15] Commemorating the birth of the Prophet.

[16] Saunders, *A History of Brunei*, pp. 184–5. Since the mid-2000s, women are no longer authorised to parade in the streets during the Maulud procession but are instead invited by the Queen (Rozan Yunus, *The Golden Warisan Brunei Darussalam* [BSB, 2009], p. 94).

construction (the main private sector industry outside hydrocarbons), 3.2%, with the remainder divided among five sectors (real estate, finance, transport, agriculture and tourism), ranging between 0.5% and 2%. This meant that apart from petroleum and indispensable services (the Raja Isteri Pengiran Anak Saleha Hospital, or RIPAS,[17] was inaugurated in August 1984), Bruneian production remained ridiculously low. On top of the lacunae of production capacity, transport infrastructure, especially roads, was inadequate. The declining oil prices since the start of the 1980s encouraged the sultanate to undertake a diversification of its productive capacity during the Fifth Plan (1986–90): to the priorities of the preceding plan (social development, 29% of the budget; communications, 20%; other infrastructure, 20%; construction of public or royal buildings, 10%) was now added the manufacturing industry, which received 10% of the budget. For the first time in the history of the sultanate, a new land law (1984) gave the "indigenous", that is, non-Malay, population access to property—under certain conditions.[18]

Monetary independence was achieved by abrogating preliminary authorisation from the currency board for exchange operations,[19] the first opportunity arising after the joint Sino-British declaration of December 1984 that set the agenda for the handover of Hong Kong to China. Uncertainties about the takeover of a bastion of regional capitalism by a power that was still largely communist upset Hong Kong finance (14% of its GDP in 1985),[20] while opening up new prospects for its Southeast Asian competitors. The bankruptcy of Hong Kong's Overseas Trust Bank had a ricochet effect on the foremost Bruneian bank, United National Finance:[21] the government, which dreamed of developing the financial sector, consolidated one of its prides, the Island Development Bank (IDB),[22] in August 1985, by increasing the royal family stake up to

[17] In 1986, a nursing college Pengiran Anak Puteri Rashidah Sa'adatul Bolkiah College of Nursing was also created.
[18] Ismail Duraman and Abdul Amin Hj Hashim, "Brunei Darussalam, developing within its own paradigm", *SAA 1998*: 57.
[19] Cleary and Wong, *Oil, Economic Development and Diversification of Brunei Darussalam*, p. 70.
[20] *Hong Kong Statistics*, Table 035, "Gross Domestic Product (GDP) by Economic Activity at Current Prices".
[21] Founded in 1975, the Island Development Bank was then led by Patrick Chiang Chen Tsong (*New Sunday Times*, 21 June 1985).
[22] Renamed the International Bank of Brunei in 1988.

51%.[23] In 1986, management of funds invested abroad by the state and royal family was entirely reconfigured: the agents of the British Crown lost their monopoly in favour of the BIA (the sovereign fund of Brunei created three years earlier). Moreover, the income drawn from overseas investments was no longer incorporated into the Bruneian budgetary receipts.[24]

Diversification was entrusted to Prince Jefri, the sovereign's younger brother, named in October 1986 as Minister of Finances and head of the BIA. But after the scandal caused by the bankruptcy in November 1986 of the National Bank of Brunei[25] due to unsecured loans made to its minority Sino-Malaysian shareholders, priority was given to tightening financial regulation, especially since QAF Holdings,[26] the nation's premier company, found itself in the red. The creation of the Brunei

[23] E. Zobel, who abandoned the presidency, kept 29% of shares, and Dai Ichi Kangyo, 20%.

[24] Cleary and Wong, *Oil, Economic Development and Diversification of Brunei Darussalam*, p. 73.

[25] The National Bank of Brunei (NBB) was founded in 1965 by Khoo Teck Puat (邱德拔), with 25% ownership by the royal family; at the end of 1985, the assets of the NBB was estimated at B $2.06 billion, generating after-tax profits of B $30 million. But at the end of 1986, Khoo Ban Hock (son of Khoo Teck Puat), now president, was accused of siphoning B $1.3 billion through undocumented, unsecured loans to companies controlled by the family group. As a result, the bank was closed and he was convicted to three years of prison, serving two-thirds of his term (see K.U. Menon, "Brunei Darussalam in 1986, in search of the Political Kingdom", *SAA 1987*: 60). At Brunei's request, the Australian assets of Khoo Teck Puat (Southern Pacific Corporation) were frozen. It seems that the deterioration of ties between the sultan and Khoo Teck Puat was also due to the sale of the Holiday Inn (in Singapore, Scotts Road) at a top price by Khoo to the sultan in 1983, just before the 1985 crisis (D.S. Ranjit Singh, "Brunei Darussalam in 1987, Coming to Grips with Economic and Political Realities", *SAA 1988*: 65). Khoo Teck Puat could nevertheless call himself a "good risk", since at his death in 2004, he held 13.51% of the Standard Chartered Bank that he had helped to keep afloat after the 1986 crisis in Hong Kong (his father, Khoo Yang Thin, was an associate of one of the most powerful Singapore banks, the Overseas Chinese Banking Corporation). See "Brunei National Bank fiasco recalled with the death of Mr Khoo", *BruneiDirect.com*, 25 February 2004, http://old.brudirect.com/public_html/DailyInfo/News/Archive/Feb04/250204/nite02.htm; and Michael Backman, "Tycoon's death signals end of an empire", *Asia on line*, 12 March 2004.

[26] Half-controlled by Prince Mohamed, it had acquired the Keppel Group in Singapore as well as several other firms. QAF also owned the *Borneo Bulletin* and the *New Straits Times*. But the loss remained modest: B $4.3 million (Ranjit Singh, ibid.: 65).

Institute of Technology in 1986, then of the Ministry of Industry and Primary Resources in December 1988, seemed to lead the way for the development of a manufacturing industry.

Skilful Diplomacy

It was its cautious diplomacy in particular that gave credit to the new state. Membership in ASEAN on 7 January 1984 was followed by the establishment of diplomatic relations with the Western block (the United States, Canada, Japan, South Korea and the EEC), combined with a first series of state visits throughout 1984 (in chronological order: Malaysia, Japan, Korea, Indonesia, Oman, Jordan and Egypt), as well as greater military cooperation with Singapore.[27] The sultan also affirmed his solidarity with Muslim countries: he personally attended the Rabat summit for Brunei's admission into the Organisation of the Islamic Conference (OIC) on 15 January 1984, and Yasser Arafat was invited to Bandar Seri Begawan in July of the same year. In his October 1984 speech in New York, when the sultanate joined the United Nations, the sultan condemned Israel and supported the right of Palestinians to a homeland. At the same time, Brunei manifested its commitment alongside the West to increase defence partnerships. An agreement was signed with Australia in November 1985.[28] After a visit by the U.S. Secretary of State George Shultz in June 1986, the American Special Forces obtained US $10 million in assistance for a particularly sensitive zone of overseas interventions in Nicaragua;[29] joint exercises (army and navy)[30] with the United States were now held each year. Once the command of the Royal Armed Forces—long held by a Briton—was transferred to a Bruneian[31] on 1 January 1986, similar exercises took place with the British navy starting in 1988.

---

[27] Military cooperation with Singapore started in 1979; the first joint exercises took place in 1983.

[28] Horton, *Turun-temurun: A Dissection of Brunei Darussalam*, p. 145.

[29] The affair was negotiated with the deputy minister of defence, YAM Pg. Hj. General Ibnu Ba'asith (Lawrence E. Walsh, *Final Report of the Independent Counsel for Iran/Contra Matters,* ch. 25, "United States v. Elliott Abrams", 1993, http://www.cfr.org/publication/11974/final_report_of_the_independent_counsel_for_irancontra_matters.html); due to a presumed American typographic error, the funds were sent to another Swiss account. They were restored to the sultan after a lawsuit in 1987.

[30] Named "Kingfisher" until 2000.

[31] General Pehin Dato Hj Mohammad bin Hj Daud.

Anticipating its independence and in conformity with the Geneva Convention of 29 April 1958[32] and the 1982 United Nations Convention on the Law of the Sea,[33] the sultanate enlarged its fishing zone on 1 January 1983 to 200 nautical miles as measured on the basis of the coastline,[34] thus claiming an area enlarged to some 34,500 km^2. This claim overlapped those of Vietnam, Malaysia, China and the Philippines south of the Spratly Islands (see map 5[35]), and relations with these three Southeast Asian countries quickly became complicated.

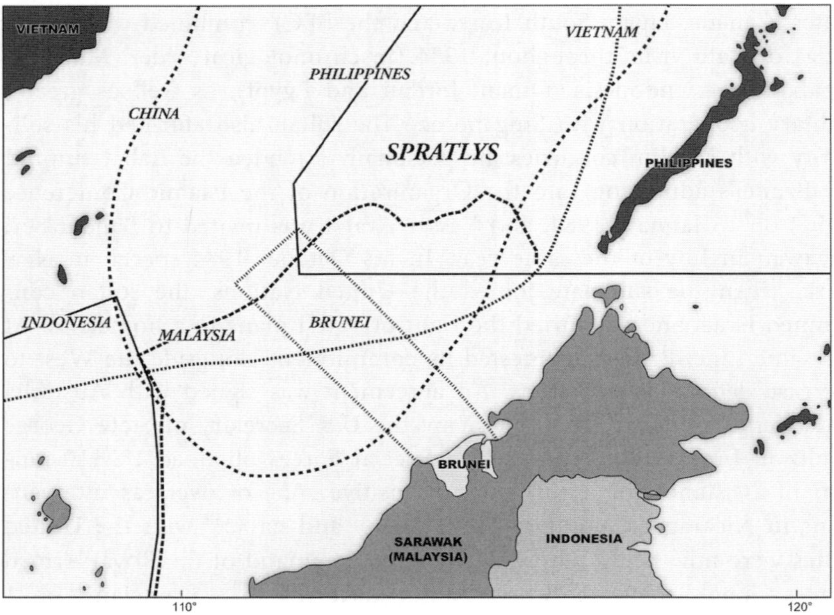

Map 5. Overlapping Claims South of the Spratly Islands

[32] U.N.T.S. No. 7302, vol. 499, pp. 312–21.

[33] UNCLOS.

[34] 18,500 square nautical miles; *Brunei Fishery Limits Act* (BLRO 1/1984, Cap. 130), cited by Renate Haller-Trost, *The Brunei-Malaysia Dispute over Territorial and Maritime Claims in International Law* (Durham: International Boundaries Research Unit, Maritime Briefing, Department of Geography, University of Durham, vol. 1, no. 3, 1994), p. 43. The exact area fluctuates depending on how it is calculated (low or high tide, etc.), see Haller-Trost, note 215.

[35] Map drawn from Leszek Buszynski and Iskandar Sazlan, "Maritime Claims and Energy Cooperation in the South China Sea", *Contemporary Southeast Asia* 29 [2007 (1)]: 162.

However, the appointment of the Bruneian Roderick Yong to the secretariat-general of ASEAN from 1986 to 1989 allowed the sultanate, whose claims had few concrete consequences, to play at appeasing its Southeast Asian neighbours without losing face. Tensions with Malaysia diminished somewhat during Prime Minister Mahathir's visit in May 1987,[36] with Brunei raising its stake in Malaysian Airlines to 10%. This, along with the granting of US $100 million credit aid to Indonesia during the sultan's official trip in September 1987, reinforced "Malay" solidarities.[37] And if the accession to power of Cory Aquino in February 1986 threw cold water on relations with Manila (due to the presumed links of the sultanate with one of Marcos' cronies, General Fabian Ver, implicated in the assassination of Benigno Aquino in 1983),[38] tensions were rapidly dissipated by Cory Aquino's state visit in August 1987.[39]

---

[36] Mahathir more or less voluntarily reopened the Limbang file. According to an article in the *Far Eastern Economic Review* (hereafter cited as *FEER)*, an (unfounded) rumour purported that Brunei had proposed buying back Limbang, which caused a nationalist outcry on the Malaysian side (K.U. Menon, "Brunei Darussalam in 1987, modernizing autocracy", *Asian Survey* 28, 2; *A Survey of Asia in 1987*, part II [Feb. 1988]: 252–8).

[37] Credit repayable over 25 years, plus a grace period of 7 years!

[38] Benigno Aquino was shot in the back while disembarking near an airplane of the Royal Brunei Airlines. Personnel of the airlines were later called to the bar. Fabian Ver (deceased in 1998), a second cousin of President F. Marcos and his chief of staff at the time, was also suspected of having transferred funds via Brunei (Saunders, *A History of Brunei*, p. 178). On the implication of F. Ver in the assassination, see Earl G. Parreño, *Boss Danding* (Quezon City, 2003), p. 176; and Republic of the Philippines, "Crim. Case 10010 & 10011", http://www.pcij.org/blog/wp-docs/Sandiganbayan_ruling_on_Ninoy_assassination.pdf.

[39] Cory Aquino participated in the ceremonies of August 1989 marking the majority (*berkhatan*) of the crown prince.

Full Steam Ahead! (1989–99)

At the start of the 1990s, the middle road taken by Brunei since independence was challenged by a dual modification to its geostrategic context. First, the implosion of the Soviet bloc and the ensuing end of the war in Afghanistan pushed hardened Islamist extremists, potential instruments of destabilisation, towards Southeast Asia (and more precisely, to the Malay world defined at its broadest, from south Thailand to Southern Philippines and the Moluccas). Second, the bursting of the speculative bubble in developed countries raised questions on the viability of constituting an income based solely on financial markets that would replace the hydrocarbons rent after a few decades. The 1990s therefore saw Brunei paradoxically both strengthening the nation's Islamic dimension and accelerating its economic development under the leadership of Prince Jefri.

Implementation of MIB

The domestic situation seemed to relax somewhat at the start of 1989 with the liberation of 34 political detainees, followed in January 1990 by the release of 6 PRB members and 2 BNDP activists. PRB's former vice-president, Zaini Ahmad,[40] who wished to return to Brunei, apologised for the 1962 uprising (while requesting for a session of the Legislative Council).

This indulgence did not, however, imply any liberalisation of the regime; it was merely a modulation of its *modus operandi* from (usually

[40] Following the request of several PRB members imprisoned since 1962.

moderate) coercion to ideology. On 15 July 1990, the rescript issued on the sultan's birthday focused on MIB, the sovereign adding in one of his October *titah* that MIB was the will of God. The MIB was now obligatory in the curriculum of all Brunei schools and the university, with its propagation delegated to the Academy of Brunei Studies. All legislation had to conform to Islam,[41] with the corollary that safeguarding the Jawi language became a cultural imperative.[42]

What followed was a strengthening of the society's Islamic dimension, the first manifestation of which was a ban in January 1991 on alcohol, which had been gradually proliferating along with drugs. In February, the sultan stated that Brunei was not a secular state and demanded a modification of the school curriculum, which was judged much too Western-oriented. In a subtle balancing game, he also banned the Malaysian fundamentalist movement Darul al-Arqam.[43] In June the sultan went again on pilgrimage to Mecca. Foreign priests, nuns and missionaries were expelled from the sultanate;[44] the celebration of Christmas was forbidden in public places; and Buddhist temples were closed or ransacked.[45] The MIB was finalised in April 1992 and was preached by the sultan in person during the solemn prayer of Hari Raya—a first in the history of Brunei. The launching of a holiday to celebrate teachers (*Hari Guru*, in September) reinforced the emphasis on education, which became the favourite instrument for (gently) conditioning the population. Chinese lost its status as a teaching language, to the benefit of Malay and English in Chinese schools, and courses in Chinese, whose content

---

[41] Horton, *Turun-temurun: A Dissection of Brunei Darussalam*, p. 150.

[42] Later all religious subjects had to be taught in Jawi (A. Mani, "Negara Brunei Darussalam in 1992: Celebrating the Silver Jubilee", *SAA 1993*: 108).

[43] Darul al-Arqam is a movement founded in 1968 in Kuala Lumpur by Ashaari bin Mohamad, originally from Rembau (Negeri Sembilan). It is tinged with Mahdism, which revolves around the figure of Syeikh Muhammad as-Suhaimi. The movement developed a large network of economic interests before being banned by the Malaysian government for heterodoxy in 1994; its founder took refuge in South Thailand. See Farahwahida Mohd. Yusof, *Al-Arqam & ajaran aurad Muhammadiah: satu penilaian* [*Al-Arqam and the teachings of the Way of Muhammadiah: An evaluation*] (Sintok: Universiti Malaysia Utara Press [UTM], 2007), 258 p.

[44] Four Western priests and nuns in 1992; 12 Protestant missionaries from South Korea in December 1992.

[45] Horton, *Turun-temurun: A Dissection of Brunei Darussalam*, p. 61.

was now set by the Ministry of Education, were added to the national programmes.[46]

Symbolically, Brunei Shell was obliged to reserve three-quarters of its internal promotions for Bruneians.[47] The sovereign made a speech before the army deploring the lingering influence of aged leaders whose behaviour did not conform to Islam.[48] The new orientation was celebrated with ostentation during the Silver Jubilee ceremonies in October 1992, culminating in the inauguration of the sumptuous state mosque Hassanal Bolkiah.[49] The department of Islamic Studies at the university was promoted to the rank of faculty, and a new religious training facility (at high-school level), the Sultan Haji Hassanal Bolkiah Quranic Studies Institute, was inaugurated in January 1993. When judicial assistance from Hong Kong magistrates came to an end on 1 January 1993, the arrangement was not renewed; instead an agreement was signed with the Sultanate of Oman to train judges for the Islamic courts,[50] which laid the bases for an Islamisation of the legislation. This was reinforced by a speech delivered by the sultan at the opening session of the Islamic Law Council (*Fiqh*) in June 1993, noting the growing importance of the shariah.[51] In 1996, prayers before take-off on Royal Brunei flights became the norm and an Islamic dress code for government employees was enforced.[52] This increased the ostentation of Muslim values, as did the launching in May 1997 of a Malay religious radio channel. On the other hand, to prevent any risk of extremism, the mufti came under the direct control of the sovereign in November 1994. In April 1999, the Institute for Islamic Education of the Ministry of Religious Affairs merged with the Faculty of Islamic Studies at UBD[53] to form—within a university

[46] Geoffrey Gunn, *Language, power and ideology in Brunei Darussalam* (Athens: Ohio University Center for International Studies, Southeast Asia series no. 99, 1997), pp. 158ff.

[47] G. Braighlinn, *Ideological Innovation under Monarchy: Aspects of Legitimation Activity in Contemporary Brunei* (Amsterdam: VU University Press, 1992), p. 48.

[48] FEER, *Asia Yearbook 1992*: 86.

[49] Constructed by the Korean Daewoo. In May of the same year, the sultan performed the hajj for the third time.

[50] Horton, *Turun-temurun: A Dissection of Brunei Darussalam*, p. 150.

[51] One of the committees of the OIC.

[52] Although the skirts worn by policewomen were not replaced by trousers until 1998.

[53] A new vice-chancellor was named to head the UBD: the jurist Dato Mahmud Saedon bin Awang Othman, a Bruneian trained in al-Ahzar, former director of the shariah department at the Ministry of Religious Affairs.

whose chancellor was (and remains) the sovereign—the Sultan Haji Omar Ali Saifuddin Institute of Islamic Studies (SHOAS IIS). The creation of a Council of National Education, led jointly by the ministries of education and religious affairs, in September 1999 sealed government control over religious education. This restructuring of education and propaganda[54] was accompanied by stricter regulation and control of halal products in April 1998.[55]

On the institutional level, rather than cede to demands from the rare activists who remained in the sultanate to reopen the Legislative Council, the government established in March 1992 two local representative bodies that were partially elected: Consultative Councils at village (*kampung*) and district (*mukim*) level,[56] supervised by the General Assembly of Districts and Villages (*Majlis Perunding Mukim dan Kampong*, MPMK), itself chaired by the minister of home affairs.[57] According to the new Islamic orientation, imams and school principals were members by right of the district councils. To forestall any social demands, an Employee Trust Fund was created in 1993 to finance the pensions of both private and public workers.[58] On April 1993, Zaini Ahmad returned to Brunei at his own risk: he was soon placed again in detention and released two years later, on 19 July 1995.[59] The MPMK's first general assembly in January 1995 was a setback for the Brunei National Solidarity Party (BNSP),[60] which was quickly stifled by a ban from any political activity slapped on its president Haji Abdul Latif Chuchu, who was thus

[54] The publication of two books by the mufti Abdul Aziz Juned within six years—*Islam di Brunei* [*Islam in Brunei*] (1992) and *Lawatan Negara: satu wadah kerama Allah* [*Visit of State: A Channel for Allah*] (July 1998), the latter financed by the Islamic Bank of Brunei—attests to the emphasis placed on religion.

[55] The "Emergency Order on Halal Meat 1998" went into force on 1 January 1999. Pork was eradicated from the sultanate in 1993.

[56] Leaders of villages and *mukim* (districts) were appointed by provincial "prefects" from four candidates elected by secret ballot by citizens and permanent residents. District leaders had to be between 30 and 65 years old and possess the equivalent of a high school degree (A. Mani, "Negara Brunei Darussalam in 1992: Celebrating the Silver Jubilee", *SAA 1993*: 98).

[57] *Brunei Times*, 8 August 2007.

[58] The employer and salaried worker each contributed up to 5% of the gross salary (Mark Cleary and Simon Francis, "Brunei, the search for a sustainable economy", *SAA 1994*: 65).

[59] Anonymous, "An Interview with Dr. Hj. Zaini Ahmad, Kuala Lumpur, 1985 (Research Notes) (Interview)", *Borneo Research Bulletin*, 1 January 2008, Borneo Research Council, 35 p.

[60] Alternatively called *Parti Perpaduan Kebangsaan Brunei* (PPKB).

forced to resign. Once opposition demands had been contained, three political detainees (including the PKB's second in command) were freed in July 1996. Pop singer Michael Jackson was even invited to give a concert in Brunei in honour of the sovereign's 50th birthday.[61] Nonetheless, although the working group on a new constitution (chaired by Prince Mohamed) handed over favourable conclusions to the sovereign,[62] no institutional reform seemed to have been taken under consideration. Nothing, however, prevented the liberation of the PKB's secretary-general.

Failures of Economic Modernisation

In fact it was the economy and not politics that changed the most at the start of the 1990s. The Sixth Plan (1991–96), whose delay might have been symptomatic of a debate within the royal family,[63] set out more ambitious goals than the preceding one: to attract US $2 billion in foreign direct investments in sectors outside hydrocarbons that would create 2,000 industrial projects[64] and 40,000 jobs by the year 2000. This did not preclude tightening control of the fuel sector, as seen by the creation in 1993 of the Brunei Oil and Gas Authority (BOGA), chaired by Prince Jefri, who also possessed his own company, Jasra International Petroleum.[65] Foreign investments were exempted from almost all taxes except for a corporate tax (30%, one of the lowest in ASEAN), from which they could be exonerated for up to eight years. The creation in 1994 of a one-stop investment centre also facilitated potential investment. For purposes of external growth, an investment fund specialising in hydrocarbons, the Primal Corporation, with Prince Sufri as majority shareholder, was launched at the start of the 1990s.[66] Meanwhile Prince

[61] The concert was attended by the sultan's two wives and many members of the royal family, but the sultan himself did not participate, as he was giving at the same moment a dinner at the Palace in honour of the Prince of Wales. On 23 February 1997, the sultan invited Céline Dion for a fee of £1.3 million.

[62] FEER, *Asia Yearbook 1997*: 92

[63] FEER, *Asia Yearbook 1992*: 87.

[64] The Trade and Industry Development Council was created in January 1992.

[65] Horton, *Turun-temurun: A Dissection of Brunei Darussalam*, p. 81. The prince lost control of Jasra, which acquired a stake in the American firm Jackson, at the end of the 1990s. The future of the company is still pending.

[66] Cleary and Wong, *Oil, Economic Development and Diversification of Brunei Darussalam*, p. 121. In August 1993, Primal invested some B $9 billion in Vietnam, spread over 19 projects lasting 21 years each (Horton, *Turun-temurun: A Dissection of Brunei* Darussalam, p. 81). There does not seem to be any traces of these projects after 1994, which could suggest that their shares were taken over by Amedeo.

Mohamed acquired a majority share (65%) in QAF Holdings in 1990,[67] which had become the third largest employer in the sultanate after the government and Brunei Shell.

The non-fuel sector that took off the fastest was construction (a new university campus, an international conference centre and a luxury hotel at Jerudong, an airport hangar); firms linked to BIA were favoured in bids.[68] Other sectors languished. The principal manufacturing sector, textiles, saw only five Malaysian and Hong Kong businesses trying to bypass Western quotas. As growth stagnated at a few percentage points a year, the government resorted to a double financial gambit:

- Launching an Islamic financial sector with the creation of the Tabung Amanah Islam Brunei (TAIB) savings bank in September 1991, followed by the reorientation in January 1993 of one of the major banks, the International Bank of Brunei,[69] which became the Islamic Bank of Brunei (IBB).[70] The latter soon created an insurance company (Takaful IBB) and an investment fund,[71] both Islamic.
- Promoting at the same time a Western-style financial sector with the creation of the Baiduri Bank (August 1994)[72] and the Development Bank of Brunei (January 1995) by Prince Jefri.

To stimulate the emergence of a modern private sector, Prince Jefri created a holding company, Amedeo, in 1994. Within a few months, it became the largest private conglomerate in Brunei, grouping 27 firms engaged in all-out development in sectors other than hydrocarbons: infrastructure (port management, electrification, telecommunications), tourism (the hotel complex in Jerudong, golf, an amusement park), real

[67] Amedeo controlled then 20 companies whose capital was entirely held by the royal family, plus shares in several other firms (Tilak Doshi, "Brunei, the Steady State", *SAA 1991*: 74); Amedeo's share was reduced to 10% in January 1993.

[68] FEER, *Asia Yearbook 1994*: 95.

[69] In 1991, the bank's capital was divided as follows: the sultan (51%); E. Zobel (29%) and Dai Ichi Kangyo (20%); see Sharon Siddique, "Brunei Darussalam 1991. The Non-Secular Nation", *SAA 1992*: 96.

[70] In August 1993, IBB offered 14 million shares destined for Muslims only (Mark Cleary and Simon Francis, "Brunei, the search for a sustainable economy", *SAA 1994*: 65); a consultancy partnership with the Bank of Singapore Securities Pte Ltd followed at the end of 1994.

[71] November 1993, in partnership with the Singaporean Nikko Capital Management (Naimah Talib, "Brunei in 1995: A New Assertiveness?", *SAA 1996*: 102).

[72] In partnership with Paribas.

estate and finance.[73] The launching of the export zone in Muara (May 1994) was followed by the start of the privatisation of the port administration, reduction of import taxes on 650 products and equipment (April 1995), and the inauguration of a container terminal[74] (also at Muara) at the start of 1996. Notwithstanding the stagnation of both national and foreign investment (aside from petroleum) due to its obsolescent tax laws,[75] Brunei—where a vast gas deposit was discovered six months earlier[76]—seemed particularly well-placed economically. In 1996, the sultanate was classified by the World Bank (which it joined in 1995) among the developed countries, a rise in ranking that was rather exceptional for a country whose wealth was based solely on hydrocarbons. The World Bank acknowledged the social progress achieved and the commitment of its government, as demonstrated by the doubling of the health budget in the Seventh Plan (1997–2001).

But the management of the Amedeo Group, where a portion of the BIA fund had been invested (c. US $4.4 billion), raised concerns in early 1997. To this were added various allegations in the Western press about the escapades of Prince Jefri, which triggered his resignation from the Ministry of Finance in February 1997. The sultan then took over the ministry. After complaints by two of the Prince's suppliers in early 1998,[77] followed by rumours about the bankruptcy of Amedeo in the British press, an audit of the management of BIA funds[78] was launched in September 1998. It revealed that up to mid-1998, some US $40 billion[79] had been transferred out of the BIA accounts.[80] The minister of justice (and Attorney General) Pg. Haji Bahrin Abas[81] and the permanent

[73] Amedeo thus controlled the Baiduri Bank.

[74] Managed by the Singapore Port Authority Corporation (PAS) and the Bruneian Archipelago Development Corporation; the contract was cancelled after six years and management taken over by the port department of Brunei. In October 1999, the port activities of Bandar Seri Begawan were moved to the new port of Muara.

[75] Naimah Talib, "Brunei in 1995: A New Assertiveness?", *SAA 1996*: 107.

[76] Selangkir 1, discovered by Brunei Shell Petroleum.

[77] The brothers Bob and Rafi Manoukian.

[78] Entrusted to KPMG.

[79] US $1 = B $1.5 at this time.

[80] US $14.8 billion was transferred to the accounts of Prince Jefri, US $8 billion to those of the sovereign, and US $3.5 billion to the government. The recipients of the remaining US $13.5 billion were not identified (Privy Council Appeal No. 69 of 2006, from the Court of Appeal of Brunei Darussalam, "Judgment of the Lords of the Judicial Committee of the Privy Council, delivered the 8th November 2007").

[81] Member of several governing boards, including that of BIA and of Brunei Shell.

secretary of the Ministry of Justice[82] were dismissed in June; the ministry itself was abolished six months later. Between July and October 1998, Prince Jefri lost control of Amedeo and its subsidiaries,[83] then BIA, which was passed to the minister of education, Pehin Abdul Aziz. Against the backdrop of the fall of Suharto in neighbouring Indonesia, the shock was all the greater when the Palace received anonymous letters demanding the resignation of several members of the royal family.[84] To sway public opinion, pensions and salaries in the public sector were increased sharply in July 1998,[85] and a body in charge of long-term planning, the Brunei Darussalam Economic Council (BDEC),[86] was established in September to steer the new development strategy. The reigning mood was grim. Prince Jefri tried without success to obtain a friendly settlement in October. Amedeo went bankrupt a year later, leaving in its wake some US $3.7 billion in debts,[87] which the BIA (it managed some 40% of the sultanate's exchange reserves)[88] had to cover to preserve the trust of international operators, although a portion of its own capital had sunk in the wreck.

Not only did the combined setbacks of Amedeo/BIA amount to a gap equivalent to almost quadruple the Bruneian GDP in 1998, the international conjuncture was also disastrous. The Asian financial crisis entailed the fall of the Singapore dollar to which the Brunei dollar had been pegged since 1967 (on 1:1 parity),[89] and so the latter lost a fifth of its exchange rate with the United States dollar from 1997–99, when the upward trend of oil and gas prices reversed until 1998 (prices fell by

---

[82] Abas Serudin, also solicitor general.

[83] Which were then given to two consultants from Andersen (FEER, *Asia Yearbook 1999*: 82).

[84] *Surat layang*, FEER, *Asia Yearbook 1999*: 83.

[85] Costing an additional B $5 million per month (Mark Cleary and Simon Francis, "Brunei Darussalam, the Outside World intrudes", *SAA 1999*: 72).

[86] The secretariat of the Brunei Darussalam Economic Council merged in March 2001 with the Economic Planning and Development Department of the Ministry of Finance to form the Department of Planning and Economic Development (DPED, in Malay JPKE), now attached to the Prime Minister's Office, that is, the sultan.

[87] Geoffrey Gunn, "Brunei Darussalam: Dynastic Fallout, Economic Crisis and Recovery?", 東南アジア研究年報 *Tonan Ajia kenkyu nenpo* [*Annual Review of Southeast Asian Studies*], 49 (2008): 1–24, http://hdl.handle.net/10069/20942.

[88] The remaining 50%–60% would be divided among foreign banking and financial institutions (Gunn, ibid.: 9).

[89] After these agreements with Singapore (1967) and the creation of a currency board, Brunei currency had no autonomy whatsoever.

37% and 25% respectively), although the two phenomena were unrelated. Meanwhile the bulk of hydrocarbons exported to East Asia dropped due to the crisis. Ultimately the Bruneian GDP fell by 4% in 1998. The disaster brought on a cure of budgetary austerity, until then unknown in the country, which triggered the bankruptcy of several major firms operating in construction.[90] To keep the state afloat, there was no choice but to draw on both the Consolidated Fund and Development Fund[91] in 1999 and 2000 to cover current expenditure and investment.

The crisis had three consequences:

1. It destroyed the sultanate's aspirations for accelerated development. According to a report from the BDEC, the government had been drawing on its reserves since 1994 to cover a huge deficit of some 15% of GDP, yet since 1985, the economic growth rate was only half that of demographic growth. The failure of diversification translated into the departure from the sultanate of some 10,000 immigrant workers. There was now no question of becoming the logistic and tourist hub of the BIMP-EAGA growth triangle that comprised Brunei, Indonesia (Sulawesi, Kalimantan and Moluccas), insular Malaysia and South Philippines, a project that had been at the heart of the Seventh Plan (1996–2000).
2. The affair increased the polarisation of the decision-making circles around the sultan, who officially made his eldest son, Prince Al-Muhtadee Billah, the Crown prince in August 1998.[92]
3. Finally, the scandal as well as the chaotic waste seriously harmed the decision-making capacity of the top level of government.

Enlargement of Partnerships

While diversification proved disappointing, foreign policy remained a success on four fronts:

1. Brunei consolidated its ties with the West by voting in favour of U.N. intervention in Kuwait (1990–91). In so doing, the sultanate managed to preserve the pivot of its security policy: its defence agreement with

[90] Mohammad Yusop Haji Damit (Haj.), "Brunei Darussalam, Weathering the Storm", *SAA 2000*: 90.
[91] The Consolidated Fund was for current expenditure, while the Development Fund was for financing the Plan.
[92] On the eve of the ceremony, Prince Jefri made public his conflict with the sultan, complaining of being under attack from both his foreign advisors and religious conservatives (FEER, *Asia Yearbook 1999*: 83).

the British (renegotiated every five years since 1983) that maintained the presence of a regiment of 1,000 Gurkhas[93] near the Seria oil fields. This support was strengthened by a state visit to London in 1992, reciprocated by Queen Elizabeth II's visit to Bandar Seri Begawan in September 1998. The army was reorganised in 1991 for various purposes (especially domestic security) to comprise five components (the three forces, logistics and training); the assistance of foreign officers also enabled the acquisition of the most recent equipment.[94] So as to diversify its military partnerships, Brunei started to conduct joint exercises with New Zealand and Australia in addition to the United Kingdom and the United States (with which cooperation was increased in November 1994).

2. The diplomatic horizon was expanded. The sultan received the Kenyan president Daniel Arap Moi in February 1989 and welcomed the minister of foreign affairs of the interim Afghan government, Gulbudin Hekmatyar, in April of the same year. Brunei Darussalam then established relations with Iran in March 1990, which was reinforced by the Iranian prime minister's visit in May and an exchange of state visits in 1994, while skilfully strengthening relations with Iran's potential targets, the Gulf States, by establishing diplomatic relations with Qatar (1991) and by visiting Kuwait (1994). An agreement was signed with Palestine in May 1994 in Kuala Lumpur. In addition, Brunei reached out to countries that were not within its geostrategic horizon: Russia, Mexico (1991) and Kyrgyzstan (1996). It also normalised relations with the most powerful nation in the region, China, in September 1991, followed by the opening of an embassy in Beijing in October 1992. A first official visit in 1993 was the occasion to recall—on the very site of the tomb of the king of Boni in Nanking—the antiquity of the two countries' relations; the visit was repeated in August 1999.
3. Faced with an increasingly assertive and domineering Chinese diplomacy,[95] the sultanate consolidated its ties with its Southeast Asian partners: in July 1992 it supported the joint declaration by the ASEAN ministers of foreign affairs[96] on the South China Sea, to

[93] The last renewal was in 2008.
[94] FEER, *Asia Yearbook 1992*: 87.
[95] See François Joyaux, *La tentation impériale, politique extérieure de la Chine depuis 1949* (Paris: Imprimerie Nationale, 1994), 426 p.
[96] The Philippines's proposal aimed to resolve the conflict over the Spratly and Paracel islands and reefs by diplomatic means.

which China also laid claim. Brunei launched into the fight over sea boundaries by transforming the 1983 fishing zone into an Exclusive Economic Zone (EEZ) in July 1993—to the dismay of Malaysia, which fiercely contested the point of extension.[97] Although the sultanate by all accounts did not have the material and human means to occupy the zones it was claiming "continuously and effectively"—according to the jurisprudence of the International Court[98]—Prime Minister Mahathir went to Brunei in August to propose the creation of a joint committee on maritime and land border issues, starting with the litigious question of Limbang. Some months later, the Malaysian proposal was accepted during Deputy Prime Minister Anwar Ibrahim's passage. The first meeting of the joint committee in 1995[99] noted the absence of major differences over the land border but difficulties in defining the water boundary, particularly in the marshy zone of Limbang. Nonetheless, the joint committee meetings enabled the opening of a regular ferry service to Labuan and Kota Kinabalu. Other talks were carried out with Singapore (Lee Kuan Yew visited in April and October 1993):[100] (1) to strengthen ties between the BIA, the Singapore Government Investment Corporation and Singapore's monetary autority, and (2) to renew the lease on the training base of the Singaporean army at Temburong, which was expiring in 1994. In August 1994, President Fidel Ramos of the Philippines made a state visit to Brunei Darussalam. Discussions within ASEAN authorised the formal constitution of the BIMP-EAGA "growth triangle" in March 1994. In August 1995, Brunei hosted the second annual meeting of the ASEAN Forum on security (ARF); the Philippines proposed the adoption of a binding code of conduct on the South China Sea, designed to reduce tensions. At the 27th ASEAN Economic Ministers Meeting on 7–8 December 1995, the sultanate suggested advancing

[97] Gerald H. Krausse, "Brunei and the Sea: Transformation of a Maritime State", in *From Buckfast to Borneo: Essays Presented to Father Robert Nicholl on the 85th Anniversary of His Birth, 27 March 1995*, ed. Victor King and A.V.M. Horton (Hull: University of Hull, 1995), pp. 363–86.

[98] Leszek Buszynski and Iskandar Sazlan, "Maritime Claims and Energy Cooperation in the South China Sea", *Contemporary Southeast Asia* 29 [2007 (1)]: 143–71.

[99] Mahathir returned to Brunei in April 1995 and the new king of Malaysia made a visit in September.

[100] Singapore also trained staff from the Bruneian port department and civil aviation, especially controllers, in 1991.

implementation of the ASEAN Free Trade Area (AFTA)—but without success.

The sultan established diplomatic relations with countries waiting to join ASEAN: Vietnam (1992), Laos and Myanmar (July 1993).[101] The Asian financial crisis was the first opportunity for Brunei to show solidarity with its neighbours: in addition to the Singapore dollar with which it had fixed parity, BIA lent support to the Malaysian ringgit in August 1997. Brunei gave emergency financial assistance (B $1.88 billion = US $1.1 billion) to Indonesia in November and contributed up to US $500 million to the IMF's plan to save Thailand (where the sultan paid a visit in April 1998). Meanwhile, Malaysia—which called on its regional partners and Japan, instead of the IMF—received almost US $600 million in investments to consolidate its financial sector. Even though the sultanate was mired in the Amedeo affair, it granted a second slice of aid to Indonesia. These good deeds were somewhat rewarded by the holding of the 20th Southeast Asian games in Bandar Seri Begawan in August 1999.

4. To these positive regional moves, Brunei added increased activity within multilateral organisations: it participated more actively in Muslim bodies (the Organization of Islamic Cooperation or OIC in Senegal, in December 1991),[102] adhered to the Non-Aligned Movement in September 1992, gave aid (under OIC auspices) to Bosnia and the Middle East in 1995, and joined the IMF in October of the same year. Generally speaking, the sultanate contributed to UN and Commonwealth agencies[103]—while regularly denouncing Israel's policies.

Thus on the eve of the third millennium, Brunei's profile was that of a country governed by a traditional Muslim monarchy, developed and well integrated into its region. Two reservations persisted nonetheless: its wealth was derived from hydrocarbon rent, and the diversification of its economy remained far from accomplished, due to the seriousness of the BIA dysfunction that had discredited the government.

---

[101] The sultan visited Rangoon in 1998.

[102] The executive committee of the Regional Islamic Da'wah [Propagation of the Faith] Council of Southeast Asia and the Pacific met in Brunei in June 1991, and the sultan participated in a Festival of Islamic Culture in Jakarta in October.

[103] In 1992, Brunei was the fourth largest contributor to the Commonwealth (FEER, *Asia Yearbook 1993*: 90).

Running Before the Wind and Tacking (2000–14)

The 2000s were marked by a strong concern about social evolution, illustrated by the emphasis placed on Islamic issues and the slowing down of economic diversification. What followed was a policy of dead reckoning, with a succession of contradictory internal measures.

Islamisation and Institutional Reform

Priority was given to social issues with the publication in June 2000 of a ten-year health plan (2000–10). The Islamisation of the administration and of official bodies continued:[104] in January 2001, all private schools, religious or otherwise, were placed under the control of public education; the lower courts were transformed into Islamic courts; and a few weeks after September 11, the sultan created a MIB Council,[105] charged with accelerating the implementation of the state ideology.[106] But the fundamentalist threat persisted—locally, as confirmed by the arrest in September 2003 of six Bruneians accused of reactivating al-Arqam,[107] and regionally, by the signing during the Bali summit in October of an

[104] The vice-chancellor of the Universiti Brunei Darussalam (UBD) Awang Hj. Mahmud Saedon bin Awang Othman, published *Keluarga bahagia: dari kacamata islam* [A Happy Family through the Prism of Islam] in February 2000.
[105] It took over from the committee created in 1984.
[106] The first cohort of Islamic law students trained in Brunei graduated in 2002.
[107] Mohammad Yusop Haji Damit (Haj.), "Brunei Darussalam: Steady Ahead", *SAA 2004*: 67.

agreement to exchange information and fight against terrorism and other crimes. The Islamisation of institutions seemed to slow down in May 2005 when minister of education Pehin Abdul Aziz,[108] who had regularly increased the importance of religion in the curricula, was replaced by the president of Brunei Shell.[109] The attorney general was also given ministerial status (although, for balance, so was the mufti). However, a new decree in 2005 imposed on non-Muslim religious groups the requirement —above and beyond registration—to provide their membership lists.[110] Two months later, the emphasis was shifted back to the MIB: a *titah* encouraged the people to support the monarchy. Then pledges were given to the most rigorous factions with the creation of an Islamic university (Universiti Islam Sultan Sharif Ali, UNISSA) in August 2007, followed by the launching of a campaign against *bomoh*, deviant shamanic practices derived from Malay tradition.[111] This did not preclude the Ministry of Education from publishing a guiding plan for 2007–11 to improve the quality of programmes and to increase its control over the body charged with training religious teachers, which was transformed into a faculty[112] within the UBD in early 2007.

As a sign of modernity, women, who formed two-thirds of the higher-education student population but could not work as civil service officers after marriage, entitled only to monthly renewable contracts, became full-fledged public servants starting in 2009. In August of the same year, a woman[113] was even appointed to the post of attorney general. Meanwhile, the government continued to finance the participation of Bruneians (outside Brunei) in various interfaith dialogues within the framework of Asia-Europe Meeting (ASEM) or other organisations.[114]

---

[108] YB Pehin Abdul Aziz bin Begawan Pehin Udana Khatib Dato Seri Paduka Haji Awang Umar, born in 1936 and graduate of the University of Birmingham (A.V. Horton, *The Top Hundred Persons of Power and Influence in Negara Brunei Darussalam A.D. 2000*, Bordesley: A.V.M. Horton, 2001, pp. 32ff).

[109] YB Pehin Abdul Rahman bin Dato Setia Haji Mohd Taib, who had already been minister of education from 1986–88 (ibid., p. 37).

[110] Christopher Roberts and Lee Poh Onn, "Brunei Darussalam: Cautious on Political Reform, Comfortable in ASEAN, Pushing for Economic Diversification", *SAA 2009*: 65.

[111] *Brunei Times*, 27 December 2007.

[112] Seri Begawan Religious Teacher College.

[113] Datin Paduka Hajjah Hayati binte Pehin Orang Kaya Shahbandar Dato Seri Paduka Hji Mohd. Salleh.

[114] Christopher Roberts and Lee Poh Onn, "Brunei Darussalam", *SAA 2009*: 65.

To satisfy the "conservatives", the MIB Council (reactivated in May 2009) was given an economic dimension, and the draconian 2005 provisions relating to the halal label[115] went into force in August 2009. The decision to make Islamic religious education compulsory for young Muslims was reaffirmed in January 2010. Finally, in October 2013, a new Islamic Penal Code (including corporal punishments or *huddud*) was promulgated and enforced in April 2014, placing Muslim women under male guardianship for their whole life.

The same to-and-fro tacking strategy was observed in politics. The press seemed somewhat liberalised with the launching in March 2000 of the *Sunday Borneo Bulletin* and particularly with the authorisation in August 2001 of the first daily newspaper in Chinese. On the other hand, new laws in January 2001 called for the immediate closing of newspapers and the banning of any foreign press deemed harmful to morality or security. A step towards ending the state of emergency (enforced since 1962) was taken at the beginning of 2003, with the study of a constitutional amendment increasing the Legislative Council (Legco), dissolved since 1984, from 29 to 45 seats; it was even envisaged that a third of the members might eventually be elected by the villages and districts leaders.[116] The amendment was promulgated by the sovereign in September 2004, during the first session of the Legislative Council held since independence. This bright spot allowed a group of Chinese to launch the *Brunei Times* in January 2005 (which in turn devoted much space to religion), then the foundation in August of the National Development Party (NDP, known as *Aspirasi*), headed by a former leader of the PRB[117] who now loudly proclaimed his loyalty to the sovereign.

The former Legco was dissolved in September 2005 and the new Council (comprising 14 members by right, mostly from the government, 3 members of the aristocracy, 7 public figures and 6 district representatives, chosen from among the elected leaders of villages or sub-districts)[118] took over in March 2006. One innovation was that the questions posed to ministers and their answers were now reported in the press, but the government still refused to convey financial information relating to the

[115] *Halal Certificate and Label Order 2005*.

[116] There were 410 villages (kampung) and 38 districts (*mukim*) in Brunei.

[117] The NDP elected its officers in April 2006.

[118] Pushpa Thampillai, "Brunei Darussalam, Consolidating the Polity", *SAA 2006*: 57–67.

BIA. Another step taken by the authorities was the granting of permanent resident status—on the condition that the applicant held a minimum of B $500,000 assets in the sultanate (May 2006).[119] At its next session (March 2007), the Legco raised a few questions about minor points of public finance[120]—at the end of 2004, an audit had revealed a total of B $380 million in back taxes owed by various agencies and departments to the government. This was essentially explained by defects in collection procedures. The same was true in 2009 after the announcement of a possible return to a budget deficit.

This restoration of a tenuous legislative practice was accompanied by a cabinet reshuffle in May 2005, marked by the nomination of a minister of energy and two deputy ministers (for finance and foreign affairs) and the appointment to the latter of a Bruneian Chinese citizen, Pehin Dato Seri Paduka Lim Jock Seng.[121] The crown prince became senior minister. The transfer of the departments of international and commercial relations from the Ministry of Industry to the Ministry of Foreign Affairs facilitated diplomatic policy by integrating both political and economic dimensions. Emphasis was also placed on good governance through the establishment of internal consultation among the various ministries in preparation of a master plan for 2035, complemented by many training programmes. Appointments to ministerial functions (including for deputy ministers) were also amended to five-year terms.

Despite these changes, political life remained lifeless. Apart from the NDP, there existed no political party worthy of the name. This was confirmed by the de-registration of two barely active bodies: the PAKAR (March 2007)[122] and the PPKB (February 2008).[123] The second national assembly of villages and sub-districts in August 2007 was just as lacklustre. Bruneians were not prone to protest because the social sector received the lion's share of the budget: 32.1% in the Ninth Plan (2006–10),

---

[119] Contrary to what was said by William Case, "Brunei in 2006—Not a Bad Year", *Asian Survey* 47, 1 (January/February 2007): 189–93, this was not a matter of citizenship but of permanent residence rights (*Brunei Times*, 8 July 2007).

[120] Notably for the purchase of official vehicles.

[121] Pehin Lim holds a degree in economics as well as a master's degree in social anthropology (LSE). His master's thesis was published in 1986 (*The Inter-Relationship of Technology, Economy and Social Organisation in a Fishing Village in Brunei* [BSB: Brunei Museum, 1986], 123 p).

[122] Brunei People's Awareness Party.

[123] Parti Perpaduan Kebangsaan Brunei (Brunei National Solidarity Party).

with an emphasis on education (8.7% of expenditure) and to a greater extent, housing (16.4%, set aside for the construction of 9,300 housing units), which was one of the main requests from nationals. At the least hike in prices on the world market, the state handed out generous fuel subsidies.[124]

Procrastinating on Diversification

The start of the 2000s signalled a brake on economic diversification as a result of the Amedeo and BIA debacle, whose repercussions were still being felt, both legally and financially.

After the failure of friendly negotiations with Prince Jefri, the Bruneian state and the BIA embarked in February 2000 on a dual lawsuit in the Bruneian courts: a criminal case against Prince Jefri for embezzling US $14.8 billion[125] from the BIA for personal purposes and a civil case against the prince, his older son Hakim and 71 other persons in their entourage, for having transferred US $40 billion out of the BIA accounts. The court asked for a freezing of their assets in Brunei and abroad. The two parties came to an agreement in May 2000, but the prince later tried to get around it by refusing to declare his holdings in totality and by multiplying procedures. The only solution left was to sell off Amedeo liabilities: in October 2001, the government transferred its ownership to a new body, Global Evergreen, which spent eight months dealing with creditors. Several procedures later—including an appeal by Prince Jefri to the British Privy Council,[126] dismissed in November 2007—the litigation between the prince and the state of Brunei Darussalam was finally settled in 2008 by a restitution of the last assets. The presence of Prince Jefri and his sons at the Hari Raya celebrations in October 2009 confirmed that the affair was closed.

Meanwhile Brunei was shaken by a loss of confidence and restructuring the financial sector became a priority again. The creation of the Brunei International Finance Centre (BIFC) in July 2000, then of a first

---

[124] In 2007 alone, these subsidies reached B $200 million (Pushpa Thambipillai, "Brunei Darussalam: Making a concerted effort", *SAA 2008*: 98).

[125] See *Privy Council Appeal No. 69 of 2006, from the Court of Appeal of Brunei Darussalam.*

[126] The last judicial link with the former colonial power, the Privy Council of London, remains to this day the ultimate authority in matters of civil litigation in Brunei, under certain conditions.

capital market at the end of 2002,[127] was an attempt to promote the sultanate as a financial centre. But it ran counter to regional dynamics,[128] battered by the financial crisis and by the slowdown in American growth. A second advance by the Islamic financial sector five years later reversed this trajectory, reaffirming the sultanate's religious commitment on economic ground, under the cover of establishing a regional market hitherto monopolised by Malaysia. The first move was the creation in January 2006 of a body to supervise the Islamic financial sectors.[129] The merger of two Islamic banks in February[130] enabled the creation of a specialised bank, the Islamic Bank of Brunei Darussalam (IBBD), which could compete with traditional banks; the state—even though it did not need much cash—issued Islamic bonds in April.[131] Five laws and amendments consolidated the financial sector in March 2006, notably by imposing a minimum capital requirement of B $100 million for banks and B $25 million for financial companies. After the Anglo-American financial crisis, the Bruneian government guaranteed bank deposits (in local and foreign currency) in October 2008 until the end of 2010, and at the same time imposed on Bruneian insurers prudential margins and the establishment of a reinsurance fund.

Diversification Once Again

Added to the setbacks of BIA were the many structural weaknesses of the Brunei economy, which were diagnosed at the end of 1999 in a report from the BDEC:[132] despite a large budget deficit (15% of the GDP on average) since 1994, GDP growth had not been able to catch up with demographic growth in the 1990s. Faced with an increase in unemployment among university graduates,[133] the government was obliged to

[127] Committed to a Singapore firm, Nesdex.

[128] In 2003, only the Royal Bank of Canada and the Infrastructure Fund (based in Jeddah) of the Islamic Development Bank were registered.

[129] Shariah Financial Supervisory Board.

[130] The Islamic Bank of Brunei (IBB), subsidiary of the Baiduri Bank, and the Islamic Development Bank of Brunei (IDBB); the latter introduced a credit card in 2003 that conformed to the principles of Islamic finance.

[131] Sukuk al-Ijarah, commercialised via Sukuk Holding Properties and Sukuk Brunei.

[132] *Report of the Brunei Darussalam Economic Council* (BSB: BDEC), September 1999.

[133] Hamzah Sulaiman, "Negara Brunei Darussalam. Socio-Economic Concern Amid Stability and Plenty", *SAA 2003*: 75.

employ more than three-quarters of the national workforce, which not only prevented it from reducing the public deficit but also seriously hurt administrative efficiency. So there was no other solution for the BDEC but to advocate a systemic reform with the creation of a Ministry of Economy and an accelerated decision-making process, notably in public tenders, permitting a minimum of coherence in implementing a combination of restructuring, diversification and privatisation. Except for the creation of a Ministry of Economy, the report's conclusions were adopted in the Eighth Plan (2001–05), but their implementation was disordered at best.

The government did effectively engage in restructuring the vital sector of hydrocarbons by creating in January 2002 the Brunei National Petroleum Company ("Petroleum Brunei"), which assumed the role of the Brunei Oil and Gas Authority (BOGA). In its wake the last two blocks for exploration were granted:[134] block J to a consortium consisting of the French Total, the Australian BHP Billiton, and the American Amerada Hess; and block K to Brunei Shell Petroleum (BSP), Mitsubishi, and Conoco Brunei.[135] To develop foreign investments in order to diversify production, the Brunei Economic Development Board (BEDB) was formed in December 2001. Certain services were also privatised: the management of the Port of Muara[136] was leased for 25 years to the Port of Singapore Authority Corporation (PSA), and telecommunications were de-nationalised in February 2003.[137] A third slice concerning services previously delivered free of charge has been envisaged since October 2009.

Yet it was not until textile quotas were ended in early 2005 and an overview of the remaining businesses was carried out, did the issue of diversification return to the agenda. In conformity with the 30-year Master Plan published in 2008, *Wawasan* [*Vision*] *Brunei 2035*, the Ninth Plan seemed to confirm three non-social axes of development:

1. Infrastructure (26.9% of the budget), particularly transportation, electricity and water treatment. Construction of a port zone at Pulau Muara Besar (on an island facing the current port of Muara,

[134] In March 2008, the Californian Nations Petroleum Brunei got 50% of the shares of block L. This implied that Loon Energy, which had until then held 90% of the shares of that block, had sold 50%, and QAF Brunei kept the remaining 10%.

[135] Half-owned by the American ConocoPhillips.

[136] A direct link with China, Thailand and Indonesia was set up in 2003.

[137] The department of telecommunications became Telekom Brunei Berhad (TelBru).

at the entry to the Brunei Bay) was completed in 2012. The Ninth Plan called for a feasibility study of a bridge linking the district of Brunei-Muara to the second portion of the sultanate, Temburong, which would avoid transit over Malaysian territory. This, however, could only be carried out after a precise delimitation of the frontier.

2. Information technologies received 12.1% of the budget (compared to 7.2% in the preceding plan), of which US $100 million solely for the workforce.
3. Activities upstream of hydrocarbons received 10.8% of the budget. With the start of one of the key BIA projects of the 1990s—the construction of the Sungai Liang industrial park—in January 2007, the development of a manufacturing industry came back onto the agenda. The BEDB signed several letters of intent for biofuels,[138] aluminium, mobile telephones, a rice processing factory,[139] and organised in Singapore (February 2008) a forum on investment in Brunei.

But despite BEDB's interest in developing activities upstream of the exploitation of hydrocarbons, there was insufficient will to seize the opportunities offered by fitting out the Muara Port and by supplying natural gas for industrial installations. To this day, only a single major industrial project has been achieved—a methanol factory fed by natural gas (a joint investment by Brunei Petroleum and Mitsubishi Gas Chemical and Itochu, US $450 million). While a second refinery is envisaged, the plan for an aluminium foundry at Pulau Muara Besar,[140] under study for seven years, has not materialised. The slowness of decision-making, already criticised in 2003 in an American study,[141] continues to hold back most initiatives.

Multilateralism and Regionalism

On the threshold of the third millennium, Brunei has succeeded in inserting itself into the concert of nations, as illustrated by the holding in November 2000 of the eighth summit of APEC, state visits by the

---

[138] With the Malaysian HDZ Biodiesel Corporation.
[139] With the Southeast Asian leader in the sector, the Thai Charoen Pokphand (CP).
[140] Proposed by Alcoa.
[141] Monitor Group (Hj. Mohammad Yusop Haji Damit, *SAA 2004*: 64).

South Korean and Chinese presidents (Kim Dae-jung and Jiang Zemin) and the signing of a trade agreement with the United States. A year later, it hosted the seventh ASEAN Summit and the first ASEAN+3 Summit. The sultanate is also recognised as a full-fledged actor in regional security, which is attested (among other things) by the joint fight against piracy led by its maritime police and the Japanese coastguard in August 2002,[142] after the number of incidents in Southeast Asia had quadrupled, and by the success of the first international defence exhibition, Bridex, organised in Brunei in 2007.[143] So it is not surprising that Brunei, which has 32 embassies abroad and maintains diplomatic relations with more than 100 countries (including East Timor), joined the Asian Development Bank (ADB) in April 2006 and the International Labour Organization (ILO) in January 2007.[144] But Brunei's good relations with western countries have recently been tarnished by the enforcement of the new Islamic penal code in April 2014.

Nonetheless ASEAN remains the privileged field of Bruneian diplomacy, as reflected in a multiplication of official missions:[145] the sultan of Brunei was the guest of honour at the jubilee ceremony for the King of Thailand in June 2006,[146] and Singapore Prime Minister Lee Hsien Loong visited Brunei in June 2007. In line with the AFTA (ASEAN Free Trade Area) agenda, customs duties among the five founding countries plus Brunei (ASEAN-6) dropped to less than 5% in January 2003. In December 2005, Brunei became a party to CAFTA, which all but eliminated custom duties[147] between China and the members of ASEAN-6[148]

---

[142] Derek Johnson and Mark Valencia, eds., *Piracy in Southeast Asia: Status, Issues and Responses* (Singapore: ISEAS, 2005), p. 93.

[143] Subsequently the event was held every other year.

[144] To remove even the slightest whiff of Marxism, Labour Day in Brunei is celebrated on 5 May and not on 1 May.

[145] The crown prince toured ASEAN countries in June 2006 and attended the fourth China-ASEAN exhibition in Nanning in October 2007.

[146] In 2002 BIA had signed a MOU with the Thai Government Pension Fund for the creation of a fund holding shares in all restructuring Thai companies, but the project came to nothing.

[147] Import taxes on Chinese products fell from an average of 12.8% to 0.6% in the six ASEAN countries; import taxes on Southeast Asian products in China, from 9.8% to 0.1%. Brunei participated in the fourth China-ASEAN Exhibition and in the China-ASEAN Economic Summit in Nanning (2007), followed by the Shanghai Universal Exhibition (2010).

[148] 2015 for the three Indochinese nations and Myanmar.

in January 2010 (with each country reserving the possibility of drawing up a list of products liable to fall outside the accord). ASEAN nations continue to benefit from the sultanate's assistance, which from purely financial in the 1990s broadened to include security and humanitarian aid in the following decade. Alongside 50-odd Malaysians, 10 Bruneian officers went to the Philippines to help frame an agreement with the Moro Islamic Liberation Front (MILF) in October 2004; in 2008 Bruneians asked to direct an international team in charge of supervising the ceasefire in Mindanao after the withdrawal of the Malaysians. Brunei provided humanitarian aid to Indonesia (Aceh in 2005, then Yogyakarta in 2006) and to Myanmar after the Nargis typhoon in 2008. It also committed to preserving its rainforest (which covers three-quarters of its territory) by including more than 60% of national land in the World Wild Life Fund's conservation project "Heart of Borneo", to preserve a third (about 220,000 km^2) of the island's surface.

Figure 5. Teapot of Abundance, Kuala Belait (close to the oilfields)

Although the king of Malaysia has paid Brunei a state visit every five years (at each new enthronement),[149] a conflict burst out when it turned out that blocks M and L, which Kuala Lumpur had granted to a consortium led by Petronas Carigali,[150] overlapped with block K and especially block J (map 6), whose exploration rights Brunei had granted in January 2002 to the Total-Fina-Elf consortium.[151] Tensions escalated in 2003 when the Malaysian and American consortium (Petronas and Murphy) discovered a large deposit that might extend to block J. The Bruneian navy chased a Murphy drilling ship in March, and the following month, the Malaysians hunted down a Total ship operating in block J, forcing the company to suspend exploration two months later.[152] Unable to resolve the boundary question, the tenth annual negotiations between Brunei and Malaysia (2006) concluded with a project to build a trans-Borneo highway and to simplify procedures for regular borders,[153] which would in time open up the sultanate to most of the trade with neighbouring Malaysia that had been transiting through Singapore.

After new advances in August 2008, an agreement on land and sea borders was finally signed in March 2009, during the 39th round of negotiations since 1995. In September 2010, a second series of agreements ratified practical protocols for exploiting blocks J and K (renamed CA_1[154]

---

[149] The Malaysian Federation is a revolving monarchy where the king (*Yang di-Pertuan Agong*) is elected every five years by the Council of Rulers, the nine sultans of Peninsular Malaysia.

[150] With the American firms Murphy Oil and ConocoPhillips and the British-Dutch Shell.

[151] With the Australian BHP Billiton and the American Amerada Hess; block K had been granted by the Bruneians to the Shell–Mitsubishi–ConocoPhillips consortium (see the website of the Brunei National Petroleum Company, http://www.pb.com.bn/Update%20-%20Blockk%20J&K.htm).

[152] Buszynski and Sazlan, "Maritime Claims and Energy Cooperation in the South China Sea", p. 163; Cutler J. Cleveland, "Energy Profile of Brunei", *Encyclopaedia of Earth* (Washington: Environmental Information Coalition, National Council for Science and the Environment, 2007, e-edition, http://www.eoearth.org/article/Energy_profile_of_Brunei).

[153] There was to be a regular traveller's card; a trial run at one of the border posts between Brunei and Sarawak proved positive for both parties.

[154] Malaysia got 10% of CA_1; Brunei kept the remaining 90%, which it granted to a consortium including Total E&P Borneo (60% of the consortium), BHP (25%) and Amerada Hess (15%), Petroleum Brunei buying back 15% of the field once the exploitation begins.

and CA_2[155]). A joint project for electricity development with Sarawak was launched in mid-2009, with plans to connect the two networks around 2015, when Malaysia is expected to export 400 megawatts per year to Brunei.[156]

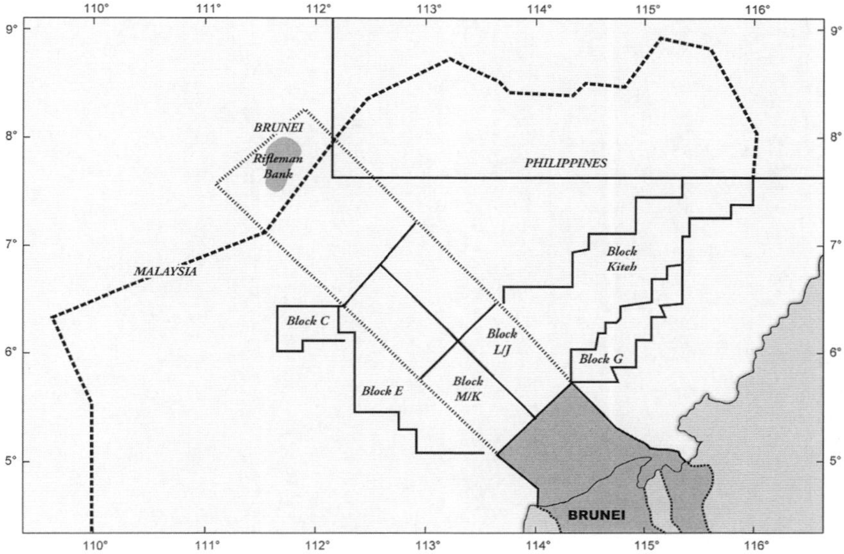

Map 6. Malaysian and Bruneian Claims (Blocks L/J and M/K)
(Buszynski and Sazlan, "Maritime Claims and Energy Cooperation in the South China Sea", *Contemporary Southeast Asia* 29 [2007]).

Finally, the strengthening of security continued with two White Papers on defence. The White Paper of 2004 stressed combating terrorism and trafficking in drugs, arms and human beings, while that of 2007 focused on cooperation with foreign security agencies.[157] Brunei's links with the United Kingdom were once again made explicit during Prince Charles' visit in October 2008.

---

[155] Block CA_2 is shared between Malaysia, 75% (45% Petronas and 30% Murphy) and Brunei, 25% (Brunei Shell 12.5%, Mitsubishi 6.25% and ConocoPhillips 25%).

[156] A second phase extended the project to Sabah in 2014.

[157] *Defence White Paper 2004: Defending the Nation Sovereignty* (BSB, August 2004), 53 p; *Defence White Paper 2007: Shaping the Forces Today* (BSB, August 2007), 53 p.

FROM HYDROCARBON RENT TO FINANCIAL RENT

The resolution of the century-old border issue with Malaysia in September 2010 opened up significant prospects for hydrocarbons; thus the matter of Brunei's survival was relegated to the distant future, when petro-gas income runs out. In order to evaluate future prospects, it is necessary to start by studying how the Bruneian economy has been working since independence, then analysing the various sources of surplus it has generated, and finally estimating in a heuristic way the amount and profitability of capital it has invested abroad.

Absolute Dominance of Hydrocarbons

Wealth and Growth

Note that the following analysis of growth (that is, increase in production) refers to GDP (Gross Domestic Product) and not to GNP (Gross National Product, nowadays Gross National Income in U.N. sources). Since 1986, income drawn from outward foreign investment is no longer included in statistics related to national income in Brunei.

Apparent Strong Growth, Both Nominal and in US Dollars

A graph of production data in nominal value and in current US dollars backs the impression of wealth: in less than 50 years, Brunei's GDP multiplied by 127 times. According to demographic growth, this means that its GDP per capita multiplied by 33 times. Therefore Brunei passed from a position slightly below the average world wealth in 1965 to the 30th spot by the end of the 2000s, placing it among the richest countries on the planet.

But at the same time, this strong progress seems relatively fragile if judged by the amplitude and frequency of fluctuations detected on the graph (graph 1), showing seven phases since 1965.

Modest Real Growth

Brunei's real growth rate of GDP (apart from inflation, on the basis of data in constant Brunei dollars)[1] reveals by contrast the mediocrity of

[1] Available only after 1975.

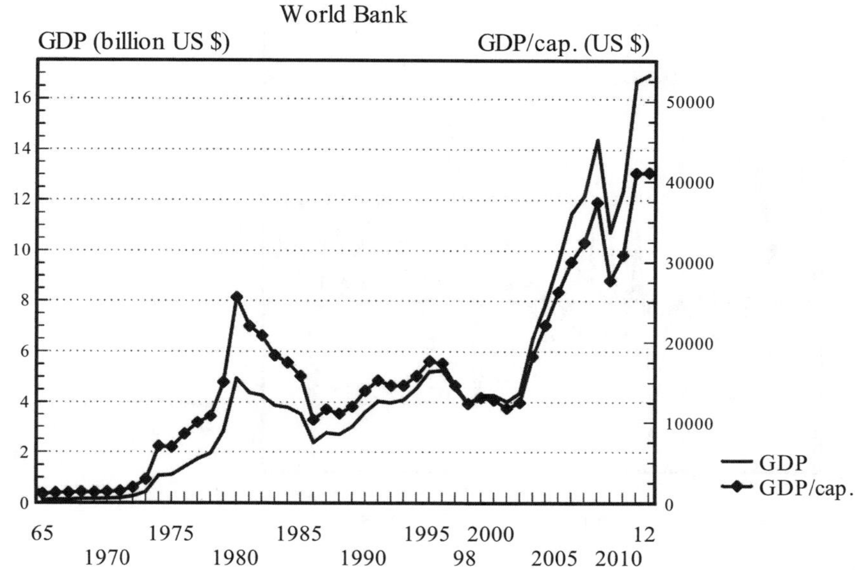

Graph 1. GDP, 1965–2012 (current US $)

Notes:

1. 1965–72, when the GDP (in both nominal value and in US $) multiplied by 2.3;
2. 1972–80, with exponential progress (× 25);
3. 1980–86, when it was divided by 2.5;
4. 1986–96, when it more than doubled;
5. 1996–2002, when it fell by almost a fifth;
6. 2002–08, when it almost tripled;
7. 2008–12, with a 25% decrease followed by a return to the 2008 level and resumption of growth.

the economic performance (see graph 2): for the period from 1975–2010, the average growth rate of Brunei, the second richest country in ASEAN, barely reached 1.9%, while that of the three best-off countries was three to four times higher—between 5.9% (Thailand and Malaysia) and 6.9% (Singapore).

The fluctuations in growth are very marked: the GDP growth rate surged to 20% in 1976, fell to below 8% in 1978, exceeded 20% in 1979, then became strongly negative for 1980–81 (–7% and –19.8%). And since 1982, growth oscillated between –4% and +4%, with five troughs: 1985–86 (–1.5% and –2.7%); 1989 (–1.1%); 1992 (–1.1%); 1998 (–4%) and 2008–09 (–1.9% and –1.7%).

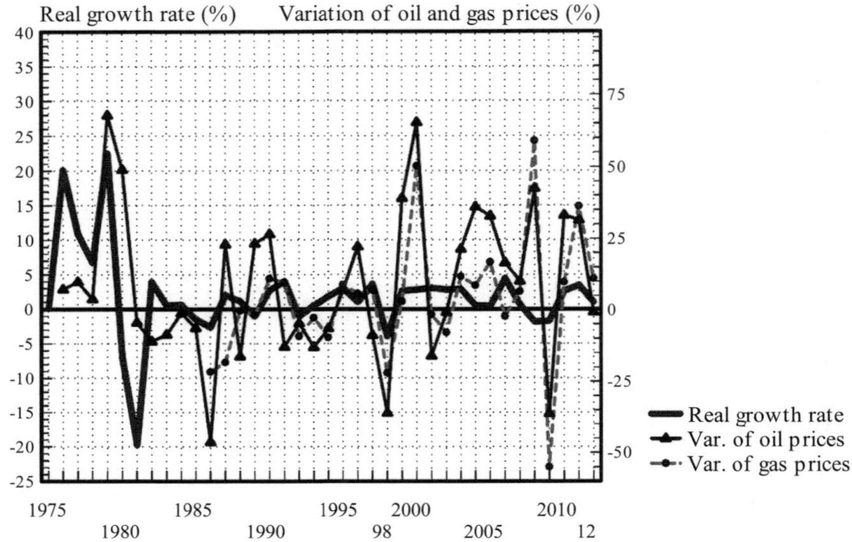

Graph 2. Real GDP Growth Rates, 1975–2012
(based on gross domestic product at constant US 2005 $)

It was undoubtedly the rise in oil prices[2] (which multiplied by 11 between 1972 and 1980) that propelled growth beyond 20% in 1976 and 1979, but their fluctuations (and those of liquefied natural gas after the mid-1980s) are by no means the sole factor that explains Brunei's meagre performance, as shown by the lack of synchrony between the GDP growth rate and oil and gas prices over two periods: 1980–83 and to a even greater extent 2001–09. The strongly negative growth in 1998 is thus the result of the conjunction between an internal crisis (the failure of Amedeo and BIA's mismanagement), the Asian financial crisis and a plunge in hydrocarbon prices.

Production Centred on Hydrocarbons

An analysis of the evolution of the productive structure since 1963 (when data was first made accessible) allows a better appreciation of the weight

[2] Annual average prices, "Crude Oil Prices from 1946–Present", InflationData.com, 14 June 2012.

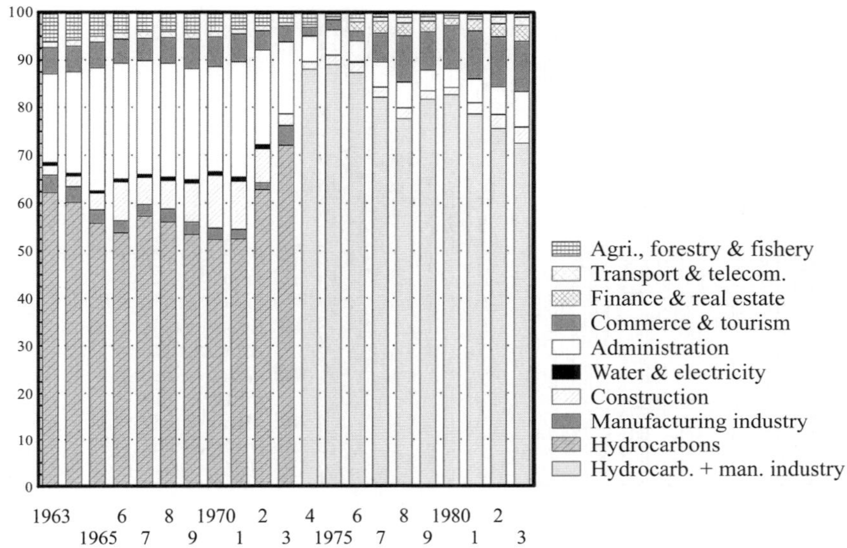

Graph 3. GDP Breakdown by Sector, 1963–83
(Source: *Annual Report, 1958-76; Yearbook 1975-86*)

of hydrocarbons in the economy by contrasting the 20 years preceding independence (1963–83), when management of the economy was essentially incumbent on the British mentors, and the following 30 years (1984–2012) when Brunei was a master of its own house. Three phases appear in each of the two periods:

(1) *1963–83* (see graph 3)

- From 1963–71, the share of hydrocarbons declined slightly from 62% to 52% of GDP; administration[3] (22%–25% of GDP) and private services[4] (6%–7% of GDP) remained stable; construction increased five-fold (from 2% to 10% of GDP); and the manufacturing industry and the primary sector,[5] down by half, represented no more than tiny fractions (respectively 2% and 3% of GDP).
- From 1971–76, the proportion of hydrocarbons increased by more than half, to represent 89% of GDP. Since manufacturing

[3] Social services (health, education, etc.) included.
[4] Commerce, real estate, finance, transport and telecommunications.
[5] Agriculture, forestry and fishery.

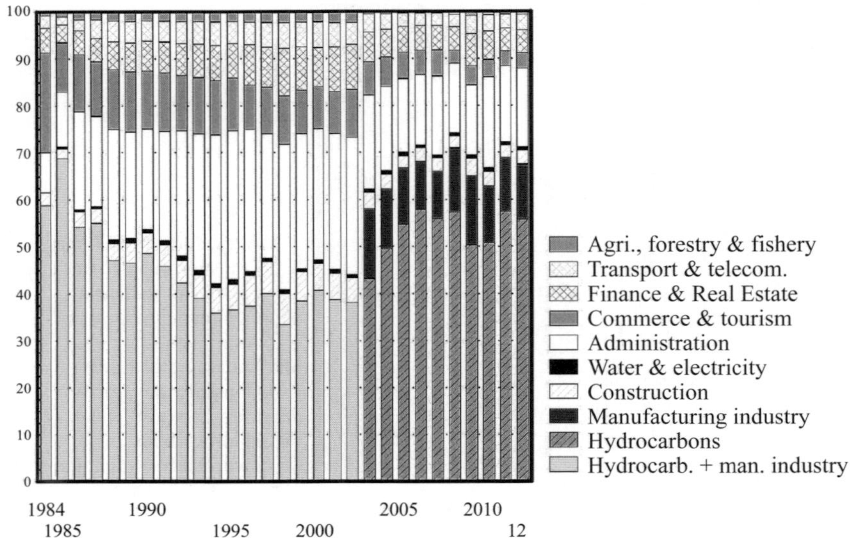

Graph 4. GDP Breakdown by Sector, 1984–2012
(Source: *Brunei Statistical Yearbook, 1986–2012*)

provided only 4% of GDP in 1973, it was added to hydrocarbons starting from 1974.[6] Administration represented 5% of GDP and commercial services, 4%–5%; the primary sector generated barely 1% of GDP.

- From 1976–83, the share of hydrocarbons (including manufacturing) dropped by a sixth to 73% of GDP, to the benefit of administration, which rose to 8%, and especially services, which reached 15% of GDP, with the primary sector continuing to represent less than 1% of GDP.

(2) *1984–2012* (see graph 4)

- These trends persisted during the first decade after independence (1984–94). The share of hydrocarbons (industry included) dropped by almost half, from 70% of GDP in 1984 to 36% in 1994, noting that, according to the Sixth Plan,[7] industry increased slightly from

[6] On 1975–84, it represented some 1% of GDP.
[7] Cited by Naimah Talib, "Brunei in 1995: A New Assertiveness?", *SAA 1996*: 105.

0.7% of GDP in 1985 to 1.7% in 1990. The decline of hydrocarbons seems to have influenced services, which diminished by a fifth (from 29% to 24% of GDP). Inversely, administration tripled (from 10% to 31%), which corresponds to the massive entry of nationals into public service; construction doubled (from 2% to 5%); and the primary sector rose slightly, while remaining almost negligible (2% of GDP in 1994).

- The productive structure remained almost stable from 1995–2002: 35%–40% for hydrocarbons and industry, about 30% for administration, 24% for services, 6% for construction and 2% for the primary sector.
- In 2003, manufacturing was again recorded separately from hydrocarbons. While no information is available in the *Yearbooks* about its composition, it obviously includes almost all the activities surrounding the extraction of hydrocarbons (refining, liquefaction of petroleum gas);[8] the IMF evaluated other industries at a negligible 1.8% of GDP.[9] On this basis, the share of hydrocarbons *stricto sensu* increased by a quarter (from 44% of GDP in 2003 to 56% in 2012), but other sectors shrank: industry diminished by a fifth (from 15% to 12%); services, which had dropped by a third in 2003 to 16% of GDP, then continued decreasing to 9%; administration slipped by a third. The primary sector was not even perceptible on the graph.

To summarise, since 1986, administration and health and education services generated between 20% and 30% of GDP; other services (since 1983), between 15% and 25%, making hydrocarbons by far the prime sector of Brunei's production, providing since the early 1960s between 40% and 90% of GDP.

No Salvation Apart from Hydrocarbons?

Gas versus Oil

From 1965 to 1973, Brunei's oil production almost tripled (see graph 5). It then stabilised between 65 and 85 million barrels per year until 1980, before sinking by almost half during the following decade. After a stepped

[8] The *Yearbooks* give the quantity produced.

[9] EIU, *Brunei, Country Profile 2007*, p. 17.

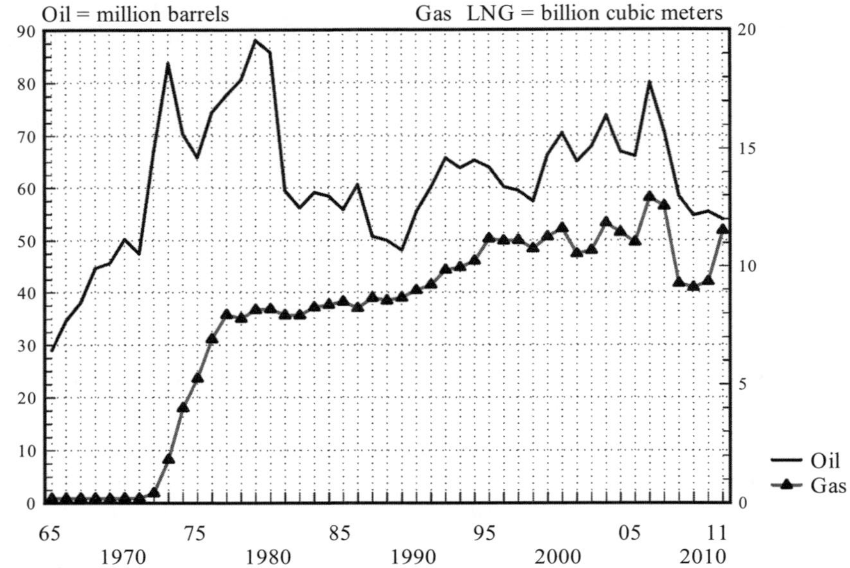

Graph 5. Hydrocarbon Production, 1965–2011

upturn and a peak of 80 million barrels in 2005, it fell again by almost 40% at the end of the 2000s.

The production of liquefied natural gas (LNG) started becoming significant in 1973 (1.8 billion m^3), then tripled in four years (7.9 billion m^3 in 1977). Its progress slowed down sharply, as the 11 billion m^3 mark was not reached until 1995, and then rose in slight stages to 12.5 billion m^3 in 2007. The years 2009 (9 billion m^3) registered a drop of about a quarter, followed by a 26% increase on 2010–11.

Until 2005, more than 95% of oil production was exported, and since then, around 90%. Between 95% and 98% of LNG production has been exported up to now, with Brunei keeping its own petroleum gas. To judge by the estimates of its reserves at the start of 2012 (1,100 million barrels of oil and 360.4 billion m^3 of gas)—and despite the drop recorded at the end of the 2000s—on 1 January 2014 and at the current rate and technology of production, Brunei possesses 18 years of oil reserves and more than 30 years of gas reserves. Added to these reserves are the deepwater blocks (J/CA_1 and K/CA_2), whose potential may be considerable by Brunei's yardstick. In short, the sultanate possesses resources that alone would justify the reluctant efforts to diversify production.

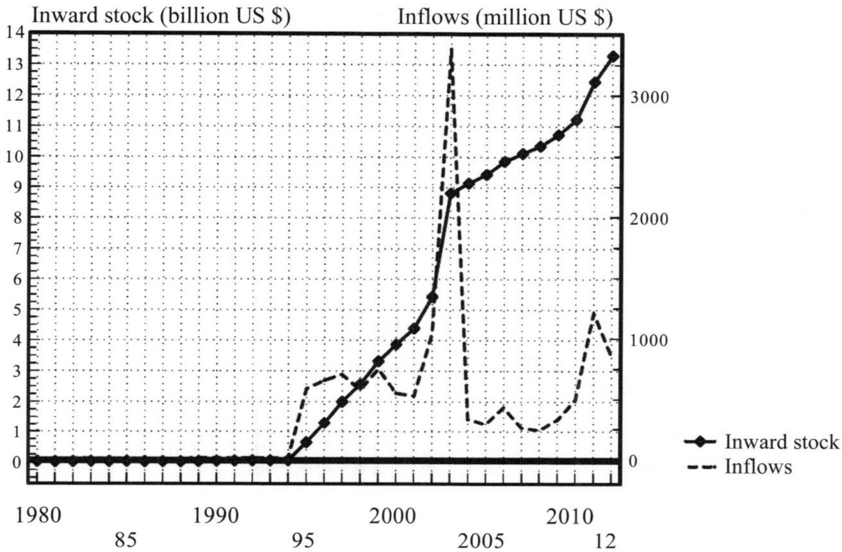

Graph 6. Foreign Direct Investment, 1980–2012
(Source: UNCTAD, World Investment Report)

Partially Foreign-financed Development of Hydrocarbons

Development of hydrocarbons was largely self-financed by local petroleum firms (Brunei Shell, etc.) from 1980 until the middle of the 1990s (see graph 6). After the difficult path to independence, the years 1980–86 even registered some disinvestments: in 1990, Brunei counted only US $33 million in foreign direct investment (FDI) stock since 1980 and a meagre $60 million in 1994.

Due to both an effective change of development policy and to the exploitation of new deposits, foreign investment exploded from 1995–2000, with US $3.8 billion in six years. The boom continued between 2001 and 2008, when FDI inflows (US $6.8 billion) doubled in eight years.

This inflow of capital means that despite its wealth, the sultanate—along with Singapore—is one of the two Southeast Asian countries most open to foreign capital. In 2012, FDI stock (realised) since 1980 (excluding investments made locally by Shell) represented 78% of Brunei's GDP, nearly twice that of Malaysia's (43%), but one third that of Singapore's (246%).

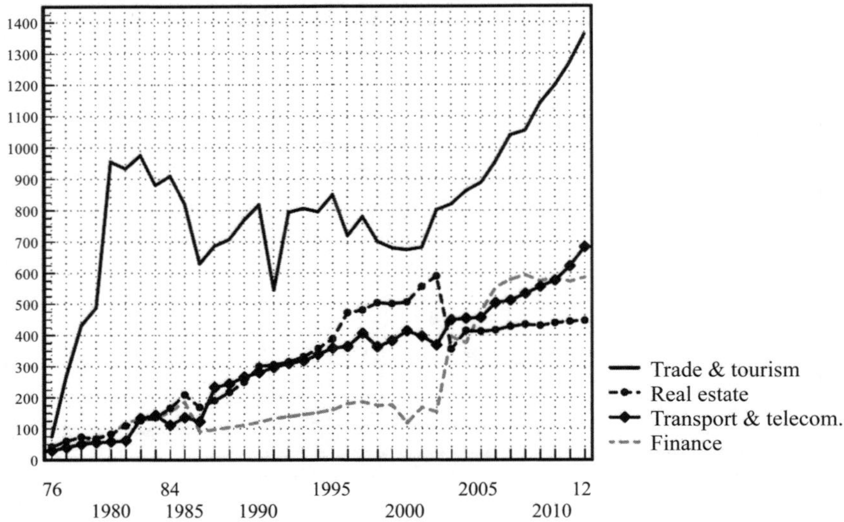

Graph 7. Commercial Services, 1976–2012

(Source: *Brunei Statistical Yearbook, 1975–2012*; *State of Brunei Annual Report, 1958–76*)

The Rise of Commercial Services

After the explosion of oil-gas revenues, Brunei became a more bourgeois and consumer society, as revealed by the evolution in commercial services (graph 7): trade (and tourism)[10] quadrupled between 1976 and 1977, then tripled from 1977 to 1980. Due to a drop in oil prices, it slid back 40% over 1980–86, to stabilise around B $800 million until 1997. If the financial jolts at the end of the 1990s translated into a slight lowering of commercial activity, subsequently it took off for good, doubling between 2001 and 2012.

Transport and telecommunications progressed in a more regular manner, on the order of a twelve-fold increase throughout the period. As for the two sectors most revealing of the enrichment of the population, real estate and finance, they evolved in opposite directions after 1986: in 13 years (1986–99), real estate tripled but finance barely doubled; after the failure of Amedeo, finance fell by 30% in 2000 while real estate stabilised; finance almost tripled between 2002 and 2007, while real estate

[10] Tourism represented between 1% and 2% of GDP.

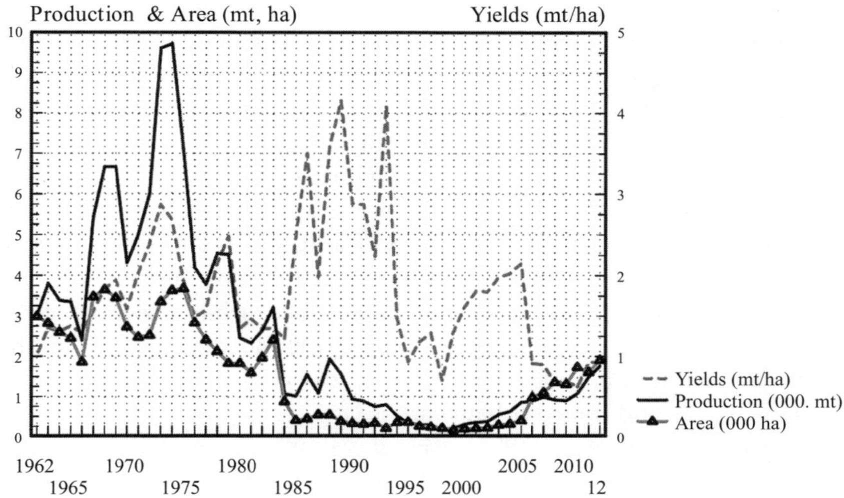

Graph 8. Rice Growing, 1962–2012
(Source: *Brunei Statistical Yearbook, 1975–2012*. Estimations 1982–83 based on average yields for years 1980, 1981 and 1984)

fell by almost a third in 2003. In short, once they become homeowners—thanks to massive state aid to Bruneian citizens who benefit from unsecured loans for housing as for automobiles (even if low-income housing remains insufficient)[11]—nationals today prefer to place their savings in a bank rather than in real estate.

Irresistible Decline of the Primary Sector

A closer examination of the data on the primary sector shows that its decline has been evident for at least half a century. In 1963, the primary sector was already of slight importance (6% of GDP), even in terms of a Malay world that traditionally imports food products (in peninsular Malaysia, agriculture, fishing and forestry still generated 38% of GDP).

(1) *Agriculture*

More precisely, as shown in graph 8, rice growing (which represented some 60% of the primary sector in value) crumbled after 1974. Rice

[11] Some 30,000 requests were still pending in 2010.

production, which had tripled (from 2.9 to 9.7 thousand tonnes) in 20 years (1955–74), was divided by 69 over the following 25 years, leaving a residue of 140 tonnes in 1998. It then multiplied by 10 over the following 12 years, crossing the threshold of 1,000 tonnes in 2011.

The oil boom has thus played against rice growing: not only did production plummet, but rural people deserted the rice fields to occupy new jobs in administration and related services, so the returns themselves were divided by more than three in 1974 and in 1998. In other words, the only rice growing that survived has been the most archaic kind on slash-and-burn fields and among remote tribes, while irrigated fields created from scratch at the instigation of the British, starting in the 1920s (Brunei-Muara and Tutong), gave way to real-estate modernity and largely air-conditioned urbanism.

Even at its apogee in 1974, rice cultivation met less than a quarter of the demand.[12] The authorities tried to stimulate the cultivation of rice at the end of the 1970s for both food security and ideological reasons: the Fourth and Fifth Plans (1975–84) proclaimed the goal of 30% self-sufficiency in rice. A doubling of returns between 1984 and 1993 could not stem the disappearance of rice cultivation: today the production of rice is lower than its 1965 level (graph 8). After 1995, domestic cultivation thus covered only 2%–3% of rice consumption, with most of the crop being homegrown.[13] This led to a renewed "promotion" of the activity in 2010. Inversely, 60% of the fruits and vegetables consumed in 2012 were produced locally, as opposed to 50% at the end of the 1970s:[14] in the year 2008 alone, vegetable production increased by a third. But until the second half of the 2000s, cultivated area occupied only 2,000 hectares,[15] of which a quarter was devoted to rice. The Sino-Bruneian joint venture for planting 700 hectares of paddy,[16] launched in November

---

[12] *Ranchangan Kemajuan Negara 1975–1979* [*The National Development Plan 1975–1979*] (BSB, 1980), p. 53.

[13] Ismail Duraman (Haj.) et al., "Achieving sustainable development in an oil-dependent economy: The case of Brunei Darussalam", *Asia-Pacific Development Journal* 5, 1 (June 1988): 108.

[14] Johannes C. Franz, *The sultanate of Brunei, oil wealth and problems of development* (Nurnberg: Wirtschafts- und Sozialgeographisches Institut der Friederich-Alexander, Universitaet Nurnberg, 1980), p. 230.

[15] See, for example, Pushpa Thambipillai and Hamzah Sulaiman, "Brunei Darussalam. After a Decade of Independence", *SAA 1995*: 117.

[16] Guangxi Wangwangda Farmers Company, in partnership with the Bruneian Wen Zhong Agro-science and Technology.

2009, increased on its own by half the rice field area, although the rice yields, which decreased at the end of the decade, are now by far the lowest of all ASEAN countries! Just as one century ago, wet rice cultivation (with the introduction of new varieties) is being developed by the Chinese!

Cattle, whose quantity remains infinitesimal (549 heads slaughtered in 2012), provides a contrast: between 1971 and 2012, the number of buffaloes has decreased by a fifth; other bovid, whose number had doubled between 1971 and 1994, then dropped by half. The sultan's Australian ranch has furnished some 40% of the demand for beef since the middle of the 1980s.[17] Given the interdiction on raising pigs in 1993, the only other husbandry to be developed in any significant way is battery farming of chickens, which has increased tenfold since it started at the end of the 1970s.

(2) *Forestry*

Forestry has witnessed a similar evolution (graph 9). The production of undressed timber, which had multiplied by eight between 1962 and 1982, stabilised around 200,000 m^3 until 1987, then dropped by half. Brunei had as many as 20 sawmills in 1974,[18] whose output remained at about 90,000 m^3 in the 1980s before dropping by half during the 1990s, after implementation of a policy to preserve the rainforest.[19] In short, interest in timber, which might have been one of the elements of the diversification sought since the 1970s, collapsed in less than a decade.

(3) *Fishing*

Only fishing and aquaculture seem to have been able to diversify the primary sector in a durable way, with production rising from some 2,000 tonnes in 1985 to some 15,000–16,000 tonnes at the end of the 2000s. Since the middle of the 2000s, half the demand for aquatic products has been covered locally.

---

[17] Sharon Siddique, "Brunei Darussalam 1991. The Non-Secular Nation", *SAA 1991*: 91.

[18] The first modern sawmill was built just after World War Two, but it had to close in 1949 because of a shortage of skilled manpower. Handsaws were then progressively replaced by mechanical saws (Cleary and Wong, *Oil, Economic Development and Diversification of Brunei Darussalam*, p. 273).

[19] Sharon Siddique, "Negara Brunei Darussalam", *SAA 1985*: 105.

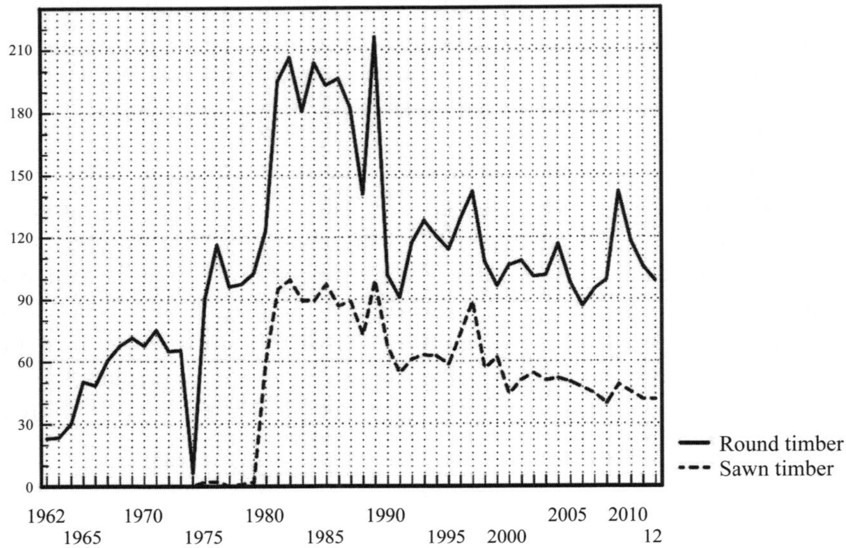

Graph 9. Timber, 1962–2012 (thousands m^3)
(Source: Brunei Key Indicators, 1975–2012)

Overview of the Primary Sector

To sum up, if 30% of nationals still earned a living in the primary sector at the start of the 1960s, only half (15%)[20] remained in the sector by the mid-1970s, 2% in 1991 and only 0.6% in 2001. The massive abandonment of the countryside and coastal zones by Bruneians means that four-fifths of the labour employed in agriculture, forestry and fishing today are immigrants,[21] which is a major brake on the expansion of the sector in view of the sultanate's immigration policy, without nonetheless threatening its survival.

[20] Johannes C. Franz, *The sultanate of Brunei, oil wealth and problems of development*, pp. 215ff.

[21] According to the 2011 census, complete data of the 2011 census having not yet been published at the beginning of 2014.

Structural Trade Surplus

Growing Surpluses

For the time being, there is no need at all for the primary sector to survive: during the oil boom, exports doubled between 1972 and 1973, then multiplied by 13 between 1973 and 1980. The drop in oil prices made exports fall by more than half (US $2 billion) in 1986, and oscillated between US $2 and 3 billion until 1999. The strong hike in hydrocarbon prices entrained a tripling of exports (US $8.7 billion in 2008), followed by a drop in 2009 induced by the fall in hydrocarbon prices, then by a 83% increase in 2010–12.

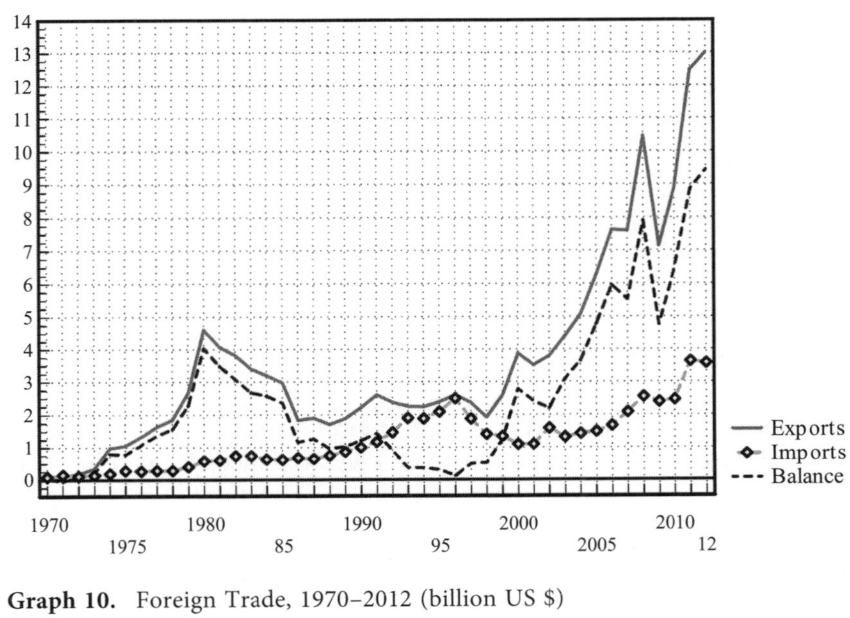

Graph 10. Foreign Trade, 1970–2012 (billion US $)

Imports progressed in a much more regular way, multiplying by around 20 in a quarter century (1970–96). As a sign of a relative financial "crisis", they halved between 1996 and 2001, tripled between 2001 and 2008, then fell in 2009 and increased again from 2010–12.

Brunei's trade (graph 10) remained structurally in surplus. And since imports stayed way below exports (except for 1996), the commercial surplus exploded twice over: from 1972 to 1980, it multiplied by 57; from 1998 to 2008, it multiplied by 11. In 2008, the commercial surplus (US $5.6 billion) thus reached 38% of GDP; and even though it dropped by a fifth in 2009, it still compensated for the mediocre growth in production, before increasing again from 2010–12.

No Hope Apart from Hydrocarbons?

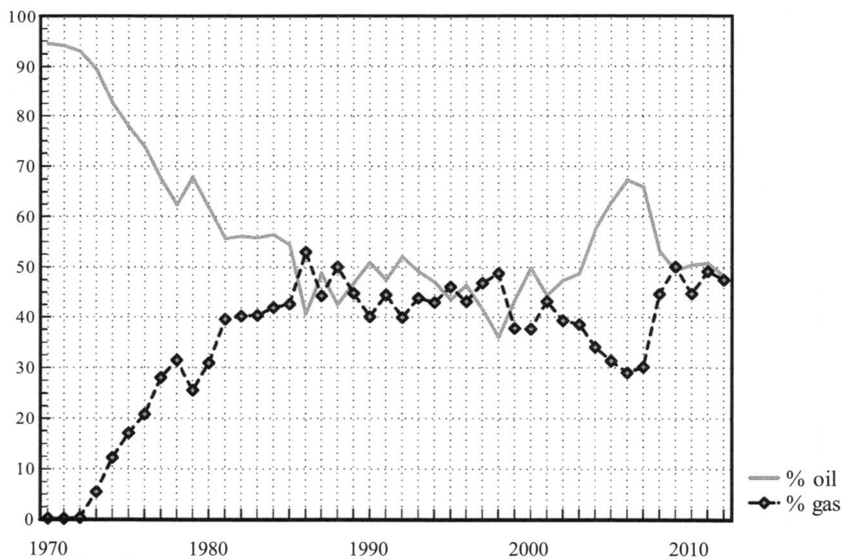

Graph 11. Exports by Commodities (%), 1970–2012

Since the 1950s, hydrocarbons have represented almost all of Brunei's exports,[22] except that gas has partially replaced petroleum: the share

[22] The second export commodity (to United States), clothing, produced in 1994 a meagre B $40 million (Naimah Talib, "Brunei in 1995: A New Assertiveness?", *SAA 1996*: 105).

of gas, negligible until the early 1970s, was more than 50% in 1986. Gas and crude oil then oscillated between 40% and 50% of exports for a dozen years (1986–98). While gas fell back below 40% in 2006, the trend seemed to reverse once more at the end of the decade—not including the future exploitation of blocks J/CA_1 and K/CA_2, which are presumed to be very rich.

Apparently Reasonable Consumption

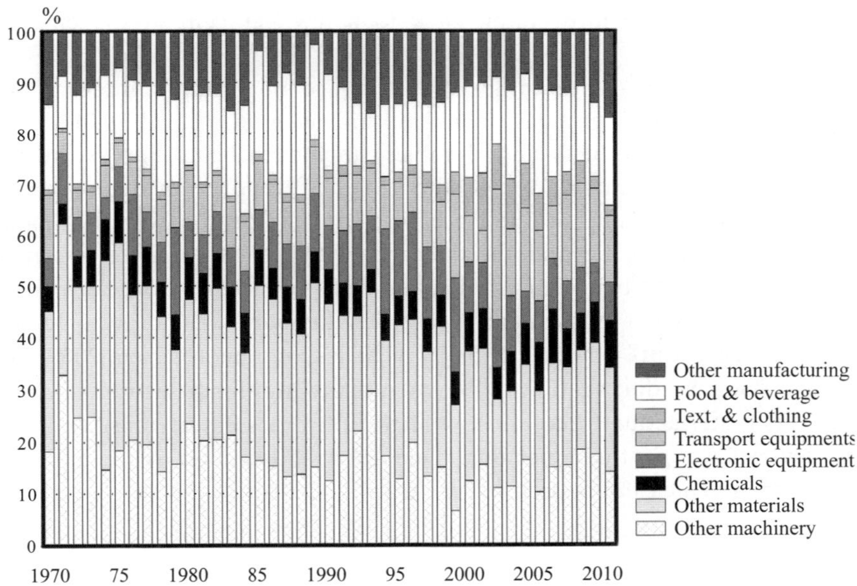

Graph 12. Imports by Commodities, 1970–2010

Given the virtual absence of a primary sector, food and beverage represented between 15% and 18% of Brunei's imports during the whole period from 1970–2010 (graph 12). Since 1978, except for years when the sultanate equipped itself with ferries or other boats (such as motorised pleasure boats sprinkled across the mouth of the Brunei River), cars represent between 8% and 15% of imports. The share of "other machinery", which had climbed to 33% in 1971, fell to some 15% at the end of the 1970s; with the re-launch of diversification in the early 1990s, it climbed back to 30% in 1993, then declined to slightly below 20%—except for 1998, when the purchase of transport vessels exceeded other equipment.

Other materials[23] (apart from textiles) that reveal developing urbanisation (with construction in the lead), totalled 40% of imports after the first oil bonus in 1975. They fell by half on the eve of the 1980s, with their share climbing to 30% at the end of the decade, then fell back below 20% in the course of the next two decades. Electronics,[24] which represented only a few percentage points of imports in 1970, climbed to 17% in 1979, then stabilised between 8% and 10%. Chemical products oscillated between 5% and 10% since 1970. Textiles and clothing remained negligible until the early 2000s, then climbed to almost 10% of imports in 2003, before falling back to a few per cent at the end of the decade.

Despite petro-gas income, the structure of Brunei's imports far from translated into excessive consumption over the period 1970–2010, since consumer products and durables (including boats but excluding electronics) represent on average about half of imports. In other words, society is modernising at the pace of financial income with no signs of Bruneians living beyond their means, with one notable exception—automobiles. Cars being an emblematic sign of success, Bruneians own several vehicles per household, even when they are used only in town. The sultanate thus counted 165,000 vehicles on the road in 2009, or almost one per adult aged over 19, when many immigrant workers (more than half the labour force, mostly single) only possess at most one car for every two or three persons. Due to a squeeze on lending,[25] the number of vehicles decreased by one third in 2010.

---

[23] According to the Standard International Trade Classification, Revision 3 (S.I.T.C Rev. 3) of the United Nations, "Manufactured Goods by Materials" include glass, ceramics, cement, sheet metal, iron rods, textiles, etc., but exclude food, beverages, tobacco and living animals.

[24] Electrical and office equipment included.

[25] Including restrictions on credit cards, cf. *The Report: Brunei Darussalam 2010* (Oxford Business Group, 2011), pp. 91–2.

Successful Regional Integration

Buyers from ASEAN+3

Although it exports only hydrocarbons (including methanol), Brunei has not ceased diversifying its customers since the 1970s, which has taken effect in four phases (graph 13):

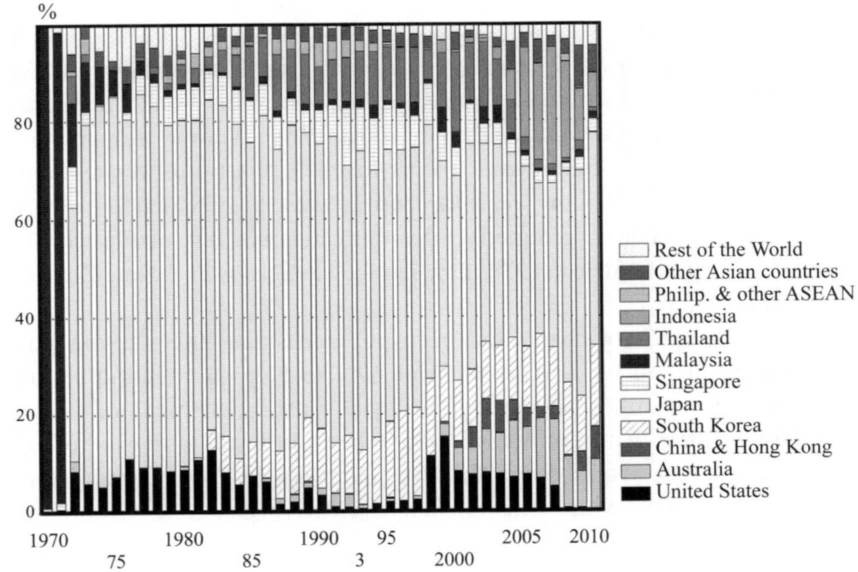

Graph 13. Exports by Destination Country, 1970–2010

(1) 1970–71: Brunei's sole client was Malaysia, or more precisely Sarawak, to which it sent all of its oil through the Lutong refinery.[26]

[26] State of Brunei, *Annual Report 1971*, p. 68; "Credit card debt to be curtailed", *Brunei Times*, 10 January 2010.

(2) The completion of the Seria oil terminal in 1971 (even after LNG had gone into production) freed it from the Malaysian hold: between 1973 and 1975, Japan became its prime client, with exports to Japan rising from 52% to 83%; inversely, Malaysia's share (already less than 12% in 1972) dropped to 5% in 1975 to the benefit of four "new" partners: Singapore (8% in 1972, 4% in 1973), Thailand (5% in 1972, 2% in 1973), Taiwan (accounting for "other Asian countries": 2%–3% of exports), and especially the United States (between 5% and 8% in 1972–74).

(3) From 1975–2002, diversification of prospective clients continued, this time to the detriment of Japan, whose share of exports fell by half (from 83% to 40%), and to a lesser extent, the United States, whose share fell to only 1% in 1988, rose to 10%–15% in 1998–99, then fell back to around 7%. This shift benefited neighbouring countries, starting with ASEAN members: Singapore (1% in 1976, then 5%–10%), Thailand (1.5% in 1979, then 10%–12% in the early 2000s) and Philippines, marginally (from 0.5% to 3%). Starting in 1982, South Korea's share rose from 4% to 12%, notably after a 1994 agreement on gas.[27] Finally, beginning in 1999, Australia's purchases reached almost 9% in 2002. When Taiwan stopped importing hydrocarbons from Brunei in 1999, the trade was assumed by India the following year. On top of these regular partners came occasional clients (grouped under the category "rest of the world") such as South Africa (1978–81), France (1979–84) and New Zealand (since 2000).

(4) Diversification of clients has been pursued since 2003. Japan's purchases did fall by a quarter (from 40% to 30%) between 2003 and 2007, but climbed above 43% in 2010, to the detriment of China/Hong Kong. And Indonesia, which became a net importer of oil, saw its share tripling in four years from 6% in 2004 to more than 20% in 2008, while Thailand's share fell below 2%. Geographic proximity played in favour of Jakarta, even if Indonesia's share decreased to 7% in 2010.

[27] Between Brunei Coldgas and Korean Gas Corporation, for a minimum of 50,000 t. of gas up to 300,000 t.

Regional Suppliers

The evolution of imports attests to a similar diversification, but this time to the detriment of developed countries:

(1) In 1970–71, Western countries—the current EU-27 (excluding former communist countries) and the United States—accounted for between 44% and 48% of the sultanate's imports. Japan's share doubled in two years (from 15% to 30%) to the disadvantage of Singapore, Brunei's traditional partner since its foundation in 1819, whose share halved from 16% to 8%. The remainder went to Malaysia, Thailand and Taiwan, the latter representing the "rest of the world" category in Bruneian statistics at that time.

(2) After 1972, Japan's share declined steadily until it represented only 10%–12% of imports at the end of the 2000s; in parallel, the shares of Europe and the United States (respectively 25% and 20% in 1972) fell by half. The exception to the rule was observed in 1993, when sale of equipment boosted Europe's share to 27% (thanks to Germany, which alone furnished 12% of imports) and that of the United States to 25%.

Taking over from the Western countries and Japan was Southeast Asia: Singapore's share climbed back to 15% in 1976, then to 26% in 1989, to oscillate between 20% and 30%, noting that the city-state played the role of commercial interface for a certain number of products.[28] Malaysia supplied 6% of imports in 1973, and between 20% and 25% since 2000. Other ASEAN countries (essentially Thailand and Philippines) supplied barely 1% of imports in 1972 and reached 10% at the end of the 2000s. And finally China (Hong Kong and the PRC), which rose from 2%–3% of imports at the start of the 1990s to some 10% at the end of the following decade.

The remaining 10% was supplied by two groups: "other Asian countries" (between 6% and 9% of imports), including Taiwan and after the middle of the 1980s, South Korea, which constituted three-quarters of the share except for 2001, when India alone furnished 6.5% of imports; and Australia, with 2% to 3% of imports after the middle of the 1990s.

[28] In 2011, 15% of imported transport equipment, mechanics and electronics came from Singapore (which has no automobile industry but deals with naval construction), 13.6% from the rest of ASEAN (essentially Malaysia and Thailand), 14.7% from Japan and 22% from the United States. See *Statistical Yearbook 2011*, table 5.7, p. 95.

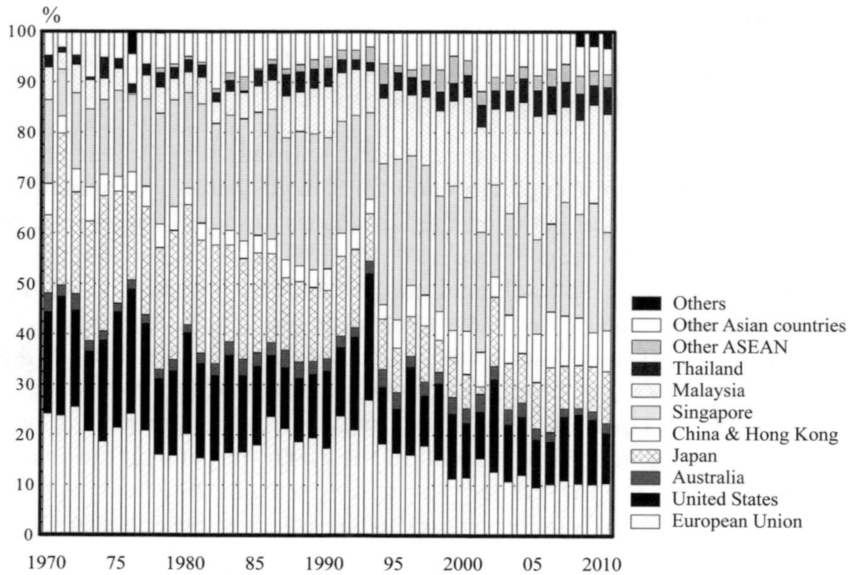

Graph 14. Imports by Country of Origin, 1970–2010

Three Rings of Partners

By founding its diplomacy on access to new clients for its oil and gas resources, Brunei has thus made foreign trade its favourite tool for regional integration. This arrangement has up to now taken the form of three concentric circles that are symmetrically inverse:

1. The first circle, in expansion, is formed by the immediate regional environment—ASEAN countries, with 14% of exports and 52.6% of imports in 2011, as opposed to 10% of exports and 25% of imports in 1975;
2. The second circle has been reduced to the dominant but declining partner of the periphery—Japan, 43.4% of exports and 7% of imports in 2011, as opposed to 78% of exports and 22% of imports in 1975;
3. The third, also in expansion, includes the "newcomers" of the periphery—China, South Korea and India, with 28% of exports and 11.5% of imports in 2011, as opposed to 3% and 9% respectively in 1975.

EVALUATING THE BRUNEIAN MODEL

To maintain this fine balance of commercial partners, Brunei needs to rely on the export of its hydrocarbons. Once petro-gas income falters, will Brunei possess sufficient rent to be able to nurture its GDP on the same bases? To answer the question, it is necessary to evaluate the surpluses accumulated by Brunei's economy, externally and internally. We can then formulate a hypothesis of the value and profitability of investment abroad, which can be refined by comparing the "Brunei model" with that of its peers, the small petro-gas states of the Arabian Gulf.

Internal and External Surpluses

Brunei's economy recurrently cumulates two types of surplus: externally, a balance of current accounts surplus, and internally, a budgetary surplus.

Balance of Current Accounts

The sultanate's balance of current accounts has been structurally positive since 1985,[1] but it has evolved in two opposite phases:

- A first phase of decrease, 1985–98, when it fell by four due to the drop in oil prices over 1981–98 and financial difficulties specific to the sultanate.
- A second phase of strong growth, when the surplus increased ten-fold over 13 years (1998–2011), led by the rise in hydrocarbon prices and the adoption of a tighter budgetary policy.

Despite the reduction by a third in the budget surplus in 2009, this latter trend is unlikely to continue: the balance swerved up again in 2010–11; following the border agreement with Malaysia in March 2009, the two hydrocarbon blocks CA_1 and CA_2 should come into operation by the end of the present decade, the sultanate keeping 90% and 25% respectively of their production.

Government Finance

To this first external source of surplus should be added a second domestic one. Brunei being without income tax, government revenue (c. 49% of GDP in 2011) comes essentially from taxes on corporate profits (c. 62%

[1] First available data.

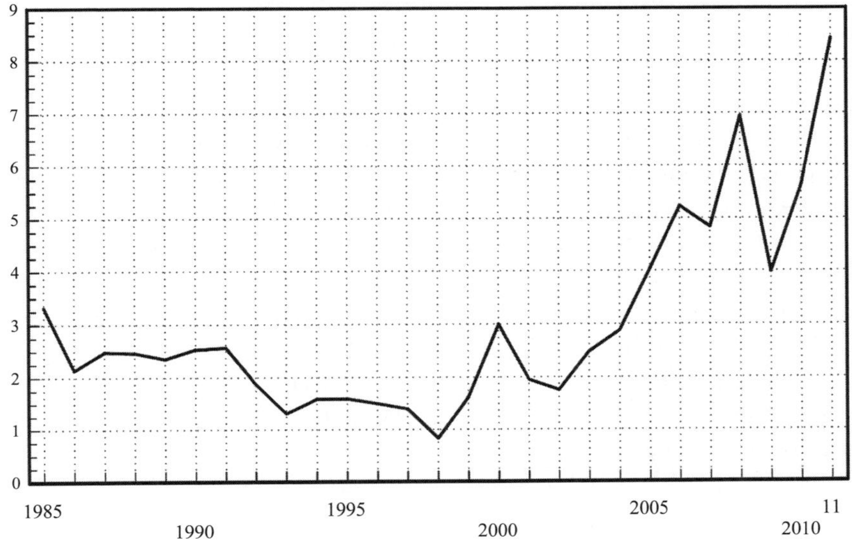

Graph 15. Balance of Current Accounts, 1985–2011 (billion US $) (Source: UNCTAD)

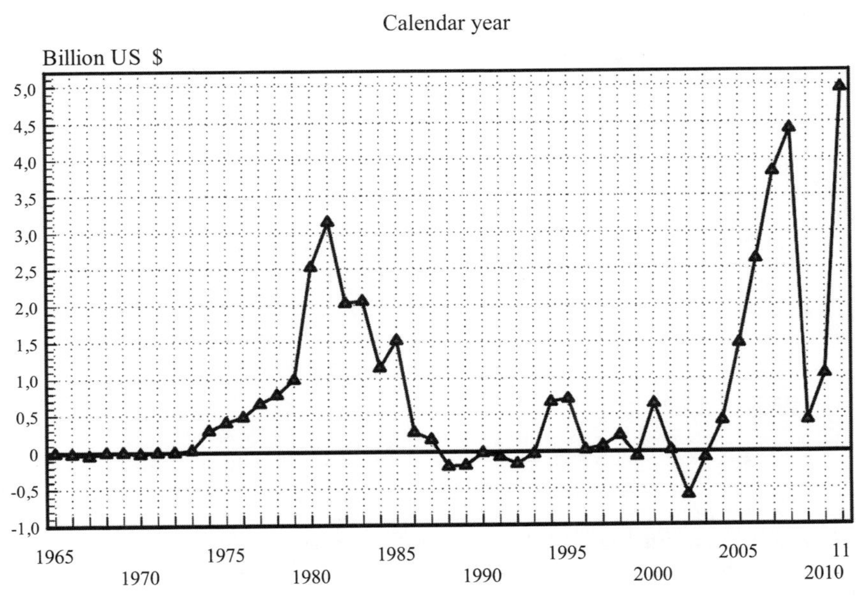

Graph 16. Budgetary Balance, 1965–2011

of government revenue) and from property income (38%); a little under half of the budget suffices to pay the salaries of government employees. Since 1973, Brunei has mostly enjoyed a comfortable budget surplus (graph 16),[2] thanks to the effect of the two oil booms (culminating in +US $3.14 billion in 1981), but the balance became negative again over 1988–93. Over 1994–97, there was a small surplus, which dropped slightly in 1999 (–US $0.06 billion). It dropped sharply in 2002 (–US $0.59 billion) but took off after 2003, rising to more than US $4 billion in 2011.[3]

Among expenditures are transfers made each year to Brunei's Development Fund (for a cumulative total of some US $11 billion at the end of 2011) and those regularly made to the Government Trust Fund.

Therefore the budget surpluses should be considered as net. Regarding the amounts already invested in the sultanate (of whatever origin), they must have been invested abroad.

---

[2] Data in B $ converted into US $ on the yearly average exchange rate.

[3] Given the shift in 2003 from a calendar year to a fiscal year running from 1 April to 31 March, the data have been recalculated on a calendar basis (the first three-quarters of the current fiscal year + the last quarter of the preceding fiscal year).

From Surplus to Assets

Accumulated Surpluses

Simple arithmetic—adding budgetary and current account surpluses (and subtracting deficits)—shows an accumulated surplus of some US $120 billion at the end of 2011: US $83 billion from current accounts and $36 billion from public finance. For the purpose of making a model and for the sake of simplicity, in the rest of this analysis all the surpluses will be considered as if they were placed in the Bruneian sovereign fund, the BIA, although this may well be an accounting abstraction, since the fund

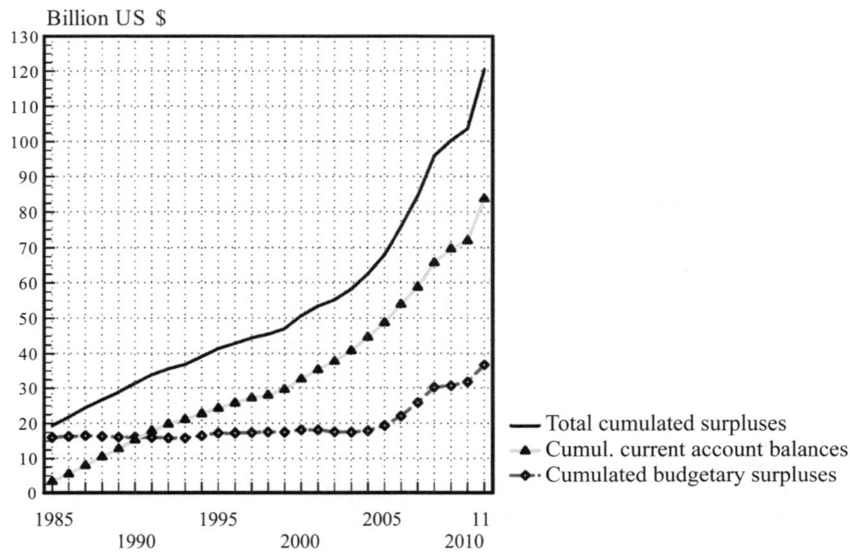

Graph 17. Financial Surpluses (Stocks), 1985–2011
(Source: Budgetary Surplus 2011. Estimate based on the first three quarters)

was described at the start of the 1990s as managing merely 40% of the foreign reserves of the sultanate.[4]

Accumulated, these surpluses at first doubled between 1985[5] and 1995, from US $20 to $40 billion, increased by only 25% between 1995 and 2000 (which evidently relativizes the "crisis" diagnosed at the end of the 1990s), and finally surged to more than double from 2000 to 2011 (from US $50 to $120 billion).

Estimating BIA's Assets

These data remains gross, however. To evaluate the BIA's assets more reliably, it is first necessary to deduce the amounts of withdrawals made under Prince Jefri's mandate (US $40 billion, which have been charged by default to the year 1995), then reintegrate the capital restituted at the end of 2007 (the minimum of US $13.5 billion paid back by the prince).

On the hypothesis that all the income generated by the fund was totally replaced in it, an estimate of the assets can then be made on the basis of the return of the capital invested. Taking into consideration the limits of the exercise, data have been computed as such:

(1) A "composite stock market index" (index c.) made of 1/5 from Nasdaq and 4/5 from Dow Jones has been calculated for heuristic purposes, on the basis of the annual variation of each of these two indices.

(2) The very object of the fund seeming to imply a preference for investment at fixed rates, this first composite index has been mixed with LIBOR, on the basis of interest rates applicable to credits of a year's maturity; and given the currency in which the hydrocarbons exports are paid, they are labelled in American dollars. Based on this, four hypotheses about returns on investment have been formulated, taking into account the composite index (index c.) and the LIBOR as follows: (A) 50% index c., 50% LIBOR; (B) 1/3 index c.,

[4] The remaining 50%–60% were split between eight banking and foreign financial institutions (Gunn, "Brunei Darussalam: Dynastic Fallout, Economic Crisis and Recovery?", p. 9).

[5] Sharon Siddique estimated the sultanate's foreign reserves at B $26 billion in 1985 ("Negara Brunei Darussalam: 'A New Nation but an Ancient Country'", *SAA 1985*: 107), an estimate officially contested by Brunei.

1/3 LIBOR; (C) 1/4 index c., 3/4 LIBOR; (D) 1/5 index c., 4/5 LIBOR.[6]

In 2011 (year end), the BIA assets can thus be estimated between 170 (rate C) and US $200 billion (rate A)[7] with some reservations, the BIA having numerous real estate holdings (in particular many hotels) whose value remains difficult to assess. If it seems reasonable to count on an average profitability of 2.5%, then the sovereign fund would be able to generate the equivalent of 28% to 31% of Brunei's GDP in 2011.

From Hydrocarbon to Financial Rent

Could the sovereign fund's revenue eventually contribute to the Bruneian GDP at the same level as hydrocarbon income during the 2000s (54% on average)? An extrapolation[8] from hypotheses about the value of BIA assets from 1985–2011, obtained on the basis of the four rates above, and of the country's GDP in current U.S. dollars suggests the following:

(1) In 2020, BIA's assets might totalise between US $170 and $230 billion, and the GDP represent some US $16 billion. Based on an average yield of 2.5% on capital invested, the BIA could generate income between 26% and 36% of GDP; for a yield of 3%, between 32% and 43% of GDP.

(2) In 2030, these assets would amount to between US $220 and $300 billion and the GDP would reach US $20 billion; with a yield of 2.5%, the revenue generated by the BIA would still amount to between 27% and 37% of GDP; and with a yield of 3%, they would amount to between 33% and 45% of GDP.

---

[6] Mode of calculation: surpluses banked in the year N + (surpluses accumulated in the year N-1 × rate A [B, C or D]).

[7] An estimate five to six times higher than that of Deutsche Bank in 2008 (Prometheus, *Mythe et réalité des Fonds Souverains*, February 2009, pp. 2, 9), which merely adopts, without citing any source, the figure of US $30 billion that appears in the specialist press, and without taking into account the fact that if the US $40 billion (Privy Council Appeal No. 69 of 2006) "special transfers" recorded in 1998 have been topped without too much hitches, BIA assets should then obviously have exceeded US $60 or $70 billion.

[8] For data relating to surpluses, I have chosen—with a view to profiling curves and the reality of the markets—to make a linear extrapolation; on the other hand, for GDP whose curve is exponential, I have used an exponential projection.

Taking into consideration the very nature of an exercise that relies on a double series of hypotheses about the capital invested and the returns, but which does not take into account the impact of any new oil and gas discovery on GDP, it appears that:

(1) Adding in the surpluses furnished by blocks J/CA_1 and K/CA_2, which were not included in the above estimates, the sovereign fund might very plausibly generate sufficient revenue to compensate for the disappearance in 2030 of deposits being exploited today;
(2) With the reservation that at least part of its revenue would continue to be reinvested in the sovereign fund after 2030 (which would obviously run counter to the very purpose of creating the fund, to take over from petro-gas income when the time comes).

Thus it is not obvious that financial income could wholly substitute for petro-gas income. Despite the slowness of the process, Brunei has good reason to engage in a diversification of its productive activities.

An Unusual Model

Brunei versus the Gulf Emirates and Kuwait

The Bruneian economic model at first sight might seem close to that of small oil states in the Persian Gulf and Kuwait. However, a comparison of economic, social and financial indicators of Brunei and the five so-called "emirates", expressed in the form of relative values (percentage of GDP, growth rate, inflation rate, unemployment rate, etc.) reveals the very different strategic choices (see table 1 and graph 18).

There are some similarities (see graph 18). Brunei's incidence of foreign trade (as a percentage of GDP) is in the middle of those of the five Middle-East states: deprived of warehouses, Brunei cannot compete with Singapore or even the ports on the west coast of the Malay Peninsula. As in the small Arab oil states, its nationals are mostly employed in the public sector (63%)—but less than in Oman (68% of nationals) and the other Gulf States and Kuwait (90%).

Table 1. Brunei versus the Gulf Emirates and Kuwait

US $/%	*GDP 2010 US $ billion*	*GDP/ capita 2010*	*GDP Growth Rate 2000–10*	*Hydrocarbons % GDP*	*Manufacturing Industry Excluding Hydrocarbons, % GDP*
Brunei	13.0	32,648	1.5	50.8	12.1
Bahrain	22.9	18,184	6.3	25.7	17.1
Kuwait	124.3	45,430	6.2	52.8	5.3
Oman	57.8	20,791	4.7	47.9	10.0
UAE	297.6	39,029	5.0	34.1	9.7
Qatar	127.3	72,498	14.2	52.2	10.6

Table 1. continued

2010	*Services % GDP*	*% Immigrants*[9]	*% Nationals Working in Public Service*	*% Unemployment (among resident workforce*[10]*)*	*Inflation Rate*
Brunei	32.4	35.1	63.0	2.7	0.3
Bahrain	59.5	24.9	90.0	3.5[11]	1.9
Kuwait	44.1	76.6	90.0	2.0	4.0
Oman	37.3	29.6	68.3	15.0[12]	3.2
UAE	48.0	43.8	90.0	4.0[13]	0.8
Qatar	33.3	74.2	88.7	0.5	-2.4

2010	*Curr. Account Net/ GDP (%)*	*Foreign Trade*/ GDP (%)*	*International Reserves/ GDP (%)*	*Inwards FDI** Stock/ GDP (%)*	*Sovereign Funds (US $ billion)*
Brunei	43.1	103.0	9.2	86.3	153.0[14]
Bahrain	3.3	140.7	19.5	66.1	13.8
Kuwait	29.6	86.3	17.2	5.2	296.0
Oman	8.8	93.0	22.5	26.2	8.2[15]
UAE	3.7	130.7	10.6	18.3	845.7[16]
Qatar	16.5	80.6	24.0	24.6	100.0

	Sovereign Funds/ GDP (%)	*Foreign Debt/ GDP (%) 2010*	*General Government Net Debt/ GDP (%) 2010****	*Domestic Credit/ GDP (%) 2010 *****
Brunei	1,176.00	10.6	0.0	25.1
Bahrain	60.2	64.4	34.0	75.2
Kuwait	35.2	43.8	10.5	66.0
Oman	24.5	14.2	6.4	37.7
UAE	284	43.5	27.6	92.3
Qatar	78.5	59.0	Net surplus: 92.3	70.4

9 World Bank Databank.

10 Including immigrant workers.

11 RAM, *Bahrain, Country Assessment Report*, April 2011, p. 4.

12 2004 estimate.

13 2008.

14 Average value.

15 Oman State General Reserve Fund + Oman Investment Fund.

16 Abu Dhabi Investment Authority + International Petroleum Investment Company + Investment Corporation of Dubai + Dubai Holding + Emirates Investment Authority + Mubadala Development Company + RAK Investment Authority (Sovereign Wealth Funds [SWF] Institute; Dubai Holding Commercial Operations Group Llc, Consolidated Financial Statements, 31 Dec. 2010).

Table 1. continued

	Foreign Debt/GDP (%) 2010	*Internet Users (%) 2010*
Brunei	10.6	50.0
Bahrain	64.4	55.0
Kuwait	43.8	38.3
Oman	14.2	62.0
UAE	43.5	78.0
Qatar	59.0	81.6

Notes: * Goods and services, ** Foreign Direct Investment, *** IMF, World Economic Outlook Database, **** Provided by the banking sector (World Bank)

However, by all the other indicators presented above, Brunei appears significantly different from its peers. Brunei differs from most of them (except for Oman) in its control of migratory inflows, limiting immigration to some 35% of the total population (c. 146,000 immigrants in 2010), while immigrants constitute 25% of the population in Bahrain, 44% in the United Arab Emirates (UAE),[17] 74% in Qatar and 76% in Kuwait. The explanation is historical: in 1962 the sultanate barely escaped from subversion and absorption into Malaysia, and since then the government has tried to maintain a comfortable demographic majority. Although strictly speaking, the Malay world (apart from Indonesia and the southern Philippines) has traditionally been a zone of demographic depression, the scarcity of workforce in Brunei means that the cost of imported labour is relatively high compared to the rest of Southeast Asia (except Singapore), making low-technology industries uncompetitive compared to rivals in Vietnam, the Philippines and China. Thus at the end of 2010, Brunei's economy remained poorly diversified: hydrocarbons generated 51% of GDP, significantly more than in the UAE and Oman, and more than double the figure in Bahrain; other industry contributed only 12% of GDP—one-third less than in Bahrain but similar to Qatar. Moreover, private services generate only 18.7% of GDP in Brunei.

[17] Immigrants accounted for 75% of UAE's workforce before the bubble burst in Dubai in November 2009.

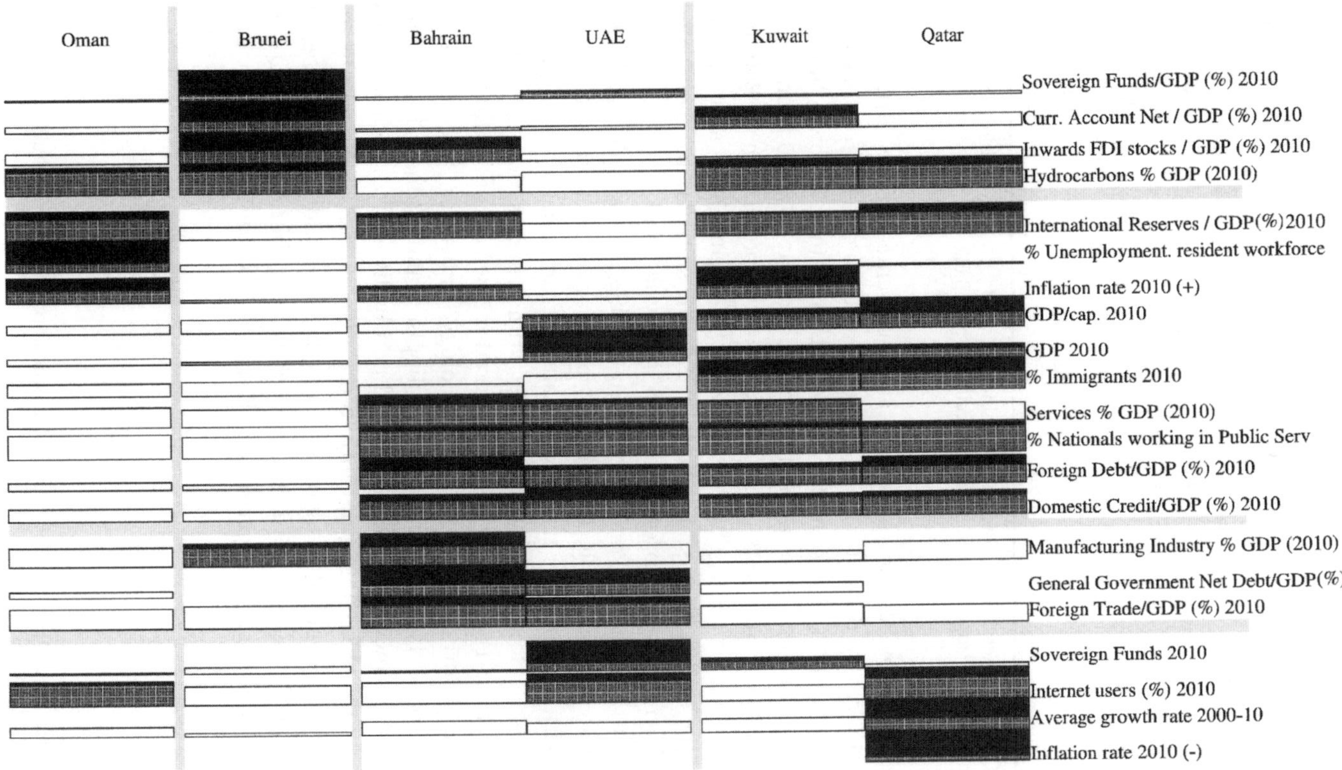

Graph 18. Brunei versus the Gulf States

(Data higher than the group average are in black, and lower figures are in grey.)

Moderate Risk-taking

Brunei is very distinct from its petro-gas peers in the moderation of its global financial risk. Inflation remains minimal (0.3% in 2010, as opposed to the range of 0.8%–4% in the UAE, Bahrain, Oman and Kuwait, and 15% in Qatar after its increase in 2009). Unlike Bahrain, government net debt is non-existent. Brunei could wait until March 2006 to issue its first bonds, which were designed for the regional Islamic bond market hitherto monopolised by Malaysia, and were issued more to assert the sultanate's religious commitment than to fill the treasury. Domestic bank loans reached only 24% of GDP, as opposed to 38% in Oman and 92% in the UAE (to give an extreme example). Foreign debt remains anecdotal, barely 11% of GDP, whereas it is two to six times more in the Gulf States excluding Oman (64% in Bahrain, 59% in Qatar). In short, Brunei's economy has a trivial amount of debt, both internal and external: its combined total debt is only 36% of GDP, with the qualification that this modest domestic indebtedness, reasonable at the national level, is inverted at the household level, where debt represents seven to eight times personal income. In January 2010, the government restricted the issue of credit cards to bank account-holders and banned their use to pay off other loans; the amount of monthly payments authorised is now a function of income.[18]

Inversely, foreign direct investment (FDI) in Brunei is quite high: inwards FDI stocks reached 86% of GDP at the end of 2010—one-third more than in Bahrain, compared to 26% in Oman, 24% in Qatar and 18% in the UAE, FDI being almost non-existent (5.2%) in Kuwait.

On top of this modest indebtedness exists a comfortable surplus from current accounts—43% of GDP in 2010—significantly more than in the most excessive "emirate", Kuwait (29.6%). The assets of the BIA (see above) could be estimated to be at least US $145 billion in 2010, or 11 times Brunei's GDP, while the combined seven funds (whose figures are available) of the most financially powerful state, the UAE, amounted to 284% of the GDP before the crash of Dubai World. Even in doubling this ratio to take account of some Dubai funds whose holdings are unknown, it would still be far from Brunei's figure. So while the Bruneian economic model seems relatively close to that of Oman (otherwise much poorer) in terms of the dominance of hydrocarbons, the percentage of

---

[18] EIU, *Brunei, Country Report*, March 2010, p. 12.

nationals working in public service and the level of immigration, in terms of sovereign fund, balance of current accounts and inwards FDI stocks (all three indicators in percentage of the GDP), it could not be more different.

But it is Brunei's choices in economic development that most distinguishes it from the UAE, Qatar, Kuwait and even Bahrain. These countries all make financial services—and correlatively indebtedness—a major axis of their development policies. By contrast, Brunei manifests caution vis-à-vis the local financial sector, which is partly explained by the past mistakes of the BIA and Prince Jefri, and favours the accumulation of surpluses, invested and managed abroad. The systemic risk presented by Brunei is thus very different from that of the UAE, whose total indebtedness (domestic bank loans plus foreign debt) reached 136% of GDP in 2010, with most of the risk still represented by Dubai, or (with growing concern) Bahrain (135% of GDP).

To sum up, Brunei's prosperity relies on both the hydrocarbon rent, whose durability is ensured at least in the medium term, and a "reasonable" development that combines slow production diversification and weak financial risk.

IV

ADAT ISTIADAT AND SOCIETAL MANAGEMENT

Seeking the Brunei Paradigm

Brunei has favoured social stability to the detriment of stronger growth in production; it has required that its nationals master the skills necessary for modernity in return for maintaining their demographic superiority. However, its massive investment in education has gone hand in hand with the reiteration of ostentatious rituals that the sultanate has preserved in their integrity, unlike most countries in the Malay world. How can the Bruneian state, which entered into technological modernity almost half a century ago and which has attained considerable socio-economic progress, hang on to such an archaic way of managing the social body? More precisely, how can a society that has free access to the material tools of modernity still cling without any apparent reservation, to such dramatisation of the monarchy, on top of a culture of secrecy and growing religious rigour?

Given that the sultanate's representative institutions—the Legislative Council (LegCo), composed almost entirely of members appointed by the sultan,[1] sits for only three-and-a-half weeks per year—are almost

[1] Since 2011, the LegCo has comprised 33 members who serve five-years term—the speaker, Pehin Isa Ibrahim; 14 ministers (including the sultan, both prime minister and minister of finance); three representatives of important sections of state and society (one *cheteria*, the mufti and the commissioner of the Royal Brunei Police Force); 7 persons who have "achieved distinction", all appointed by the king; 8 representatives of districts (*mukim*) elected by *penghulus*, village heads and heads of long houses from all 4 districts ("Voting to Elect LegCo members", *Borneo Bulletin*, 28 March 2011). Village chiefs, who must be male, are elected for a term of five years ("Bolkiah 'A' Elects New Village Chief", *Brunei Times*, 29 September 2008). Their terms can be renewed until they reach the age of 65—at the discretion of the sultan, with or without elections. Candidates must be between 30 and 60 years old.

identical to those of the smaller Middle Eastern oil states, whose democratic tropism seems equally weak, the answer must lie elsewhere. In fact, the heart of what seems like the veritable instrument of social management (considering the time devoted to it in the calendar year), is *adat istiadat*, which has become the brand of the "Bruneian exception" among countries that are equally culturally Malay.

To understand the terms of the problem, Bruneian society must be read from the inside. This entails: analysing the weight of its historical core, the Malay component, in today's population, both quantitatively (ethnic structure) and qualitatively (education and employment); evaluating the adequacy of *adat istiadat* for Brunei's social texture; and finally trying to identify the mainstay of the country's political paradigm.

Melayu Islam Beraja

ORANG MELAYU, ORANG BRUNEI?

Demographic Expansion

Multi-ethnic Substratum

Like most societies of the Insulindian world, Brunei is a multi-ethnic society gathering Malays, other indigenous ethnic groups from West Borneo and representatives of various foreign mercantile communities (Indo-Muslims, Chinese, Persians, Bugis, etc.).

To start with the "indigenous" (that is, Austronesian) and contemporary dimension, a dozen ethnic groups, with ethnonyms derived from the rivers whose estuaries and banks they lived on, were officially registered at the beginning of the 20th century. In addition to the Brunei Malays, the 1931 census (the most precise of the three surveyed before 1945) identified as "indigenous" the Kedayan, Tutong, Dusun, Belait, Murut[2] and Bisayah. Furthermore, it mentioned that the Dayak[3] were recent immigrants, while the Dusun and Bisayah belonged to the same group.[4] The 1947 census added to the ethnic listing the Melanau

[2] Or Lun Bawang.

[3] In Sarawak, Brunei and Sabah, the ethnonym "Dayak" refers to the "Sea Dayaks" who live along the coast or the riverbanks of West Borneo, the Iban of postwar sources (Benedict Sandin, *The Sea Dayaks of Borneo: Before White Rajah Rules* [East Lansing: Michigan State University Press, 1968]). Sandin is himself Iban, see the review of his book by A. Hudson, *American Anthropologist* 71 (1969): 945–6. See also Norman C. Scott, *A Dictionary of Sea Dayak* (London: School of Oriental and African Studies, 1956, 218 p).

[4] Bisayah and Dusun are two variants of a single group, see Victor T. King, "What is Brunei Society? Reflection on a conceptual and ethnographic issue", *SAR* 2, 2 (September 1994): 191–2, *dusun* meaning "from the village" (cf. Malay *desa* and Javanese *dusun* = village).

(numbering 100) and the Punan (only 30).[5] The 1931 nomenclature was adopted 30 years later by the Brunei government, whose 1959 constitution designated as indigenous (*puak jati*) the same seven groups as in 1931.

This ethnic diversity is the result not only of a dispersal of the habitat induced by the dense forest but also of linguistic (mostly lexical) specificities that, combined with elements of the material culture (habitat, activities, technologies, etc.), enable the ethnic groups to be differentiated. While in the 1990s, the Brunei Malays had 84% of their vocabulary in common[6] with "standard Malay" and the Kedayan[7] had 80%, the proportion was only 40% for the Dusun/Bisayah, 33% for the Tutong, 29% for the Belait, and 24% for the Murut.[8] Despite their close linguistic proximity (94% of the vocabulary in common),[9] the Brunei Malays and the Kedayan were distinguished by their habitat and economic activities: the former lived along the coast where they traditionally fished, while the latter were scattered along the rivers where they practised slash-and-burn cultivation. Today the Malays, Kedayan, Tutong and Belait are all Muslims, but this is not yet the case with the Murut, Dusun/Bisayah and Dayak, who are on their way to Islamisation (their cultures have been widely documented by Brunei Museum ethnologists).[10]

---

[5] Also called *penan* in later sources, *punan/penan* being the standard term used in Borneo/Kalimantan to characterise itinerant hunter-gatherers groups (Bernard Sellato, *Innermost Borneo: Studies in Dayak Culture* [Paris and Singapore: SevenOrients; Singapore University Press, 2002], pp. 56ff).

[6] For a survey of language in the first half of the 20th century, see Sidney H. Ray, "The Languages of Borneo, Sarawak", *SMJ* 1, 4 (1913); H.S. Haynes, "A List of Brunei-Malay Words", *Royal Asiatic Society Straits Branch Journal* [*RASSBJ*] 34–37 (1900–02): 39–48; H.B. Marshall, "A Vocabulary of Brunei Malay", *RASSBJ* 83–84 (1921): 45–74; G.T. MacBryan, "Additions to a Vocabulary of Brunei-Malay", *RASSBJ* 85–86 (1922): 376–7.

[7] For a discussion of the Kedayan, see P.M. Shariffuddin, "The Kedayans", *BMJ* 1, 1 (1969): 15–23.

[8] Peter W. Martin, "Some Views of the Language Ecology of Brunei Darussalam", in *From Buckfast to Borneo: Essays Presented to Father Robert Nicholl on the 85th Anniversary of his Birth, 27 March 1995*, ed. V.T. King and A.V.H. Horton (Hull: Centre for South-East Asian Studies, University of Hull, 1995), pp. 236–51.

[9] "Bahasa melayu dialek Brunei", http://melayuonline.com/culture/?a=bXVWei9zVEkvUXZ5bEpwRnNx=&l=bahasa-melayu-dialek-brunei.

[10] Norazah binti Pengiran Haji Muhammad, "Government mechanism for safeguarding intangible cultural heritage: Brunei Darussalam", Asia-Pacific Database on Intangible Cultural Heritage, Asia-Pacific Cultural Centre for UNESCO, Sub-Regional Experts Meeting in Asia on Intangible Cultural Heritage: Safeguarding and Inventory-Making Methodologies, Bangkok, 13–16 December 2005.

Demographic Expansion

Global Demographic Evolution

The colonial authorities carried out a census every decade starting from 1911,[11] but the data for 1911 and 1921 are still very approximate, as registry offices were not created until 1922. After an interruption due to the Second World War (the departure of the Japanese and the return of the British), counting resumed in 1947; a census was taken every ten years after 1960 and this was maintained after independence (1984).[12]

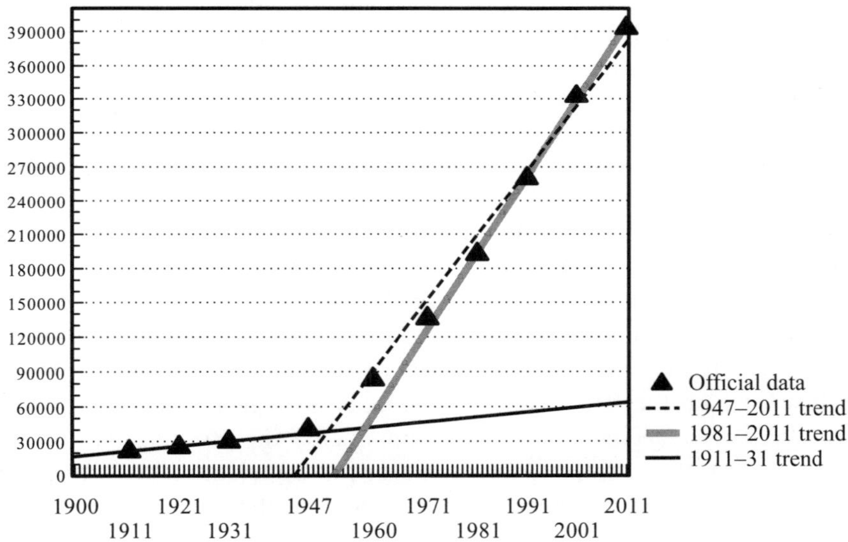

Graph 19. Population, 1911–2011
(Source: Censuses. Extrapolations based on linear trends.)

[11] For the years 1911–80, the present analysis is based on statistical sources collected by Jacques Népote since the late 1970s, particularly during a mission of ERA 855 conducted in Singapore, Malaysia and Brunei in 1981. See "Les grands traits de l'histoire démographique de Brunei (fin XIXe début XXe s.)", paper presented at Denys Lombard's research seminar, 1982, 7 f. unpublished.

[12] For an ethnic breakdown in 1911 and 1921, see *Brunei Annual Report 1911*, p. 11 and *Brunei Annual Report, 1921*, pp. 6–8; State of Brunei, *Annual Report 1938*, pp. 4–5 for the 1931 census and *Annual Report 1947*, pp. 4–5 for that of 1947; *Brunei Statistical Yearbook 1974/75* (BSB, 1976), pp. 6–7, for the censuses of 1911–71; *Brunei Darussalam Statistical Yearbook 2007* (BSB, 2008), p. 13, for those of 1960–2001.

It is thus possible to describe the evolution of the Brunei population since the beginning of the 20th century.[13]

The first thing to remark from graph 19 is the change in demographic dynamics brought about by World War Two. The relative flat curve of the first years of the 20th century reflects in human terms the decline of the sultanate. Not until 1960 (more than a century later) did the population catch up with its mid-1850s level (estimated at 25,000 inhabitants),[14] after the amputation of four-fifths of the national territory. Extrapolating from the trends of the years 1911–31, the population—which could be estimated to be about 17,000 inhabitants in 1900—should have been at most 65,000 inhabitants in 2011; it was six times as large, with more than 393,000 inhabitants. Overall, demographic growth has been six times faster since 1945 than during the preceding half-century; the sultanate's population has multiplied by 19 in a century.

In fact, the growth rate, which increased slightly between 1911 and 1947 (1.5% in 1911–21; 1.7% in 1921–31; 1.9% in 1931–47), almost tripled (5.3%) over the period 1947–61. The rate then diminished regularly until the start of the 21st century: 3.5% in 1961–71; 3% in the following two decades (1971–91); 2.5% in 1991–2001; and 1.7% in 2001–11.[15]

The steep rise of the demographic curve after 1947 indicates the combination of a high natural growth rate[16] (at least until the 1990s, with the birth rate not falling below 2% before 2005) and a positive migratory balance, which the Brunei authorities began to regulate as soon as they recovered their decision-making autonomy after the promulgation of the 1959 constitution. However, with a growing population, the closer we get to present time, the steeper gets the slope of the demographic curve, even with a falling birth rate: an extrapolation from the post-Second World War trend (1946–2011) would give a projection of 355,000 inhabitants in 2015, extrapolating from the short-term trend (1981–2011), 395,000 inhabitants, in other words, a difference of 40,000 individuals (almost 10% of total population).

---

[13] For the preliminary results of the 2011 census, see *Laporan Awal, Preliminary Report, Banci Penduduk dan Perumahan, Population and Housing Census 2011* (BSB: JPKE, 2012), 87 p.

[14] Horton, *Turun-temurun: A Dissection of Brunei Darussalam* (1998), p. 21.

[15] *Laporan Awal, Preliminary Report, Banci Penduduk dan Perumahan, Population and Housing Census 2011*, p. 3.

[16] Ratio of birth rate to death rate.

The Pace of Immigration

Therefore the immigration question holds a central place in Brunei's demographics. How did it evolve and on what basis? This is not an easy question to answer, for the most accessible statistics in Brunei[17] give no information about the number of nationals in the overall population, thus proving (by default) the sensitivity of the issue. At best, they mention the ethnic composition, although the definition of "Brunei Malays" and other "indigenous peoples" has constantly been modified over time,[18] with the former gradually incorporating the latter[19] as they become Islamised, while the latter includes a growing number of immigrants from Malaysia (and to a lesser degree from Singapore).

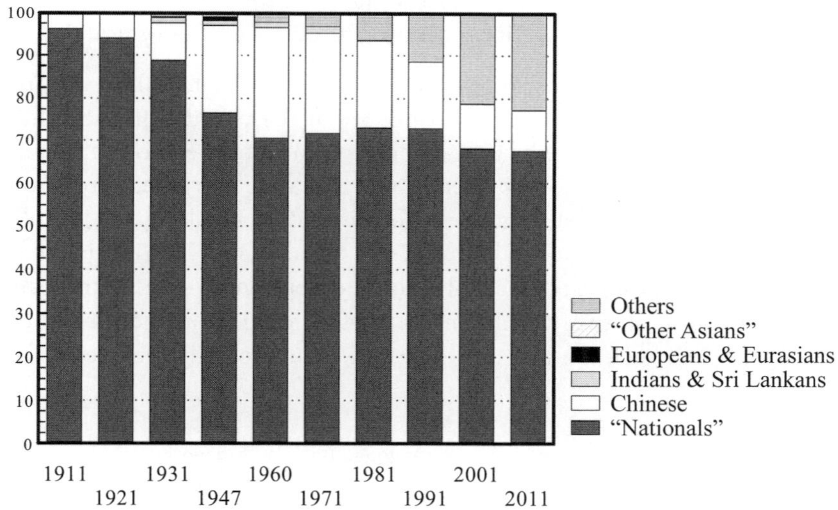

Graph 20. Ethnic Breakdown, 1911–2011, "Nationals" versus "Foreigners" (Source: *Annual Reports* and *Brunei Statistical Yearbook*)

---

[17] *Brunei [Darussalam] Statistical Yearbook. Brunei Darussalam Key Indicators*, published by the Department of Statistics, Department of Economic Planning and Development (JPKE), provides data relating to immigration only since 2008.

[18] See the change in definitions, in B.A. Hussainmiya and N. Tarling, *Brunei: Traditions of Monarchic Culture and History, R.H. Hickling's Memorandum upon Brunei Constitutional History and Practice* (BSB: Yayasan Sultan Haji Hassanal Bolkiah, 2011), p. 151.

[19] See *Brunei Statistical Yearbook 1974/75*, p. 6, n. 1; and *Brunei Darussalam Statistical Yearbook, 2008*, p. 13, n. 1–4.

This ethnic breakdown is complicated by the effects of naturalisation, which is granted to adults after a serious test of their knowledge of "Bruneian culture".[20] From 1962–2014, some 35,100 persons[21] have obtained Bruneian nationality, equivalent to 8.5% of the population, to which should be added the children of these new Bruneians. Very few non-*Melayu* have thus obtained citizenship—some by marriage with a Muslim spouse (implying conversion to Islam) and others for their deeds, among them some 7,500 Chinese by the end of 2009[22] (23% of new citizens).

Despite the lack of information about the demographic impact of naturalisations, it is still possible to read the data on the basis of official records by considering all "Malays" and other Borneo indigenous as "Brunei nationals". However imperfect the counting may be, it reveals the three phases of the evolution of immigration to Brunei (graph 20):

1. A first phase of almost 60 years (1911–69), when the share of presumed "nationals" decreased from 96% of the population to slightly more than 70%—a reduction of more than a quarter, to the benefit of the Chinese, whose presence more than quadrupled, from 6% to 26%. In parallel, immigration diversified, making graphically visible first the "Indians"[23] (1.2% of residents in 1931, including some Ceylonese), and then—but only exceptionally—the Europeans (nearly 1% of the population in 1947). Having abandoned their assets in Brunei, the heirs of the Brookes temporarily required more

---

[20] This involves not only a mastery of the language but also a deep knowledge of the culture, with questions ranging from poetry (*pantun*) to marriage rites and names of the various parts of the traditional wooden house, cooking recipes, etc. Many Bruneians of Malay origin would be unable to pass the test (Rozan Yunos, "Brunei Citizenship", *Brunei Resources*, 4 November 2006, http://bruneiresources.blogspot.com/2006/11/brunei-citizenship.html).

[21] Naturalisation became a little easier in the years 2001–06, with an annual average of 738 residents—16% more than during the preceding period (*Brunei Times*, 8 July 2007). Overall 29,658 persons were naturalised from 1962 to mid-2007, which would give a total of some 35,400 naturalisations by the end of 2014 at the rate of 2001–06. Some 7,505 permanent residents were naturalised from 1962 to 2009, mostly of Chinese origin (*Brunei Times*, 18 March 2010).

[22] Rao Shangdong (aka Niew Shong Tong, mand. Jao Shang-tong 饒尚東/饶尚东), "汶莱华人的本土化与归属感 *Wen Lai hua ren de ben di hua yu gui shu gan* [*The Settlement and Identity Perception of the Chinese of Brunei*]", ISSCO 7th International Conference, 9 May 2010, Nanyang Technological University, Singapore.

[23] Essentially Dravidians (Tamil and Malayalam).

British and Dutch (the latter to put the Shell installations back in operation) to recover them. A small Javanese community also makes it appearance: 165 in 1931, 234 in 1947,[24] which becomes slightly visible on the graph.

2. A second phase of 30 years (1960–91), when the percentage of Chinese in the population plummeted to 15.6% in 1991 (a diminution of about a third, which was due less to a drastic reduction in Chinese immigration than to the inverse effect of Chinese emigration out of Brunei). This did not benefit "nationals" (whose share barely increased, settling at 73% at the end of the period) but a new category, "others", which went from 2.1% of the population in 1960 to 11.4% in 1991, noting that this category now included Indians (several thousand of them), Europeans (several hundred) after 1981,[25] and by all accounts, the Gurkha regiments under British or Bruneian authority (c. 2,000–2,500 men),[26] and probably Indonesians and Filipinos too.
3. A third phase took place from 1991 to 2011, which saw a slight weakening of "nationals" whose share fell to 65.7%, a drop by another third among the Chinese (10.3% in 2011), and the appearance of the category "others" (corresponding partly to the development of immigration from Philippines and Indonesia), which have now reached 24%.

The British presence and later on the discovery of hydrocarbons both stimulated immigration, first (in line with what was observed in the Malay Peninsula) by the Chinese until 1971, then by "other Asians" (who made up the biggest portion of the "others" category), composed mostly of Indonesians (47,000 in 2010)[27] and Filipinos (22,000),[28] plus some Bangladeshis. The demand for resident visas by nationals (or "visa farming"), supposedly to increase their direct employees, became a very

[24] *Annual Report 1947*, p. 5.

[25] The 1971 data aggregates Indians with other non-Chinese foreigners.

[26] Eight to nine hundred "British" Gurkhas, plus two Gurkha reserve infantry battalions and their support, directly placed under the command of the sultan, estimated in 2008 at 2,100 men (Christopher Roberts and Lee Poh Onn, "Brunei Darussalam", *SAA 2009*: 68), plus their families.

[27] 47,368 Indonesians in August 2010 (*Brunei Times*, 6 August 2010).

[28] "Sultan Bolkiah commutes death sentence of a Filipino man, granting the request of Gloria Arroyo", *The Inquirer*, 1 February 2009.

lucrative activity. *Bumiputera*[29] (Malaysian autochthonous) immigrants, being included in the "*Melayu*" category since 1981,[30] swells the number of actual or potential nationals in the sultanate. Various professionals working in Brunei agree that the number of immigrants could easily exceed the figures found in official sources.[31]

Ethnicity and Assimilation

To understand the dual question of ethnicity and nationality, it is necessary to shift the focus from presumed immigrants ("foreign" ethnic groups) to the potential "indigenous" population—Malays and other ethnic groups called as such in official statistics.[32]

The 1911, 1921 and 1931 censuses recorded, in addition to Malays, eight[33] Borneo "indigenous ethnic groups": Kedayan, Tutong, Dusun/Bisayah, Belait, Murut, Dayak and Melanau. The 1947 census added Punan (nomadic groups of a few dozen individuals). These groups are designated in the graph 21-1 on page 213 by their initials; the first five groups could be characterised as autochthonous from Brunei.

The Tutong disappeared suddenly from official records after the 1947 census.[34] Their presence had obviously been under-estimated in these records since their numbers had dropped by 12.4% in 16 years (1931–47), while the Kedayan, with similar living conditions, increased by more than 14%. This statistical evaporation of the Tutong—which can only be explained by their incorporation into the Malays—was followed in 1960 by that of a portion of the other "indigenous ethnic groups" (the Dusun/Bisayah, Murut and Kedayan).[35]

From 1971–91, statistical records were thus limited to four groupings: Malays, "other indigenous" (non-Malays, meaning non-Muslims), Chinese and "others" (Indians, Westerners and other Asians). But the

---

[29] *Bumi* = earth; *putra* = son.

[30] *Statistical Yearbook 2008*, p. 13, n. 3.

[31] On the age pyramid in Brunei at the beginning of the years 1990s, see Warwick Neville, "The Population Composition of Brunei", *Singapore Journal of Tropical Geography* 11, 1 (1990): 27–42.

[32] See Roger Kershaw, "Ethnic minorities in late twentieth century Brunei, a survey of errors and imbalances in foreign analysis", *Borneo Research Bulletin* 41 (2010): 250–75.

[33] Grouping together Dusun and Bisayah, which are distinct in the sources.

[34] *Annual Report 1959*, p. 7.

[35] *Statistical Yearbook 1974/75*, p. 6, n. 1.

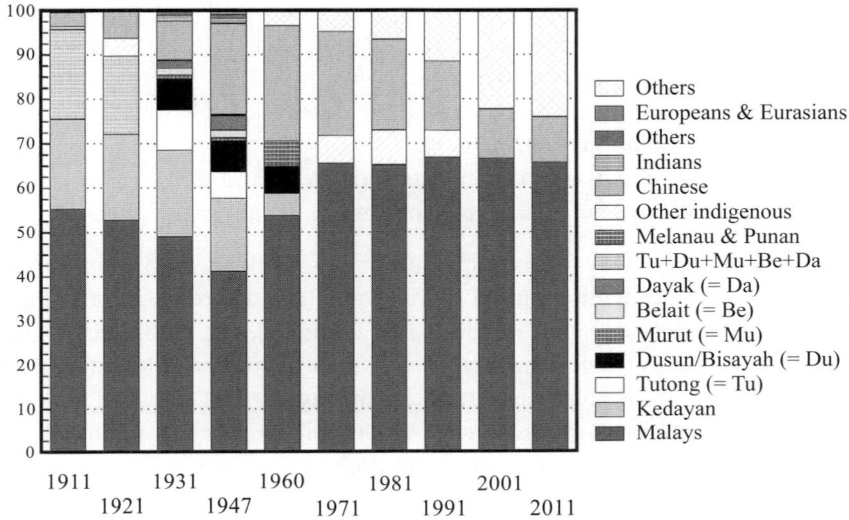

Graph 21-1. Population Ethnic Breakdown, Official Data, 1911–2011
[Source: *Annual Reports* (State of Brunei) and *Brunei Statistical Yearbook*]

relevance of the statistics is strongly compromised by the fact that categories and definitions changed from one census to another: in 1971, the remainder of the Belait, Dusun, Murut, Kedayan and Bisayah groups were included as "Malays", and the category "other indigenous" was not spelt out (it probably included the Dayak, who were considered as "non-indigenous" in the 1950s and so did not get the same treatment as other Bruneian tribes, plus the non-Muslim indigenous immigrants from Sarawak and Sabah). In 1981, "Malays from other countries" (Malaysia and Singapore)[36] were included in the same category as the Brunei Malays.

A last change occurred in 2001, when only three statistical "races" were retained ("Malays", "Chinese" and "others"), due to the merger of the two categories, "other indigenous" and "others".

A first graph (21-1) drawn from official data shows a three-phased evolution of the share of the Malays in the total population, bearing in mind the multiple statistical redefinitions of the category:

[36] *Statistical Yearbook 2001*, p. 9. The 1971 census mentioned the presence of 298 Malays born in Singapore (25.9% of all residents born in Singapore) (*Laporan banchi pendudok Brunei 1971, Report on the census of population 1971* [BSB: The Star Press, 1973], p. 54).

(1) The share of the Malays constantly decreased in the first half of the 20th century, from 55% of the population in 1911 to 41% in 1947.
(2) The successive enlargements in 1960 and 1971 of the category reversed the trend, by increasing the percentage of Malays to two-thirds of the population in 1971.
(3) New enlargements of the category in 1981 and 2001 ensured the stabilisation of the Malays' predominance at this same level.

While the prickly nationality question is avoided as the published statistics make no distinction between nationals and foreigners (although public service jobs are still reserved for nationals), the traditional elites are able to boost their undeniable historical mandate with statistical legitimacy: a comfortable demographic majority.

However, these figures are not as significant as they might seem, since they gather under the same label populations whose ethnic breakdown differs from one census to another. To get a clearer picture of the ethnic issue, it is thus necessary to start by evaluating the true demographic weight of the promoters of the Brunei state, the "ethnic", as opposed to "statistical", Malays of Brunei.[37]

Table 2. Religious Data (per cent)

	1947	*1960*	*1971*	*1981*	*1986*[38]	*1991*	*2001*	*2011*
Muslims	67.0	60.2	62.1	63.4	66.4	67.1	75.0	78.8
Christians	4.3	8.1	7.6	9.7	8.9	9.9	9.4[39]	8.7
Buddhists[40]	28.6	31.6	13.4	14.0	11.8	12.8	8.5	7.8
Others			16.7	12.8	12.7	10.0	6.9	4.7

The sources available are the four ethnic censuses (from 1911 to 1947), the annual natural (excluding immigration) demographic growth rates, and the totals by large masses ("Malays" and "other indigenous"), plus religious statistics (see Table 2). Knowing that Malays are all

[37] Statistical manipulations already pointed out by Roger Kershaw, "Ethnic minorities in late twentieth century Brunei, a survey of errors and imbalances in foreign analysis", *Borneo Research Bulletin* 41 (2010): 250–75.
[38] Statistical survey.
[39] 4/5 Catholics, 1/5 Anglicans (Mgr. Cornelius Sim, interview, November 2008).
[40] Animists, Hindus and followers of Chinese cults were grouped with Buddhists in 1947 and 1960.

Muslims, it is possible to reconstitute the evolution of Brunei's ethnic structure up to the start of the 21st century in a relatively precise way, through the following steps:

1. Estimate the diverse components of the "indigenous" population. For the years 1947–2001, based on the last detailed (in terms of ethnicity) census of 1947 and average annual natural growth rates (excluding immigration), and calculate by category for each census, and doing so for each census up through 2001. For the years 1911–21, proceed in the same way, but on the basis of the first detailed census, that of 1931, following a statistical regression up to 1911.
2. Estimate Muslim immigration by deducing from the total number of Muslims[41] (Table 2) data relating to Malays and other Bruneian Muslim ethnic groups.
3. The first estimate of presumed Muslim immigrants to Brunei remains over-evaluated because it includes non-*bumiputera* Muslim immigrants (such as Indonesians, Bangladeshis, etc.), who are already incorporated under the heading "Others" in official ethnic statistics.
4. Once these data relating to Muslim immigrants are integrated into demographic counts, the estimation of the total population (P4) is thus higher than that of the census (PR), as non-*bumiputera* Muslim immigrants are counted twice (as immigrants and as Muslims).
5. To obtain the correct number of *bumiputera* Muslim immigrants from Malaysia (and marginally from Singapore), it suffices to subtract from Muslim immigrants the difference between the population listed in official statistics (PR) and the totals previously obtained (P4).

On these bases, graph 21-2 shows a four-phased evolution of the so-called "indigenous" population:

1. A first phase of 50 years (1911–60) when the share of ethnic "Malays" (following the pre-World War Two definition) in the total population decreased by a quarter, from 55% to 42%. It is not surprising that the authorities, both colonial and local (the latter

---

[41] *Annual Reports 1951 to 1960* and *1971* (p. 11); *Brunei Darussalam Statistical Yearbook 2007*, p. 21.

culturally Malay), checked this decline with two measures: (a) demographic, by opening the doors to immigration from the British territories of Borneo and Malaya[42] in the 1950s (7% of the population in 1960); and (b) statistical, by partly absorbing under the "*Melayu*" heading in 1960 the six indigenous ethnic groups hitherto registered separately.

2. A second phase of 30 years (1960–91) when the immigration of Malaysian Malays, whose proportion tripled from 7% to 22% of the total population, largely compensated for the prolonged decline of the Brunei Malays (from 42% to 34%). Thanks to the former, the proportion of ethnic Malays rose from 46% to 55% of the Brunei population, so that they became a majority. A new statistical definition followed, incorporating *Melayu* immigrants into the "Malay" category.
3. A third phase of 20 years (1991–2001), when the share of ethnic Malays seemed to increase again—all the more as some 20,000

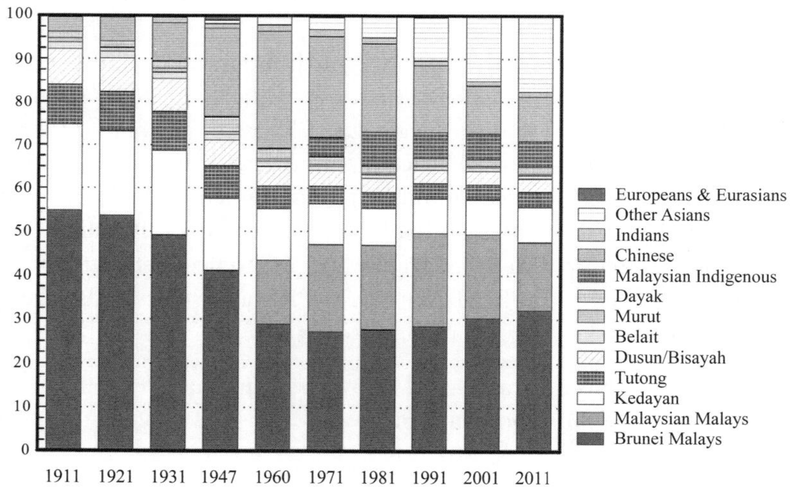

Graph 21–2. Population, Reconstitution of Ethnic Breakdown, 1911–2011 (based on censuses and demographic growth rates)

[42] This is evidenced in the annual records of entries and exits to and from Brunei, categorised by ethnic group until 1974. Since these tend to overestimate immigration, the only reliable estimates are still those of the censuses, as even local statisticians admit (*Annual Report 1970*, p. 16).

Malaysian Malays secured Bruneian citizenship between 1961 and 2001. Official statistics thus stopped aggregating new groups to the "Brunei Malays" following the definition of the 1991 census, the only new contribution to this category being other Southeast Asian Muslims (essentially Indonesians, plus a few Filipinos), or non-Muslim Southeast Asians (mostly from the Philippines). Their low educational level and specific religious practices means that the Indonesians are considered unlikely to be assimilated, while the Filipinos have the additional drawback of their Christianity or, for the Muslim minority, their presumed political risk (the Moros).

4. A fourth and current phase that began in 2001 and whose duration is unpredictable. Even if the share of Brunei Malays has risen slightly (from 30% to 32%), the share of ethnic Malays decreased anew to less than half (48%) of the population, while "other Asians" (two-thirds Indonesians, one-third Filipinos) has reached 17%.

To sum up, according to the previous data computing, 72% of Brunei's population would be identified by the authorities as "indigenous" in 2011, divided as follows:

- The ethnic groups considered as autochthonous would represent some 48% of Brunei's total population: ethnic Malays, 32%; Kedayan, 8%; other groups (Murut, Belait, Dusun/Bisayah and Tutong), 8%. It should be noted that the Kedayan (mostly city dwellers today) are hard to distinguish from the Brunei Melayu, and that the other groups are on the way to rapid assimilation. This implies that most of them now speak Brunei Malay.
- The Malays originating from Malaysia (and to a lesser degree from Singapore), would constitute a mere 16%, notwithstanding that half of them obtained Bruneian citizenship in the last 50 years;
- and the "others indigenous"[43] (Dayak as a whole, plus a few Bisayah and Melanau) from Sarawak or Sabah, 8%.

Behind the obvious manipulation of demographic data in order to play down the migration phenomenon and to inflate the proportion of "Malays" in the population of the sultanate, it is truly necessary to consider the distance separating Brunei from the concepts of state and citizenship imported by its British mentor. The statistical recording reveals

[43] In Brunei's demographic sources.

the unfolding of a cultural process of Malay-isation, which consists in grouping people for purposes of integration. The change in appellations is due less to a conscious desire to skew the data than to adopt political concepts specific to the Bruneian state, with the aim of refurbishing the traditional sultanate in terms consistent with modernity. This approach is reminiscent of the Indianisation process in which Southeast Asian populations, strongly heterogeneous, ended up adhering to the reference values of the dominant group (such as in Thailand, where only 30% of the population spoke Siamese in 1900). To understand the Bruneian society, it is thus essential to take into account all its components:[44] characterising oneself as "Brunei Malay" is as much the result of individual or familial choices as a political process of assimilation. Nevertheless, these racial identifications persist in the leaders' social framework, as attested, for example, by recruitment for the armed forces.[45] Moreover, the Dusun and other indigenous ethnic groups who have converted to Islam continue to be referred to as *mualap* (new convert),[46] a discriminatory term. The converted Chinese receive the same treatment, with a longer probationary period.

Subjects versus Nationals

The approximate 28.4% of immigrants officially registered in 2011 include: 9% of non-naturalised "Malays" (Malaysian and Singaporean); 8% of Chinese of various provenances; 1% of "other Malaysian indigenous"; 17% of "other Asians" (mostly Filipinos and Indonesians); plus a few hundred Westerners.

---

[44] Following the analysis of V. King, "What is Brunei Society? Reflexion on a conceptual and ethnographic issue", *SAR* 2, 2 (September 1994): 176–98.

[45] Royal Brunei Armed Force Recruiting Office, "Organisation and the role of the Recruiting Office, Royal Brunei Armed Force", 3 March 2009, Ministry of Defence website, which mentions on p. 2 that in order to be recruited into the Brunei army, one has to be either a natural-born Brunei citizen belonging to one of the following groups (Brunei, Belait, Tutong, Kedayan, Dusun, Murut and Bisayah—excluding Bruneian Chinese or Indians as well as Dayak), or else born in Brunei as ethnic Malay Muslim and naturalised.

[46] For the Dusun, see Kershaw, Eva Maria, *A Study of Brunei Dusun Religion: Ethnic Priesthood on a Frontier of Islam*, Phillips (ME), Borneo Research Council, Monograph series no. 4, 2000, ch. 11.

Permanent residents represent 6.6% of the total population and temporary residents, 21.8%.[47] The foreign population is split between roughly a fifth (23.2%) holding permanent residential status and almost four-fifths who are temporary residents. Permanent residents are either nationals of other countries or stateless, that is, born in Brunei of parents who were already permanent residents (almost all of whom are Quemoy Chinese) and possessing an international identification certificate.[48]

[47] *Laporan Banci Penduduk dan Perumahan, Population and Housing Report, Ciri-Ciri Demografi, Demographic Characteristics* (BSB, JPKE, November 2012), p. 2.

[48] They must pay B $50 each year for the right to enter the country and B $10 for a visa, for their comings and goings not to be subject to restriction (*Brunei Times*, 18 March 2010).

Education as a Recent Phenomenon

The evolution of different masses of the demographic structure takes on greater meaning when these ethnic statistics are correlated with data about education, which are qualitative in nature.

In Brunei, education is a recent phenomenon. Unlike the Buddhist kingdoms of the Peninsula where the dissemination of pagodas sustained monastic schools and enabled a diffusion of written culture (which contrasted with the heterogeneity of Buddhist influence),[49] and unlike certain Islamised states reputed for their literary tradition, the sultanate's culture remained largely oral until the arrival of the British. The decline of Brunei in the 19th century translated to the quasi-disappearance of indigenous scholars[50] in the 1870s, as they lacked the means to study abroad,

[49] To get an idea of the strong heterogeneity of Buddhism, see Jacques Népote, "Pour une approche sociohistorique du monachisme theravada—I. Les grandes tendances du monachisme", *Péninsule* 1 (1980): 94–135; "—II. La mise en place des signes du monachisme", *Péninsule* 2–3 (1981): 119–84; "— III. La résistance à la bouddhisation", *Péninsule* 4–5 (1982): 135–88; IV. "—Les marges statistiques relatives", *Péninsule* 8–9 (1984): 137–96.

[50] Brunei has some 626 manuscripts in Jawi: 135 in the *Dewan Bahasa dan Pustaka*, 110 in the Brunei Museum and about 400 in the national archives (Gunn, *Language, Power and Ideology in Brunei Darussalam*, pp. 52–4), not to mention manuscripts that may still be in royal or private hands. By way of comparison, the British Library holds some 100 Malay manuscripts, most of which are much older than those in Brunei, and Malaysia, 3,590 (National Library of Malaysia, *Malay Manuscript, Cultural Heritage of the Malays*, e-publication, http://www.pnm.my/collections/manuscript%20melayu.pdf, p. 3). However, if one divides this last figure by the number of sultanates in the Peninsula (nine), Brunei owns at least 50% more manuscripts than the average Malay sultanate (398), which indeed proves the existence of a solid tradition of scholars in the sultanate, which was in distress in 1904.

especially as part of the pilgrimage to Mecca.[51] And even if the trend was somewhat reversed in the 1880s, Brunei at the start of the 20th century possessed, other than a mosque, only a small number of *surau* or *balai* in Kampung Ayer offering learning of the Koran by rote, and no schools in the rest of the sultanate. The first "modern" primary school for Malays did not open until 1914; in 1918, the sultanate counted four primary schools[52] that taught in both Jawi and in Romanised scripts,[53] using textbooks and curricula conceived in the Malay Peninsula, including a course on religious instruction. A 1928 study revealed that only 12% of boys were educated in the capital. The following year, education from the age of 7–14 was made compulsory, on condition of proximity (less than two miles) to a school and only for boys. Religious teaching was introduced in Malay schools in 1931. Not until 1930 was a first English school established in Belait, and on the eve of the war (1938) a second one opened in Brunei Town. Because of their confessional nature, they recruited massively among the Chinese and Indians. Malays were for the first time sent to pursue their education in Malaya at the Sultan Idris Training College (SITC)[54] of Perak in 1930; in 1932, Pengiran Muda Omar Ali Saifuddin and two of his cousins entered the Malay College of Kuala Kangsar, where they completed their secondary studies at the end of 1936; others went to the Agricultural School in Serdang. This resulted in growing awareness of a Malay cultural identity (attested by the success of a theatrical genre perceived as specifically Malay, the *bangsawan*, and the development of printing), which would give birth a decade later to Bruneian nationalism.[55] In 1939, the sultanate had some 1,740 pupils, of whom 1.7% were girls.[56]

With the Japanese, Jawi disappeared from education to make way for a new transcription of Malay in the Roman alphabet that would constitute the basis of post-war spelling. Meanwhile all civil servants had to

---

[51] Gunn, *Language, Power and Ideology in Brunei Darussalam*, p. 65.

[52] In Brunei Town, Muara, Tutong and Belait.

[53] Programmes defined by R.O. Winstedt; Romanisation by R.J. Wilkinson.

[54] Among the former students of SITC are the current Pehin Mohd. Jamil al-Sufri, who studied there in 1939–41 and 1948–49.

[55] Through a variety of movements such as the *Persekutuan Guru-Guru Melayu Brunei* (PGGMB, the association of Brunei Malay teachers) and the *Kesatuan Melayu Brunei* (KMB, Union of Brunei Malays), presided by the *Pengiran Muda*, Omar Ali Saifuddin (Gunn, *Language, Power and Ideology in Brunei Darussalam*, p. 83).

[56] Rozan Yunos, *The Golden Warisan Brunei Darussalam*, vol. 1 (BSB: PDBPB, 2009), p. 170.

learn Japanese. To allow Bruneians to continue secondary school after the closing of the English college in Labuan, a college was opened in 1942 in Brunei Town,[57] which closed down two years later. The Japanese trained numerous teachers, notably graduates of SITC, and sent the most brilliant ones to Japan.[58] This laid the bases for the elites of the 1950s and 1960s.

Educational Stake

Mass Education, Girls Included

The period from 1950 to 1971 saw the start of mass education and the access of girls to the educational system. With the return of the British, 18 Malay schools reopened at the end of 1945. But Brunei had a considerable lag in education: in 1947, only 41% of males over the age of nine and 8% of females, a ratio of one female to five males (graph 22), could read. Once colonial institutions were restored, education became a priority, signified by the appointment of a British head in 1949, then the opening of a first secondary school in 1951. With the approach of the deadline for the end of British residency and the stirring of Malay nationalism, the first development plan (1953–58) strengthened education by increasing the number of Malay schools and creating a teacher training college (1956) designed to supply *bumiputera* teachers—hitherto they had been imported from Malaya—and to supervise their training. In 1959, the sultanate had 52 Malay primary schools and 8 Chinese schools, plus 8 religious schools and 3 public and Anglophone secondary schools.

However, more than half of the population remained illiterate in 1960 (graph 22); while almost two-thirds (64%) of males could write, the rate was only 29% (less than half) for females. Even if the percentage of literate women had almost quadrupled in 13 years, the sultanate still remained seriously backward. Subsequently the pace of education accelerated: in 1971, the literacy rate reached 65% (78% for men and 58% for women), and in 1981, it reached 86.3% for men and 73.3% for women.

---

[57] Led by the Indian V.A. Georges; among its graduates was Azahari, later sent by the Japanese to study in Bandung (Western Java).

[58] The most famous being the future YAM Pg. Setia Negara Haji Mohd. Yusuf bin Pg. Abdul Rahim, who after his appointment as a teacher at Miri (when he was 18), was sent in 1943 to Japan, first to Tokyo, then to Hiroshima, where he was living at the moment of the explosion, still alive in May 2014.

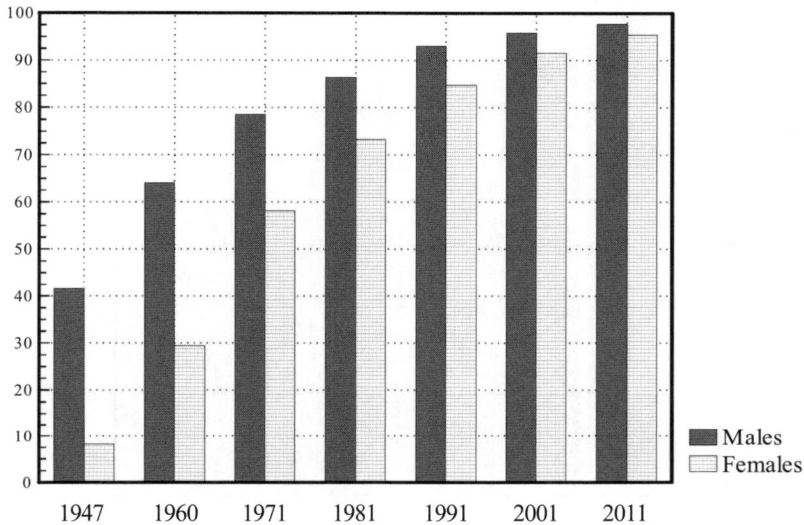

Graph 22. Literacy Rate, 1947–2011
(Source: Censuses and Ministry of Education)

The threshold of 90% was reached in 1991 for men (93%), with the rate for women hovering around 85%. The gap between men and women was reduced by a few percentage points in 2001, with a literacy rate of 95.8% for men and 91.5% for women. By the start of the 2010s, there was no longer any difference between genders in this respect.

Ethnicity and Education

Access to free education depends on nationality—today secondary school and university education is free for Bruneians, while permanent residents have to pay B $140 in school fees for college and between B $2,800 and $3,500 for university.[59] This discrimination is essentially a historical inheritance, for access to mass education did not take place at the same pace for everyone (graph 23), with "indigenous" (to stick to official categories) and Malays[60] showing a considerable lag until the years 1960–70.

59 Rao Shangdong, "汶莱华人的本土化与归属感 [The Settlement and Identity Perception of the Chinese of Brunei]", 2010.

60 "Malays" here includes the Kedayan, Bisayah, Dusun, Murut, Belait and Tutong; "Other indigenous" covers the remainder: the Iban, Melanau, Punan, etc. See above for the evolution of the statistical concept of "Malays".

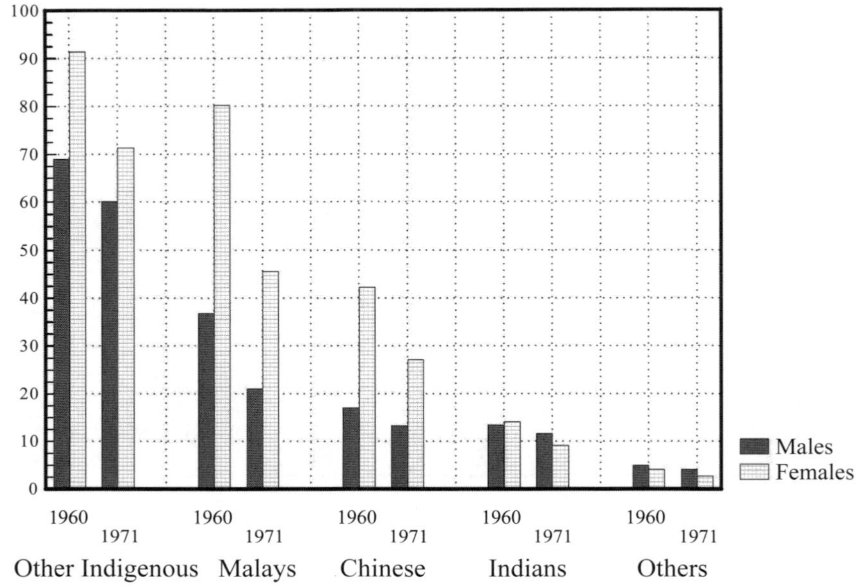

Graph 23. Illiteracy Rate by Ethnic Group, 1960–71
(Source: Censuses and Ministry of Education)

In 1960, 80% of the non-Malay indigenous population aged above nine was illiterate and among them, 90% female; in 1971, they remained very poorly schooled since 60% of the men and 70% of the women were still illiterate. This meant that schools had barely reached the peripheral zones—the coastal stretches between Muara and Kuala Belait—apart from the interior of the country and Temburong. For Malays, the situation was markedly better in 1960 for men, whose literacy was twice as high as the indigenous population, but was scarcely more favourable for women (80% illiterate). The education effort that got underway in the 1950s in the *bumiputera* milieu did bear fruit, since the rate of illiteracy among Malay men fell to 20% in 1971 and to 45% among Malay women.

Non-*bumiputera* foreigners, already largely literate in 1960, saw their illiteracy rate drop below 10% in ten years. Among the Chinese, illiteracy shrank from 17% to 13% for men and from 42% to 27% for women between 1960 and 1971, a level of education twice as high as among Malays. Educational advancement among Indians was even more marked, since their illiteracy rate (only 13%–14% for both sexes in 1961 —a third of the rate for the Chinese) fell in 1971 to 11.6% for men and to 9.1% for women. In fact, the Chinese who emigrated to Brunei (60% were Hokkien originating from Quemoy)[61] were mostly poor and uneducated, whereas the Indians, ten times less numerous in 1960, filled the intermediate ranks of colonial administration. The category "Others", which encompassed the Nepalese (Gurkhas), South Koreans, Japanese and Westerners, twice as numerous as the Indians, included a tiny fraction of illiterates, probably a few Gurkhas who had escaped the severity of recruiters.

Westerners supplied the upper echelons, and the Nepalese the basic military force, and thus it was largely Indians and Chinese who staffed the sultanate's administration in 1969–70. Although Brunei enjoyed greater autonomy and the principle of independence had been accepted since 1959, on the threshold of the 1970s native Bruneians (apart from the reigning family) were still unable to take complete charge of managing their society.

However, acquiring the instruments of modernity exceeded mere access to writing, for in a society undergoing full modernisation, management of economic activity required the acquisition of expertise far beyond the Malay curriculum defined by Winstedt at the start of the 20th century and adopted by the British in Brunei, which apart from the "3 Rs",[62] was content with initiation to hygiene and to a few basic crafts.[63]

In fact, the take-off of general secondary education started in the mid-1960s (graph 24). Over the decade from 1965–75,[64] the number of pupils more than tripled, but only doubled over the next 20 years (1975–95). Between 1995 and 2010, it only progressed by 50% (in 13 years)—half of the demographic growth rate over the same period (31%). Those who did not finish the general curriculum were directed toward vocational training, created in 1966. Pupils in "technical" branches tripled in ten years, quadrupled from 1975–95, then doubled between 1995 and

---

[61] Economic and Cultural Office of Taipei, Brunei.

[62] Reading, writing and arithmetic.

[63] Initially drawing and later, in some schools, gardening and basketry, the latter recognised for centuries as the finest craft artisanship in the sultanate (Rozan Yunos, *The Golden Warisan* [2009], vol. 1, p. 169; also Gunn, *Language, Power and Ideology in Brunei Darussalam*, p. 74).

[64] Asbol bin Haj Mail, Dr. Hj. Awg., "Persekolahan Melayu Brunei Darussalam 1950–1984: Perubahan dan cabaran [Malay education in Brunei Darussalam 1950–1984: Transformation and Challenge]", *Seminar Sejarah Brunei III, sempena Ulang Tahun Kebangsaan Negara Brunei Darussalam ke-22 tahun 2006* (BSB, 2006), 17 p.

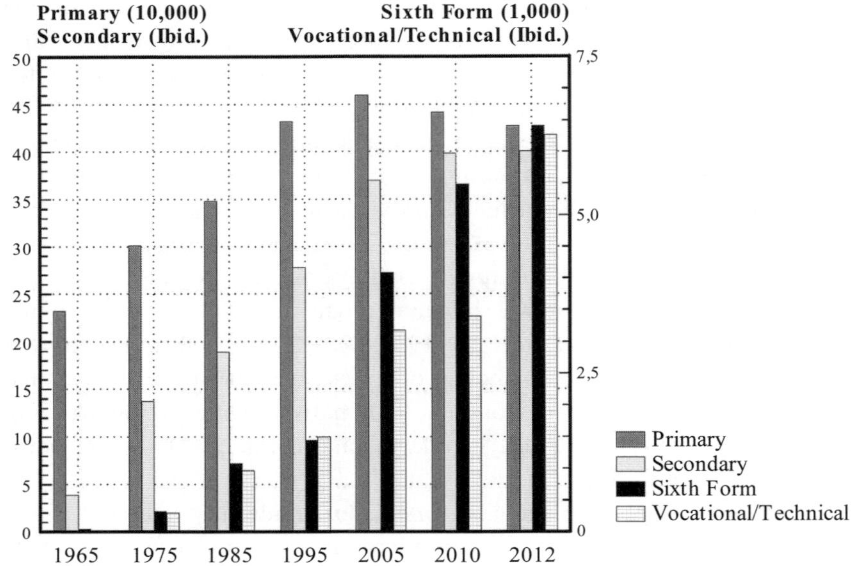

Graph 24. Enrolment by Level, 1965–2012

2010.[65] Today vocational schools welcome a quarter of the boys as well as girls.

While secondary education became general at the end of the 2000s, three problems remained:

1. Terminal pupils (Sixth form I & II) represented only 3.3% of those in secondary schools in 2001, which means that only one pupil in five finished general secondary curriculum;[66] the ratio reached one out of three in 2012.
2. Teaching methods did not evolve from that used in the *surau*, relying essentially on the memorisation of questions and answers[67] and not on critical analysis as promoted in the Western type of education.

[65] Today Brunei has four vocational schools that offer training certificates: Sultan Bolkiah Vocational School, Pusat Latihan Mekanik, Business School and Wawasan Vocational School.

[66] Given that there are six forms, if all the pupils reached the final year, then those in the sixth form I and II would logically represent close to 1/7 (14%) of all secondary enrolment (Sources: *Statistical Yearbook* for the Year 2000-12).

[67] Gunn, *Language, Power and Ideology in Brunei Darussalam*, pp. 171ff.

3. Most importantly, the educational system ran up against a cascade of language barriers, aggravated by the generalisation of English bilingual teaching in 1984.[68]

Multiple Diglossia

Since the 1959 Constitution, the official language has been Malay (*bahasa Melayu*); in 1983, Brunei adopted the Romanised spelling used in both Indonesia and Malaysia.[69] The decree on citizenship in 1961 requires the passing of a stiff examination in Malay.[70] The bureau of language and literature also launched the promotion of Jawi, the use of which became official in 1988.

However, the native vehicular language of Brunei is not Malay but *bahasa Brunei*,[71] whose pronunciation and enunciation differ significantly from standard Malay. Paradoxically, the Chinese, who have settled for several generations in Brunei and whose schooling took place in Malay, are better masters of Malay than native Bruneians,[72] whose language is furthermore contaminated by local dialects. The situation is rendered all the more complex by the Court's requirement to use the royal language, *bahasa dalam*,[73] the difficult and delicate mastery of which is a mark

[68] Noor Azam, *The Evolution of Multilingualism in Brunei*, The Language Centre, Department of English Language & Applied Linguistics, Universiti Brunei Darussalam [ca. 2005], 17 p.

[69] Set up in 1972 in both countries.

[70] Rozan Yunos, "Brunei Citizenship", *Brunei Resources*, 4 November 2006, http://bruneiresources.blogspot.com/2006/11/brunei-citizenship.html); see note 18.

[71] Bahasa Brunei might itself be defined as an ensemble of dialects; see Ataim Bakar, *Morfologi dialek Brunei: satu tinjauan kajian lampau* [*Morphology of the Brunei dialect: a survey*] (BSB: DBPB, 2000), 152 p; Jaludin Chuchu, *Morphology of Brunei Malay* (Bangi: Universiti Kebangsaan Malaysia, 2000), 162 p; H.S. Haynes, "A List of Brunei-Malay Words", *RASSB* 34–7 (1900–02): 39–48; *Kamus Bahasa Melayu Brunei* [*Dictionary of the Brunei Malay*] (BSB: DBP, 2nd ed., 2007).

[72] Lim Jock Seng, *The Inter-Relationship of Technology, Economy and Social Organisation in a Fishing Village in Brunei* (BSB: Brunei Museum Monography no. 6, 1986), p. 33.

[73] See, for example, the document titled "*Bahasa Dalam*, Part of Court Language" that was prepared by the Jabatan Adat Istiadat Negara (Bureau of National Tradition and Custom) and distributed to all foreign diplomatic staff in 2008. This is not as unusual as it may seem, for the use of court language is not specific to Malay but exists in all Southeast Asian kingships. In Thailand, the directives of the Central Bank are still written in royal language, requiring the specialised bank services to translate

of status. Add to this various kinds of Malay speech, and the fact that English has become the default vehicular language of the elite and is broadcast by the media through the mouths of presenters who are not native English speakers. Of the many languages of immigration, only Mandarin Chinese[74] was widely taught. The result is that apart from the Singaporeans and Indians whose forefathers had settled in the sultanate, only Bruneians who have studied abroad are really bilingual in English and their mother tongue. The sole vehicular language that is really mastered by *bumiputera* nationals is the Brunei dialect,[75] which is unwritten.[76] In short, the linguistic landscape resembles that of Singapore.

Training Elites

Channels to Success

Despite its small population, the sultanate wanted not only to generalise secondary schools but also to form modern elites. The first channel was teacher training, whose content became more demanding over time, ending with its integration into higher education in 1985. This was followed three years later by the creation of a Faculty of Education within the Universiti Brunei Darussalam (UBD). Between 1965 and 1975, the number of apprentice teachers doubled from 300 to 600. It stabilised for 30 years at around 400 plus candidates, then doubled again between

them into ordinary language. Similarly, in Cambodia, after the restoration of the monarchy in 1993, King Sihanouk reminded the country of the need to re-learn royal vocabulary (for a description of this vocabulary in ancient Khmer, see Suppya Nut, *Étude du Vocabulaire royal khmer* [Université Sorbonne Nouvelle-Paris III: Master thesis, 1995], 62 p).

[74] Bruneian Chinese have the same desire for linguistic homogeneity as native Bruneians. Influenced by Singapore and by radio broadcasts (which used to combine Hokkien, Cantonese and Mandarin), they have started to broadcast exclusively in Mandarin since 1983 (Gunn, *Language, Power and Ideology in Brunei Darussalam*, pp. 198ff).

[75] See especially P. Martin, "Brunei Malay and *Bahasa Melayu*: A Sociolinguistic Perspective", in *Language Use and Language Change in Brunei Darussalam*, ed. W. Martin, Conrad Ozóg and Gloria Poedjosoedarmo (Athens: Ohio University Center for International Studies, 1996), pp. 27–36.

[76] As mentioned in the article "Bruneians", *Brunei Resources*, 28 July 2006, which enumerates 69 distinctive traits of Bruneian: "40% have bad *bahasa melayu* even though you have been studying it for your whole life".

2005 and 2010. In parallel, the creation of three technical institutes after 1988[77] opened up vocational courses destined for industry, in addition to the upgrading of paramedical training.

But generally speaking, it was the university that was called upon to form the modern functionaries of the sultanate (graph 25). While the first intake of UBD in 1985 was only 176 students, the number increased tenfold in ten years (1995) and more than doubled over the subsequent decade (1995–2005), before stabilising around 3,500 (bearing in mind that UBD included the Faculty of Education, which trains most teachers, after 1988). Brunei has been endowed with a second university since 2007, Universiti Islam Sultan Sharif Ali (UNISSA), with an enrolment of 478 in 2010, where learning is conducted in Malay and Arabic. It is an option for students who cannot enter the Sultan Haji Omar Ali Saifuddin Institute of Islamic Studies at UBD.

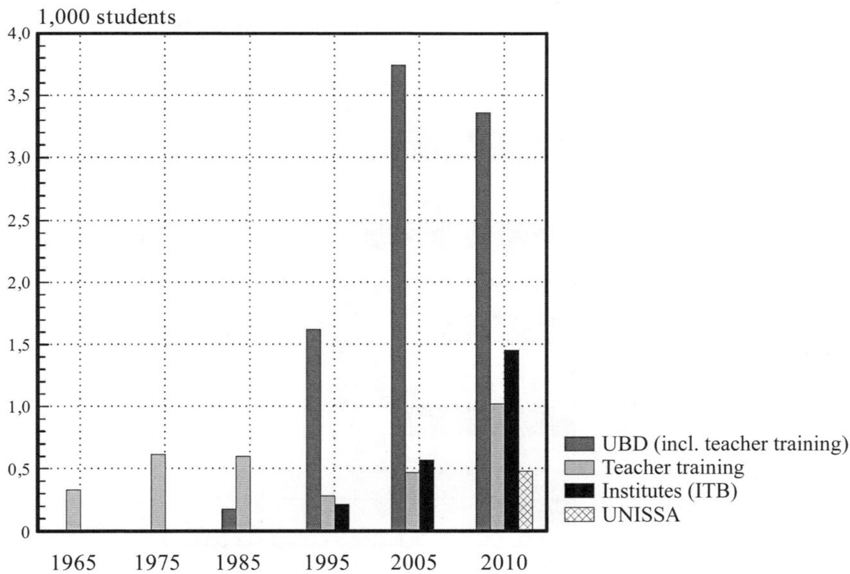

Graph 25. Tertiary Education, 1965–2010

[77] Sultan Saiful Rijal Technical College and Jefri Bolkiah College of Engineering are at the sixth-form level; the Institut Teknologi Brunei (ITB) is higher-level.

Female Predominance

The new elites formed through this channel are overwhelmingly female. Some 60% of pupils in the final year of secondary schools are girls. Some of them are headed for traditionally female jobs like nursing or midwifery, where they represent almost four-fifths of the staff. More surprisingly, in various technological institutes (apart from paramedics), where boys formed the majority until 2007, girls have edged into the majority (51%) in 2010. More encouraging still, although the access of girls to education met with much resistance, girls were actually more than twice as numerous (69%)[78] as boys at the university in 2010. The university is by far the prime site for the "gestation" of modern elites, with 2.5 times more students than Institut Teknologi Brunei (ITB) and ten times more than the nursing school. Moreover, to the sultanate's student body should be added about 2,000 scholarship holders (60% of whom are females), whose studies abroad are financed by the government. Upon their return, these scholars constitute Brunei's intellectual elite.

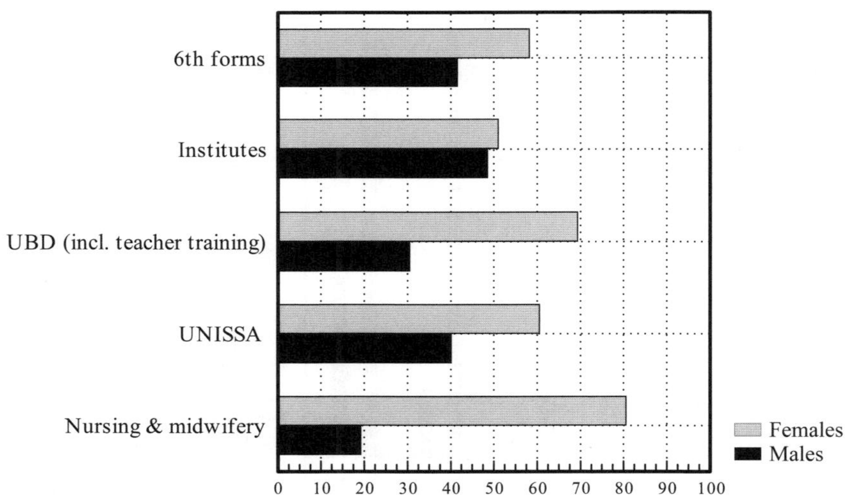

Graph 26. Tertiary Education and Sixth Forms, Breakdown by Gender, 2010 (%)

[78] Azman Ahmad and Azri Kifle, *Country Report, Brunei Darussalam: Quality Assurance for Higher Education*, 21st SEAMEO RIHED Governing Board Meeting, Bangkok, 21–22 September 2010, 12 p.

Malays = Civil Servants

Although women represent more than two-thirds of the graduates educated in Brunei, they made up only 49% of the total active population having residential status (permanent residents and nationals combined) in 2010. If the relatively high rate of female employment (compared to 46% in the United Kingdom)[79] attests to the speed of social change, it also reveals the end of a form of discrimination against women in public administration—by 2011 they occupied 51% of jobs, mostly reserved for nationals.[80] On the other hand, women represented only 27% of the total workforce in the private sector in 2010.[81]

Employment and Ethnicity

These figures are not sufficient to describe Brunei's labour market, which is highly dependent on importing manpower, judging from the census of 2001 (whose results will probably barely differ from the 2011 census which have not yet been fully published). Due to the sultanate's migration policy, nationals represented in 2011[82] 46.8% of the active population; permanent residents 7%, and temporary residents 46.2%.

According to the data available in the 2001 Census,[83] certain kinds of jobs appear to be reserved for Malays regardless of their citizenship

[79] EUROSTAT, http://www.insee.fr/fr/themes/document.asp?ref_id=T12F039 [accessed 1 Aug. 2012).

[80] *Brunei Darussalam Statistical Yearbook 2011*, p. 55.

[81] Ibid., pp. 47–8.

[82] Including employment in the private sector, in the security forces (around 5,700 men in the army and 2,500 men in the police force), and in the government.

[83] Most of the results of the 2011 Census had not yet been published by the time of the completion of the book in early 2015.

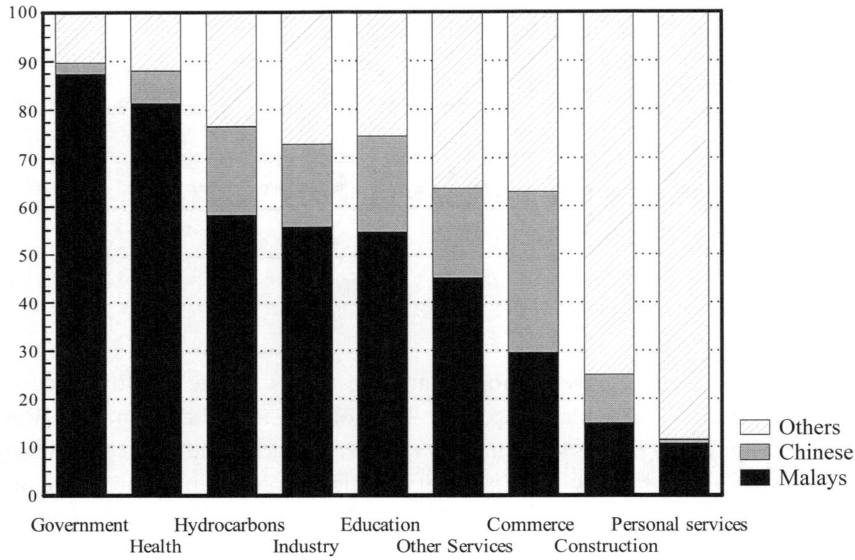

Graph 27. Employment and Ethnicity, 2001 Census

(graph 27): public administration and defence, where they occupy almost 90% of posts, and health (80%). This holds true too, although less perceptibly, in hydrocarbons, industry and education, where they occupy between 50% and 60% of the jobs. The participation of Malays falls to 45% in "other services",[84] to 30% in commerce and 15% in construction. Despite the sultanate's considerable efforts in education, Malays occupy barely more than half of the jobs in the key sectors of Bruneian development, industry and services, and are hardly more present in the sector generating most of the sultanate's income—hydrocarbons. Therefore, while 30% of the Chinese residing in the sultanate were still engaged in 2001 in traditional activities such as retail trade and crafts, 30% held skilled jobs and another 25% had highly qualified jobs (professionals and upper management, key posts being reserved for Chinese with Bruneian nationality), notably in the financial sector, although banking regulations limit the employment of foreigners to half of the workforce.[85]

[84] Tourism, transport, finance, real estate, and public and private services, apart from household staff.

[85] Rao Shangdong, "汶莱华人的本土化与归属感 *Wen Lai hua ren de ben di hua yu gui shu gan [Localisation and Perception of Identity of the Brunei Chinese]*", p. 4.

More generally, Bruneian nationals still represent only 25.7% of employment in the private sector in 2010:[86] there is a real problem of adequacy between the educational system, particularly higher education, and the sultanate's labour needs.

A Plethora of Administration

Thus in 2010, 74% of the jobs in the private sector (hydrocarbons included) was occupied by foreigners.[87] Inversely, the public service, strictly speaking, which provided 30.4% of all jobs in 2011,[88] was the employer of 64% of the population who are effectively active[89] and of Bruneian nationality, that is to say, of almost all Bruneian Malays. Moreover, to palliate a possible rise in unemployment among nationals, the administration has constantly created government jobs: for example, it increased its staff by 9.2% in five years (2007–11), by more than 1% per year (3.1% in 2011 alone). With 1 civil servant[90] (excluding the security forces) for every 12.4 inhabitants (infants included) in 2011, the government is tremendously overstaffed, which considerably slows down its functioning and seriously hampers its efficacy.[91] One illustration (among many others) is the underspending of budgets granted by the development plans: 55% for the Sixth Plan (1991–95), 64% for the Seventh Plan (1996–2000), 25% for the Eighth Plan (2001–06) and 43% for the Ninth Plan[92] (2007–12).

[86] *Statistical Yearbook 2011*, table 2.9, p. 55.

[87] Ibid., pp. 48–9.

[88] Including military and police; the total active population (apart from jobseekers) was estimated to 182,700 persons in 2011, *Statistical Yearbook 2011*, table 2.2, p. 34.

[89] Some 89,000 persons in 2011.

[90] On the payroll of the various ministries.

[91] For a toned-down assessment of the question, see "Dynamic and Sustainable Development in Brunei Darussalam's Civil service in the Era of Globalisation", Country Paper for the 11th ASEAN Conference on Civil Service Matters (ACCSM), Hanoi, 2001, http://www.bruneiresources.com/pdf/accsm11_brunei_countrypaper.pdf; and between the lines, Azaharaini Hj. Mohd Jamil, "Performance Management in the Brunei Civil Service; Issues and Challenges", BSB, 52nd Europa Seminar, 14–17 November 2006.

[92] Between the fiscal years 2007 and 2011, B $4.095 was spent on development, out of the B $9.5 billion allocated to the 9th Development Plan.

ADAT ISTIADAT

The Malay takeover of the civil service, like the gradual acquisition of material comfort by most nationals since the 1950s, could not, however, guarantee the preservation of consensus. The decay of the sultanate in the 19th century and the territorial losses that followed, and the British residency in the 20th century, had dissociated the foundations of governing, which once operated through the land-riverine rights, *kerajaan*, *kuripan* and *tulin*, from those of kingship. As soon as they had the means to do so, sovereigns tried to restore a direct link with the people on the symbolic level—by restoring a royal tradition that had fallen into decrepitude. They reactivated and "improved"[1] ancient rituals by systematically collecting documentation about palatine customs, drawn from both Malay sources and Western writing, to invoke practices going back to Malacca. For example, to reconstruct the *Lapau* (ceremonial hall), destroyed during the Second World War, they looked to the sketches in Frank S. Marryat's book for inspiration.[2] In general, they made the ostentation of the social hierarchy an instrument of the integration of modern elites into traditional sociology, thereby reconciling the modernisation of the state apparatus with the maintenance of the symbolic order inherent in such curial systems.

---

[1] "*Adat istiadat Diraja itu [...] hendaklah dibisaikan, dielokkan dan diperbaiki* [*The custom of the Kingdom [...] should be embellished, groomed, and improved*]", Pehin Dr. Hj. Mohd. Jamil al-Sufri, *Adat istiadat diraja Brunei* (BSB: Jabatan Adat Istiadat Negara, 2002), frontispiece.

[2] *Borneo and the Indian Archipelago: With Drawings, Costumes and Scenery* (London: Longman, Brown & Green, 1848), p. 110. J. Népote, interview, *Jawatan Adat Istiadat*, 26 September 1981.

Evolution of Royal Custom

Starting in 1954, Sultan Omar Ali Saifuddin III engaged in a redeployment of monarchical symbolism,[3] establishing a department of customs (*adat istiadat*), religious affairs and social protection, which he made explicit three years later in 1957 in a first rescript (*titah*).[4] It is likely that nascent awareness of Bruneian identity and the necessity of political reconstruction as a preliminary for eventual independence played a determining role in the operation. The layout of royal custom was confided to Pg. Mohamed Yusuf,[5] at the time responsible for information and former vice-president of the nationalist movement BARIP.[6] He compiled a first series of written and oral information about *adat istiadat* with the stated objective of improving, enriching and reorganising it, without "modifying its foundations"[7]—in the very same terms as the sultan's speech. The work was published in Jawi (Arabo-Malay) in 1958,[8] a year before domestic autonomy and its constitutional corollary, which

[3] "Role of *Adat Istiadat Negara* Department", Powerpoint presentation to diplomatic staff, 2009.
[4] Pehin Dr. Hj. Mohd. Jamil al-Sufri, *Adat istiadat diraja Brunei.*
[5] He was the one sent by the Japanese to Hiroshima in 1943; he also wrote the lyrics of what was to become the Brunei national anthem in 1947, which was officially adopted during the coronation of Sultan Omar Ali Saifuddin III in May 1951 (*Bendera dan lagu kebangsaan Brunei* [*The Brunei State Flag and National Anthem*] [BSB: no date], p. 15). He became *menteri besar* from 1967 to 1972. For his biography, see A.V. Horton, *The Top Hundred Persons of Power and Influence in Negara Brunei Darussalam A.D. 2000* (Bordesley: A.V.M. Horton, 2001), pp. 77–8.
[6] Founded in 1946 and close to the palace.
[7] In the *rumi* edition (Romanised transliteration) of 1975 "[...] diperbaiki, di-tambah dan di-susun", Pg. Mohd. Yusuf, "*Adat Istiadat diraja Brunei Darus-Salam* [*Custom of the Kingdom of Brunei Darussalam*]", *BMJ* 3, 3 (1975): 43.
[8] Ibid., p. 52.

restored to the sultan his traditional prerogatives of appointing ministers and administrative directors.[9] In 1959 the department was separated from religious affairs, then in 1962 from social welfare. If the operation seems paradoxical next to the forced modernisation undertaken by the sultanate, it actually belongs to a long series of "refoundations" of the polity, as illustrated among other examples by the genealogies (*silsilah*) of the present dynasty.

Refoundation at the Start of the 17th Century

To judge by the various versions of the *Silsilah Raja-Raja Berunai*,[10] the first institutional "refounding" mentioned in Malay textual sources—beyond the Islamisation of the kingdom—was undertaken by Sultan Hassan[11] after the Spanish destructions at the start of the 17th century, following the signature of the peace treaty with Spain in 1599. The reform affected the law and the political apparatus. The sultan drew up the first legal code of Brunei,[12] which was almost identical[13] to that of

[9] D.E. Brown, *Brunei: the structure and history of a Bornean Malay Sultanate*, p. 127.

[10] P.L. Amin Sweeney, "*Silsilah Raja-Raja Berunai* [Genealogy of the kings of Brunei]", *JMBRAS* 41, 2 (1968): 1–82; "Errata and Short note", *JMBRAS* 42, 2 (1969): 222–4; Hugh Low, "*Selesilah* (Book of Descent) of the Rajas of Bruni", *JMBRAS* 5 (June 1880): 1–36; P.M. Shariffuddin and Abdul Latif Hj. Ibrahim, "Batu Tarsilah; the Genealogical Tablet of the Sultans of Brunei", *BMJ* 3, 2 (1974): 253–64.

[11] Today's official historiography dates the death of Sultan Hassan to 1599, while in the 1970s it was dated to around 1625 (Pehin Dato Awang Hj Mohd. Jamil Al-Sufri, *Chatatan sejarah perwira² dan pembesar² Brunei* [*Notes on the history of dignitaries and titled persons of Brunei*], Jilid II [Brunei: Dewan Bahasa dan Pustaka, 1973], p. 37). Various sources in Brunei ("*Batu Tarsilah*..." etc., see preceding note) all mention that Sultan Hassan set up a government inspired by that of the Acehnese Sultan Iskandar Muda who, according to both Malay and Western sources, did not accede to the throne until 1607 and died in 1636.

[12] Brown, *Brunei: The structure and history of a Bornean Malay Sultanate*, p. 128.

[13] R.O. Winstedt signals in "A Brunei Code", *JMBRAS* 1 (1923), 2nd ed., in *Papers Relating to Brunei*, ed. Cheah Boon Kheng (Kuala Lumpur: MBRAS Reprint 18, 1998), p. 27, that the "[...] Romanised copy of a code of laws formerly enforced under the Brunei sultans" [whose] "[...] original belonged to the Orang Kaya di-Gadong Sri Lela Muhammad Hussin and was dated A.H. 1121" sent by G.C. Woolley to *JMBRAS* was a copy of *Undang Undang Melaka*. Windstedt's copy in all probability is the one kept at the Museum of Sarawak (cf. Dato' Dr Haji Mahmud Saedon Awang Othman, *Perlaksanaan dan Pentadbiran Undang-Undang Islam Di Negara Brunei Darussalam, Satu Tinjauan* [*Application and management of Islamic law in Brunei Barussalam, an Assessment*] [BSB: Dewan Bahasa dan Pustaka, 1996], p. 21).

Malacca (*Hukum Kanun Melaka*).[14] Compiled in 1523 after the fall of the sultanate, it had been implemented by Malacca's "legitimate" dynastic heirs, Johor and Perak. And as Sultan Hassan allied with Johor's main rival,[15] Aceh, he was inspired by the latter's authoritarian modes of government,[16] specifically that of Iskandar Muda, referred to in sources by his posthumous name "Ma[h]kota Alam".[17] This influence is corroborated by the presence of hundreds of Aceh manuscripts in the royal collections.[18]

Four Great Officers

The administrative structure of Brunei formalised at the start of the 17th century therefore reproduced the pattern prevailing in Malacca, the oldest Islamic political entity in the Malay Peninsula. This was characterised by the presence of four great dignitaries at the summit of a structure that revolved around the sultan. But a comparison between the functions and titles prevailing in Malacca, Aceh and Brunei reveals the specificity of the Bruneian model:

[14] Malacca had two codes, one civil, *Undang Undang [Hukum Kanun] Melaka,* and the other maritime, *Undang-Undang Laut Melaka*; the former was translated by Liaw Yock Fang, *Undang-undang Melaka = The laws of Melaka* (Den Haag: M. Nijhoff, 1976).

[15] Low, "*Selesilah* (Book of Descent) of the Rajas of Bruni", p. 17.

[16] "Sultan Hassan itu-lah yang keras di-atas tahta kerajaan-nya [mengikut] perintah Sultan Mahkota Alam yang di-negeri Acheh [Sultan Hassan is the one who strongly on the throne of his kingdom (followed) the rules of Aceh's Sultan Mahkota Alam]", *Batu Tarsilah* (genealogy engraved on a stele dated 1807, following the date given by Amin Sweeney, pp. 168ff). The *Batu Tarsilah* was translated by Low, ibid., p. 23, translation revised by P.M. Shariffuddin and Abd. Latif Hj. Ibrahim, "Batu Tarsilah: The Genealogical Tablet of the Sultans of Brunei", in *Papers relating to Brunei,* ed. Cheah Boon Kheng (Kuala Lumpur: MBRAS Reprint, 1998), p. 162.

[17] Teuku Iskandar, "Aceh as a Muslim-Malay Cultural Centre (14th–19th Century)", *First International Conference of Aceh and Indian Ocean Studies*, Banda Aceh, 24–27 February 2007, p. 17, http://www.ari.nus.edu.sg/docs%5CAceh-project%5Cfull-papers%5Caceh_fp_teukuiskandar.pdf.

[18] "600 Naskah Aceh Kuno Tersimpan di Brunei Darussalam [600 ancient Aceh manuscripts in Brunei Darussalam]", *Nusantara,* 26 August 2009, http://www.serambinews.com/news/view/12419/600-naskah-aceh-kuno-tersimpan-di-brunei-darussalam.

Table 3. Malacca, Aceh and Brunei: Political and Administrative Hierarchy (17th Century)

Rank	*Malacca*[19]	*Aceh*[20]	*Brunei*[21]
1.	*Bendahara* "Prime Minister"	*Leubè Kita Kali* *[Qadi Malik al-Adil]* Minister of religion and of justice	*Pg. Bendahara Seri Maharaja Permaisura* "Prime Minister"
2.	*Temenggong*[22] Minister of police and justice	*O.K.*[23] *Maharaja Sri Maharaja* Minister of state affairs	*Pg. Temenggong Sahibul Bahr* [master of the sea] Minister of trade
3.	*Penghulu bendahari* Minister of trade	*O.K. Laksamana perdana menteri (panglima dalam)* Minister of defence and home affairs	*Pg. Di Gadong Sahibul Mal* [master of the treasury] Minister of home affairs
4.	*Laksamana*[24] Minister of defence	*Penghulu (panglima) Bandar* Minister of trade	*Pg. Pemancha Sahibul Rai wal-mashawarat* Head of the council

Malacca was run by four "state ministers": the *Bendahara*, the *Temenggong*, the *Penghulu Bendahari* (who looked after the various *shahbandar)* and the *Laksamana*. This terminology represented the historical strata of societies around the Straits: Sanskrit (*bendahara*

[19] Andaya and Andaya, *A History of Malaysia* (London: Macmillan, 1982), pp. 46ff.

[20] L. Andaya, "Aceh's contribution to Standards of Malayness", *Archipel* 61 (2001): 52ff.

[21] P.L. Amin Sweeney, *Silsilah (A)*, pp. 17–8.

[22] Originally, the *Penghulu bendahari* was in the second position, but he was supplanted by the *Temenggong*, whose function became an obligatory step to accede to the post of *Bendahara*, who came from the same family (Andaya and Andaya, *A History of Malaysia*, pp. 46ff).

[23] *Orang Kaya.*

[24] Liaw Yock Fang, *Undang-undang Melaka = The laws of Melaka*, placed the *shahbandar* in the fourth position, in the rank of the *laksamana*, although the first Portuguese witnesses mention the presence of four *shahbandar* in Malacca: one for the Gujratis; one for the Keling, Peguans and Pasai; one for the Malays; and the last for the Chinese, Tonkinese and Filipinos (Richard O. Winstedt, *The Malays; A Cultural History* [Singapore: Kelly & Walsh, 1947], p. 65).

and *laksamana*);[25] Javanese (*temenggong*);[26] Malay (*penghulu*);[27] and Indo-Muslim (with the vocable *shahbandar*, a term of Persian origin[28] referring to customs officers who took charge of the merchant communities from which they originated). The *Bendahara* did not belong to the royal family but to another prestigious (and sometimes competing) lineage[29] to which he was related by marriage. The *Temenggong* (in charge of justice and police) served as an avenue to the highest administrative offices and was often issued from the same lineage as the *Bendahara*. The sultanates of the Malay Peninsula that claimed filiation to Malacca,[30] notably Perak, had a similar political structure.[31]

In Aceh, at least since Sultan Iskandar Muda, this usual Malay hierarchy shifted downward by one head, as the *Bendahara*, designated by the title of *Maharaja Sri Maharaja*,[32] ceded primacy to the religious head, the *Qadi Malik al-Adil* [Judge-King of Justice], who took charge of justice—a function that was elsewhere devolved to the *Temenggong*. The *Laksamana* kept his traditional military duty, to which was added in Aceh internal security. The equivalent of the *Penghulu bendahari*, the *Penghulu bandar*, was thus retrograded to fourth place. And there was no longer a *Temenggong*, for his function had been emptied of content.

On the other hand, in Brunei, although the sultanate claimed both the Aceh model and a founding alliance with Johor[33] (that is, with

---

[25] From the Sanskrit *bhāṇḍāgāran*, treasury, which became "treasurer" in Malay; and *lakṣamaṇa*, younger brother of Râma in the *Rāmāyana*, which became "admiral" in Malay (Russell Jones, ed., *Loan-words in Indonesian and Malay* [Leiden: reprinted KITLV, 2007], pp. 36, 178).

[26] See Lexicon in the Appendices.

[27] Chief; etymologically, the man who controls upstream (*hulu*).

[28] "Master" of the port (*bandar*).

[29] The competition between the *Bendahara*'s and the Sultan's lineages is demonstrated by the assassination of the *Bendahara* of Malacca in 1510 by the last sultan, Mahmud Shah (Winstedt, *The Malays; A Cultural History*, p. 137); or by the origins of the sultanate of Terengganu, founded by a descendant of the first *Bendahara* of Malacca (M.C. Sheppard, "A short history of Terengganu", *JMBRAS* 22, 3 [June 1949], reprinted Kuala Lumpur: MBRAS 19, 1983: 1–74).

[30] Excluding Kedah, Selangor, Perlis and Negeri Sembilan.

[31] R.O. Winstedt and R.J. Wilkinson, *A History of Perak* (Kuala Lumpur: MBRAS Reprints, 1974), pp. 137ff.

[32] Ibid., p. 138.

[33] *Sya'ir Awang Simawn*, part IV (Maxwell, 2006, p. 14).

Malacca), whence the royal carillon and *nobat* (orchestra),[34] the titles of the four great dignitaries in the 17th century differed from those above: while the first was indeed the *Bendahara* and another the *Temenggong*,[35] the other two dignities, *Di Gadong*[36] and *Pemancha*, were specific to Brunei. These four posts were occupied by members of the royal family,[37] as shown by the fact that their holders bore the title of *pengiran* and not *orang kaya* (*O.K.*). In this aspect, the structure formalised in Brunei in the 17th century was inspired by a model reminiscent of the Javanese empire of Majapahit, where the three great dignitaries of the kingdom were princes of high rank,[38] rather than the Malacca or Acehnese model. Moreover, the title of *Pemancha*[39] evokes the five components (*mancapat*) of the ancient Javanese administrative system. Following certain courts in 17th-century Java, in particular Banten (for a while),[40] the unique *shahbandar* was also a *pengiran*; at the end of the 16th century, he was the fourth of the four great dignitaries of the kingdom[41] and later found himself relegated to the fifth position after the creation of the *Pemancha*.

---

[34] *Silsilah (A)*, p. 11 (f. 1); the *Batu Tarsilah* (P.M. Shariffuddin and Abdul Latif Hj. Ibrahim, "Batu Tarsilah: The Genealogical Tablet of the Sultans of Brunei", p. 162) mentions a second *nobat* coming from Andalas (Minangkabau), whose status would be lightly lower since it is not—at least in this part of the text—depicted by the *Silsilah (A)* as *pesaka* (*regalia*), ibid., p. 14, f. 6).

[35] In Sweeney, *Silsilah (A)*, the order of precedence after the *Bendahara* fluctuates: the *Di Gadong* is in second position on p. 14 (f. 8), p. 19 (f. 14), p. 22 (f. 23), p. 30 (f. 35); the *Temenggong* is in second position on p. 16 (f. 16), p. 18 (f. 13), p. 29 (f. 31); and in third position on p. 31 (f. 35), p. 44 (f. 61), etc.

[36] The function had already been mentioned in the "*Boxer Codex*" at the end of the 16th century (Carroll, "Berunai in the *Boxer Codex*": 6), so it was not created by Sultan Hassan, as asserted by Hugh Low, "List of the Mahomedan Sovereigns of Brunei, or Borneo Proper", p. 17, and adopted by contemporary Bruneian historians with no further examination.

[37] The elder brother of Sultan Hassan but born of a concubine became *Temenggong*; another of his brothers, *Di Gadong*, yet another, *Shahbandar*, and the son of his sister, *Bendahara* (*Sisilah [A]*, p. 21, ff. 16–7).

[38] In Majapahit, the three great officers bore the title of *dyah* (equivalent in Brunei to *Pengiran Anak)*, reserved for direct descendants of sovereigns (Slametmuljana, *A Story of Majapahit* [Singapore: Singapore University Press, 1976], pp. 150ff).

[39] *Manca* also means foreigner.

[40] In Banten, the post was held by the *Pangeran* Kidul between 1674 and 1677 (Kidul —[ruling on the] South), *D.R.*, June 1674, p. 159 and February 1677.

[41] Carroll, "Berunai in the *Boxer Codex*": 6.

Another specificity is that except for the *Bendahara*, the five foremost dignities mentioned in the various enumerations of the *Silsilah (A)* all bear a dual denomination, in Sanskrit-Malay and in Arabic, which is apparently unknown among the titles of the Peninsula. This attests to an Islamisation of institutions, plausibly under the influence of Aceh. Thus the *Di Gadong* is named in Arabic "master of finance"; the *Pemancha* is "master of courage and counsel"; the *Temenggong* is "master of the sea"; the same is true of the *Shahbandar*, called *Sahibul Bandar*, "master of the port".[42]

On top of these particularities is the terminology for river rights, *kuripan* (tied to the office) or *tulin* (personal properties). The first vocable, *kuripan*, is a Malay term fallen into desuetude for camphor,[43] the kingdom's principal resource; the term *tulin*[44] refers to the princes' personal heirlooms and signifies "own". While the constitution of rivers (*sungai*) *kuripan*[45] might be assumed to reproduce another major river system (Srivijaya), and *tulin* probably existed in the rest of the zone, these terms are specific to Brunei, where the ultimate foundation of power was not so much control of rivers as of the people (and their goods) who moved along them.

Two Circles of Cheteria and Menteri

Despite the discordances between the various listings of the genealogy (A) and between the latter and genealogy (B), as correctly noted by D.E. Brown,[46] the oldest sources[47] collected in the *Kitab Risalat al-Marhum fi Adati 'l-Marhum* (*Sisilah A*), 17th-century data compiled in 1735,[48] have not preserved a trace of major changes at the summit of the hierarchy. At lower levels, they do describe a hierarchy of three degrees:

[42] I thank Louis Le Vert, former ambassador of France to Brunei Darussalam, for his translations from Arabic.
[43] Before it was soaked; W.J.S. Poerwadarminta, *Kamus umum bahasa Indonesia* [*General Dictionary of Indonesian*] (Jakarta: Balai Pustaka, 1976), p. 543. Not to be confused with the ancient Javanese kingdom of the same name.
[44] *Tulén,* ibid., p. 1098, also called *pesaka.*
[45] Peter Leys, "Observations on the Brunei Political System, 1883–1885", *JMBRAS* 41, 2 (1968): 124.
[46] Brown, *Brunei: The structure and history of a Bornean Malay Sultanate*, pp. 184ff.
[47] Ff. 7–15 of the *Silsilah (A)* (ibid., p. 184).
[48] Sweeney, "Silsilah Raja-Raja Berunai [Genealogy of the kings of Brunei]", p. 2.

the *Bendahara* and the *Temenggong*, each controlling a first level of 8 *Cheteria*,[49] followed by a second tier of 8 *Menteri*[50] of lesser rank[51]—a total of 16 *Cheteria* and 16 *Menteri*. Thus the Brunei polity followed a design of the Mandalaic type, characteristic of Indianised Southeast Asian kingdoms[52] and which the Nusantarian world kept long after the 18th century. One illustration of the persistence of this model is the seal of the sultans used in Aceh until the start of the 20th century. Despite the ostentatious Muslim orthodoxy prevailing in the sultanate since the 17th century, it represented a mandala with eight petals;[53] the four great dignitaries were also flanked by eight *uleebalang*. Further corroborating the persistence of this cosmology in Brunei is the fact that under Sultan Hassan, Kota Batu was protected by eight huge cannons, each given a name[54] (plus several hundred small ones).[55]

A Pattern Partially Applied in Brunei

However, at the time, this cosmological design applied in Brunei to only half the arrangement (*Bendahara*/*Temenggong*). The *Temenggong*, as the head of justice and trade, would have assumed (at least formal) control

[49] A design markedly different from that prevailing in the Malay Peninsula, where the four great dignitaries were usually followed by a second circle of eight dignitaries of lesser importance, but the circle was not doubled (J.M. Gullick, *Indigenous Political Systems of Western Malaya* [London: The Athlone Press, 1958], pp. 51, 90–1).

[50] Malacca had four (R.J. Wilkinson, "The Malacca Sultanate", *JMBRAS* 13, 2 [1935]: 29–33).

[51] *Silsilah (A)*, p. 16 (f. 9).

[52] S.J. Tambiah, "The Galactic Polity", in *World Conqueror & World Renouncer*, ed. S.J. Tambiah (London: Cambridge University Press, 1976), pp. 102–31.

[53] Called *cap Sikureung* (seal "9", or 8 petals + the centre). See, for example, the 1733 letter presented by Annabel Teh Gallop, "Gold, Silver and Lapis Lazuli: Royal Letters from Aceh in the 17th Century", *First International Conference of Aceh and Indian Ocean Studies*, Asia Research Institute, National University of Singapore & Rehabilitation and Construction Executing Agency for Aceh and NIAS, 24–27 February 2007, p. 46. It was still in force at the start of the 20th century (cf. the seal of the last sultan Tuanku Muhamāt Dawōt, in Snouck Hugrongje, *The Acehnese*, vol. I [Leiden: Brill, 1906], p. 9).

[54] *Silsilah (A)*, p. 20 (f. 17).

[55] *Meriam* (cannons) and *bedil* (culverins); Brunei is said to have possessed more than 200 pieces of artillery at the moment of the Spanish attack (D.E. Brown, "Spanish accounts of their expeditions against Brunei in 1578–79", *BMJ* 3, 2 [1974]: 203).

of the three religious great officers[56] and of the *Shahbandar*.[57] For the other half, the *Di Gadong* was responsible for a number of subordinates who represented the riverine estates that made up the sultanate and which were not a multiple of eight: since the middle of the 17th century, he took charge of two *OK Di Gadong* (*Seri Nara Indera* and *Seri Laila*), each metaphorically in charge of one of the riverbanks that served as interface with local chiefs (called *menteri darat*), the *OK Di Gadong Seri Laila*[58] post having been created by Sultan Muhammad Ali[59] to accord some status to one of his half-brothers born of a concubine. The *Pemancha*, less regularly cited than the three other great dignitaries, did not have direct subordinates.

First Extension of the *Notitia Dignitatum*

While the last list elaborated in 1807[60]—which is also the date of the raising of the *Batu Tarsilah*—did not mention any major change at the top of the administration, except that the four great dignitaries were called wazirs,[61] the number of dignitaries at lower levels had grown:[62] the *cheteria* increased from 16 (2 × 8) to 22,[63] and the number of *menteri* and other non-princely officers more than doubled, from 20 to more than 50, and the document stated that this "titling [is] in vigour in Johor".[64]

This inflation of dignities might be explained in Johor-Riau by the need to formally integrate the Bugis chiefs and clans who took effective control of the Straits in the 1720s into a ranked society.[65] It is hard to guess the reasons that pushed Brunei to such an overload in the lower

---

[56] *Datu Imam Malikul Adil* (*Silsilah (A)*, p. 36 [f. 36]), *Siraja Khatib* and *Udana Khatib* (ibid., p. 16, f. 10).

[57] *Silsilah (A)*.

[58] The *Boxer Codex* mentions the presence of three *OK Di Gadong* in 1588, under the orders of the *Di Gadong* (Carroll, "Berunai in the *Boxer Codex*": 6).

[59] Son of Sultan Hassan, Pg. Mohd Yusuf, *Adat Istiadat diraja Brunei Darus-Salam* [*Custom of the Kingdom of Brunei Darussalam*], p. 52.

[60] From the middle of f. 64 to the middle of f. 69 of the *Silsilah (A)*, and followed by the list of religious dignitaries.

[61] *Silsilah (A)*, p. 48 (f. 68).

[62] Ibid., pp. 47–8 (ff. 66–8).

[63] Here called *raja*.

[64] *Silsilah (A)*, p. 48 (f. 68).

[65] Leonard Andaya, *The Kingdom of Johor (1641–1728)* (Kuala Lumpur: Oxford University Press, 1975), pp. 279ff.

ranks of the *Notitia Dignitatum*, if not for, once again, the need to grant more positions to local chiefs and especially to Bugis, who intermarried within the royal family in the course of the 18th century.[66] In fact, it was under Sultan Omar Ali Saifuddin I (1740–95)[67] that the post of Perdana *Menteri* was created—apparently temporarily and for a "Malay" of Perak[68]—even though the ranks of *menteri* were supposed to be full. In this way, the opening of the ranks became the procedure by which new non-Malay and non-noble elements might be integrated into the palatine hierarchy.

To judge from the available sources, the system did not seem to modify significantly during the 19th century, although the most important of the *menteri* were now titled *pehin*, as shown for the first time in a part of the *Silsilah (B)* dated 1841,[69] and the four wazirs henceforth had eight *cheteria* under their orders[70] (and probably as many *menteri*).

Formalisation of a Double Hierarchy

The modernisation unleashed by the establishment of the British residency a century later caused a reconfiguration of dignities, attested to by the last pages of the *Silsilah (B)*, recopied in 1936,[71] which described the four-part structure from the summit of the hierarchy to the lower levels.

---

[66] The *Silsilah Melayu dan Bugis dan Sekalian Raja Raja nya* [*Genealogy of Malays, Bugis and all the Kings*], translated by Hans Overbeck, *JMBRAS* 4, 3 (1926) mentions on p. 343 the marriage of a daughter of the Bugis chief Upu Daeng Manabun and of the princess Kesumba (daughter of the sultan of Sukadana Muahamad Safiyu'd-din), with Pangeran Kapur [Ghafur], "first cousin of the sultan of Brunei"). The *Tufat-al-Nafis* (V. Matheson and B. Watson Andaya, *The Precious Gift*, p. 29), calls Pangeran Abd al-Ghafur the "king of Brunei". Respectively dated 1865 and 1866, these two works were written by the same Raja Ali Haji Ibn Ahmad.

[67] Official date of the reign of Sultan Omar Ali Saifuddin I (Pehin Dr. Hj. Jamil al-Sufri, *Tarsilah Brunei, the Early History of Brunei up to 1432 AD* [BSB: Brunei History Centre, 2000], p. 47). His lengthy reign (55 years) might have been arranged to mask the 18th-century "gap".

[68] Pg. Mohd. Yusuf, *Adat Istiadat diraja Brunei Darus-Salam*, p. 62. This "Malay" official was plausibly of Bugis origin, in light of the situation prevailing in Perak.

[69] *Silsilah (B)*, p. 70 (f. 32).

[70] Spenser St. John's, *Life in the Forest of the Far East* (London: Smith, Elder & Co., 1862) vol. II, p. 247.

[71] List copied by Pehin OK Di Gadong Awang Aminiddin and completed for the genealogical part by Abdul Ghaffar bin Abdul Mu'min in 1936 (*Silsilah [B]*, p. 70, f. 31).

At the top of the palatine hierarchy were the four great princely dignitaries, in order of precedence: the *Bendahara*, the *Di Gadong*, the *Pemancha* and the *Temenggong*.[72] The *Cheteria* were split into two levels: at the summit was a first group of "Four *Cheteria*" (*Cheteria Empat*)—the *Shahbandar*, "head of all the *cheteria*" and three other *cheteria* of very high rank—followed by 14 *cheteria* of lesser rank. The commoner *menteri* were reorganised according to the same pattern, with a first group formed of three *menteri*—the *perdana* (prime) *menteri*, flanked by two *menteri*-in-chief (*kepala menteri*); a second tier of four *menteri* of prime rank (*Menteri Empat*); and finally a third tier of 24 *menteri* of lower rank. The latter tier remains non-exhaustive and largely open.[73]

Thus under Sultan Ahmad Tajuddin a ceremonial, statutorily asymmetrical, diarchy took shape combining nobles, who held (theorically, regarding the British) decision-making power and their inferiors, the commoners, who actually administered the country:

Table 4. Formalisation of a Dual Hierarchy (1930s)

NOBLES *Holders of political power*	*COMMONERS* *Officers*
4 Wazirs	1 *Perdana Menteri*
Bendahara	2 *Kepala Menteri*
Di Gadong	*OK Di Gadong Seri Léla*
Pemancha	*OK Di Gadong Seri Nara*
Temenggong	
Cheteria Empat	*Menteri Empat*
Shahbandar	*Seri Maharaja di Raja Betara Dalam*
Maharaja Lela	*Pekerma Raja Betara Luar*
Paduka Tuan	*OK Laksamana*
Seri Dewa Maharaja	*OK Shahbandar*
Other *Cheteria*	Other *Menteri*

[72] On the evolution of their functions, see Haj. Awg. Asbol bin Haji Mail, "Institusi Wazir, Ceteria dan Manteri pada Abad ke-19: Struktur dan Kuasa Elite dalam Pentadbiran Kesultanan Melayu Brunei [The institution of wazirs, cheterias and menteris in the 19th century: Structure and power of the elite in the administration of the Malay sultanate of Brunei]", *Sosiohumanika, Jurnal Pendidikan Sains Sosial dan Kemanusiaan* 1, 2 (2008): 79–114.
[73] *Silsilah (B)*, p. 75 (f. 41).

The system was made coherent by linking the two parallel hierarchies of nobles and commoners through the intermediary of four *menteri*:

a. The fourth and fifth *menteri*, who were the chief *menteri* of the *Di Gadong*;[74]
b. The two leaders of the *Bendahara*'s and *Temenggong*'s[75] *menteri* who were part of the *Menteri Empat*.

While the *Temenggong* and *Di Gadong* posts remained vacant and effective executive power remained in the hands of the British Resident, there was a need to incorporate, at least symbolically, the "modern" administrators into the traditional hierarchy. This could explain the formalisation of the diarchy.[76] Since all decisions were taken in the name of the sultan, this reinforced his moral authority while the *pengiran* lost theirs when deprived of their land-river rights. More importantly, by playing on hierarchy, the sultan now had the means to reconstitute the social linkage between the two halves of society, commoners and nobles—ties that had been harmed by the over-exploitation of riverine populations[77] and their being auctioned off by the core elite of the kingdom during the previous century.

Transposition of a System Characteristic of Western Borneo

This hierarchical dualism was unknown in the Malay courts of the Peninsula, which gathered aristocrats and commoners into a single pattern. It was evidently inspired by the social organisation of the hierarchical societies from the west and centre of Borneo, especially the Kenyah, among whom exists a stratification in five degrees, spatially inscribed in the long house[78] on either side of the highest aristocrat living in the

---

[74] At least since the 17th century.

[75] The *Pemancha* did not appear to supervise any *menteri*. This corroborates the previous data in *Silsilah (A)*, which mentioned that the office was created after the other three, under Sultan Hassan.

[76] On the overall structure of Bruneian society before colonisation, see Brown, *Brunei: The structure and history of a Bornean Malay Sultanate*, pp. 79–118, and in particular the figures on pp. 85, 87, 89.

[77] Called "*hamba tulin*", personal slaves (Peter Leys, "Observations on the Brunei Political System, 1883–1885", *JMBRAS* 41, 2 [1968]: 122).

[78] Bernard Sellato, "Note préliminaire sur les sociétés 'à maison' à Bornéo", in *De la Hutte au Palais, Sociétés 'à maison' en Asie du Sud-Est insulaire*, ed. C. Macdonald (Paris: Presses du CNRS, 1987), pp. 15–44.

centre: (1) nobles of high rank; (2) nobles of lesser rank; (3) wealthy commoners; (4) ordinary commoners; (5) slaves and their descendants, the latter occupying the two ends of the longhouse. In fact, the Bruneian term for nobles of the second rank is *cheteria damit* ("small" in the dialect of Brunei), while the Kenyah call their second rank *deta'u* (Malay *datu*[79]) *dumit*; among the Kenyah (and Kayan) commoners are designated by the term *panyin*,[80] which paradoxically refers to the highest title to which they can accede in Brunei,[81] that of *pehin*.[82]

The interface between second-rank nobility and the most qualified (statutorily speaking) of the commoners thus became the junction for social mobility.[83]

[79] The relation between the Kenyah *deta'u* and the Malay *datu*, with the introduction of an aspirate, is similar to that between the Malay doublon *perahu/prau*, the transformation of "*pepet*" 'e' into 'a' being a variant attested by Malay dialectology. On the validity of the hypothesis *datu/deta'u*, see V. King, correspondence with the author, 31 January 2011.

[80] Bernard Sellato, *Innermost Borneo: Studies in Dayak Cultures* (Singapore & Paris: Singapore University Press & SevenOrients, 2002), pp. 74–5.

[81] The title of *pehin* has been maintained in Sarawak since the arrival of the Brookes until today.

[82] A mechanism that recalls, *mutatis mutandis*, the semantic shift in the West from *sine nobilitate* (somebody "deprived of nobility") to "snob" (someone trying to emulate aristocrats), even if linguistic data seem not allowing the Bruneian lexeme *pehin* to be derived directly from the Kenyah *panyin*.

[83] Victor King, "Social Rank and Social Change among the Maloh of West Kalimantan", in *The Real and Imagined Roles of Culture in Development*, ed. M.R. Dove (Honolulu: University of Hawaii Press, 1988), pp. 219–53.

Opening Up of the Hierarchy (1958–2014)

Multiplication of Hierarchical Levels (1958)

In 1958, as the residency closed, this proliferation of ranks culminated in the creation of four levels of multiples of four among the *cheteria* and *menteri*.[84]

Table 5. Multiplication of Hierarchical Levels (1958)

Nobles	*Commoners*
4 Wazirs	1 *Perdana menteri*
	2 *Kepala Menteri*
Cheteria Empat (4)	*Menteri Empat* (4)
Cheteria Besar (*Cheteria* 8)	*Pengalasan Besar* (*Menteri* 8)
Cheteria Pengalasan (*Cheteria* 16)	*Pengalasan Biasa* (*Menteri* 16)
Cheteria Damit (*Cheteria* 32)	*Pengalasan Damit* (*Menteri* 32)

While the titles of wazirs, *cheteria* 4 and *menteri* 4 remained practically the same as in 1936,[85] the numbers of *cheteria* and *menteri* each rose to 60, whereas the 1936 list mentioned only 18 and 34 respectively. This inflation of dignities (tripling the *cheteria* and doubling the *menteri*,

[84] Pg. Mohd. Yusuf, *Adat Istiadat diraja Brunei Darus-Salam*, pp. 43–108, who compiled the various *Silsilah* of the royal family to which he had access thanks to his high ranking, as well as British works about the history of the Malay Peninsula.

[85] The second *cheteria empat*, the *Pg. Maharaja Laila* was given an Arabic title: *Sahibol kahar*, "master of the conquest".

meaning that more than half of the titles cited were unknown in previous Bruneian sources)[86] enabled enlarging the *Notitia Dignitatum* to include a growing number of aristocrats and commoners and thus take into account the demographic growth (among the princes as among the administration). Meanwhile the PRB of Azahari was perpetually agitating—Brunei was supposed to be evolving toward a constitutional monarchy. But the link between the two halves, nobles and commoners, had disintegrated: the two *Kepala menteri OK Di Gadong* were no longer attached to the *Di Gadong* (whose office was moreover vacant) and of the four *menteri besar*, only the *OK Shahbandar* was still chief *menteri* of one of the four great officers (the *Bendahara*), although this mission now receded to the third level of his attributions.[87]

The *Notitia Dignitatum* lost its final functional elements while strengthening its symbolic task, which was to place the sovereign at the heart of a cosmological structure of four degrees and four concentric circles, of which he constituted both the centre and the pivot,[88] the throne today being one of its representations.[89] This symbolism is reinforced by implementing a similar pattern among religious dignitaries, with the *Pehin Datu Seri Maharaja* reigning over four imams,[90] though it extends to neither the representatives of foreign businessmen, who remain three in number,[91] nor the several dozen minor officials with the rank of *menteri*.

This pyramid of four degrees reproduces the system instituted in Perak by a decision of the State Council in 1905 that fixed the titles of

---

[86] 66% of the title-holders of *cheteria* and 36% of *menteri*, up to *menteri* 32 included (see the confrontation of various *Notitia Dignitatum* in Brown, *Brunei: The structure and history of a Bornean Malay Sultanate*, pp. 199ff).

[87] Pg. Mohd Yusuf, *Adat Istiadat diraja Brunei Darus-Salam*, p. 53.

[88] This structure, in which the four cardinal points are multiplied four times to constitute a mandala with four circles, and centred around the sovereign, arises from an Indianised cosmology (encompassing 32 gods plus Indra, the king of the gods), making the sovereign in his kingdom the earthly transposition of the celestial world (see R.O. Winstedt, *Malaya and its History* [London: Hutchinson, 1948], p. 85).

[89] *Pat(a)rana*, in Pehin Dr. Hj. Mohd. Jamil al-Sufri, *Adat istiadat diraja Brunei*, p. 131.

[90] Pg. Mohd. Yusuf, *Adat Istiadat diraja Brunei Darus-Salam*, pp. 57ff.

[91] Responsible respectively for Chinese of Bruneian nationality, Chinese residing in Brunei and Indians (ibid., p. 59). The latter is called *saudagar* (from the Persian *saudagar*, "merchant"), as in 17th-century Aceh (Andaya, "Aceh's Contribution to Standards of Malayness", p. 52).

the three lower ranks.[92] In Aceh style, the 8, 16[93] and 32 Perak chiefs were titled *orang kaya kaya*. As the study by Winstedt and Wilkinson on the history of Perak had been published in 1934 and the widow of Sultan Ahmad Tajuddin of Brunei (a princess of Selangor) married in a third marriage (in full observation of the *adat istiadat*) a prince of Perak in 1956, we can safely presume that Perak's custom was well known to the Brunei authorities, as well as to the compiler of Brunei's *adat*, Pg. Yusuf, who had himself studied in Perak at the Sultan Idris Training College. Yet the two systems present one significant difference, which is the existence of a single hierarchy in Perak (where the *Bendahara* was in most cases the sole wazir of princely origin), whereas Brunei preserved its diarchy.

New Extension of the *Notitia Dignitatum* (1968–2011)

Table 6. New Extension of the *Notitia Dignitatum*

Nobles (all Pengiran)[94]	*Commoners (all Pehin)*
1 *Perdana Wazir Sahibul Himmah Wal-Waqar*[95]	1 *Perdana Menteri*
4 *Wazirs*	
2 *Kepala Cheteria Sahibun Nabalah & Sahibun Najabah*[96]	2 *Kepala Menteri*
Cheteria Empat (4)	*Menteri Empat* (4)
Cheteria Besar (*Cheteria* 8)	*Pengalasan Besar* (*Menteri* 8)
Cheteria Pengalasan (*Cheteria* 16)	*Pengalasan Biasa* (*Menteri* 16)
Cheteria Damit (*Cheteria* 32)	*Pengalasan Damit* (*Menteri* 32)

92 Winstedt and Wilkinson, *A History of Perak*, pp. 145–58. This system is unchanged down to the present day (see the sultan's website, http://sultan.perak.gov.my/English/32.htm).

93 Counting in multiples of 4 up to 32 goes back not only to Malacca (Panuti HM Sudjiman, *Adat Raja Raja Malayu* [Jakarta: Penerbit Universitas Indonesia], 1982, 279 p), but also to Indianised kingship. Robert Heine-Geldern ("Conceptions of State and Kingship in Southeast Asia" [Ithaca: Cornell University, Southeast Asia Data Paper no. 18, 1942], pp. 1–13) mentions that according to the New History of the Tang, Java was divided into 28 provinces, which gave a total of 32 great dignitaries (the 28 chiefs of provinces plus the four ministers), thus making the kingdom the microcosm of the universe.

94 Jamil Al-Sufri, *Adat istiadat diraja Brunei*, "Lampiran [Annexe] D", pp. 593–630.

95 Or Prime Wazir "master of grand goals and objectives, and of dignity".

96 Master of the nobility; [second] master of the nobility.

The perpetuation of ranks continued after the accession of Sultan Hassanal Bolkiah in 1967, with the creation of two *Kepala Cheteria* in 1968 and 1974[97] and a *Perdana Wazir* designed for Prince Mohamed [Bolkiah] in 1969.[98] With the addition of a new echelon to the *cheteria*, the two hierarchies (nobility and commoners) became strictly symmetrical (in functional but obviously not in statutory terms) at the five lower levels, which isolated the wazir echelon. Since 2000, 3 supplementary dignities have been created among the *cheteria*[99] and 11 among the main[100] *menteri* (thus up to *menteri* 32 altogether), within which were interposed the 5 great religious dignitaries[101] (previously listed separately) and 6 new grades. Granting the title of *cheteria*[102] does not depend on the presence of *cheteria* in the close ascendants or among siblings, although this might be taken into account, but tends to acknowledge favour as much as merit. On the other hand, since the present reign, the title of wazir has been reserved for the *Pengiran Anak*—first-rank princes, sons or brothers of sovereigns and *garaha* (those born of a princely mother).

However, the posts are far from being filled: the positions of *Temenggong* and of *Pemancha* have remained vacant since 1976 for the first and 1982 for the second; 64% of the posts of *cheteria* and 31% of

---

[97] Intended respectively for one of the sons of minor rank of Sultan Hashim, Pengiran Anak Hj Khamis (in 1968), then for the brother-in-law of the reigning sultan, the husband of his sister Princess Masna (in 1974).

[98] Prince Mohamed was made *Temenggong* in 1967, with precedence over the *Bendahara* and *Pemancha* (*State of Brunei Annual Report 1967*, p. 6); he became *Perdana Wazir* in 1969 (*Brunei Annual Report 1969*, p. 274), the offices of *Temenggong* and *Di Gadong* remaining vacant. In 1971, Pengiran Anak Hj Khamis, until then *Kepala Cheteria*, became *Di Gadong*, and Pengiran Hj Mohammed bin Pg. Piut succeeded Prince Mohamed to the office of *Temenggong* (*Brunei Annual Report 1971*, p. 367).

[99] *Sanggarama Diraja*, between 4s and 8s; *Penggawa Laila Bentara Istiadat Diraja Dalam Istana* and *Laila Kanun Diraja*, between 16s and 32s.

[100] Among several others.

[101] *Kepala Menteri Ugama*, after the *Perdana menteri*; *OK Penggawa Laila Bentara Diraja*, *OK Penggawa*, *OK Laila Setia Bakti Diraja*, *OK Laila Wijaya*, between the two *Kepala Menteri 4* and the *Menteri 4*; *Datu Imam*, *Siraja Khatib*, *Tuan Imam* and *Udana Khatib* (dignities previously listed in the notice of religious dignitaries), *OK Paduka Setia Raja* and *OK Paduka Seri Utama*, between the *menteri 4* and the *menteri 8*.

[102] The title *cheteria* does not lead to any specific allocation.

those of *menteri*[103] (*menteri* 32 included) were also vacant in January 2009.[104]

It is thus the very existence of the hierarchical structure that is symbolically pertinent: it allows a distinction between the Court honours —which are not empty shells since their title-holders must perform various ceremonial tasks during important palatine rituals (coronation, marriages)—and holders of government offices. And as, unlike government offices, these honours are perennial (the only possible mobility being upward), both the lengthening of lifespans as well as the need for promotion necessitated the regular creation of new dignities. Yet, the vacancy of many grades maintains the flexibility of the system while permitting competition within the curial elites, strengthening the power of the sovereign.

The non-princely members of the government occupy a modest place in the *Notitia Dignitatum*: in 2010, except for the minister of religious affairs (second of the *menteri* 4), most of them belonged to the category of *menteri* 16 or 32—or even beyond. Real responsibilities are thus quite distinct from the dignities, as illustrated by the case of Pehin Lim Jock Seng, second minister of foreign affairs, president of Brunei National Petroleum and of Royal Brunei Airlines, etc., who has occupied only the 23rd rank of *menteri* 32 since 2004![105] On the other hand, the system enables the awarding of decorations on merit (15 in all),[106] the title of *Dato* (*Datin* for a woman) being conferred by the first two classes.

To stretch the analysis a little farther, honours prevent a situation where positions are systematically granted to persons "of quality" who may not be competent; at the same time they make space for competent people, however low, in the statutory grid.[107] It would be difficult to find a more skilful and cheaper way to integrate modernity and to neutralise the Court than this system, which could be compared to the court of

---

[103] Without counting the *menteri* lower in rank than the *menteri* 32, where in certain categories all the titles have been attributed, and in others, like the *menteri dagang* (= of commerce, titles reserved for non-Malay foreigners), only 12%.

[104] *Senarai nama-nama gelaran dan orang-orang yang dikurniai gelaran* [*List of titles and persons to whom they were granted*] [BSB, January 2009], 33 p.

[105] Titled *Pehin Orang Kaya Pekerma Dewa Dato Seri Setia.*

[106] Rozan Yunus, *The Golden Warisan Brunei Darussalam*, vol. 2, pp. 171ff.

[107] Naimah S. Talib, "A Resilient Monarchy: The Sultanate of Brunei and Regime Legitimacy in an Era of Democratic Nation-States", *New Zealand Journal of Asian Studies* 4, 2 (December 2002): 137.

Versailles under King Louis XIV. The "invention of tradition"[108] has thus been put at the core of the process of socio-economic modernisation for a century.

The Museum of Malay Tradition

The sultanate has kept intact ritual procedures going back to the dawn of its history. Even today, during the enthronement ceremony, dignitaries recite the corresponding *chiri*, a half-Arabic, half-Malayo-Sanskrit formula written in Jawi, whose origin dates back to the *Sejarah Melayu*, when the title of Sri Tri Buana, "Lord of the Three Worlds", was conferred upon the Raja of Singapura.[109] This practice is conducted in all the sultanates of the Malay Peninsula[110] and is mentioned in the oldest part of the *Silsilah (A)*.[111] The *chiri* (written on a paper so its efficacy is augmented[112]) is recited in the same way as before,[113] in the presence of a Muslim cleric who plays the role once performed by Brahmins. The esoteric character of the formulas[114]—which always mention "Seri [Tri] Buhana" (Lord of the Three Worlds)[115]—endows them with a strong apotropaic element. The colours of the parasols and standards used by the prime dignities are the same as in the 16th or 18th centuries: white

[108] Eric J. Hosbawm and Terence Ranger, *The Invention of Tradition* (Cambridge: Cambridge University Press, 1983).

[109] By Bat'h, born of the foam coming out of the mouth of a cow (Brown and Roolvink, *Sejarah Melayu 'Malay Annals'*, p. 15 [f. 56]).

[110] Winstedt, "Kingship and Enthronement in Malaya", p. 141; J.M. Gullick, *Indigenous Political Systems of Western Malay* (London: Athlone Press, 1958), pp. 44–64.

[111] *Silsilah (A)*, pp. 22–4 (f. 20–3) mentions that it was the Dato Imam who read the *chiri*, as the dignitaries were usually illiterate.

[112] In a society that traditionally uses talismans and other charms, the writing down of the *chiri*, as recorded several times in the *Silsilah (A)*, confers on it a "magical" value.

[113] The rank of the cleric before whom the *chiri* is read depends on that of the recipient (Jamil Al-Sufri, *Adat istiadat diraja Brunei*, p. 368).

[114] See the translation of the Malayo-Sanskrit terms in Jamil al-Sufri, ibid., pp. 637ff.

[115] Cf. the enthronement formula of Pg. Hashim at one of the *cheteria* grades in H. 1272 (1856) (W.E. Maxwell, *An Account of the Malay 'Chiri', a Sanskrit Formula* [London: RAS, January 1881], 22 p), used in Jamil Al-Sufri, "Chiri gelaran di-Brunei", *Bahana* (1981), pp. 671ff, who adds a third *chiri* to the two Bruneian *chiri* of Maxwell. The Bruneian *chiri* present a preamble in Arabic while those in use up to today in Perak do not, which should be related to the presence of an Arab complement in the titles of the principal Bruneian dignitaries.

(*Bendahara*), green (*Di Gadong*), black (*Pemancha*) and red (*Temenggong*),[116] and as in the Theravadin courts of the Indochinese Peninsula, yellow for the sovereign. These five colours are the very ones found in the symbolic system of the *Orang Petalangan* in Riau, where they correspond to the five components of the human body: white for the spinal column, yellow for the flesh, green for the veins, red for the blood and black for the skin.[117] The use of *nobat* (royal orchestras) for palatine celebrations, which also goes back to the foundation of Malacca[118] and whose most sacred elements are the drums, and more generally the coronation rite as a whole (see the ancient crown on the next page),[119] belong to the same cultural background.[120]

---

[116] With an insertion of yellow in the middle to recall the primacy of the sovereign. On the colours, see Spenser St. John's, *Life in the Forest of the Far East*, vol. II, pp. 259. We find the same four colours in Sulu, where they corresponded to the four-part division of the land, referring back to the four cardinal points.

[117] Tenas Effandy, "The Orang Petalangan of Riau and their Forest Environment", in *Tribal Communities in the Malay World*, ed. Benjamin Geoffrey and Cynthia Chou (Singapore: ISEAS, 2003), pp. 375–6.

[118] Brown and Roolvink, *Sejarah Melayu*, pp. 19, 84, 137, 177, describe all the uses of the *nobat* [ff. 59, 120, 168 and 204 of Brown's manuscript]. Three *nobat* are in use in Brunei today, the most sacred being the "Nobat Iskandar" (*Silsilah [A]*, p. 18 [f. 13]), which perform during coronation ceremonies and whose name refers to Sultan Iskandar Shah, the last sultan of Malacca.

[119] *Istiadat Berpuspa, Kebawah Duli yang Maha Mulia Paduka Seri Sultan Hassanal Bolkiah Mu'izzaddin Waddulah* [*The Coronation Ceremony of His Majesty…*] (Bandar Brunei, 1 August 1968), p. 53. A first crown (likely the original) had been destroyed in the 17th century during the conflict between the usurper Abdul Mubin and the legitimate Sultan Muhiuddin, *Silsilah (B)*, p. 64 (f. 22); the one in Fig. 6 was in turn destroyed during the Australian bombing of 1945.

[120] *Berpuspa* in the dialect of Brunei, based on skt. *puṣpa* = flower, "one who wears flowers", meaning the Crown garlanded with flowers. The coronation rite begins with the bath and the lustration of the sovereign in a pavilion dedicated to this purpose, also found in Cambodia and Siam, which is of Vedic origin. During the *puja* (skt. ceremony) of enthronement, the *Bendahara* pronounces seven formulas, intermingled with the sound of the Nobat Iskandar, successively enthroning the sovereign as (1) King; (2) first; (3) ruler; (4) protector; (5) pillar; (6) Yang Di-Pertuan (he who was made sovereign); (7) mounting the throne of Brunei. The three-tiered crown that was destroyed in 1945 (G.E. Cator, "Brunei", *Asiatic Review* 21 (1935): 1–25) obviously evoked the "Three Worlds" [*Tri Buana*] mentioned in the *chiri*. The crowned sovereign's parade through the capital in a processional carriage reiterates the circumambulation of the ancient Indianised monarchs, etc. See also *Memperingati ulang tahun ke-10 Perpuspaan 1968–1978, Commemorating the 10th anniversary of the Coronation* (BSB: Muzium Brunei, 1978). All the stages of the ritual are punctuated with prayers (*Doa Selamat*), cf. Jamil al-Sufri, *Adat istiadat diraja Brunei*, pp. 303ff.

Figure 6. Crown of Sultan Mohammad Jamalul Alam II, with its three tiers that bestow on the sovereign status of Sri Tri Buana, Lord of the Three Worlds. Brunei was at the time the only Malay sultanate to have kept a crown similar to those used in Malacca [*Istiadat Berpuspa, Kebawah Duli Yang Maha Mulia Paduka Seri Sultan Hassanal Bolkiah Mu'izzaddin Waddulah (Ceremony of Coronation of His Majesty the Sultan Hassanal Bolkiah Mu'izzaddin Waddulah)*. Bandar Brunei, 1 Aug. 1968, p. 53].

As in the 17th century,[121] the processions that took place during princely marriage ceremonies or coronations carried the various royal insignia in multiples of four.[122] The use of *bahasa dalam* (court language)[123] and the formalism of public relations that it conveys,[124] were not only maintained but widely promoted for the purposes of building national identity[125]—to the point that they might in time constitute a level of language that is used regularly, such as the Javanese *kromo inggil*.[126] Finally,

[121] See *Silsilah (A)*, pp. 32–6 (ff. 38–46).

[122] Jamil al-Sufri, *Adat istiadat diraja Brunei*, pp. 306ff.

[123] On the persisting use of *bahasa dalam* in Malaysia, see Laurent Metzger, *Les sultanats de Malaisie, un régime monarchique au XXe siècle* (Paris: L'Harmattan, 1994), pp. 107ff.

[124] The use of the *bahasa dalam* is mentioned by Spenser St. John's, *Life in the Forest of the Far East*, p. 267, and the extreme formalism that accompanies it by W.H. Treacher, *British Borneo, Sketches of Brunai, Sarawak, Labuan, and North Borneo* (Singapore, reprint from the *JSSBRAS*, 1891), pp. 20–1.

[125] Pg. Dr. Hidop bin Pg Hj Samsuddin, "The Significance and Substance of Brunei's Court Language" (BSB, draft, 2009), 19 p; "Bahasa Dalam [Part of Court language]", note sent to the diplomatic corps, 2009.

[126] Fatima Awang Chuchu, "The Palace Language of Brunei", in *Language use and language change in Brunei Darussalam*", ed. W. Martin, Conrad Ozóg and Gloria Poedjosoedarmo, pp. 89–104. The *kromo inggil* is today the third and last level of the Javanese language (after *ngoko* and *kromo*), reserved for conversation with an interlocutor of high rank.

while tradition tries to link the royal emblem (the *panji*[2] strikingly present at the centre of the flag), which appears for the first time on a coin struck in 1865[127] but is mentioned in the *Silsilah (A)*,[128] to Sultan Sharif Ali of the 15th century,[129] it is more likely to be directly inherited from Sassanid numismatics of the first century of the Hegira.[130]

Figure 7. Dirham dated the 75th year of the Hegira (693 BCE)

Figure 8. *Piti* (tin alloy), Brunei, 1865

The crown on the first Muslim coins up until 698, when Caliph Abd al-Mâlik abandoned human representation on currency, is itself derived from that of Sassanid sovereigns, which questions the introduction of this type of representation in Brunei more than a half millennium after the Hegira.[131] Land where the "Malay" tradition[132] has been re-invented, Brunei is also that of its conservation.

[127] Abdul Latif Haji Ibrahim, *Sejarah Rengkas Panji*[2] *Negeri Brunei: A Short History of the Brunei State Crest]* (BSB: Muzium Brunei, 1972), p. 2.
[128] *Silsilah (A)*, p. 18 (f. 13) and p. 35 (f. 44).
[129] It is mentioned by Pigafetta (Nicholl, *European Sources*, p. 9).
[130] Cf. Cécile Beurdeley, *Sur les routes de la Soie, le grand voyage des objets d'art* (Paris: Seuil & Freiburg, Office du Livre, 1985), p. 145, fig. 147, coin of 693 CE.
[131] One hypothesis is that this type of coin was introduced by Arab or Persian merchants and some were kept among the regalia. This is plausible considering the discovery of a tenth-century gold Persian coin among the "treasure of Limbang" (Harrisson, "The Golden Hoard of Limbang", p. 59). However, in the tenth century, Persian coins were all aniconic.
[132] See Eric J. Hosbawm and Terence Ranger, *The Invention of Tradition* (Cambridge: Cambridge University Press, 1983), 332 p.

Tradition as an Instrument for Managing Society

Playing on Proximity and Preserving Distance

This customary conservatism comes along with many celebrations that are, by contrast, mostly innovations. Muslim festivals and civilian ceremonies regularly put the sovereign in contact with his subjects, as a way of strengthening the social linkage rebuilt during the 20th century. This runs against the practice related by Pigafetta, in which the sovereign only communicated with his subjects by means of a bamboo,[133] symbolising the distance separating the proxy of the gods from the world of men, a sovereign who frequently lived in seclusion, as confirmed too by later sources.

Thus in September 2010, during Hari Raya,[134] which celebrates the end of the fasting month and the start of the month of Shawal, 100,000 people, children and immigrants included—the equivalent of more than a quarter of the sultanate's population—paraded for three days to pay respect to the sovereigns, with men paying respect to the sultan and women to the queen. Almost all the inhabitants of the capital region made their way to the Palace, plus some from Kuala Belait at 100 km away, participating as individuals and families. The sultan in his capacity as chancellor of the university personally presents university diplomas during graduation ceremonies. He also attends the Friday prayer in a

[133] Pigafetta, in Nicholl, *European Sources*, p. 10. The use of bamboo is a symbolic reference to the descent of gods from Mont Meru, also evoked in the Negeri Sembilan. Under the ancient palace hung an oblong pillar held by a rope that did not touch the ground (Winstedt, "Kingship and Enthronement in Malaya", p. 136).

[134] On the evolution of the celebration, see Rozan Yunos, *The Golden Warisan*, vol. 1, pp. 239ff.

different mosque each week. He is equally present at the inauguration of factories or important administrative or community buildings; this is interspersed with lesser manifestations by the crown prince or the wazirs, Prince Mohamed and Prince Sufri, etc.

Regardless of the emphasis on hierarchy, the royal family remains close to its subjects, without reducing the considerable statutory distance between the people and the sovereign. This is evident in the abundant protocol and the use of *bahasa dalam*, for example, the use of *peramba* for the first person singular (from the lexeme *[h]amba* = slave) when addressing an ordinary *pengiran*, even if the speaker is himself a *Pehin*.

Recognition of Constituted Bodies

The multiplication of celebrations helps to promote modern governance through constituted bodies, which are paraded during religious festivals such as *Maulud* (the birth of the Prophet)[135] or civilian ones such as National Day.[136] These celebrations feature representatives of the various components of society, present not on the sole basis of their rank but through their work and the institution to which they belong. If the sultan's birthday[137] is indeed officially celebrated by a parade in the morning followed by a dinner at the palace, he is also invited in the following days by the main corporate bodies of the kingdom—ministries, institutions, foreign representations and the biggest companies such as Brunei Shell. The sultan also tours the four provinces whose leaders—all appointed by him—pledge anew their loyalty to him, drinking the water of the oath of allegiance, an age-old ritual.[138]

---

[135] Ibid., vol. 2, pp. 92ff.

[136] See, for example, *Konsep dan format, upacara perhimpunan Agung Hari Kabangsaan Negara Brunei Darussalam, kali-ke 24, 16 Safar 1429–23 Februari 2008* [*Conception and format, Ceremony of the great gathering of the 24th national anniversary of Brunei Darussalam*...], 2008; Kula Haji Md. Noor. (Hj.), *Kata dan bentuk bahasa dalam dalam konteks pentadbiran beradat di Negara Brunei Darussalam* [*Words and terms of address in Court language in the customary administration of Brunei Darussalam*], BSB, DBPB, 2007, 180 p). Fixing National Day on 23 February, date of the official celebration in the presence of foreign leaders, and not on 1 January (date of independence) has avoided linking the existence of the nation to the retrocession of full regalian powers thanks to independence (G. Braighlinn, *Ideological innovation under monarchy: aspects of legitimation activity in contemporary Brunei*, p. 24).

[137] On 15 July.

[138] Braighlinn, *Ideological innovation under monarch*, p. 47.

Tradition as a Substitute for Parliamentary Representation?

Adat istiadat[139] becomes the means to simultaneously: (1) celebrate the monarchy; (2) nurture the linkage between subjects and the monarch through festivals that restore the proximity to the crown; (3) recognise the status, no matter how minor, of managers of the social body and thus their participation in the social order;[140] (4) strengthen the primacy of the Malays while multiplying the scope of social promotion, thanks to a dissociation between honours and offices; (5) promote an "organic" implementation that relies on corporate bodies and not on individuals, the latter being considered as potential troublemakers. Celebrating over and over again the cohesiveness of society compensates for the absence of representation[141] of its components, the whole system proceeding from a world view that is specifically Southeast Asian, where "the measure of all things, in other words the law, order, the working of the world and its representation in the widest sense, is obtained by making a hierarchy of ranks [...]".[142]

---

[139] Donald E. Brown, "Mechanism for the Maintenance of Traditional Élites in Brunei to the Eve of Independence", in *From Buckfast to Borneo: Essays Presented to Father Robert Nicholl on the 85th Anniversary of his Birth, 27 March 1995*, ed. King and Horton, pp. 408–19.

[140] Pg. Dr. Hidop bin Pg. Hj Samsuddin, "Tatasusila mendukung keharmonian dan memengkin pembangunan [Moral rules sustain harmony and permit development]" (BSB: Penolong Yang Di-Pertuan Adat Istiadat, Jabatan Adat Istiadat), 46 p.

[141] The powers of the sovereign were strengthened even further when Brunei gained full independence, as demonstrated by the following excerpts dating from 1984, of the *Dokumen-Dokumen perlembagaan, Constitutional Documents* (BSB, 8 November 2008), Part III, 4 §3, p. 51: "His Majesty may appoint from among citizens of Brunei Darussalam any numbers of Ministers [...] who shall be responsible solely to His Majesty [...]"; Part IV, 5 § 3, p. 55: "Every Appointed Member of the Privy Council shall hold office during His Majesty the Sultan and *Yang Di-Pertuan*'s pleasure [...]"; and Part VI, 31 §1, p. 81: "Every member of the Legislative Council shall hold his seat during His Majesty the Sultan and *Yang Di-Pertuan*'s pleasure [...]".

[142] Grégory Mikaelian, speaking of Cambodia, in his book review "Oknā Veang Thiounn, *Voyage du roi Sisowath en France en l'année du cheval, huitième de la décade, correspondant à l'année occidentale 1906*", translated from Khmer, introduced and annotated by Olivier de Bernon, *Péninsule* 56 (2008): 213.

MELAYU ISLAM BERAJA

Such celebration of *adat istiadat* might appear artificial to the grandchildren of the voters of Azahari's PRB in 1962, were it not in turn encased in a wider framework, not just of a symbolic order but also an ideological one: the *Melayu Islam Beraja* or MIB, which over-signifies the Crown's "organic" legitimacy, the Crown being the only master of the synthesis of Custom (*adat Melayu Brunei*) and of Religion, thus warding off the traumatic shift to modernity by the re-inscription of the sultanate into a cultural continuum. The apparently anodyne title that defines Malay identity as Muslim and monarchic (the official English translation —*Malay Islamic Monarchy* being a semantic shift) conceals the gradual application of a state ideology that innervates the whole public sphere. The legitimising rewriting of history and the imposition of an "orthodox" Islamic behavioural norm thus become the foundation of a "Bruneian" cultural identity in which the monarchy, exemplary as well as legitimate, proves to be the privileged instrument of the divine project for the sultanate of Brunei Darussalam. The sultan is jointly Head of State, Head of Religion and Head of *Adat Istiadat*.[1]

[1] "Ideology and Public Administration: MIB perspective" (English title, Malay text), http://www.docstoc.com/docs/23848748/ceramah_pg_dr_bakardoc, c. 2010.

The Making of History in the Service of Power

Origins of MIB

While the very concept of MIB was launched at the start of the 1950s by Sultan Omar Ali Saifuddin III, it was not formalised by a doctrinal corpus until the early 1970s. However, a first modern book of a historical nature[2] was published in Brunei in 1958 by Yura Halim (alias Pg. Mhmd. Yusuf, the reviver of royal custom, whose *adat istiadat* was published the same year) and Jamil Umar (al. Jamil al-Sufri). As soon as it acquired internal autonomy in 1959, Brunei created a publishing house, Dewan Bahasa dan Pustaka (DBP),[3] to promote Malay culture through the development of publishing in Romanised Malay. The premises of re-writing history were laid after the abdication of the *Begawan*, when the 1967 *Annual Report* interpreted the paragraph in the 1905 agreement with the British, as reserving *adat* and religion for the sultan's intervention alone,[4] although it was not until 1959 that this became effectively the case for *adat*. The text of the agreement at the end of the same volume lists the many measures taken—in the name of the sultan—with regard to taxable property (*tulin*), previously managed on the basis of custom, during the first decades of the residency.

[2] Yura Halim and Jamil Umar, *Sejarah Brunei* [*History of Brunei*] (Kuala Belait: Percetakan Brunei, 1958), 53 p.
[3] Language and Literature Bureau.
[4] Braighlinn, *Ideological innovation under monarchy*, p. 26. Also *Annual Report 1967*, pp. 321, 336–7.

The organisation of the coronation ceremonies of the new sultan was entrusted to the *Pemancha*, Pengiran Hj. Mohammad Alam (father-in-law of the young sovereign[5] and brother-in-law of the *Begawan*), whose deputy was none other than the *Menteri Besar* Pg. Mhmd. Yusuf.[6] And it was the Dewan Bahasa dan Pustaka—under the direction since 1965 of Jamil al-Sufri,[7] who was granted the title *Pehin* in 1968—who was tasked with organising the coronation of the new sultan, via a working group created for this purpose whose deputy director was Abdul Aziz bin Haji Umar,[8] younger brother of the same Pehin Jamil. The orchestration of MIB was thus the deed of a triumvirate—Pengiran Mhmd. Yusuf, Jamil al-Sufri and his brother Aziz.

A new step toward the sultanate's rewriting of its own history was taken in 1973 with the publication by the same Jamil al-Sufri of the second historical book produced in Brunei, *Chatatan Sejarah*,[9] prefaced

---

[5] Also his maternal uncle, since the *Begawan* had married his sister; later when he became widowed he would marry her youngest sister.

[6] Istiadat Berpuspa, *Kebawah Duli yang Maha Mulia Paduka Seri Sultan Hassanal Bolkiah Mu'izzaddin Waddulah*, p. 10.

[7] Born in Kampung Ayer in 1921, Pehin Mhd. Jamil al-Sufri is the son of the Udana Khatib, the fourth dignitary of the Muslim religion in the sultanate. After two years at the SITC of Perak (1939–41), he went back to Brunei, started his career as a teacher and became deputy director of primary schools. During the war, he resumed his studies at Kanri Yosezyo Training Centre of Kuching (1944–45). Back in Brunei, he became the general secretary of BARIP (Youth Front, which was close to the Pengiran Muda, the future sultan Omar Ali Saifuddin) in 1946. He returned to SITC in 1948–49, pursued his studies at the Agricultural College of Selangor (1950–51), then completed his training in England where he enrolled in a history course at the Teachers College of Worcester (1956–57). See his biography in Muhammad Abd. Latiff, *Monograf Jurnal Generasi, Pehin Jawatan Dalam Seri Maharaja Dato Seri Utama Dr. Haji Awang Mohd. Jamil al-Sufri: ensiklopedia bergerak sejarah Brunei: satu pengenalan ringkas* [*Monograph, Journal of a generation, Pehin… Jamil Al-Sufri: an encyclopedia in movement of the history of Brunei, a short study*] (BSB: Pusat Sejarah, 2008), 212 p.

[8] Pehin Dato Abdul Aziz, born in 1936 (cf. Horton, *The Top Hundred Persons of Power and Influence in Negara Brunei Darussalam A.D. 2000*, pp. 32–3, 75–6), acting *menteri besar* from 1981 to December 1983, minister of education (1989–2005), minister of health (1998–2002), is today the third of four *menteri* placed just above the *menteri* 4.

[9] *Chatatan sejarah perwira² dan pembesar Brunei* [*Notes on the history of dignitaries and titled persons of Brunei*], Jilid II (Brunei: Dewan Bahasa dan Pustaka, vol. 1 [1971], 86 p and vol. 2 [1973], 190 p).

by the *Begawan*. This consisted of a compilation of Malay and Western documents, the sources of which were usually not mentioned. In the second volume can be found pell-mell: the history of the Bendahara Sakam taken from the *Silsilah (B)*;[10] an interesting biography of Sultan Hassan,[11] based on information from *Silsilah (A)* and *(B)*[12] and from Spanish archives;[13] a very long and undated genealogy of Pehin O.K. Di Gadong Seri Nara (whose origin would be worth knowing since it mentions the female side of his parentage);[14] the genealogy of the sultans of Sulu;[15] a legal code; and lastly, the biography of the Perdana Menteri Ibrahim bin Mohd. Jahfar (pp. 157–88). This compendium is accompanied by an adornment of facts: while *Silsilah (B)* mentions that Bendahara Sakam was the son of a *Bajau* without going into any other details, the *Chatatan Sejarah* states that his mother was a Bajau "princess".[16] Moreover, the first volume based itself on a new version of the *Silsilah* discovered in 1971, so as to demonstrate the historic anteriority of Brunei in relation to Malacca. It asserted that the founder of Singapura (and heir of Srivijaya) Sri Tri Buana was the author of the conversion and coronation (in *Singapura*) of the first sultan, Awang Alak Betatar,[17] whereas none of the *Silsilah* versions edited by Sweeney or Low, nor the *Batu Tarsilah* contain any trace of this, any more so than the *Sya'ir Awang Simawn*, which mentions that the first sultan was crowned in Brunei.[18]

---

[10] *Silsilah (B)*, pp. 54–5 (ff. 6–8).

[11] Despite an error (p. 27) regarding the date of reign of Sultan Iskandar Muda of Aceh, which is not 1612–31, but 1607–36 (Denys Lombard, *Le Sultanat d'Aceh au temps d'Iskandar Muda [1607–1636]* [Paris: EFEO, 1967], 297 p).

[12] *Silsilah (A)*, p. 12 (f. 3) & *(B)* p. 56 (ff. 9–10), plus excerpts (pp. 39–40) from the maritime codes contained in the *Silsilah (A)* pp. 39–49 (ff. 51–63).

[13] Providing notably the transliteration of a 1599 letter from the sultan to Don Francisco Tello, hitherto only known through the English translation of the Spanish translation (Nicholl, *European sources*, pp. 93–4).

[14] Pp. 43–97.

[15] Pp. 97–112, taken from the work by Najeeb Saleeby, *The History of Sulu* (Manila: Bureau of Printing, 1908), reprint Nabu Press, 2010.

[16] "Anak raja Bajau Sabah" (Jamil Al-Sufri, "The Story of Bendahara Sakam", *BMJ* 3, 3 [1975]: 109–15).

[17] P. 6, cited by Braighlinn, *Ideological innovation under monarchy*, p. 30.

[18] Maxwell, "Accessing the Epic Status of the Brunei Malay Sya'ir Awang Simawn", episodes [67] to [69], p. 14.

This work of official historiography led to the publication of a first series of history textbooks designed for secondary education in 1976.[19] Thus was established an official chronology, although the coronation booklet of 1968 contained a genealogy of the sultans[20] with no date prior to the start of the 19th century.

Highjacking History: The Creation of the *Pusat Sejarah*

To boost the creation of a Bruneian historical personality and in order to claim a scientific approach, the Pusat Sejarah (History Centre)[21] was created in 1982 under the leadership of Pehin Jamil Al-Sufri, who left the DBP (although he remained an advisor to the publishing house).

The objective of the History Centre is, as its name (*pusat*) shows, constitute the focal point for researching the history of the sultanate. Most importantly, the Centre aims to become a "source" (*pusat sumber*) of historical production after the systematic collation of materials inside and outside the country—in short, to constitute a consensual pole for the "reconciliation" of viewpoints and to become the sole acknowledged authority[22] on the matter. In other words, the goal is not so much to support or undermine any hypothesis or still less to compare hypotheses in the classic scientific way, but rather to establish a dogma. This kind of history is foremost that of sovereigns and their families, leaders and titled people,[23] hence the attention to genealogies (princely or otherwise),[24] which remain to this day the principal textual sources of Brunei.

---

[19] With two editions, in Malay and in English, for example, DBP, *Sejarah Brunei untok tingkatan menengah rendah & History of Brunei for Lower Secondary Schools*, 1976, 79 p which devotes a third of its content to the Western discoverers of Brunei, with a reproduction of the statue of Pigafetta (p. 29).

[20] *Istiadat Berpuspa, Kebawah Duli yang Maha Mulia Paduka Seri Sultan Hassanal Bolkiah Mu'izzaddin Waddulah* [*Coronation of HM…*], pp. 56–7.

[21] Or Centre on the History of Brunei (Horton, *Turun-temurun: A Dissection of Brunei Darussalam*, p. 36).

[22] "Pusat rujukan yang autoritif", http://www.history-centre.gov.bn/visi.htm [accessed May 2014]. The English version of the site presents significant differences from the Malay version, translating "Pusat rujukan yang autoritif" to "authorised institution", a "recognised" institution, and not "institution for 'reconciliation' having authority [over others]", which is the true meaning in Malay.

[23] "Objektif", § 1, http://www.history-centre.gov.bn/Objektif.htm.

[24] The first unit of the Centre is dedicated to genealogies.

The department of epigraphy, essentially of funerary steles, another major source, occupies the third position within the Centre's organisational structure, followed by architectural vestiges,[25] which are more limited due to the repeated destructions of 1578, during the 19th century and World War Two. Other archaeological information—ceramic shards and artefacts from the collection *in situ* of material sources—is not mentioned and remains the province of the National Museum; neither are Chinese or oral (*puak sakai*)[26] sources to be found. The pre-Islamic period is only interesting to the Centre as an illustration of the antiquity of the Bruneian polity, because the time factor—as with the rest of the Malay world and in Southeast Asia in general—offers a legitimising value. One example among others is the genealogy of the sultans of Kedah, drawn from the *Hikayat Merong Mahawongsa*, presented on the website of the sultanate.[27] Apart from the classic tasks of collecting data, publishing and training, the Pusat Sejarah is thus the sole actor in a re-appropriation of the "history of the country and people of Brunei, to avoid its alteration by foreign authors",[28] who are obviously not considered true historians.[29]

A Key Policy Instrument

Invested with the mission to "correct the errors in the writing of Brunei's history and make it conform to the country's aspirations (that is, Brunei-centric)",[30] the Pusat Sejarah had published 32 books by the end of 2010:

---

25 "Bahagian-bahagian", http://www.history-centre.gov.bn/b_penyelidik.htm.

26 Etymologically, the "savages" and "aborigines" of Bruneian mythography, those considered as being the oldest inhabitants of the land, whose presence is thus essential for major royal rites.

27 The royal dynasty of Kedah is supposed to go back to 1136, according to the *Hikayat Merong Mahawonsa*, composed c. 1821 (http://kdymmtuankusultan.kedah.gov.my/index.php?id=5&sub=0).

28 "[…] sejarah negara dan bangsa Brunei agar tidak diselewengkan oleh penulis-penulis asing", http://history-centre.gov.bn/Objecktif.htm.

29 On the beginnings of Bruneian historiography, see Sanib b. Said, "The Development of Brunei Historiography, a Survey and evaluation", Conference of the International Association of Historians of Asia, 27–31 October 1986, Singapore.

30 "[…] Membetulkan penyelewengan penulisan sejarah Brunei supaya selaras dengan aspirasi negara (Brunei-sentrik)", http://history-centre.gov.bn/strategi.htm, reprinted in "Books on Brunei should be more 'Brunei-centric': minister", *Brunei Times*, 25 February 2011.

a third of its publications were general history books reconstructing the chronology of the sultanate since its origins; another third were historical monographs; and the rest were four biographies, three books devoted to Islam, three to the MIB and the Romanised edition of the *Sya'ir Rakis*, composed on the occasion of the cession of the island of Labuan to the British.

Four of the six volumes published in English are translations of Malay reference works: a chronology of the sultanate before Islamisation, a historical synopsis, the march toward independence and Islam in Brunei. Twenty of these 32 volumes—almost the whole general history section—are authored by Pehin Jamil al-Sufri: the edification of official historiography is thus the product of one individual, whose position of authority on the subject is at least as strong as that occupied by the mufti on the doctrinal level.

History has become one of the key instruments of policy-making,[31] inasmuch as it draws an "easily comprehensible" picture of the past, able to hammer out a collective consciousness that is "loyal and loving toward the immemorial Royalty"[32] and grounds "a feeling of belonging to the Nation and the country". Rather than gauging history by the standards of methodologies and referents used in the West, it is foremost a re-writing of the *Silisilah Raja Raja Brunei* that belongs to the purest Malay tradition.[33]

---

[31] See the presentation of the latest publications of the Pusat Sejarah in the "History Centre launches New Book", *Brunei Times*, 25 February 2011 and http://narawahana.blogspot.com/.

[32] "[…] yang berbalankan [*balan* signifies 'to forge' in the dialect of Brunei, *Bahana*, 6/16, 1971, p. 978], taat setia dan perasaan kasih sayang kepada Raja yang telah dipusakai turun-menurun […]", § 4, http://www.history-centre.gov.bn/Objektif.htm.

[33] See A.H. Johns, "The Turning Image: Myth and Reality in Malay Perceptions of the Past", in *Perceptions of the Past in Southeast Asia*, ed. Anthony Reid and David Marr (Singapore: Heinemann, 1979), pp. 43–67.

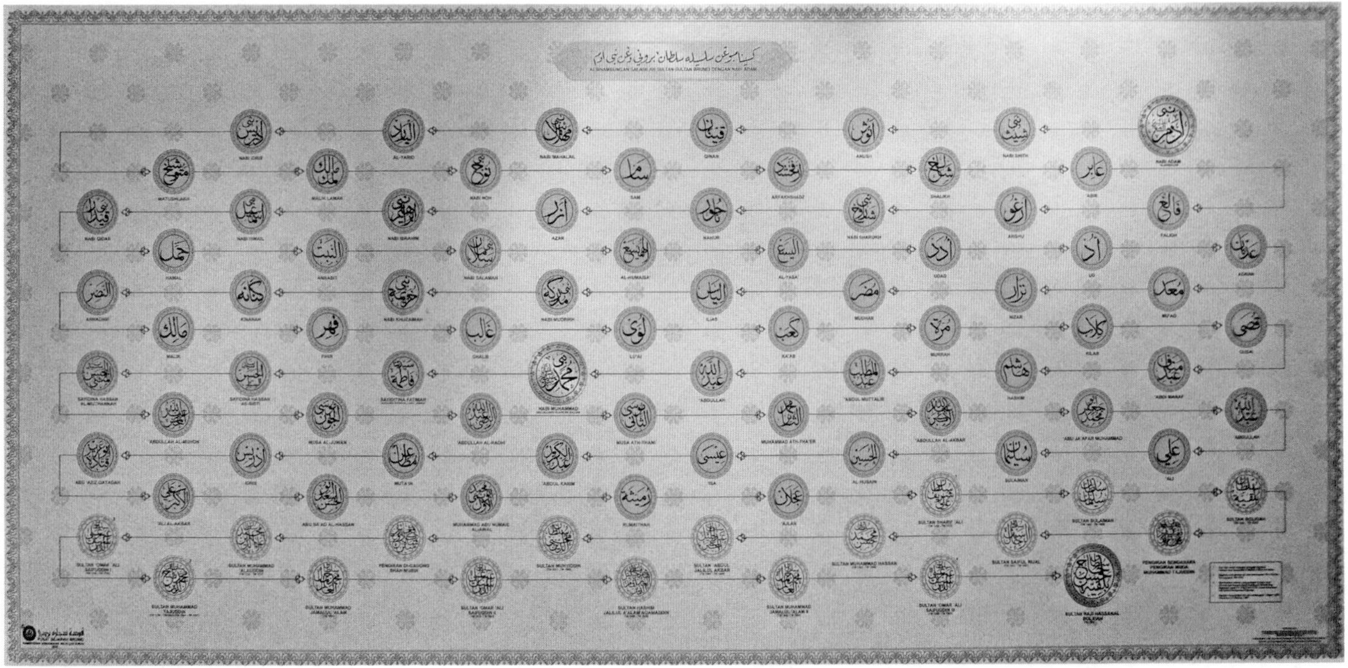

Figure 9. Pusat Sejarah, Genealogy of HM the Sultan Hassanal Bolkiah until Nabi Adam (above right) (Photo by the author, June 2012)

Power at the Service of Religion—And Vice Versa

This re-writing of history with the aim of legitimising the dynasty goes hand in hand with the strengthening of the Islamic framework of society.

Increasing Instruments for Religious Practice

The multiplication of instruments for the practice and propagation of religion has kept pace with the enrichment of Brunei. Muslim religious schools went from 7 in the mid-1950s to more than 80 in 1971. While they increased by only 28% from 1971–83, the relay was taken over by mosques, whose number grew by almost half. After independence, the construction of mosques matched demographic growth, averaging one mosque for 2,500 inhabitants,[34] and likewise for Muslim schools.

Staff under the supervision of the Ministry of Religious Affairs (including teachers in religious schools) tripled between 1983[35] and 2010. As for the *hajj*, the pilgrimage to Mecca[36] that constitutes one of the five obligations of believers, it is today subject to the quota allotted to each

[34] In addition to the two national mosques (Omar Ali Saifuddin and Hassanal Bolkiah), Brunei had 11 great mosques, 25 district mosques (*mukim*), 53 village mosques, 7 oratories (*surau*) and 11 prayer halls (*balai ibadat*) in 2010. Each building or group of administrative buildings also has its own *surau*, which is not counted in these statistics.

[35] *Penyata tahunan 1983, Jabatan hal ehwal ugama Negara Brunei Darussalam*, Ramadhan 1404, Jun [*sic*] 1984, p. 3.

[36] The *hajj* can only take place during the month of pilgrimage *Dhu al-Hijjah*, a pilgrimage during other periods of the year (*umrah*) is not considered a substitute.

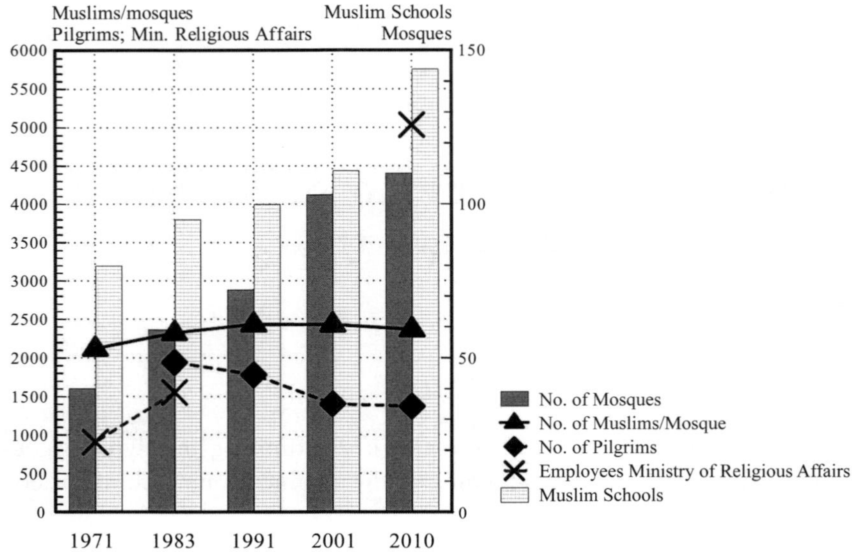

Graph 28. Islam in Brunei, 1971–2010

country by Saudi authorities, which explains why the number of pilgrims dropped by a quarter between 1991 and 2001 before stabilising.[37]

Religion under Political Supervision

The most noteworthy aspect of this management of religion is that religion in Brunei has come under the control of the public administration more so than in any other Southeast Asian country where the population is mostly Muslim: integrated into the *menteri* hierarchy and given the title of *pehin*, religious dignitaries are part and parcel of the state apparatus.[38] While Brunei had been without a mufti plausibly since the start of the 1930s,[39] in April 1962 Sultan Omar Ali Saifuddin recruited

[37] Except for the years 2008 and 2009 when the number of pilgrims dropped by 50% after the bird flu epidemics.

[38] Arifin Mansurnoor, "Socio-religious changes in Brunei during the British Residency (1906–1959)", 1998.

[39] The *Silsilah (B)*, p. 76 (f. 44) mentions the nomination in 1913 of Imam Al-Haj Muhiuddin ibnu Nahoda Jembul Burong Pingai [the religious quarter in Kampung Ayer] to the post of Datu Seri Maharaja Mufti of Brunei.

the chief *kadi* (religious judge) of Johor.[40] Given the backdrop of major political turbulence and the return of young graduates from Al-Azhar University in Cairo,[41] the mission of the new mufti was clear: to give weight to the official religion and to "issue *fatwa*, regulations, points of law, etc., for the peace of Bruneians and of the country".[42] The mufti is thus placed under the double tutelage of the Department of Religious Affairs and of the Council of Islamic Religion, the latter being involved each time a regulation is issued. But the context underlying the management of religion was shattered during the 1970s. On the Malay Peninsula, the imminent disappearance of traditional rural society, upset by the New Economic Policy and its positive discrimination in favour of the *bumiputera*,[43] combined with the rise of parliamentary monarchies, which gradually confined sovereigns to a symbolic role, entailed a return of Islamic activism and the flourishing of various movements, including the Darul al-Arqam.[44] The latter had great success in Brunei—to the point of being finally banned in February 1991.

Consequently, in the mid-1980s the Brunei authorities engaged in a showdown with religious extremists,[45] which meant strengthening the

[40] He held the post from April 1962 to March 1965, then reassumed it in March 1967 until his death in February 1993. The recruitment of a mufti in Johor paradoxically refers to the foundation myth, the *Sya'ir Awang Simawn*, which confers on Johor the legitimising function of presenting the regalia.

[41] Among them, the future minister of religious affairs Mohammad Zain, who helped furnish the Islamic doctrinal corpus part of the MIB in the early 1970s [Arifin Mansurnoor, "Socioreligious changes in Brunei during the British Residency (1906–1959)", p. 19].

[42] Rescript [*titah*] of Sultan Omar Ali Saifuddin III in January 1961, "Latar belakang lantikan Mufti [The context of the installation of the Mufti]", http://www.brunet.bn/gov/mufti/pengenalan/latarbelakang.htm.

[43] In Malaysia, the most important of Muslim associations, the *Angkatan Belia Islam Malaysia* (ABIM) or Movement of Muslim Youth of Malaysia, created by Anwar Ibrahim in 1971, already counted 35,000 members in 1980. Anwar Ibrahim spent two years in prison (1979–81) under the Internal Security Act, then joined UMNO (1982), became minister of education (1983), minister of finance (1991) and finally vice-president of UMNO (and thus presumed heir to Mahathir) in 1993, before being ousted on the occasion of the 1997 financial crisis.

[44] See Part IV.

[45] On the importance attached to this threat, Robert Nicholl (letter to J. Népote, 7 December 1984, J. Népote Fund) relates that Bruneian students abroad (600 in the United Kingdom alone) were firmly warned in 1984 by the sultan to "avoid all contact with the fundamentalists in Europe".

institutions of control. In October 1986, the department of religious affairs became a full ministry and the mufti was placed under the Office of Shariah; a deputy mufti post was created in 1989. To counter the threat represented by a Southeast Asian Islamic radicalism forged in the Afghan conflict[46] (whose fighters went back to their countries of origin after the Soviet collapse), the authorities justified the growing control of the religious apparatus by the ostentatious reaffirmation of the central character of religion within the MIB. In November 1994, on the pretext of asserting the primacy of the Islamic faith,[47] the mufti's office was placed directly under the orders of the prime minister, that is, the sultan. If the mufti's first mission is undoubtedly to "implement God's Law", the second is explicitly to sustain the king's position.[48] The mufti is thus in charge of writing—under the sultan's supervision—the unique Friday sermon that is read in all the mosques in the country. The sultan is both "head of religion and the highest authority in the country",[49] and so the mosque becomes the "channel of the King's command",[50] his privileged vehicle. Attendance of the Friday sermon is obligatory for all Muslim males, under threat of a penalty fine. All clerics are appointed by the sultan and responsible to him alone; they are tasked with "giving a proper comprehension of the teaching of Islam",[51] in conformity with the directives of the Council of Islamic Religion.[52] The sovereign's role in religion[53] belongs to a Malay tradition that not only makes the sultan

---

[46] The Filipino Muslim leaders of the MNLF, MILF and Abu Sayyaf, of the Indonesian Laskar Jihad, and several movements of South Thailand trained there.

[47] "Penubuhan ini sangat bermakna kepada syiara dan status Islam di Negara Brunei [...] [This establishment strongly attests to the law of Islam and its status in Brunei...]", http://www.brunet.bn/gov/mufti/pengenalan/jabatan%20mufti.htm.

[48] "Mendukung Wawasan Raja" (ibid.), the second of eight attributes of the mufti.

[49] "[...] ketua agama dan pemerintah tertinggi [...]", in Ismail Bin Haji Abd Manap (Hj.), "Masjid Wadah Kepimpinan raja: pengalaman negara Brunei Darussalam [The Mosque, channel of royal authority, the case of Brunei Darussalam]", *Seminar Institusi Masjid, 19–21 July 2004* (BSB: Majlis Ilmu), http://www.majlisilmu.org.bn/ilmu2004/archieve/kklat.htm.

[50] *Seminar Institusi Masjid, masjid Wadah Kemimpinan* [*Seminar on the Institution of the Mosque, Mosque channel of authority*], Majlis Ilmu [Scientific Counci], attached to the Prime Minister Office, 19–21 July 2004.

[51] Majlis Ugama Islam, http://www.religious-affairs.gov.bn./index.php?tpl=th003_english_org.

[52] Attached to the Ministry of Religious Affairs.

[53] "Obey the king and adhere to Islamic Teachings: Sermon", *Brunei Times*, 19 February 2011.

(like any man) the guardian of God's trust (*amanah*), but also "the shadow of God in this world [*zillu'llahi fil 'alam*]"[54]—although this title has never been used in Brunei. The authorities' religious involvement is hard to contest: on top of training five graduates in religion and two doctorates,[55] constructing seven new religious schools and two bilingual Arab schools in five years, permitting each year 0.5% of Muslim residents who have not done so to undertake the *hajj* and registering 20% more participation in religious education by adults per year, etc., the last governing plan (2010–14) of the Ministry of Religious Affairs called for dispensing religious education to all children above the age of seven and using all possible methods of dissemination opened up by virtual social networks (Twitter, Facebook, etc.).

A Persistent Worry

Yet, beneath the roundabout discourses and the ensuing concrete measures exists a persistent worry about radical Islam. With the elevation of the MIB to the rank of official ideology in July 1990, the sultanate embarked—ten years after Malaysia and for the same reasons—on an Arabisation of religious practice. This translated to a multiplication of neologisms of Arab origin (on top of the borrowings that have existed in Malay for centuries)[56] and the obligation for women to adopt Middle Eastern dress codes that more or less reproduce the dress codes of the Bruneian aristocracy in the 19th century.[57] Architecture (except for the mosque on the campus of the Universiti Brunei Darussalam) has pursued the movement unleashed by the construction of the Omar Ali Saifuddin Mosque, completed in 1958, which substituted the wooden tiered roofs

[54] Hussain Othman, "Malay concept of Man in History", *Jurnal Perabadan Melayu* 5, 2008, electronic edition, p. 9, citing the *Hikayat Raha Raja Pasai* [*History of the Kings of Pasai*] and the *Sejarah Melayu* [*History of the Malays*] among others, the title of *zillu'llahi fil 'alam* itself being borrowed from the Ottoman caliphate.

[55] Within the Kolej Universiti Perguruan Ugama Seri Begawan (*KUPUSB*) or Seri Begawan University College of Teachers of Religion.

[56] Sven A. Schottmann, "'Melayu Islam Beraja': The Politics of Legitimisation in a Malay Islamic Monarchy", *Review of Indonesian and Malaysian Affairs* 40, 2 (2006): 130.

[57] W.H. Treacher, *British Borneo, Sketches of Brunai, Sarawak, Labuan, and North Borneo*, p. 40: "Ladies of rank and wealth substitute silk and gold brocade for the cotton material used by their poorer sisters and, in lieu of a hat, cover their head and the greater part of the face with a *selendang*, or long scarf of gold brocade."

of traditional Malay mosques with golden cupolas and ceramics. Some traditional arts now survive only marginally, such as the *gulintangan*, a percussion orchestra ressembling the Javanese *gamelan*.[58]

However, despite many promises of full adherence to the values and codes of the Arab Peninsula meant to cut the ground from under the feet of possible fundamentalists, the mufti still judged it necessary in July 2010 to mention, backed by citations from religious texts, the "Islamic character of the defence of the monarchical institution" and the role "of safeguarding the teachings of Islam in the preservation of Malay sovereignty". He also denouced out of the blue Western ideologies such as communism and capitalism and even nationalism "ala Hatta" (in other words, Indonesian, but without naming a brother country), castigating free speech, critical thought and democratic practice as threats against royal sovereignty.[59] Thus were believers reminded for the umpteenth time that they ought to obey both God and their leader—a repeat of the reminder issued four years ago in July 2006, during the annual Scientific Council seminar[60] entitled "The king reigns, the country is blessed and the people is at peace".[61] In the eyes of Southeast Asian Shafi Muslims, treason (*derhaka*, the term used for the 1962 troubles) is truly the most abject of crimes, traditionally punishable by death.[62]

---

[58] Mahmud Haji Bakyr, "Tinjau ringkas gulintangan Brunei [Brief survey of the *gulintangan* of Brunei]", *Iktisar Budaya* (BSB, DBP, 1976), pp. 38–43.

[59] "Stand strong against ideologies that threaten our monarchy system", *Borneo Bulletin*, 27 July 2010. Six months later, the *Brunei Times* would repeat on the occasion of National Day: "Not by name alone is Brunei Islamic. Imams spell out nation's priority", stating in the article that "It is our responsibility to be loyal to the Monarch, practise Islam as a way of life, protect sovereignty of the nation [...]", 19 February 2011.

[60] Under the Prime Minister's (i.e. the sultan's) Office.

[61] Md. Zain bin Haji Serudin, Dr. Ustaz Haji Awang (minister of religious affairs), "Raja berdaulat, negara berkat, rakyat selamat", contribution to the seminar "Raja berdaulat, negara berkat...", Majlis Ilmu, 20–23 July 2006, p. 2, http://www.majlisilmu.org.bn/ilmu2006/archive/index.htm. And Braighlinn, *Ideological innovation under monarchy*, p. 52.

[62] Notably by referring to authors such as al-Mawardi, deceased in Baghdad in 1058 (Schottmann, "'Melayu Islam Beraja': The Politics of Legitimisation in a Malay Islamic Monarchy", p. 133); and *Silsilah (A)*, p. 13 (ff. 5–6).

State Ideology—
But with Rule of Law

Tuning the MIB

The "national philosophy" or MIB anchors the legitimacy and governance of the absolute monarchy, whose power derives from divine devolution, to the two pillars of religion and tradition. So it is not surprising that the MIB Supreme Council gathers almost all of the top brass[63] except for the prime minister (the sultan) and the ministers of foreign affairs and health. The approach is quite similar to Indonesia's during the *Orde Baru* period (1966–98), which saw the five principles (*Panca Sila*) of the prologue to the 1945 constitution converted to state ideology. Concretely it comprises diffusing via the educational channel a package of knowledge about culture and institutions, *adat istiadat* and Islam, by adapting them to the age of recipients, ranging from the first year of secondary school to university. This consists of a mixture of elementary civic and religious instruction, manuals of protocol[64] and ethnographic snapshots usually cut off from any context (these pedagogic instruments are reminiscent of the "learning about things" method practised in French primary schools in the 1960s).

[63] The Supreme Council of the MIB includes the ministers of education, religious affairs, *adat istiadat*, culture, communications, home affairs, and those in the Prime Minister's Office; the deputy ministers of finance, education and defence; the mufti; the Grand Chamberlain; the attorney-general; the vice-chancellor of UBD; the Chief Justice; the deputy to the head of Islamic tribunals; the permanent secretaries of the ministries of education and those from the Prime Minister's Office.

[64] See, for example, the class textbook of the Second Form, *Melayu Islam Beraja menengah II* [*MIB, class II*] (BSB: Jabatan Perkembangan Kurikulum, Kementerian Pendidikan, 1998), 209 p.

As soon as the MIB's status as national ideology was proclaimed, the sultan announced in July 1990 the creation of the Akademi Pengajian Brunei (APB, Academy of Brunei Studies) within the Universiti Brunei Darussalam (UBD). The goal was to confer on the MIB a scientific character that was essential in a society aiming to make education the pivot of its modernisation. To judge by the university's catalogue, some 42 books and documents have been published by the APB since 1991: 14 on history, 9 on the MIB,[65] 5 on social matters, 5 on ethnography,[66] 5 on the UBD (APB included), 2 on Islam, and 2 anthologies of miscellanea. The re-writing of history thus confirms its central role in the elaboration of the MIB, without the APB inflecting the theses of the Pusat Sejarah; on the contrary, it tries to promote its academic reputation[67] by organising colloquia where foreign participants—who mostly come from the Malay world, that is, Brunei's potential clients—are scarce. But alongside the hack exercises of history books or those about the MIB, do appear works touching on sensitive subjects such as rape[68] or marriage with foreigners,[69] which one might not expect to be treated.

The MIB constitutes as much a code of conduct[70] as a way of instilling Melayu Brunei culture: sessions of indoctrination are regularly organised by the administrators or supervisors of various official bodies, public or private (such as Brunei Shell), in which Bruneians must participate if they wish to advance in their careers.[71] The same is true in a

[65] For example, the proceedings of the *Seminar Kebangsaan Calak Brunei* [*Seminar on the national melting pot of Brunei*], 24–27 January 2006, in collaboration with the MIB Supreme Council and UBD.

[66] Including the proceedings of two conferences on history, and of one devoted to Kampung Ayer.

[67] See Roger Kershaw, "Academic Correctness under Monarchy: Universiti Brunei Darussalam and its Research", *BRB*, 2003.

[68] Hj Suriati binti Hj Ali/Yusof, *Rogol: kes kajian di Negara Brunei Darussalam* [*Rape: study of a case in Brunei Darussalam*] (BSB: APB, UBD, 2005/06).

[69] Jumat/Mohd Ramlee bin Abas, *Perkahwinan wanita warga Brunei darussalam dengan lelaki warga asing: kes kajian di Mukim Sengkurong, Daerah Brunei dan Muara* [*The Marriage of Bruneian women with foreigners, the case of the district of Sengkurong and province of Brunei-Muara*] (BSB: APB, UBD, 2001).

[70] In short, the MIB is supposed to be a "way of life" (*Brunei Times*, 15 August 2008).

[71] See the session organised for teachers and the awarding of a certificate for assiduousness to a director of a Chinese school, "Key for everyone to understand MIB philosophy", *Brunei Times*, 9 June 2010.

minor way of the initiation into Islamic law, considered as correlative to MIB.[72]

State Ideology and Rule of Law

But this endless harping on of the MIB, and the censorship that accompanies it,[73] cannot hide a genuine rule of law, which in the Southeast Asian landscape, is at least as characteristic of Brunei as the strong emphasis placed on the hierarchisation of social relations.

As in Malaysia or in Singapore (at least for Malays), Bruneian law arises from adherence to two juridical systems: shariah (following the Shafi'i school) for family law and inheritance, and British common law for the rest of civil matters and for criminal cases. In the absence of law specific to Brunei, English legal principles have the force of law.[74] Based on the British model, the ordinary magistracy founded on common law has four levels: county court, intermediate court,[75] high court and a court of appeal.[76] Since 1995,[77] the British Privy Council is no longer used as a Supreme Court except in the case of civil litigation—if the two

[72] Nabil Daraina Badaruddin, Hj., "Challenges to legal education in a changing landscape—Brunei", *Eighth ASEAN Law Association General Assembly 2003*, Singapore, Workshop III: Challenges to Legal Education in a Changing Landscape (Singapore: Tweddle Litho), pp. 93–9, http://www.aseanlawassociation.org/docs/w3_brunei.pdf.

[73] In addition to radio and television, all the printed press, including foreign, is controlled. This makes it impossible to distribute in Brunei any publication in a language that the censors do not understand, for example, French. Authorisation of various cultural events is subject to "viewing" prior to censorship, etc. ("Every manuscript we receive is screened for censorship, but not all manuscripts have elements against MIB", *Brunei Times*, 28 February 2011, p. 3).

[74] Azrinah Binti Haji Abdul Rahman, *Legal System in Brunei Darussalam after the Signing of the Supplementary Agreement 1905/1906 between Brunei and Great Britain*, BSB, Working Paper for National Day Seminar 2006, p. 14.

[75] The first is authorised for suits below B $30,000; the second for those between B $15,000 and $100,000.

[76] Formed respectively of the Chief Justice and two justices, the president of the Court of Appeals and two appeal judges. Following an agreement with Hong Kong, these posts were filled by magistrates from the colony's Supreme Court. Despite the end of the agreement in 1993, to this day the sultan continues to recruit magistrates for the Court of Appeals from among former magistrates of the Hong Kong Supreme Court.

[77] Roger Kershaw, "Brunei—Malay, Monarchical, Micro-state", in *Government and Politics in Southeast Asia*, ed. John Funston (Singapore: ISEAS, 2001), p. 23.

parties request for it and only if the sultan agrees. Religious tribunals,[78] which became Shariah Courts in 2000 and had their remit extended to put them on par with the jurisdictions of a British court, have only three levels: lower, higher and appeal courts.[79] The magistrates come from the two highly heterogeneous legal schools. Judges of the "High Court" are chosen among Bruneian lawyers—most often of British or Australian training—or as visiting magistrates, among English magistrates or magistrates from countries with the same legal tradition; those of the Court of Appeal are for the time being from the United Kingdom or Hong Kong. For the common law, there is no choice but to study in the United Kingdom or one of its dominions: only the British version of texts is in force and English is the language of civil tribunals. By contrast, the training of Islamic magistrates takes place in Brunei, at the Sultan Haji Omar Ali Saifuddin Institute of Islamic Studies (SHOAS IIS), which delivers licences and master's degrees, as well as the certificates in Islamic law necessary for lawyers in the civil courts to appear before the religious tribunals,[80] in which the language of reference is Malay. The most traditionalist jurists have lobbied for years in favour of a sole—Islamic—law and the withdrawal of the common law.[81] In March 2011 the sultan took a first step towards the generalisation of Islamic law, in order to deal with attacks on religion.[82] On October 2013, he officially promulgated the Syariah Penal Code Order, which was enforced in

[78] The old *kadi* courts gave way to Shariah Courts in 2000. Unlike their predecessor, the Shariah Courts were given exclusive jurisdiction over crimes relating to the shariah, Islamic family law and all matters over which they have been accorded authority by the law (Azrinah Binti Haji Abdul Rahman, *Legal System in Brunei Darussalam*, p. 23).

[79] As in most countries of the world, Brunei has military tribunals offering almost the same guarantees as the civil courts.

[80] Nabil Daraina Badaruddin, Hj., "Legal Education in ASEAN in the 21st century: Brunei Perspective", *Eighth ASEAN Law Association General Assembly 2006*, Singapore, p. 7ff.

[81] This is the thesis of the Malaysian Dr. Haji Mahmud Saedon bin Awang Othman, doctor in Islamic law at the University al-Azhar (1976), expert in religious affairs. First published in Malay in 1996, his thesis was reprinted in English in 2008 (*A Review on the Implementation and Administration of Islamic Law in Brunei Darussalam* [BSB: Islamic Da'wah Centre, 2008], 165 p). Media coverage for the English edition of the book showed that the debate was far from over, cf. "A call for one court of Islamic law for all Brunei", *Brunei Times*, 12 April 2009.

[82] *Brunei Times*, 18 March 2011.

April 2014. *Huddud* (corporal punishments) is thus applied to Muslim offenders above the age of 15 years old (the penal majority in Islamic law), for religious,[83] food,[84] family[85] and sexual[86] offenses, as well as for common law crimes.[87] The law places a woman under the control of a male legal respondent throughout her whole life. In addition, for some offenses, the offender could be charged jointly by both the religious and civil courts.

---

[83] Absentees from the Friday prayer are fined B $200 (US $160) for a first infringement, B $300 for a second and B $1,000 (US $800) for repeat offenders. Propagation of a religion other than Islam to Muslims or people without a faith is liable to a B $20,000 fine plus five years' imprisonment (*Borneo Bulletin*, 24 October 2013). Denigration, irony or insult of the Koran or *hadith* by a Muslim is liable to 30 or 40 years' imprisonment ("Introduction of Syariah penal approved in Brunei", *Jakarta Post*, 23 October 2013). Apostasy is punished by death. The practice of black magic is liable to a B $20,000 fine (US $16,000) plus five years' imprisonment; the hiring of a pratician, to a B $8,000 fine and two years' imprisonment.

[84] Consumption of alcohol or drugs is liable to 40 strokes of the whip, 80 for a second infringement, and 80 strokes and two years' imprisonment for a repeat offender. The sale of food, drink or tobacco, for immediate consumption in a public place during Ramadan, is liable to a B $4,000 fine (US $3,200) and/or one year's imprisonment ("A Look Into some of 'Hadd' Punishment", *Borneo Bulletin*, 24 October 2013).

[85] Any person carrying publicly clothing of the opposite sex is liable to a B $4,000 fine and/or one year of prison. An unmarried woman who leaves her parents or legal tutors without valid reason will be liable to a B $1,000 fine and/or a year of imprisonment. Any person encouraging a Muslim woman to desert the conjugal home or to leave her parents or legal tutors will be liable to a maximum fine of B $8,000, and/or two years of imprisonment. Abortion is punished (for the pratician) by a B $12,000 fine and/or a maximum of three years of prison. Any person found guilty of attempting an abortion is liable to a fine not exceeding B $4,000 and/or imprisonment for a term not exceeding one year.

[86] Intimacy between unmarried people of opposite sexes (*khalwat*), even without any sexual relations, is liable to a fine of B $40,000 (US $32,000) and one year of prison. False denunciation of adulterous or homosexual relations is liable to 80 strokes. Sexual relations between people who are not married (*zina*) is liable to 100 strokes plus one year of prison if one of the two parties was still a virgin. For adultery (if one of the two offenders is married and has already had sexual relations), the punishment is lapidation, as for homosexuality or sodomy. Rape is liable to lapidation (of the rapist) if the victim is already married, liable 100 strokes and one year's imprisonment if the victim has never had sexual relations.

[87] If the value of the stolen good is equivalent or higher than the amount of the *nisab* (minimum assets requiring payment of *zakat* [alms]), robbery is punishable by joint amputation of the right hand from the joint of the wrist and of the left foot up to the ankle, plus a fine in the case of physical offence.

Apart from the fact that religious tribunals do not recognise the testimony of non-Muslims and the validity of forensic evidence such as DNA tests, the Islamic Penal Code also penalises the most vulnerable class—temporary residents—who are liable to be denounced at any time for trafficking in alcohol or for extra-marital sexual relations. On the other hand, the Syriah does not address modern criminality, extortion, embezzlement, corruption, cybercrime, etc.—all of which was unknown in 7th-century Arabia. Its harshness aside, Bruneian religious lawyers insist on the dissuasive character of the Islamic Penal Code and point out its requirements as regards proof, such as the absence of doubt about culpability, which implies the presence of "credible" witnesses on the spot of the offense.[88] According to them, it seems that the new law will be applied in a cautious and "modern" way, for only a very small number of cases.[89]

Notwithstanding the restrictions on the competence of civil courts in 2000 and 2014, the legal system is recognised by all protagonists as functioning quite satisfactorily, meaning that legal proceedings are equitable in all courts.[90] Not only are the Court of Appeal judges, being foreigners, removed from possible local pressure, the sultan—unlike in many authoritarian regimes—also makes it a point of honour to ensure the neutrality and equity of the judicial body, religious as well as civil. The values of the civil courts[91] are those of Anglo-Saxon law,[92] which ironically are spared the criticism of Western decadence recurrent in official media.[93] Corruption is also heavily punished if the offender is caught

---

[88] For example, four witnesses are required in the case of adultery, two for robbery.

[89] "Syariah Judge: Allah's Laws have their purpose", *Borneo Bulletin*, 13 November 2013. The death penalty, also present in the previous penal code, has never been applied since 1957.

[90] On the other hand, Brunei possesses neither administrative tribunals of the French type nor the equivalent of the British "Queen's Bench". The only recourse against an administrative decision is a measure of grace, without any guarantee that the case will be really examined, especially for people who are not government officials.

[91] In Malaysia and in Indonesia, the religious tribunals are reputed to be much less corrupt than their civil homologues.

[92] See Justice Datin Paduka Hayati Salleh, "Brunei Darussalam: Independence of the Judiciary Revisited and Towards More Effective Case Management", *Eighth ASEAN Law Association General Assembly 2006*, Singapore, pp. 7ff.

[93] Braighlinn, *Ideological innovation under monarchy*, p. 52.

with his hand in the till, whatever his rank. But nobody really knows how and to what extent the new Islamic legislation will be implemented.

The Two Faces of Janus

The double face of Brunei is not limited to the legal domain but can be detected in the whole societal field. The formation of elites at UBD is largely spared this ideological formatting in so far as the formal codes are ostensibly respected. Its library carries several copies of publications dedicated to Bruneian studies that are critical of, or even downright caustic about, the regime. These publications cannot be found in bookstores in the sultanate, which tend to be poorly stocked and subject to censorship. Moreover, the sultanate finances the studies abroad (principally in the United Kingdom) of almost 2,000 scholarship students a year, despite the potential corrosive cultural impact of this operation. Brunei has an increasing number of nationals who have the potential to perform in a growing number of fields:[94] they should be tomorrow's *menteri*.

At the same time, employees of the government or of companies whose capital is in public (or royal) hands must devote a good third of their time to interminable celebrations—a multiplication of ceremonial tasks prevents the plethora of Crown attendants from engaging in potentially subversive inaction. Above all, any personal initiative or decision-making implies taking a certain risk in a society where the *bahasa dalam* and protocol combine to evacuate from discourse the least expression of any problem:[95] a single person has the power to say "yes" while all the others have the power to say "no"—if only out of simple inertia.

[94] In 2010, some ten Bruneians were first-year students at the Karlsruhe Institute of Technology.

[95] See "Bahasa Dalam [Part of Court Language]", note sent to the diplomatic corps, 2009.

CONCLUSION

DURABLE CONSENSUS?

The survival of the sultanate of Brunei Darussalam depends on the sustaining of consensus, secured by a hydrocarbon rent capable of financing both a "welfare monarchy" and a royal dynasty.

In the medium term, its income is not under threat: as of the start of 2014, Brunei can count on 12 years of oil reserves and more than 30 years of gas at the current rate, to which can be added reserves from deep water blocks. Today income generated by the sovereign fund (BIA) already represents some of 30% of GDP and based on projections of the last 20 years will probably increase by 2030, the financial risk remaining well under control.

This rent continues to sustain a "welfare monarchy" that takes care of its nationals from birth to death: circumcision and the *hajj* are organised and subsidised in part; public education and medical care are free; and multiple preferential loans (with no collateral) and university grants are freely dispensed. Bruneians need only leave the sultanate to realise to what extent Bruneian citizenship is a privilege—one that gives access to a golden cocoon where daily life has no constraints other than bowing before the MIB and where the workload is light. Unfortunately, leisure options are scarce, although this is easily palliated by trips to neighbouring Malaysia—except for civil servants who must request authorisation to leave the country two weeks in advance. As long as nationals feel there is an equitable sharing (which does not mean *equal* shares) of the petro-gas income and remain confident in rigorous management by the state, the risk of social explosion stays minimal. This is the state of affairs unambiguously conveyed by many Bruneian blogs, which benefit from very wide access to the web. Indeed, this is something the sultan—who can boast of a real popularity—is mindful about, since the "various" category in the national budget (which is the code for the royal family's expenditure) has diminished from 20.3% in the Eighth Plan to 2.9% in the Ninth Plan.

The duality of ranks assures the insertion of modern national elites into the traditional social space without displacing the aristocracy, thus precluding the secular threat of a palace revolution. As for immigrants (whose number remains limited to some 35% of the total population, or slightly more than one out of two employees—way behind the United

Arab Emirates or Qatar), they are too ethnically fragmented and too financially dependent to constitute a proletariat, especially since the two foremost contingents, Malaysians and Indonesians, are not united but follow divergent strategies: the former, on condition of being *bumiputera*, can aspire to naturalisation, whereas the latter dream at best of an extension of their visas.

What is urgent is not to accelerate the development of downstream hydrocarbons but rather to free upstream the decision-making circuits, which are caught in the twists and turns of a ponderous and plethoric civil service (despite the retirement age set at 55 years, gradually raised to 60 starting in 2010). Therein lies the only serious threat of a systemic crisis: administrative blockage, aggravated by the government's chronic shilly-shallying. As the sovereign fund (BIA) will probably not suffice to finance consumption after the disappearance of the petro-gas rent, getting out of the administrative deadlock is a prerequisite for any preparation for the post-hydrocarbon era. Much more than the challenges of a democracy whose premises are barely laid and whose implementation in the region seems for the time being to be disconcerting on more than one point, this will be the principal strategic stake a generation from now. Responding to this challenge implies compatibility between societal and productive choices, arbitrating between ideology and efficiency, and simply giving people access to information that is not pre-digested, if only to prepare for a world that is "increasingly competitive and based on knowledge", as expressed in *Wawasan Brunei 2035*.

To evaluate the durability of Brunei's political entity, it is necessary to change the analytical grid and to penetrate the mysteries of the "model". The sultanate is awash with paradoxes: it is a mix of state ideology and rule of law; a society of ranks and proximity of the royal family; and the "invention" of the *Melayu Brunei* tradition and adherence to a Middle Eastern norm that was unknown in the Malay world[1] until the start of the 1980s and partially reinvented. Brunei combines supervision of the population and a potentially deleterious rise in the number of overseas students; effective regional integration and a silent withdrawal into itself; British military support and repeated denunciation of Western intervention in Iraq and Afghanistan.

---

[1] With the exception of the Aceh sultanate, cf. Lombard, *Le sultanat d'Atjeh au temps d'Iskandar Muda, 1607–1636* (Paris: EFEO, 1967), 297 p.

Is the Brunei paradigm culturally tenable in the long term, given that the penal Islamic law (and its *hudud*) have been implemented since April 2014, with apparently scarce support from Bruneian nationals though criticism cannot be publicly expressed?[2] In other words, is there not a risk of the implosion of referents, or else collective awareness of the country's contradictions should a shock from the outside (an attack on foreign personnel or installations, a crisis in the whole region) or a succession crisis arise?

[2] As shown by the debate generated by the paper "Let's have a healthy debate on syariah law". Out of the eight participants in the discussion, six were against the new law, including several Bruneian Malay (as shown by the language, Brunei Malay, in which they wrote), www.brudirect.com/national/whats-hot/have-your-say-hot-topics/10581-let-s-havea-healthy-debate-on-syariah-law [accessed October 2013].

APPENDICES

Weights, Measures and Currency

Some Traditional Measures and Currencies

Weight

1 *bahar*	= 181.5 kg[1] = 3 *picul*
	= 200 Malay *catty*
	= 300 Chinese *catty* = 600 Siamese *catty*
1 *picul*	= 60.5 kg = 100 Chinese *catty*
1 *Chinese catty*	= 0.6 kg
1 *Siamese catty*	= ½ Chinese *catty* = 0.3 kg

Currencies

– 1 *tael* (silver) = 37.8 g = 10 *mas* = 1,000 *piti*[2]

Currencies Used in Brunei[3]

Straits Settlements (SS) $	1906	SS $1 = 2 shillings 4 pence = £0.11 = US $0.533
	1916	SS $1 = 2 shillings 4 pence = £0.11 = US $0.52
	1926	SS $1 = 2 shillings 4 pence = £0.11 = US $0.56
	1936	SS $1 = 2 shillings 4 pence = £0.11 = US $0.58

[1] In the Malay world, the weight of the *bahar* changes from one port to another [Ferrand, Gabriel, *Les poids, mesures et monnaies des mers du sud aux XVI*[e] *et XVII*[e] *siècles*, extraits du Journal Asiatique (Paris: Imprimerie Nationale, 1921), 271 p].
[2] Tin coinage (see Annabel Teh Gallop, "Camels, Seals and the Early Tin Coinage of Brunei").
[3] See Measuring Worth, "Exchange rates between the United States Dollar and forty-one currencies", http://www.measuringworth.com/datasets/exchangeglobal.

Malayan (M) $	1950	M $1 = SS $1 = 1 shilling 2 pence = £0.12 = US $0.33
	1960	M $1 = SS $1 = 1 shilling 2 pence = £0.12 = US $0.33
Brunei (B) $	1967	B $1 = Singapore $1[4] = £0.12 = US $0.32 = FF 1.47
	2014	B $1 = Singapore $1 = £0.47 = US $0.79 = €0.58

[4] http://www.x-rates.com/table/?from=SGD&amount=1.00.

Lexicon

Etymology of terms below:
Ar. [Arabic]; Bru. Mal. [Brunei Malay]; Jav. [Javanese]; Mal. [Malay]; Per. [Persian]; Skt. [Sanskrit]; Tam. [Tamil]

Adat, adat istiadat	Custom [Ar.]
Agama	Religion; see also *ugama* [Skt.]
Anak	Child [Mal.]
Astana	Palace; see also *istana* [Skt.]
Awang	Ancient Malay title, today meaning Mister [Mal.]
Awangku	Title of young male nobles before marriage [Bru. Mal.]
Bahasa	Language [Skt.]
Bahasa Dalam	Royal language used when addressing members of the reigning family [Skt.]
Bandar	Seaport [Per.]
Bangsa	Ethnic group [Skt.]
Batu	Stone [Mal.]
Bendahara Seri Maharaja Permaisura	The first of the four wazirs; from Sanskrit *bhāṇḍāgāran*, treasurer;[5] *śrī* (honorific); *mahārāja* (great king); *permaisura* (king) [Skt.]

[5] For all etymologies, see Russell Jones, ed., *Loan-words in Indonesian and Malay* (Leiden: KITLV, 2007).

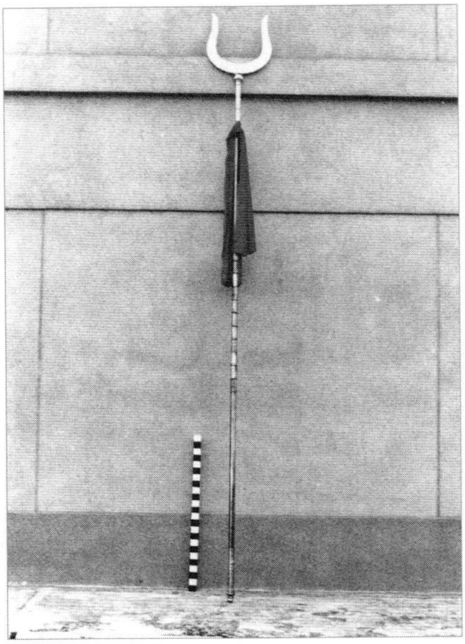

Figure 10. *Changkah*
(Photo by R. Nicholl, Coll. J. Népote)

Figure 11. *Nobat*
(Source: Muzium Brunei, *Memperingati Ulang Tahun ke-10 perpuspaan 1968–1978, Commemorating the 10th Anniversary of the Coronation*)

Figure 12. *Puspa* (coronation, just after the crowning)

(Source: Muzium Brunei, *Memperingati Ulang Tahun ke-10 perpuspaan 1968–1978, Commemorating the 10th Anniversary of the Coronation*)

Batang	River [Mal.]
Bedil	Small cannon; *deveṭi* [Tam.]
Bezoar	Concretion inside the body (bladder) of certain animals used as medicine; from *padzahr* [Per.]
Bin	Son of [Ar.]
Binte (abbr. *bnt*)	Daughter of [Ar.]
Bongsu	Youngest of the siblings [Mal.]
Bumiputera	Son of the Earth—autochthonous. Initially used to qualify native Malays, extended since 1960 to other indigenous ethnic groups of Brunei [Skt.]
Changkah	Etymologically, a two-pronged spear; in Brunei a ceremonial weapon borne by the *Shahbandar* and the *Temenggong* during coronation. The object resembles the *Du-shâké*, the ceremonial insignia of the "king of the Caravan" under the Ming dynasty.[6] Its Chinese origin is confirmed by a red cloth hung from the pole and by its shape similar to the two-pronged spears used in Chinese martial arts, notably in Shaolin. A weapon of the same type with almost the same name, *tjanga*, is described among the regalia of Kota Waringin in 1860[7] [Mal.]
Cheteria (empat, delapan, enambelas, tiga puluh dua)	Title of nobility, comprising four ranks, *cheteria empat (4)*, *cheteria delapan (8)*, *cheteria enambelas (16)* and *cheteria tiga puluh dua (32)* [Skt. + Mal.]
Chiri	Formula for enthronement in a grade or a title, in Brunei half-Sanskrit, half-Arabic [Mal.]
Dalam	Inside; refering to the palace [Mal.]

[6] Aly Mazahéri, *La route de la Soie* (Paris: Papyrus, 1983), p. 65, n. 72, data signalled by R. Nicholl in a letter to J. Népote, 3 March 1984.

[7] J. Pijnappel, "Kota Waringin in the 19th century", in *Hikajat Bandjar: A Study in Malay Historiography*, ed. J.J. Ras (The Hague: Bibliotheca Indosinica, Martinus Nijhoff, 1968), p. 620.

Datin	Equivalent of *datu* for a woman [Mal.]
Dato/datu	Traditional Malay title given to local chiefs. Since independence, title granted to holders of the two first classes of decorations [Mal.]
Dayang	Madame [Bru. Mal.]
Dayangku	Title of young noble female before marriage or women of princely rank who have married a commoner [Bru. Mal.]
Di Gadong Sahibul Mal	Title based on the word *gadong* ("green" in the Brunei dialect[8]), to which is added the prefix *di* (locative). "Gadong" refers to an affluent of the Kedayan River, whose waters are greenish, itself the affluent of the Brunei River. The current Kampung Ayer, where most Bruneians lived, is located at the confluence of the Kedayan and the Brunei Rivers. [Bru. Mal. + Ar.]
Doa selamat	Prayer that opens and closes all public ceremonies in Brunei [Ar.]
Gahara	Princes qualified to succeed the sultan, those whose lineage is princely on both the maternal and paternal sides. From *gṛhya*, "of royal birth" [Skt.]
Haji	Man who has performed the pilgrimage to Mecca [Ar.]
Hajjah	Woman who has performed the pilgrimage to Mecca [Ar.]
Hamba	Slave, servant [Mal.]
Hari Raya Aid-ul-Fitri	One of the most important festivals of Brunei that marks the end of Ramadan (the fasting month) and the entry into the month of Shawal, characterised by many parties and open houses [Ar.]

[8] "Perbendaharaan-kata Melayu Brunei", *Bahana* 7, 18 (April–June 1972): 1111.

Hikayat	Chronicle [Ar.]
Hukum	Law [Ar.]
Hukum Kanun	Islamic code [Ar.]
Ibni	Child of; term reserved for the aristocracy [Ar.]
Istana	Palace; from *āsthāna*, palace [Skt.]
Jawi	Arabo-Malay script, based on Persian script [Ar.]
Kadi, Kathi	Judge in religious courts [Ar.]
Kepala	Chief (etymologically, "head") [Skt.]
Kampung	Village [Mal.]
Kampung Ayer	Water Village, the former capital of Brunei at the confluence of the Brunei River and of the Kedayan [Mal.]
Kanun	Legal Code [Ar.]
Kerajaan	Based on *rāja*, king, land-river rights of the sovereign, attached to his office [Skt.]
Ketua	Chief [Mal.]
Khatib	Religious dignitary in charge of reading the sermon at the mosque [Ar.]
Kuripan	Land-river right conferred on great dignitaries during the exercise of their offices; etymologically, ancient Malay term referring to camphor before it is soaked[9] [Bru. Mal.]
Laksamana	Title; from Sanskrit *lakṣmaṇa*, name of Râma's brother in the *Rāmāyana*, here admiral [Skt.]
Laut	Sea [Mal.]
Ma[h]kota	Crown, from *makuṭa* [Skt.]
Melayu Islam Beraja or *MIB*	"[Being] Malay is [being] Muslim and monarchical", the national ideology of Brunei. Official translation into English with a semantic shift: 'Malay Islamic Monarchy'

[9] Poerwadarminta, W.J.S., *Kamus umum bahasa Indonesia* [*General dictionary of Indonesian*] (Jakarta: Balai Pustaka, 1976), p. 543.

Menteri, manteri	Honorific title conferred on commoners who assume administrative posts, includes four principal grades: *menteri empat (4)*, *menteri delapan (8)*, *menteri enambelas (16)* et *menteri tiga puluh dua (32)*, all titled *pehin*. From the Sanskrit *mantri*, someone who masters the *mantra* (Skt. formulas) [Skt.]
Muara	Estuary [Mal.]
Mufti	Top dignitary of the Muslim religion [Ar.]
Mukim	District [Ar.]
Nakhoda	Captain of a ship [Per.]
Negara	Country [Skt.]
Negeri	Territory [Skt.]
Nobat	Ceremonial orchestra that is part of the regalia, composed of a timbal (*nakara*), two drums (*gendang*) and three flutes (*serunai*) [Per.]
Orang	Man, person [Mal.]
Orang Kaya	Etymologically, "rich man", title or partial one granted to commoners [Mal.]
Padian	Woman selling goods on a pirogue in the water market of Kampung Ayer; by extension, the water market itself [Bru. Mal.]
Paduka	His Highness—"person whose shoes are touched",[10] from the Sanskrit *pādukā*, shoe [Skt.]
Pegawai	Civil servant [Mal.]
Pehin	Title granted to commoners in acknowledgment of their deeds, to the 64 *menteri* or to various ethnic dignitaries such as the two heads of the Chinese community [Bru. Mal.]

[10] The practice of touching the feet of the interlocutor with the right hand as a sign of respect is still widespread in India today.

Pemancha Rae' Wal-Mashuarah	The third of the four wazirs, called in Arabic "master of courage and counsel" [Jav. + Ar.]
Penghulu	Head of district (*mukim*); etymologically, one who controls upstream (from Malay *hulu*, upstream) [Mal.]
Pengiran	Male aristocrat descending from a sultan; etymologically, one who controls downstream (from Malay *hilir*, downstream) [Mal.]
Pengiran Anak	Prince or princess of the first rank, title conferred on adult children or grandchildren (male or female) of the sovereign (=Royal Highness) [Bru. Mal.]
Pengiran Isteri	Title conferred by the present sultan on his secondary wives, who were commoners by birth (=Serene Highness) [Bru. Mal.]
Pengiran Muda	Title traditionally given to the Crown Prince; since 1998, the Crown Prince Al-Muhtadee Billah is titled *Pengiran Muda Mahkota*, and his young son Abdul Muntaqim is now titled *Pengiran Muda*.
Perdana Wazir	First wazir, head of the four wazirs [Skt. + Ar.]
Pesaka, pusaka	Personal property (heirloom) [Skt.]
Puak jati	Brunei indigenous, belonging to one of the seven groups considered by the sultanate's government as autochthonous: Malays, Kedayan, Dusun, Bisayah, Tutong, Belait and Murut, the last six officially registered as Malays since the 1960s [Mal. + Skt.]
Puak sakai	The expression *puak sakai* is typically Bruneian. *Puak* means "group" in Malay and *sakai*, etymologically, "savage", "Barbarian", peoples of inferior status, which R.O. Winstedt[11] summarises as "savage" or "slave". W.J.S. Poerwadarminta[12] gives as an example the Negritos, the "aborigines" in royal Bruneian mythography and rituals [Mal.]

[11] *Kamus Bahasa Melayu* [*Malay Dictionary*] (Kuala Lumpur: Marican, 1970), p. 264.
[12] *Kamus Umum Bahasa Indonesia*, p. 851.

Pulau	Island [Mal.]
Pusat	Centre [Mal.]
Puspa	Coronation, from Skt. *puṣpa*, flower, the king being "one who bears the flowers", the Crown being traditionally garnished with flowers (as are crowns of Balinese or Javanese dancers even till today) [Skt.]
Raja Isteri	Queen consort, the King's spouse, born into a royal family, the only one to be crowned after the king during the coronation rite[13] [Skt.]
Rakyat	People [Ar.]
Sabda	Speech given by crown princes, wazirs and their wives; from *śabda*, statement from a noble personage [Skt.]
Shahbandar	"Master of the port", traditionally the foremost of the four *Cheteria*; before the 17th century, the fourth of the wazirs [Per.]
Sejarah	History [Ar.]
Silsilah, Salasilah, Salsalah	Genealogy [Ar.]
Sungai	River [Mal.]
Sy'air, syair, sjair	Poem composed in a sequence of quatrains, each with the same rhyme [Ar.]
Shariah, syariah	Islamic law, in Brunei of Shafi'i obedience [Ar.]
Tarsilah	Genealogy, see also *Silsilah* [Ar.]
Temenggong [Temenggung, Tumenggung] Sahibul Bahar	From the Javanese basis *taŋgöŋ*, "decided, firm", with the infix *um* realised (in Javanese) as *em*, etymologically, somebody who is sure of himself.[14] The fourth and last of the four wazirs, titled in Arabic "Master of the sea" [Jav. + Ar.]

[13] *Borneo Bulletin*, 5 October 2007.

[14] Zoetmulder, P.J. and S.O. Robson, *Old Javanese-English Dictionary* (Den Hague: Martinus Nijhoff, 1982): 1939.

Titah	Term used for the first time in 1371 to translate the Arabic *amr* [= command] into Malay,[15] and widely adopted. In Brunei, speech having the status of a command given by the king or queen, here translated as "rescript", "response given in a particular case to a civil servant or a judge [by imperial authority and with executive value]",[16] which seems to correspond best to its usage in Brunei [Mal.]
Tulin	Princely personal property (portion of river), assignable and transmissible by inheritance [Bru. Mal.]
Ugama	Religion; see also *Agama* [Skt.]
Umat	The community of believers in the Muslim world [Ar.]
Wazir	High princely dignitary traditionally four in number, before the creation of a fifth, the *Perdana Wazir* (prime wazir) [Ar.]
Yang Di-Pertuan	"The one who has been made chief", one of the many royal titles borne by the Sultan, Your Majesty [Mal.]

[15] In the *Hikayat Badan Budiman*, in relation with Malay kingship, Malay Concordance Project, http://mcp.anu.edu.au/cgi-bin/tapis_w.pl.
[16] Jean Gaudemet, "Romain [Roman law]", in *Encyclopædia Universalis 2007*, e-edition.

Thematic Bibliography

List of Abbreviations

ANU	Australian National University
BEFEO	*Bulletin de l'École Française d'Extrême Orient*
BMJ	*Brunei Museum Journal*
BRB	*Borneo Research Bulletin*
BSB	Bandar Seri Begawan
DBP	Dewan Bahasa dan Pustaka
ISEAS	Institute of Southeast Asian Studies (Singapore)
JHKRAS	*Journal of the Hong Kong Branch of the Royal Asiatic Society*
JIAEA	*Journal of the Indian Archipelago and Eastern Asia*
JMBRAS	*Journal of the Malay(si)an Branch of the Royal Asiatic Society*
JSAS	*Journal of Southeast Asian Studies*
JSSBRAS	*Journal of the Straits Settlements Branch of the Royal Asiatic Society*
MBRAS	Malay(si)an Branch of the Royal Asiatic Society
PEFEO	*Publications de l'École Française d'Extrême Orient*
RASMB	Royal Asiatic Society Malayan Branch
RASSBJ	*Royal Asiatic Society Straits Branch Journal*
UBD	Universiti Brunei Darussalam
UP	University Press
SAA	*Southeast Asian Affairs*
SAR	*Southeast Asia Research*
SMJ	*Sarawak Museum Journal*

Reference Works

Bibliographies

Combrink, Hans J.B., Craig Soderberg, Michael E. Boutin and Alanna Y. Boutin. *Indigenous groups of Sabah: an Annotated Bibliography of Linguistic and Anthropological Sources (Part I, Author Index)*. Kota Kinabalu: SIL e-Book, 2008, 299 p.

Engelen Krausse, Sylvia and Gerald H. Krausse. *Brunei*. Santa Barbara: Clio Press (World Bibliographical Series 93), 1988, 249 p.

Francis, Simon. *Brunei Checklist: A Bibliography of English-languages References Relating to Brunei Darussalam*. Hull: University of Hull, Centre for Asian Studies, 1993, 283 p.

Horton, A.V.M. *A Critical Guide to Source Materials Related to Brunei (with special reference to the British residential era, 1906–1959)*. Bordesley: AVM Horton, Oct. 1994, 203 p.

Joo, Monica Kuak Sim and Che Puteh binti Ismail. *Prehistory and Archaeology of Malaysia and Brunei: A Bibliography*. Kuala Lumpur: Perpustakaan Universiti Malaya, 1982, 41 p.

King, Victor T. *Register of Current United Kingdom Research on Maritime South-East Asia: Malaysia, Singapore, Indonesia and Brunei Darussalam*. Association of South-East Asian Studies in the United Kingdom (ASEASUK), 1992, 92 p.

Mulliner, Kent and John A. Lent. *Brunei and Malaysian Studies: Present knowledge and research trends on Brunei and on Malaysian anthropology, mass communication and women's studies*. Williamsburg: Department of Anthropology, College of William and Mary, 1994, ix, 143 p.

Roff, William R. (coll. Margaret L. Koch). *Southeast Asian Research Tools: Malaysia, Singapore, Brunei*. Honolulu: Southeast Asian Studies, University of Hawaii, 1979, 61 p.

Simanjuntak, S. Hasnah, compiler. *Bibliografi mengenai sejarah, politik, dan pemerintahan Negara Brunei Darussalam [Bibliography on history, politics, and government of Brunei Darussalam]*. BSB: Perpustakaan UBD, 1987, bil. Malay/English, 45 p.

Biographical and Historical Dictionaries

Horton, Anthony Vincent. *Negara Brunei Darussalam: A Biographical Dictionary (1846–1998)*. Bordesley: A.M. Horton, 1999, 4th ed., 2 vols., 1120 p.

———. *The Top Hundred Persons of Power and Influence in Negara Brunei Darussalam A.D. 2000*. Bordesley: A.V.M. Horton, 2001, 196 p.

Singh, D.S. Ranjit and Jatswan Sindhu. *Historical Dictionary of Brunei Darussalam*. Lanham: Scarecrow Press, 1997, 178 p.

General Presentation of Brunei

All Periods

Crawfurd, John. *History of the Indian Archipelago*. Edinburgh: Archipel Constable, 1820, 3 vols., 520, 563, 532 p.

———. *A descriptive dictionary of the Indian islands & adjacent countries*. London: Bradbury & Evans, 1856. Rep. Kuala Lumpur & New York: Oxford University Press, 1971, 459 p.

King, Victor and V.M. Horton, eds. *From Buckfast to Borneo: Essays Presented to Father Robert Nicholl on the 85th Anniversary of His Birth, 27 March 1995*. Hull: University of Hull, Centre for South-East Asian Studies, 1995. Rep. Kuala Lumpur: Sarawak Literary Society, 2009, xxi, 643 p.

Wadley, Reed L. *Histories of the Borneo Environment: Economic, Political and Social Dimensions of Change and Continuity*. Leiden: KITLV Press, 2005, 315 p.

Wright, Leigh. "Brunei: An Historical Relic", *JHKBRAS* 17 (1977): 12–29.

Contemporary Brunei

Abu Bakar Hamzah. "Brunei Darussalam, continuity and tradition", *SAA 1989* (1990): 91–104.

Azman Ahmad. "Brunei Darussalam, towards reforms and Sustainable Progress", *SAA 2005* (2006): 99–109.

Brunei Shell Petroleum. *Brunei, the land and its people*. Seria: Brunei Shell Petroleum, 1978, 136 p.

Case, William. "Brunei in 2006", *Asian Survey, a Monthly Review of Contemporary Asian Studies* 47, 1 (Jan./Feb. 2007): 189–93.

Cleary, Mark and Simon Francis. "Brunei, the search for a sustainable economy", *SAA 1994* (1995): 59–75.

______. "Brunei Darussalam, the Outside World intrudes", *SAA 1999* (2000): 67–76.

Crosbie, A.J. "Brunei in Transition", *SAA 1981* (1982): 75–92.

Doshi, Tilak. "Brunei, the Steady State", *SAA 1991* (1992): 71–80.

Fulton, S.J. "Brunei: past and present", *Asian Affairs* 15 (1) (Feb. 1984): 5–14.

Hamzah Sulaiman. "Negara Brunei Darussalam. Socio-Economic Concern Amid Stability and Plenty", *SAA 2003* (2004): 71–9.

Horton, A.V.M. "Negara Brunei Darussalam. Economic Gloom and APEC Summit", *SAA 2001* (2002): 95–109.

______. "Brunei in 2004: window-dressing an Islamizing sultanate", *Asian Survey, a Monthly Review of Contemporary Asian Studies* 45, 1 (Jan./Feb. 2005): 180–5.

International Seminar on Brunei Malay Sultanate in Nusantara 1994, proceedings. BSB: Yayasan Sultan Haji Hassanal Bolkiah dan APB, UBD, 1996, 2 vols.

Ismail Duraman and Abdul Amin Hj Hashim. "Brunei Darussalam, developing within its own paradigm", *SAA 1998* (1999): 53–67.

Mani, A. "Negara Brunei Darussalam in 1992, celebrating the Silver Jubilee", *SAA 1993* (1994): 95–109.

Menon, K.U. "Brunei Darussalam in 1986, in search of the Political Kingdom", *SAA 1987* (1988): 85–101.

______. "Brunei Darussalam towards a new era", *SAA 2007* (2008): 88–104.

Mohammad Yusop Haji Damit (Haj.). "Brunei Darussalam, Weathering the Storm", *SAA 2000* (2001): 87–97.

______. "Brunei Darussalam: Steady Ahead", *SAA 2004* (2005): 63–70.

______. "Brunei Darussalam towards a new era", *SAA 2007* (2008): 88–104.

Naimah Talib. "Brunei in 1995: A New Assertiveness?", *SAA 1996* (1997): 101–10.

Ong, Timothy Teck Mong. "Modern Brunei, some important issues", *SAA 1983* (1984): 71–84.

Roberts, Christopher and Lee Poh Onn. "Brunei Darussalam: Cautious on Political Reform, Comfortable in ASEAN, Pushing for Economic Diversification", *SAA 2009* (2010): 61–82.

Saunders, Graham. "Brunei: A vision for the Future?", *SAA 1997* (1998): 67–79.

Siddique, Sharon. "Negara Brunei Darussalam: 'A New Nation but an Ancient Country'", *SAA 1985* (1986): 99–108.

______. "Brunei Darussalam 1991. The Non-Secular Nation", *SAA 1992* (1993): 91–100.

Singh, D.S. Ranjit. "Brunei Darussalam in 1987, Coming to Grips with Economic and Political Realities", *SAA 1988* (1989): 63–70.

Thambipillai, Pushpa. "Brunei in ASEAN: The Viable Choice?", *SAA 1982* (1983): 105–12.

______. "Brunei Darussalam: Consolidating the polity", *SAA 2006* (2007): 57–70.

______. "Brunei Darussalam: Making a concerted effort", *SAA 2008* (2009): 88–104.

Thambipillai, Pushpa and Hamzah Sulaiman. "Brunei Darussalam. After a Decade of Independence", *SAA 1995* (1996): 111–23.

UBD. *Purih: Universiti Brunei Darussalam dalam satu dekad, kumpulan esei mengenai Negara Brunei Darussalam = A collection of essay[s] on Brunei Darussalam*. BSB: APB, UBD, 1996, xviii, 354 p.

World Market Research Centre. *Brunei Country Risk Summary* (19 Dec. 2003).

Zainal Kling. "The changing international image of Brunei", *SAA 1990* (1991): 89–100.

Anthropology and Demographic Data

Ethnic Groups

Bantong Antaran. "Costumes and Textiles of Brunei: History and Evolution", *SPAFA Journal* 11, 2 (2001): 11–9.

Kershaw, Eva Maria and Roger Kershaw. "The Mundane and the Mystic: Constructions of Human Relations in the Animal World in Brunei-Dusun and Other Bornean Folktales", *Indonesia and the Malay World* 34, 99 (July 2006): 151–95.

Lim, Jock Seng. *The Inter-relationship of technology, economy and social organisation in a fishing village in Brunei*. BSB: Brunei Museum, 1986, 123 p.

Maxwell, Allen R. "Urang Darat: An ethnographic study of the Kadayan of Labu Valley, Brunei". Ph.D. dissertation, Yale University, 1980, 271 p.

Pudarno Binchin. "'Race against time': Problems and prospect of anthropological research on Brunei Dusun". Mimeographed. BSB: Universiti Brunei Darussalam, 2005.

Sellato, Bernard. *Forest, resources and people in Bulungan: Elements for a History of Settlement, Trade and Social Dynamics in Borneo 1880–2000*. Jakarta: Centre for International Forestry Research, 2001, 183 p.

______. *Innermost Borneo: Studies in Dayak Culture*. Paris & Singapore: Seven Orients & Singapore University Press, 2002, 221 p.

Shariffuddin, P.M. "The Kedayans", *BMJ* 1, 1 (1969): 15–23.

Winzeler, Robert L., ed. *Indigenous peoples and the state: Politics, land, and ethnicity in the Malayan Peninsula and Borneo*. New Haven: Yale University Southeast Asia Studies, 1997, xii, 316 p.

Population and Demography

Amaluddin Bakeri. "Sejarah hubungan petempatan Kampung Air di Limbang, Sarawak dengan Kampong Ayer Brunei Darussalam [History of the Relations between Limbang's Kampung Ayer and Brunei Darussalam's]", *SMJ* 58, 79 (2003): 141–61.

Jones, L.W. *The population of Borneo, a study of the Peoples of Sarawak, Sabah and Brunei*. London: Athlone Press, 1966. Reprint, Kota Kinabalu: Opus Publication, 2007, 213 p.

Laporan Awal, Preliminary Report, Banci Penduduk dans Perumahan, BSB, Jabatan Perangkaan, Jabatan Perancangan dan Kemajuan Ekonomi, Department of Statistics, Department of Economic Planning and Development, Jan. 2012, 87 p.

Laporan Banci Penduduk dan Perumahan, Population and Housing Report, Ciri-Ciri Demografi, Demographic Characteristics, BSB, JPKE, Nov. 2012, 10 p.

Neville, Warwick. "The Population Composition of Brunei", *Singapore Journal of Tropical Geography* 11, 1 (1990): 27–42.

Niew, Shong Tong (Jao Shang-Tung, mand. Rao Shandong) 饶尚东 (饒尚東). "The population geography of the Chinese communities in Malaysia, Singapore and Brunei". Ph.D. dissertation, University of London, 1969.

______. *Demographic trends in Negara Brunei Darussalam*. BSB: Educational Technology Centre, UBD, Department of Public Policy and Administration, 1991, 132 p.

Dialectology

Bakar, Mataim. *Morfologi dialek Brunei: satu tinjauan kajian lampau* [*Morphology of the dialect of Brunei: Overview*]. BSB: DBP, 2000, 152 p.

Collins, James T. "Pengkajian bahasa Melayu Brunei: tinjauan kemajuan [Studies of the Malays of Brunei: Assessment of advances]", *Dewan Bahasa* 43, 3 (1999): 253–61.

Dewan Pustaka. Dialek memperkaya bahasa [*Dialect enriches the language*]. BSB: DBP, 1995, 258 p.

Haynes, H.S. "A list of Brunei-Malay Words", *RASSB* 34–7 (1900–02): 39–48.

Jaludin Chuchu. *Morphology of Brunei Malay*. Bangi: Universiti Kebangsaan Malaysia, 2000, 162 p.

———. *Dialek Melayu Brunei dalam salasilah bahasa Melayu purba* [*The Malay dialect of Brunei in the genealogies in ancient Malay*]. Bangi: Universiti Kebangsaan Malaysia, 2003, 262 p.

Kamus Bahasa Melayu Brunei [*Dictionary of Brunei Malay*]. BSB: DBP, 2007, reprint, 358 p.

Kamus Kedayan-Melayu, Melayu-Kedayan [*Dictionary Kedayan-Malay, Malay-Kedayan*]. BSB: DBP, 2006, 343 p.

MacBryan, G.T. "Additions to a vocabulary of Brunei-Malay", *RASSBJ* 85–6 (1922): 376–7.

Marshall, H.B. "A vocabulary of Brunei Malay", *RASSBJ* 83–4 (1921): 45–74.

Martin, W., Conrad Ozog and Gloria Poedjosoedarmo. *Language use and language change in Brunei Darussalam*. Athens: Ohio University Center for International Studies, 1996, 373 p.

Martin, Peter W. "Some views on the language ecology of Brunei Darussalam", in *From Buckfast to Borneo: Essays Presented to Father Robert Nicholl on the 85th Anniversary of his birth, 27 March 1995*, ed. Victor T. King and A.V.M. Horton. Hull: University of Hull, Centre for South-East Asian Studies, 1995, pp. 236–51.

Mataim Bakar and Faridah Haji Mohammad. *The Phonotactics of Brunei Malay: An optimality theoretic account*. BSB: DBPB, 2007, 275 p.

Mukul, Saxena. "Multilingual and Multicultural Identity in Brunei Darussalam", in *Language Policy, Culture and Identity in Asian Contexts*, ed. Amy B.M. Tsui and James W. Tollefson. London: Lawrence Erlbaum Associates, 2006, pp. 143–62.

Ramlee Tunggal (Hj.). *Struktur Bahasa Tutong* [*Structure of the Tutong language*]. BSB: DBP, 2005, 1st ed. Reprint 2009, 234 p.

Ray, Sidney H. "The Languages of Borneo", *SMJ* 1, 4 (1913), 196 p.

History

Ancient Historical Sources Relating to Borneo and Brunei (9th–18th Centuries)

Malay Sources

Brown, C.C. and R. Roolvink. *Sejarah Melayu 'Malay Annals'*. Kuala Lumpur: Oxford University Press, 1976, reprint, 273 p.

Gallop, Annabel Teh. "Malay Sources for the History of Brunei Darussalam in British Collections". Seminar Sejarah Brunei kali dua, masa silam sarana masa depan, 26–29 Aug. 1995, 9 p.

Low, Hugh, "*Selesilah* (Book of Descent) of the Rajas of Bruni". *JMBRAS* 5 (June 1880): 1–36. Reprinted in *Papers relating to Brunei*, ed. Cheah Boon Kheng. Kuala Lumpur: MBRAS reprint, 1998, pp. 1–24.

Manguin, Pierre-Yves and Ian Proudfoot. *Hikayat Hang Tuah* [*Malay text of the 17th century, according to the printed edition of the Dewan Bahasa dan Pustaka, 1975*]. E-publ., edition revised and expanded for the Malay Concordance Project, 1994, 224 p.

Marre, Aristide. *Sadjârah malâyou, le Livre des chroniques Malayses depuis les origines jusqu'à la conquête de Malaka par les Portugais, en 1511*. Vaucresson, 1900, pp. 81–311.

Matheson, V. and B. Watson Andaya, eds. *The Precious Gift (Tuhfat al-Nafis), translated from Raja Ali Haji Ibn Ahmad*. Kuala Lumpur: Oxford University Press, 1982, 476 p.

Maxwell, Allen R. "Who is Awang Simawn?", in *From Buckfast to Borneo: Essays Presented to Father Robert Nicholl on the 85th Anniversary of his birth 27 March 1995*, ed. Victor T. King and A.V.M. Horton. Hull: University of Hull, Centre for South-East Asian Studies, 1995, pp. 178–206.

______. "Accessing the Epic Status of the Brunei Malay Sya'ir Awang Simawn". Paper presented at the Tenth International Conference on Linguistics, 17–20 Jan. 2006, Puerto Princessa (Palawan), http://www.sil.org/asia/Philippines/ical/papers.html, 20 p.

Rahim Dulani, ed. *Hikayat Awang Kamaruddin*. BSB: DBPB, Kementerian Kebudayaan, Belia dan Sukan, 1992, 133 p.

Raja Ali Haji Ibn Ahmad. "*Silsilah Melayu dan Bugis dans Sekalian Raja Raja nya*, [*Genealogy of Malays, Bugis and all the kings*]". Translated by Hans Overbeck. *JMBRAS* IV, 3 (1926): 339–81.

Ras, J.J. *Hikajat Bandjar: A Study in Malay Historiography*. The Hague: Bibliotheca Indosinica, Martinus Nijhoff, 1968, 651 p.

Reece, Bob. "The *Syair Saribas* Project", *BRB* (2/01/2002), http://findarticles.com/p/articles/mi_hb036/is_33/ai_n28974321.

Shariffuddin, P.M. and Abdul Latif Hj. Ibrahim. "*Batu Tarsilah*; the Genealogical Tablet of the Sultans of Brunei", *BMJ* 3, 2 (1974): 253–64.

Situmorang, T.D. and A. Teeuw. *Sejarah Melayu menurut terbitan Abdullah (Ibn Abdulkadir Munsji)* [*History of Malays according to the edition of Abdullah (Ibn Abdulkadir Munsji)*]. Jakarta: Djambatan, 1952, 359 p.

Sweeney, P.L. Amin. "*Silsilah Raja-Raja Berunai*", *JMBRAS* 41, 2 (1968): 1–82.

______. "*Silsilah Raja-Raja Berunai*, Errata and Short note", *JMBRAS* 42, 2 (1969): 222–4.

Syair Awang Simaun [*Koleksi Muzium*]. BSB: DBP, 2010, 247 p.

Winstedt, R.O., ed. "The Malay Annals; or *Sejarah Melayu*", *JMBRAS* 16/3 (1938), 226 p.

Winstedt, R.O. and P.E. de Josselin de Jong. "The Maritime Laws of Malacca", *JMBRAS* 29, 3 (1956): 22–59.

Arab and Chinese Sources

Brown, Carrie C. "An Early Account of Brunei by Sung Lien", *BMJ* 2, 4 (1972): 219–31.

———. "Two Ming texts concerning King Ma-na-je-chia-na of P'o-ni", *BMJ* 3, 2 (1974): 222–31.

Groeneveldt, W.P. *Notes on the Malay Archipelago and Malacca compiled from Chinese sources*. Batavia: Verhandelingen van het Bataviaasch Genootschap van Kunsten en Wetenschappen, XXXIX, 1880, 111 p.

Kurz, Johannes L. *Boni in Chinese Sources: Translations of Relevant Texts from the Song to the Qing Dynasties*. BSB, E-publ., 2008, 66 p.

Liu, Xinsheng 刘新生. 中国与文莱关系史科江编 *Zhong guo yu wen lai guan xi shi ke jiang bian* [*The Collection of historical documents related to bilateral relations between China and Brunei Darussalam*]. Beijing: World Affairs Press 世界知识出版社 Shi jie zhi shi chu ban shi, 2006, 218 p.

Mills, J.V. "Arab and Chinese Navigators in the Malaysian waters in about A.D. 1500", *JMBRAS* 47, 2 (1974): 1–82.

Nicholl, Robert. *Notes on Early Brunei History*. Mimeographed. BSB, Dec. 1986, 66 p.

Tibbetts, G.R. *A Study of the Arabic texts containing material on Southeast Asia*. Leiden: Brill, 1979, 294 p.

Wade, Geoff, translated by. *Southeast Asia in the Ming Shi-lu* [明實錄]*: An open access resource*. Singapore: Asia Research Institute and the Singapore E-Press, NUS, 2005, http:// epress.nus. edu.sg/msl.

Dutch Sources

Chijs, A. van der, ed. *Dagh Register gehouden in't Casteel Batavia 1624–1682*. The Hague: M. Nijhoff, 1887–1931, 31 vols.

Coolhaas, Willem P., ed. *Generale missiven van Gouverneurs-generaal en raden aan Heren XVII der Verenigde Oostindische Compagnie, 1627–1737*. The Hague: M. Nijhoff, 1960–85, 9 vols.

Goor, Jurrien van, ed. *Generale missiven van Gouverneurs-generaal en raden aan Heren XVII der Verenigde Oostindische Compagnie, 1737–43*. Reprint Vol. X. The Hague: R.G.P., 2004, 1159 p.

Oosterling, Judith E., ed. *Generale missiven van Gouverneurs-generaal en raden aan Heren XVII der Verenigde Oostindische Compagnie, 1750–1755*. Reprint Vol. XII. The Hague: 2007, 698 p.

Schooneveld-Oosterling, J.E., ed. *Generale missiven van Gouverneurs-generaal en raden aan Heren XVII der Verenigde Oostindische Compagnie, 1743–1750.* Reprint Vol. XI. The Hague: R.G.P., Grote Serie, vol. 232, Instituut voor Nederlandse Geschiedenis, 1997, 949 p.

s'Jacob, H.K., ed. *Generale missiven van Gouverneurs-generaal en raden aan Heren XVII der Verenigde Oostindische Compagnie, 1756–1761.* Reprint Vol. XIII. The Hague, 2007, 698 p.

Valentyn, François. "A description of Borneo and our trade there", in *Oud en Nieuw Oost Indies*, François Valentyn. Dordrecht: Joannes van Braam, 1726. Book 3, Ch. 1–3 reproduced in *BMJ* 4, 2 (1978): 67–93.

Iberian Sources

Brown, D.E. "Spanish accounts of their expeditions against Brunei in 1578–79", *BMJ* 3, 2 (1974): 180–221.

Carroll, John S., ed. "Berunai in the *Boxer Codex*", *JMBRAS* 55, 2 (1982): 1–25.

______, ed. "Francisco de Sandes' invasion of Brunei in 1578: An anonymous Spanish Account", *BMJ* 6, 2 (1986): 47–71.

Nicholl, Robert, ed. *European Sources for the History of the Sultanate of Brunei in the Sixteenth Century.* BSB: Brunei Museums, 1st ed. 1975, 3rd ed. 2007, 119 p.

______. *Sources for the History of Brunei.* 2 vols. Mimeographed, unpublished. Vol. I, *To 1515*; Vol. II, *1515–1619*. Hull: Archives of the Brynmor Jones Library, University of Hull, DX 1991 & 1992.

Other Western Sources

Anonymous. "Notices of the city of Borneo and its inhabitants, made during the voyage of the American brig Himmaleh in the Indian Archipelago, in 1837", *Chinese Repository* 7 (1838): 121–36, 177–93.

Cameron, Charlotte. *Wandering in South Eastern Seas.* London: Fisher & Unwin, 1924, pp. 35, 81–5.

Earl, John Windsor. *Voyages and adventures in the Indian Archipelago in 1832–33–34.* London: H. Allen & Co., 1837, pp. 316–21.

Francis, Simon. *Pictures of the Palace, travellers' accounts of the Brunei of Sultan 'Abdu'l Momin and Sultan Hashim between 1881 and 1906.* Hull: University of Hull, Centre for South East-Asian Studies, 1993, 52 p.

Khoo, Kay Kim, ed. "Agreement between Her Majesty's Government and the Sultan of Brunei for the establishment of a British protectorate over the State of Brunei", in *Sabah: History and Society.* Kuala Lumpur: Malaysia Historical Society, 1981, pp. 27–32.

Moor, J.H. "Borneo proper", in *Notices of the Indian Archipelago*, ed. J.H. Moor, 1837, pp. 1–4, 13–4, 93–7.

St. John's, Spenser. *Life in the Forest of the Far East*. London: Smith, Elder & Co., 1862, vol. II, pp. 245–79.

Whitehead, John. *The Exploration of Kinabalu*. Singapore: Graham Bash, 1992 (1st publ., 1893), 317 p.

Other Historical Works

General Historical Works

Abdul Latif Haji Irahim, partly translated by Lim Jock Seng. *Photographic exhibition*. BSB: Muzium Brunei, 1970, 52 p.

Andaya, Leonard and Barbara Watson Andaya. *History of Malaysia*. London: Macmillan, 1982, 350 p.

Blundell, Peter. *City of Many Waters*. London: J.W. Arrowsmith, 1923, 223 p.

Brown, D.E. *Brunei: The structure and history of a Bornean Malay Sultanate*. Brunei: Brunei Museum, 1970, 239 p.

———. "Brunei in comparative perspective", *SMJ* 26, 47 (1978): 135–60.

Cheah Boon Kheng, ed. and introduced by. *Papers relating to Brunei*. Kuala Lumpur: Malaysian Branch of the Royal Asiatic Society, 1998, vi, 186 p.

Graaf, H.J. de. *Geschiedenis van Indonesië*. The Hague: W. van Hoeve, 1949, 516 p.

Horton, A.V.M. *The development of Brunei during the British residential era, 1906–1959: A sultanate regenerated*. Boston Spa: British Library Document Supply Centre, 1985, 2 vols.

———. *A new sketch of the history of Brunei Negara Darussalam*. Bordesley: AVM Horton, 1996, 61 p.

———. *Turun-temurun: A Dissection of Brunei Darussalam*. Bordesley: AVM Horton, reprint 1998, 280 p.

Jamil al-Sufri (Pehin Orang Kaya Amar Diraja Dato Sri Utama Dr. Haji Awang Mohd.). *Tarsilah Brunei, Sejarah Awal dan Perkembangan Islam* [*Genealogy of Brunei, ancient history of the expansion of Islam*]. BSB: Pusat Sejarah, 1990, 154 p.

———. *Tarsilah Brunei: The early history of Brunei up to 1432 AD*. Trans. by Awang Haji Mohamad Amin bin Hassan. BSB: Brunei History Centre, 2000, 138 p.

Lombard, Denys and Henri Chambert-Loir. "Guide Archipel VI: Le sultanat de Brunei Darussalam", *Archipel* 39 (1990): 19–34.

Marr, D.G. and A.D. Milner, eds. *Southeast Asia in the 9th to 14th centuries*. Singapore: ISEAS & Canberra: Research School of Pacific Studies, ANU, 1986, 416 p.

Marryat, Frank S., *Borneo and the Indian archipelago: Drawings, costumes and scenery*. London: Longman, Brown, Green & Longmans, 1848, pp. 104–17.

Monks, T.S. *Brunei Days*. Lewes: The Book Guild, 1992, 193 p.

Reid, Anthony. "Trade and State power in XVIth and XVIIth century South-East Asia". Mimeographed. Lecture at the Seventh Congress of Asia, Bangkok, Aug. 1977, 26 p.

______. *Southeast Asia in the Age of Commerce 1450–1680*, Vol. 1 *The Lands Below the Winds*; Vol. 2. *Expansion and Crisis*. New Haven: Yale University Press, 1988 & 1993, 272 & 380 p.

______, ed. *Southeast Asia in the Early Modern Era: Trade, Power, and Belief*. Ithaca: Cornell University Press, 1993, 286 p.

Rutter, Owen. *The Pirate Wind: Tales of the Sea-Robbers of Malaya*. Singapore: Oxford University Press, 1986 (Orig. Publ., 1930), 308 p.

Saunders, Graham. *A History of Brunei*. Kuala Lumpur: Oxford University Press, 2nd ed. 2002, 226 p.

Treacher, W.H. "The Genealogy of the Royal Family of Brunei", *JMBRAS* 15 (June 1880).

Turnbull, Mary C. *A History of Malaysia, Singapore, and Brunei*. Sydney & Boston: Allen & Unwin, 1989, 330 p.

Wright, Leigh. "Brunei, an historical relic", *JHKBRAS* 17 (1977): 12–29.

From the Origins to the 16th Century

Bastin, J.S. and Robin W. Winks, eds. "The Early Malacca and Brunei Sultanates", in *Malaysia: Selected Historical Readings*, 2nd ed. Nendeln: KTO Press, 1979, pp. 14–6.

Beavitt, P., E. Kurui and G. Thompson. "Confirmation of an early date for the presence of rice in Borneo: Preliminary evidence for possible Bidayuh/Asian links", *BRB* 27 (1996): 29–37.

Bellwood, Peter. *Man's conquest of the Pacific: The Prehistory of Southeast Asia and Oceania*. New York: Oxford University Press, 1979, 262 p.

Boxer, C.R. *South China in the Sixteenth Century: Being the narratives of Galeote Pereira, Fr. Gaspar da Cruz, O.P., Fr. Martin de Rada, O.E.S.A. (1550–1575)*. London: Hakluyt Society, 1953, xci, 388 p.

Braddell, Roland. "A Note on Sambas and Borneo", *JMBRAS* 22, 4 (1949): 1–12.

______. *The study of ancient times in the Malay Peninsula and straits of Malacca*. Kuala Lumpur: MBRAS, 1980, 522 p.

Chen Dasheng. "Une pierre tombale du début du XIVe s. retrouvée à Brunei", *Archipel* 42 (1991): 47–52.

Ferrand, Gabriel. *L'empire sumatranais de Çrîvijaya*. Paris: Imprimerie Nationale, 1922, 190 p.

Franke, Wolfgang and Ch'en T'ieh-fan. "A Chinese tomb inscription of A.D. 1264, discovered recently in Brunei, a preliminary Report", *BMJ* 3, 1 (1973): 91–104.

Gallop, Annabel Teh. "Camels, seals and early tin coinage of Brunei", *Archipel* 70 (2005): 261–80.

Hall, Kenneth R. *Maritime Trade and State development in Early Southeast Asia*. Honolulu: University of Hawaii Press, 1985, 368 p.

Harrisson, Barbara. "Sungai Lumut: A 15th century burial ground", *BMJ* 1 (1969): 24–56.

Harrisson, Tom. "50,000 years of stone age culture in Borneo", in *The Smithsonian Report for 1964*. Washington, 1965, pp. 521–30.

———. "The Golden Hoard of Limbang", *BMJ*, no. 1 (1969): 57–71.

———. "Further radio-carbon (C-14) dates from Kota Batu, Brunei—back to 12,500 B.C.", *BMJ*, no. 2/4 (1972): 209–17.

Harrisson, Tom and Barbara. "Kota Batu in Brunei (Introductory Report)", *SMJ* 7/8 (new series), no. 23 (1956): 283–318.

———. *The prehistory of Sabah*. Kota Kinabalu: Sabah Society Journal Monograph, Vol. 4, 1971, xviii, 272 p.

Harrisson, Tom and S.J. O'Connor. *Gold and megalithic activity in prehistoric and recent West Borneo*. Ithaca: Southeast Asia Program, Cornell University, 1970, xiv, 331 p.

Hendrick, Jim. "Ceramics found at Sinaut Agricultural Training Centre", *BMJ* 7, 3 (1991): 1–9.

Hornell, J. "Sea Trade in Early Times", *Antiquity* 15 (1941): 233–56.

Jamil Al-Sufri (Pehin Dr. Awang Haji Mohd.). "The story of Bendahara Sakam", *BMJ* 3, 3 (1975): 109–15.

———. "Batu Nisan di perkuburan orang-orang Islam di Subok, Bandar Seri Bagawan [Muslim Funerary Steles of Subok, Bandar Seri Begawan]", *BMJ* 5, 4 (1984): 1–3.

———. *Sultan Sharif Ali*. Tajuk kertaskerja [Working paper], Seminar Sejarah Brunei [Seminar on the History of Brunei]. BSB: Jabatan Pusat Sejarah, 28–31 Aug. 1989, 51 p.

Kalus, Ludwig and Claude Guillot. "Les inscriptions funéraires islamiques de Brunei", *BEFEO* 90–1 (2003–04): 229–72.

———. "Les inscriptions funéraires islamiques de Brunei (deuxième partie)", *BEFEO* 93 (2006): 139–81.

Karim bin Pengiran Haji Osman. "Notes on a blue-and-white shard (with Arabic inscriptions) found at Kota Batu archaeological site", *BMJ* 7, 3 (1991): 10–25.

———. "A report on archaeological excavation and exploration on Pulau Terendak and its surrounding area", *BMJ* 7, 4 (1992): 18–48.

———. *Sungai Limau Manis: Tapak Arkeologi Abad Ke-10-13 Masihi* [*Sungai Limau Manis, an archaeological site from the 10th–13th centuries A.D.*]. BSB: Jabatan Muzium-Muzium Brunei, Kementerian Kebudayaan, 2004, 175 p.

Kratz, Ernest Ulrich. "Silsilah raja-Raja Sambas as a source of history", *Archipel* 20 (1980): 255–67.

L'Hour, Michel. *La mémoire engloutie de Brunei: une aventure sous-marine*. Paris: Textuel, 2001, 3 vols., 142, 175 & 47 p.

Matussin bin Omar. *Archaeological excavations in proto-historic Brunei.* BSB: Muzium Brunei, 1981, ix, 116 p.

______. "Archaeology and the reconstruction of Brunei's Early History", *BMJ* 9, 1 (1994): 1–12.

Manguin, Pierre-Yves. "Research on the ships of Śrîvijaya (and of first millennium A.D. Southeast Asia)", in *SPAFA Consultative Workshop on Archaeological and Environmental Studies on Śrîvijaya, Final Report.* Bangkok: SEAMEO, 1985, pp. 291–306.

______. "Shipshape societies: Boat symbolism and Political Systems in Insular Southeast Asia", in *Southeast Asia in the 9th to 14th centuries*, ed. D.G. Marr and A.D. Milner. Singapore & Canberra: ISEAS & ANU, 1986, pp. 187–213.

______. "Palembang et Sriwijaya: anciennes hypothèses et recherches nouvelles (Palembang Ouest)", *BEFEO* 76, 1 (1987): 337–402.

______. "The Merchant and the King, Political Myths of Southeast Asian Coastal Polities", *Indonesia* 52 (1991): 41–54.

Miksic, John N. "Evolving Archaeological perspectives in Southeast Asia, 1970–95", *JSAS* 25/26 (March 1995): 46–62.

Nicholl, Robert. "The Mission of Father Antonino Ventimiglia to Borneo", *BMJ* 2, 4 (1972): 183–205.

______. "Ibn Batuta and Borneo", *BMJ* 4, 2 (1978): 34–45.

______. "Notes on some controversial issue in Brunei History", *Archipel* 19 (1980): 25–41.

______. "The Sribuza of Captain Buzurg", *BMJ* 5, 2 (1982): 1–11.

______. "Brunei rediscovered: A survey of early times", *BMJ* 4, 4 (1980), reprint *JSAS* 14, 1 (March 1983a): 32–45.

______. "The Letter of Bras Bayão", *BMJ* 5, 3 (1983b): 51–60.

______. "The Tomb of Maharaja Karna of Brunei at Nanking", *BMJ* 5, 4 (1984): 35–45.

______. "Myth and Legend in Brunei History", *BMJ* 6, 1 (1985): 32–41.

______. "The Quest for Iabadiou", *BMJ* 6, 2 (1986): 26–43.

Ongkili, James P. "Pre-Western Brunei, Sarawak and Sabah", *SMJ* 20, 40–1 (1972): 1–19.

Ptak, Roderich. "Possible Chinese References to the Barus Area (Tang to Ming)", in *Histoire de Barus, Sumatra: Le site de Lobu Tua, vol. I: Études et documents*, ed. Claude Guillot. Paris: Cahiers d'Archipel, 1998a, pp. 120–5.

______. "From Quanzhou to the Sulu Zone and Beyond: Questions Related to the Early Fourteenth Century", *JSAS* 29, 2 (1998b): 269–94.

______. "Camphor in East and Southeast Asian Trade, *c.* 1500: A Synthesis of Portuguese and Asian Sources", in *Vasco da Gama and the Linking of Europe and Asia*, ed. Anthony Disney and Emily Booth. New Delhi: Oxford University Press, 2000, pp. 142–66.

Sanib Said (Awang). *Pembentukan kerajaan Brunei lama: huraian teori penghijarahan [The structures of the ancient kingdom of Brunei, an analysis of the theory of migration*]. BSB: DBP, Sebuah kertas kerja yang dibentangkan di dalam Seminar Antarabangsa, Bahasa, Kesusasteraan dan Kebudayaan Melayu di Bandar Seri Begawan, 3–8 Aug. 1987, 32 p.

Smith, R.B. and W. Watson, eds. *Early South East Asia: Essays in archaeology history & historical geography*. New York & Kuala Lumpur: Oxford University Press, 1979, 628 p.

Stargardt, Janice. "L'isthme de la péninsule malaise dans les navigations au long cours: nouvelles données archéologiques", *Archipel* 18 (1979): 15–39.

Van Leur, J.C. *Indonesian trade and society, essays in Asian social and economic history*. Reprint. Leiden: KITLV, 1983, 465 p.

Wade, Geoff, ed. "The Zheng He voyage, a reassessment", *JMBRAS* 78, 1 (2005): 37–58.

———. *Southeast Asia-China Interactions: Reprint of articles from the Journal of the Malaysian Branch*. Kuala Lumpur: MBRAS, 2007, 620 p.

———. *China and Southeast Asia*. New York: Routledge, 2008, 2432 p.

Wiseman Christie, Jan. "State Formation in Early Maritime Southeast Asia: A Consideration of the Theories and the Data", *Bijdragen tot de Taal-, Land- en Volkenkunde* 151, 2 (1995): 235–88.

Wolters, O.W. *Early Indonesian commerce: A study of the origins of Srivijaya*. Ithaca: Cornell University Press, 1967, 404 p.

———. *The Fall of Śrîvijaya in Malay History*. Kuala Lumpur: Oxford University Press, 1975 (Orig. publ. 1970), 274 p.

17th–mid-19th Centuries

Anonymous. "British authorities in Borneo: Forcing the Brunei River, the capture of forts and the town of Borneo (Bruni) and the complete success of British policy", *The Chinese Repository* (19 Aug. 1846), 6 p.

———. "Six weeks on the coast of Borneo", *The United Service Journal*, Part III (1847): 1–8.

Andaya, Leonard. *The Kingdom of Johor (1641–1728), Economic and Political Developments*. Kuala Lumpur: Oxford University Press, 1975, 394 p.

———. *Leaves of the Same Tree: Trade and Ethnicity in the Straits of Melaka*. Honolulu: Cambridge History of Early Modern Southeast Asia & University of Hawai'i Press, 2008, 320 p.

Blumentritt, Frederick. "Spain and the island of Borneo", *BMJ* 4, 1 (1977): 82–96.

Braddell, T. "On the History of Acheen"; "Translations from the Majelis Ache", *JIAEA* 5 (1851): 15–25, 26–32.

Brown, D.E. "Brunei and the Bajau", *BRB* 3, 2 (1971): 55–8.

Davidson, J.A. "Brunei coinage", *BMJ* 4, 1 (1977): 43–81.

Dijk, Kees van. "From Raja to Prime Minister. Strange Rulers and Economic Exploitation in Borneo and the Pacific in the Nineteenth Century", *Moussons* 12 (2008): 103–35.

Dijk, L.C. van. "Relations of the East Indian Company with Borneo (Brunei), the Sulu Archipelago, Mindanao, etc.", *BMJ* 5, 4 (1984): 6–34.

Forrest, Capitaine. *Voyages aux Moluques et à la Nouvelle Guinée fait sur la galère le Tartare en 1774, 1775 & 1776 par ordre de la Compagnie Anglaise.* Paris: s.n., 1780, 470 p.

Fry, Howard T. *Alexander Dalrymple and the Expansion of British Trade.* Toronto: Royal Commonwealth Society, by University of Toronto Press, 1970, xxvii, 330 p.

Hunt, J. "Sketch of Borneo, or Pulo Kalamantan", in *The expedition to Borneo of H.M.S. Dido for the suppression of piracy, with extracts from the Journal of James Brooke*, ed. Sir Henry Keppel. New York: Harper & Brothers, 1846, vol. II, Appendix II, pp. lvii-lix.

Keppel, Sir Henry. *The expedition to Borneo of H.M.S. Dido for the suppression of piracy, with extracts from the Journal of James Brooke.* New York: Harper & Brothers, 1846, 414 p.

Logan, J.R. "Borneo"; "Notices of European intercourse with Borneo Proper prior to the establishment of Singapore in 1819"; "Traces of the origin of the Malay Kingdom of Borneo, with notices of its condition when first discovered by Europeans, and at later periods"; "Notices of Chinese intercourse with Borneo Proper prior to the establishment of Singapore in 1819", *JIAEA* 2 (1848): 495–97, 498–512, 513–27, 611–5.

______. "The piracy and slave trade of the Indian Archipelago", *JIAEA* 3 (1849): 276–7, 581–8, 629–36; 4 (1850): 45–52, 144–62, 400–10, 617–68, 734–46; 5 (1851): 374–82.

Manguin, Pierre-Yves. "Brunei trade with Macao at the turn of the 19th century, à propos of a 1819 letter from Sultan Khan Zul Alam", *BMJ* 6, 3 (1987): 16–25.

Marryat, Frank S. *Borneo and the Indian Archipelago: With drawings, costumes and scenery.* London: Longman, Brown & Green, 1848, pp. 104–20.

Matassim Haji Jibah. "Pangiran Indira Mahkota Shahbandar Muhammad Saleh and James Brooke in the History of Brunei", *Brunei History Journal* (1979): 38–51.

Moor, J.H. "Borneo Proper", in *Notices of the Indian Archipelago, and adjacent countries: Being a collection of papers relating to Borneo, Celebes, Bali, Java, Sumatra, Nias, the Philippine islands, Sulus, Siam, Cochin China, Malayan Peninsula*, ed. J.H. Moor. Singapore: F. Cass & Co., 1837, pp. 1–4.

Nicholl, Robert. "Relations between Brunei and Manila A.D. 1682–1690", *BMJ* 4, 1 (1977): 128–76.

______. *Raja Bongsu of Sulu: A Brunei hero in his time.* Kuala Lumpur: MBRAS, monograph no. 19, 1991, 78 p.

Noorduyn, J. "A Bugis inscription in the Udok-Udok cemetery, Brunei", *JMBRAS* 66 (1993): 103–12.

Nort d'Utrecht, Sr. Olivier [Olivier van Noort]. *Description du pénible voyage faict entour de l'univers ou globe terrestre*, translated from Flemish into French. Amsterdam: C. Claesz, 1602, 62 p.

Reece, Bob. "Two missionaries in Brunei in 1837: George Tradescant Lay and the Revd J.T. Dickinson", *SMJ* 52, 78 (2002): 179–204.

Short, Brook. "Brunei, Sulu & Sabah", *BMJ* 1 (1969): 133–46.

Warren, James F. *The Sulu Zone 1968–1898: The Dynamics of External Trade, Slavery, and Ethnicity in the Transformation of a Southeast Asian Maritime State*. Singapore: Singapore University Press, 1981, 390 p.

Watson Andaya, Barbara. *Perak: The Abode of Grace, a study of an eighteenth century Malay State*. Kuala Lumpur: Oxford University Press, 1979, 444 p.

Mid-19th Century–1960

Arifin Mansurnoor (Dr. lik). "Socio-religious changes in Brunei during the British Residency (1906–1959)". 13th Conference of the International Association of Historians of Asia, Sophia University, Tokyo, 3–9 Sept. 1994, 16 p.

Baring-Gould, S. and C.A. Bampfylde. *A history of Sarawak under its two white Rajahs 1839–1908*. Kuala Lumpur: Synergy Media, 2007, 523 p. (Orig. publ. London: Henry Sotheran, 1909).

Black, I.D. "The Ending of Brunei Rule in Sabah 1878–1902", *JMBRAS* 41, 2 (1968): 176–92.

Crisswell, Colin N. "Some historical aspects of local and sovereign rights in Nineteenth Century Brunei", *Journal of Oriental Studies* 10, 1 (1972): 51–61.

______. "Pg Anak Hashim's role in Brunei affairs prior to his accession to the Throne in 1885", *SMJ* 26, 46 (1977): 41–54.

______. *Rajah Charles Brooke, monarchs of all, he survived*. Kuala Lumpur: Oxford University Press, 1978, 253 p.

Francis, Simon. *Pictures of the Palace: Traveller's account of the Brunei of Sultan Abdul Momin and Sultan Hashim between 1881 and 1906*. Hull: University of Hull, Centre for Asian Studies, 1993, 52 p.

Gallop, Annabel Teh. "Sultan Abdul Mubin of Brunei: Two literary depictions of his reign", *Indonesia and the Malay World* 25, 73 (Nov. 1997): 189–220.

______. *Malay seal inscriptions: A study in Islamic epigraphy from Southeast Asia*. London: University of London, School of Oriental and African Studies, 2002, 3 vols.

Horton, A.V.H. *The British residency in Brunei, 1906–1959*. Hull: University of Hull, Centre for Southeast Asian Studies, Occasional papers no. 6, 1984, 95 p.

______. "The development of Brunei during the British residential era, 1906–1959: a sultanate regenerated". Ph.D. dissertation, University of Hull, 1985, 2 vols.

______. "British administration in Brunei 1906–1959", *Modern Asian Studies* 20, 2 (1986): 353–74.

______. *Report on Brunei in 1904 by M.S.H. McArthur, introduced and annotated by*. Athens: Ohio University Centre for International Studies, Centre for Southeast Asian Studies, 1987a, 283 p.

______. "The disturbances in the Tutong and Belait Districts of Brunei (1899–1901)", *JSAS* 18, 1 (1987b): 93–107.

______. "M.S.H. McArthur and Brunei, 1904–1908, or 'A Dying Kingdom' Reprieved", *BMJ* 6, 24 (1988): 1–32.

______. "The British resident murdered (Ernest Maundrell and Brunei 1915–1916)", *Sarawak Gazette* CXV, 1506 (Dec. 1988): 14–20.

______. "Aspects of finance in Brunei during the British residential era 1906–1959", *BRB* 22, 1 (1990a): 26–32.

______. "Brunei seventy-five years ago", *SMJ* 41, 62 (Dec. 1990b): 271–83.

Hussainmiya, B.A. *Sultan Omar Ali Saifuddin III and Britain, the making of Brunei Darussalam*. Kuala Lumpur: Oxford University Press, 1995, 447 p.

______. *Brunei revival of 1906, a popular history*. BSB: Brunei Press, 2006. [Book reviewed by Graham Saunders, *The Journal of Asian Studies* 56, 1 (Feb. 1997): 258–9].

Hussainmiya, B.A. and Nicholas Tarling. *Brunei: Traditions of Monarchic Culture and History, R.H. Hickling's Memorandum upon Brunei Constitutional History and Practice*. BSB: Yayasan Sultan Haji Hassanal Bolkiah, 2011, 204 p.

Keith, H.G. *The United States Consul and the Yankee Raja*. BSB: Museum Monograph 4, 1980, 256 p.

Leys, Peter. "Observations on the Brunei Political System, 1883–1885", *JMBRAS* 41, 2 (1968): 117–30.

Mills, L.A. *British Malaya 1824–67*. Singapore: 1925, *JMBRAS*, Vol. III. 2nd ed. completed by C.M. Turnbull (bibliography) and D.K. Bassett (introduction). Singapore & Kuala Lumpur: Oxford in Asia, 1966, 391 p.

Monks, T.S. *Brunei Days*. Lewes: Book Guild, 1992, 193 p.

Porritt, Vernon L. *British Colonial Rule in Sarawak, 1946–1963*. Kuala Lumpur: Oxford University Press, 1997, 424 p.

Singh, D.S. Ranjit. "Brunei in international cross-currents 1946–63", *Jurnal Hubungan Antarabangsa* 2 (1974/75): 95–109.

______. *Brunei 1839–1983: The problems of political survival*. Singapore: Oxford University Press, 1984, 272 p.

______. "Brunei and the Hinterland of Sabah: Commercial and Economic Relations with Special References to the Second Half of the Nineteenth Century", in *The Southeast Asian Port and Polity, Rise and Demise*, ed. J. Kathirithamby-Wells and John Villiers. Singapore: Singapore University Press, 1990, pp. 231–45.

Stubbs, Edward (Sir). "Two Colonial Office Memoranda on the history of Brunei", *JMBRAS* 41(II), 214 (Dec. 1968): 83–116.

Standard catalogue of Malaysia-Singapore-Brunei coins and paper money (1828–1981). Kuala Lumpur: International Stamp and Coin Agency, 1978, 137 p.

Tarling, Nicholas. *Britain, the Brookes & Brunei*. Kuala Lumpur: Oxford University Press (Oxford in Asia), 1971, 578 p.

Tatu, Frank. "The United States Consul, the Yankee Raja, Ellena and the Constitution: A historical vignette", *Archipel* 40 (1990): 79–90.

Treacher, W.H. *British Borneo, Sketches of Brunai, Sarawak, Labuan, and North Borneo*. Singapore: Reprinted from the *JSSBRAS*, 1891, 165 p.

Tregonning, K.G. "The Partition of Brunei", *Journal of Tropical Geography* 11 (1958): 83–9.

Walker, J.H. *Power and Prowess: The Origins of Brooke Kingship in Sarawak*. Crow's Nest: Allen and Unwin & Honolulu: University of Hawaii Press, 2002, 300 p.

Willi, Johannes. "Early relations of England with Borneo to 1805". Ph.D. dissertation, Berne, Langesalza, 1922, 146 p.

Wright, Leigh R. *The origins of British Borneo*. Hong Kong: Hong Kong University Press, 1970, 237 p.

1960–2014

Abdul Rahman Putra Al-Haj, Tunku. *Malaysia, the road to independence*. Subang Jaya: Pelanduk, 2007, 195 p.

Angel, J.R. "The Proposed Federation of Sarawak, North Borneo and Brunei: The development and decline of the British Borneo concept". MA dissertation, unpublished, Sydney University, 1963.

Anonymous, "An Interview with Dr. Hj. Zaini Ahmad, Kuala Lumpur, 1985 (Research Notes) (Interview)", *Borneo Research Bulletin*, 1 Jan. 2008, Borneo Research Council, 31 p.

Harrisson, Tom. *Background to a Revolt: Brunei and the surrounding territories*. Brunei City: Light Press, 1963, 38 p.

Harun Abdul Majid. *Rebellion in Brunei: The 1962 revolt, imperialism, confrontation and oil*. London: Tauris, International library of twentieth century history no. 14, 2007, 200 p.

Horton, A.V.M. *Brunei: An occasional news-sheet*. Bordesley: A.V.M. Horton, 1999–2001, 4 vols.

Krausse, Gerald H. "Brunei and the sea: Transformation of a maritime State", in *From Buckfast to Borneo: Essays Presented to Father Robert Nicholl on the 85th Anniversary of His Birth 27 March 1995*, ed. Victor King and V.M. Horton. Hull: University of Hull, 1995, pp. 363–86.

Leake, David. *Brunei: The modern Southeast-Asian Islamic sultanate*. Jefferson: McFarland, 1989, 178 p. [Reviewed by James F. Warren, *The Journal of Asian Studies* 49, 4 (Nov. 1990): 1004–5].

Majid, Harun Abdul. *Rebellion in Brunei: The 1962 revolt, imperialism, confrontation and oil*. London: I.B. Tauris, 2007, 200 p.

Mansurnoor, Iik A. "Brunei new town: Social change and proliferating networks 1950–1983", *SMJ* 56, 77 (2001): 235–74.

Menon, K.U. "Brunei Darussalam in 1987, modernizing autocracy", *Asian Survey* 28, 2, "A Survey of Asia in 1987", Part II (Feb. 1988): 252–8.

Mohamad Abu Bakar. "Politik Brunei menjelang penubuhan Malaysia [Brunei's Policy towards Joining Malaysia]", *Malaysia Dari Segi Sejarah* 10 (1981): 117–41.

Mohamad Yusop. "The Malaysia Plan and the first Brunei elections, 1962", *JMBRAS* 71, 1 (1998): 57–74.

Mohamed Bolkiah, H.R.H. Prince. *Remember, remember—the 8th of December: A journey to 1962*. Berakas: Brunei Press, 2007, 263 p.

Ongkili, J.P. *The Borneo response to Malaysia, 1961–63*. Singapore: Donald More, 1967, 147 p.

Poulgrain, Greg; prefaced by Pramoedya Ananta Toer. *The genesis of "Konfrontasi": Malaysia Brunei Indonesia 1945–1965*. Bathurst: Crawford House and London: Hurst, 1998, 321 p.

Sabihah Osman, Abdullah Muhamad Haji and Sabullah Hj. Hakip. *Sejarah Brunei menjelang kemerdekaan* [*History of almost independent Brunei*]. Kuala Lumpur: Dewan Bahasa dan Pustaka, 1995, 247 p.

Tan, Pek Leng et al. *Essays on modern Brunei history*. BSB: UBD, 1992, 176 p.

Historiography

Brown, D.E. "Hugh Low on the History of Brunei", *BMJ* 1, 1 (1969): 147–55.

Harrisson, T. "Brunei in the Sarawak Museum Journal", *BMJ* 1, 1 (1969): 180–9.

Horton, A.V.M. "Robert Nicholl's contribution to the historiography of Brunei: An assessment", in *From Buckfast to Borneo: Essays Presented to Father Robert Nicholl on the 85th Anniversary of His Birth 27 March 1995*, ed. Victor King and V.M. Horton. Hull: University of Hull, 1995, pp. 349–62.

Kratz, Ernest Ulrich. "*Yang tersurat dan yang tersirat*, Historicity and historical Truth", *Archipel* 60 (2000): 22–44.

Nicholl, Robert. "Some problems of Brunei chronology", *JSAS* 20, 2 (Sept. 1989): 175–95.

Sanib b. Said. "The Development of Brunei Historiography, a Survey and evaluation". Singapore: Conference of the International Association of Historians of Asia, 27–31 Oct. 1986, 19 p.

Managing the Society

Bruneian Periodicals

Borneo Bulletin (daily)
Brunei Times (daily)
Sunday Borneo Bulletin (weekly)

General Information

Kershaw, Roger. "Illuminating the Path to Independence, political themes in *Pelita Brunei* in 1983", *SAA 1984* (1985): 67–85.

______. "Brunei–Malay, Monarchical, Micro-state", in *Government and Politics in Southeast Asia*, ed. John Funston. Singapore: ISEAS, 2001, pp. 1–34.

Matassim Hj. Jibah. "Political development in Brunei with reference to the reign of Sultan Omar Ali Saifuddin III (1950–1967)". MA dissertation, University of Hull, 1985, 91 p.

Samsuddin B.P.H.M. Yusuf. *Political development of Brunei since 1945*. BA dissertation, University of Newcastle, 1984.

Vienne, Marie-Sybille (de), "L'état du Brunei en 2008", in *L'Asie du Sud-Est en 2009*. Bangkok: IRASEC, 2009, pp. 97–110.

______. "L'état du Brunei en 2009", in *L'Asie du Sud-Est en 2010*. Bangkok: IRASEC, 2010, pp. 113–29.

______. "Brunei, accroissement de la richesse, renforcement de l'idéologie", *in L'Asie du Sud-Est 2012*. Bangkok: IRASEC, 2012, pp. 113–29.

______. "Brunei, plus l'on brille, mieux l'on prie?", in *L'Asie du Sud-Est 2013*. Bangkok: IRASEC, 2013, pp. 131–49.

______. "Brunei, des pieds, des mains et l'ASEAN", in *L'Asie du Sud-Est 2014*. Bangkok: IRASEC, 2014, pp. 147–65.

Identity and Ethnicity

Brown, D.E. "The Social Structure of Nineteenth Century Brunei", *BMJ* 1, 1 (1969): 166–79.

______. "Hereditary Rank and Ethnic History: An Analysis of Brunei Historiography", *Journal of Anthropological Research* 29, 2 (1973): 113–22.

Gunn, Geoffrey. *Language, power, and ideology in Brunei Darussalam*. Athens: Ohio University Center for International Studies, Southeast Asia Series no. 99, 1997, 284 p.

Kershaw, Roger. "Ethnic minorities in late twentieth century Brunei, a survey of errors and imbalances in foreign analysis", *Borneo Research Bulletin* 41 (2010): 250–75.

King, Victor T. "What is Brunei Society? Reflections on a conceptual and ethnographic issue", *SAR* 2, 2 (Sept. 1994): 176–98.

Maxwell, Allen R. "Malay polysemy and political power: Census categories, ethnicity and citizenship in Brunei Darussalam", *SAR* 9, 2 (2001): 173–212.

Rozan Yunus. *The Golden Warisan Brunei Darussalam*. BSB, 2009, 2 vols., 238 p & 332 p.

Melayu Islam Beraja

Abdul Aziz bin Awang Juned (Pehin Tuan Imam Dato Paduka Seri Setia Ustaz Haji Awang). *Islam in Brunei: During the reign of His Majesty Sultan Haji*

Hassanal Bolkiah Mu'izzaddin Waddaulah, Sultan and Yang Di-Pertuan of Brunei Darussalam. BSB, 1st ed., 1992; 2nd ed. trans. by Haji Mohamad Amin bin Hassan, Ministry of Youth, Culture & Sports, 2008, 227 p.

Abdul Latif bin Haji Ibrahim, Hj. *On Melayu Islam Beraja, the state ideology of Brunei; collected articles*. BSB: APB, UBD, 2003, xi, 226 p.

Black, Ann. "Ideology and Law: The Impact of the MIB Ideology on Law and Dispute Resolution in the Sultanate of Brunei Darussalam", *Asian Journal of Comparative Law*, vol. 3/1 (2008): 1–41.

Braighlinn, G. *Ideological Innovation under monarchy: aspects of legitimising activity in contemporary Brunei*. Amsterdam: VU University Press, Comparative Asian Studies no. 9, 1992, 105 p.

Chalfont, Lord Alun. *By God's will: A portrait of the Sultan of Brunei*. London: Weidenfeld & Nicolson, 1989, 200 p.

Hashim bin Abd. Hamid (Awang Haji). *Melayu Islam beraja: rantai kesinambungan kebudayaan Brunei [Malay Islamic Monarchy, guiding thread of Bruneian culture]*. BSB: DBP, 1987, 71 p and 18 p.

Jamil al-Sufri, Pehin Jawatan Dalam Seri Maharaja Dato Seri Utama Haji Awang Mohd. "Islam di Brunei [Islam in Brunei]", *BMJ* 4, 1 (1977): 35–42.

———. *Perlaksanaan dasar negara Melayu Islam Beraja [Implementation of the foundations of a Malay, Islamic and Monarchical State]*. BSB: Pusat Sejarah Brunei, 1996, 99 p.

———. *Melayu Islam Beraja, hakikat dan hasrat [Malay, Islamic and Monarchical, Principles and Expectations]*. BSB: Pusat Sejarah, 2008, 263 p.

Mak, Lau-Fong. *Modeling islamization in Southeast Asia: Brunei and Singapore*. Taipei: Academia Sinica, PROSEA research paper no. 29, 2000, 49 p.

Moehammad Nazir, Hj. *Melayu Islam Beraja sebagai falsafah Negara Brunei Darussalam [Malay, Islamic and Monarchical, as a philosophy of Brunei Darussalam]*. BSB: Akademi Pengajian Brunei, UBD, 1993, 2nd ed., 64 p.

Mohammad bin Pengiran Haji Abd. Rahman (Pengiran Haji). *Islam di Brunei Darussalam [Islam in Brunei Darussalam]*. BSB: DBPB, 2001, 250 p.

———. *Islam di Brunei Darussalam zaman British, 1774–1984 [Islam in Brunei Darussalam in the British Era, 1774–1884]*. Berakas: DBPB, 2007, xxiv, 462 p.

Mohd. Zain bin Haji Serudin. *Melayu Islam Beraja: suatu pendekatan [An approach to Malay Islamic Monarchy]*. BSB: DBPB, 1998, 347 p.

Muzaffar Dato' Hj. Mohamad, Hj. *Melayu Islam Beraja: menggali hakikat leluhur, suatu manisfesto Melayu [Malay Islamic Monarchy: Rediscovering the essence of ancestors, a Malay manifesto]*. Kuala Lumpur: Pustaka BSM Enterprise, 2003, 136 p.

Népote, Jacques. "Brunei et Cambodge", in *Carte des Musulmans dans le Monde*, ed. Raymond Delval. Leiden: Brill, 1984, 19 p.

———. "Brunei [L'Islam à]", *Archipel* 29 (1985): 75–80.

Schottmann, Sven Alexander. "'Melayu Islam Beraja': The Politics of Legitimization in a Malay Islamic Monarchy", *Review of Indonesian and Malaysian Affairs* 40, 2 (2006): 111–39.

Talib, Naimah S. "A resilient monarchy: The Sultanate of Brunei and regime legitimacy in an era of Democratic Nation-States", *New Zealand Journal of Asian Studies* 4, 2 (Dec. 2002): 134–47.

Adat Istiadat

Abdul Latif bin Haji Ibrahim (Awang Haji). *Perubahan, simbolisme dan peranan bedil Brunei* [*The evolution, symbolism and role of Brunei's small cannons*]. BSB: DBPB, 1987, 16 p.

______. *Konsep legitimasi penabalan kesultanan Melayu* [*The concept of legitimation in the enthronement ritual of the Malay sultanates*]. Beijing: Foreign Studies University (BFSU), Kertas Kerja untuk Persidangan Antarabangsa Pengajian Melayu, 20–4 May 1996, 19 p.

______. "Kesultanan Brunei Abad ke-19: Sistem Politik dan Struktur Pentadbiran [The sultanate of Brunei in the 19th century, political system and administrative structures]". Ph.D. dissertation, unpublished, University of Malaya, Kuala Lumpur, 2004.

______. "Institusi Wazir, Ceteria dan Menteri pada Abad ke-19: Struktur dan Kuasa Elite dalam Pentadbiran Kesultanan Melayu Brunei [The institution of Wazirs, Cheteria and Menteri in the 19th century: Structure and power of elites in the administration of the Malay sultanate of Brunei]", *Sosiohumanika, Jurnal Pendidikan Sains Sosial dan Kemanusiaan* 1, 2 (2008): 79–114.

Braddell, T. "Ceremony Observed at the Court of Acheen", *JIAEA* 4 (1850): 728–33.

Gullick, J.M. *Indigenous Political Systems of Western Malaya*. London: Athlone Press, 1958, 150 p.

Ibrahim b. Mohd. Jahfar. "Brunei Adat [Customs of Brunei]", *BMJ* 1 (1969): 5–9.

Ikhtisar Budaya [Summary of the culture]. Brunei: DBP, 1976, reprint 1982 & 1986, 95 p.

Istiadat Berpuspa, Kebawah Duli Yang Maha Mulia Paduka Seri Sultan Hassanal Bolkiah Mu'izzaddin Waddulah [*Ceremony of Coronation of His Majesty the Sultan Hassanal Bolkiah Mu'izzaddin Waddulah*]. Bandar Brunei, 1 Aug. 1968, 59 p.

Ito, Takeshi. "The World of the Adat Aceh: A Historical Study of the Sultanate of Aceh". Ph.D. dissertation, Australian National University, Canberra, 1984, 460 p.

Jamil al-Sufri, Pehin Jawatan Dalam Seri Maharaja Dato Seri Utama Dr. Hj. Mohd. *Chatatan sejarah perwira² dan pembesar² Brunei* [*Notes on the history of dignitaries and titled persons of Brunei*]. BSB: DBP, Vol. 1 (1971), 86 p & Vol. 2 (1973), 190 p.

———. "Chiri gelaran di–Brunei [Formulas of enthronement in Brunei]", *Bahana* (1981): 670–9.

———. *Adat istiadat diraja Brunei* [*Customs of the Kingdom of Brunei*]. BSB: Jabatan Adat Istiadat Negara, 2002, 774 p.

Liaw, Yock Fang. *Undang-undang Melaka* [*The Laws of Melaka*]. The Hague: M. Nijhoff, 1976, 211 p.

Memperingati ulang tahun ke-10 perpuspaan 1968–1978, Commemorating the 10th Anniversary of the Coronation. BSB: Muzium Brunei, 1978, 50 p.

Sambutan ulang tahun Hari Kebangsaan Negara Brunei Darussalam kali ke-24 [*Rehearsal of the 24th Anniversary of Brunei Darussalam's National Day*]. BSB: Tunas Bangsa, 2008, 184 p.

Sudjiman, Panuti HM. *Adat Raja Raja Malayu* [*Customs of Malay Souvereigns*]. Jakarta: Penerbit Universitas Indonesia (UI-Press), 1982, 279 p.

Winstedt, Richard O. "The Founder of Malay Royalty and his conquest of Saktimuna the serpent", *JRASMB* 4, 3 (1926): 413–9.

———. "Bendaharas and Temenggungs", *JMBRAS* 10, 1 (1932a): 55-66.

———. "The Early Rulers of Perak, Pahang and Acheh", *JMBRAS* 10, 1 (1932b): 32–44.

———. "A History of Johore, 1365–1895 AD", *JMBRAS* 10, 3 (1932c): 1–159.

———. "History of Negeri Sembilan", *JMBRAS* 12 (Oct. 1934): 41–111.

———. "Kingship and Enthronement in Malaya", *JRAS* 77, 3/4 (1945): 134–45.

———. *The Malays, a Cultural History*. Singapore: Kelly & Walsh, 1947, 162 p.

——— and R.J. Wilkinson. *A History of Perak*. 1st ed., Vol. XII, Part 1, *JMBRAS* (June 1934), repr. Kuala Lumpur: MBRAS, 1974, 226 p.

——— and P.E. Josselin de Jong. "The Maritime Laws of Malacca", *JMBRAS* 29, 3 (1956): 51–9.

Yusuf, Pengiran Mohammed. *Adat Istiadat diraja Brunei Darus-Salam* [*Customs of the Kingdom of Brunei Darussalam*], *BMJ* 3, 3(1975): 43–108 (reprint of the 1958 Jawi edition).

Law and Institutions

Azrinah Binti Haji Abdul Rahman. *Legal System in Brunei Darussalam after the Signing of the Supplementary Agreement 1905/1906 between Brunei and Great Britain*. BSB: Working Paper for National Day Seminar 2006, 29 p.

Dokumen-Dokumen Perlembagaan, Constitutional Documents, printed under the power conferred on the Attorney General by section 18A of the Law Revision Act (Chapter 1); all amendments prior to 8 November 2008 have been incorporated. BSB, Nov. 2008, 333 p.

Hedges, Robert Yorke, ed. *The Laws of Brunei*. Brunei: Brunei Press, 1973, 2 vols., revised edition, 1268 & 68 p.

Hussainmiya, Bachamiya Abdul. "Manufacturing Consensus: The Role of the State Council in Brunei Darussalam", *JSAS* 32, 2 (2000a): 321–50.

______. *The Brunei Constitution of 1959, a Short History*. BSB: Brunei Press, 2000b, 81 p.

______. "Constitutional Practice in Brunei as highlighted in the 1955 memorandum of R.H. Hickling", *JMBRAS* 79, 2 (Dec. 2006): 23–38.

Mahmud Saedon Awang Othman, Dato' Dr Haji. *Perlaksanaan dan Pentadbiran Undang-Undang Islam Di Negara Brunei Darussalam, Satu Tinjauan [Implementation and Management of the Islamic Law in Brunei Darussalam, an Assessment]*. BSB: DBPB, 1996, 106 p.

______. *Characteristics of Islamic Management: Principles and implementation*. BSB: Civil Service Institute, Department of Public Service, 2004, x, 206 p.

Udang² Taraf Kebangsaan Brunei, 1961 [*The Brunei Nationality Enactment, 1961*]. BSB: 1973, 35 p.

Economy

Primary Sources

Brunei Darussalam Economic Council (BDEC). *Report of the Brunei Darussalam Economic Council*. BSB: September 1999, 53 p.

Brunei Darussalam Statistical Yearbook, 1984 to *2013*. BSB: Department of Economic Planning and Development, 1985–2014.

Brunei Statistical Yearbook, 1974/75 to *1983*. BSB, 1976–84.

Negeri Brunei, State of Brunei. *Laporan banchi pendudok Brunei 1971, Report on the Census of Population 1971*. BSB: The Star Press, s.d., 260 p.

Ranchangan Kemajuan Negara 1975–1979, The National Development Plan 1975–1979. BSB: s.n., 1980, 63 p.

Report for 1919 on the State of Brunei, presented to the Parliament by command of His Majesty. London, December 1920, 7 & iv p.

State of Brunei Annual Report, 1958–1976. BSB: Brunei Daily Newspaper & Print, 1959–77.

General

Ali, Ameer. "Industrialization or industries? The vision and the viability of Brunei Darussalam", in *Sumbangsih UBD*, ed. Dato Seri Laila Jasa Awang Haji Abu Bakar bin Haji Apong. BSB: Akademi Pengajian Brunei, 1992, pp. 196–205.

______. *From penury to plenty: Development of oil rich Brunei, 1906 to present*. Perth: Murdoch University, Department of Economics Research, 1996, vii, 229 p.

Arief, Siritua. *The Brunei economy*. East Balmain: Rosecons, 1986, xiii, 233 p.

______. *An Economy of Brunei*. BSB: UBD, 2002, 230 p.

Blomqvist, Hans C. "The Endogenous State of Brunei Darussalam: The Traditional Society Versus Economic Development", *The Pacific Review* 11, 4 (1998): 541–59.

Colclough, Christopher. "Brunei: Development problems of a resource-rich State", *Euro-Asia Business Review* 4, 4 (Oct. 1985): 29–32.

Daniar Hj Abdullah. *The structural change in Brunei economy since the 1960's.* Middlesex: Middlesex Polytechnic, 1986, 50 p.

Economist Intelligence Unit. *Brunei, Country Profile, 2007–2013.*

______. *Brunei, Country Report, 2007–2013.*

Fadilah bin Sheikh Ahmad. *Brunei Darussalam: Its economy and the issue of diversification.* East Anglia: University of East Anglia, 36 p.

Franz, Johannes C. *The sultanate of Brunei, oil wealth and problems of development.* Nurnberg: Wirtschafts- und Sozialgeographisches Institut der Friederich-Alexander, Universitaet Nurnberg, 1980, 335 p.

Heeks, Richard. *Small enterprise development and the 'Dutch disease' in a small economy: The case of Brunei.* Manchester: Institute for Development Policy and Management, University of Manchester, 1998, 50 p.

Ismail bin Haji Duraman. "Development in Brunei Darussalam: Sustainable growth and development of an oil-based economy". Ph.D. dissertation, School of Economics, The University of Queensland, 1998, xiv, 247 p.

Ismail Duraman (Haj.), Clem Tisdell and John Asafu-Adjaye. "Achieving sustainable development in an oil-dependant economy: The case of Brunei Darussalam", *Asia-Pacific Development Journal* 5, 1 (June 1988): 247–73.

Lee, Yong Leng. *North Borneo, a study in settlement geography.* Singapore: Eastern University Press, 1965, 156 p.

Levy, Walter J. *A review of the economy of Brunei, with particular reference to the arrangements concerning government revenues from oil producting operations.* Zug: s.n., 1962, 61 p.

Mohamad Yussof bin Hji Mohiddin and Dr. Law Sam. *Empowering the people to develop the agro-economy of Brunei Darussalam: focussing on the broiler industry—its success stories, challenges and the way forward.* BSB: Department of Agriculture, Ministry of Industry and Primary Resources, 2004, 316 p.

Nur Amni Alyani Bte Haji Abd Rahman. *The history of Brunei economy during SOAS III rule (1950–1967).* BSB: UBD, 2008, 51 p.

Obben, James and Tan Siew Ee, eds. *Readings on the economy of Brunei Darussalam.* BSB: UBD, Department of Economics, 2002, 335 p.

Porter, Michael and Monitor Company Group. "Improving the competitiveness of Brunei Darussalam's economy", *Manager International* (2003), 13 p.

Rao, Shangdong (Niew Shong Tong 饶尚东). 汶莱经济多元化的发展道路 *Wen Lai Jing ji duo yuan hua de fa zhan dao lu [Brunei, the path of economic diversification]*. Miri (Sarawak): 拉让出版社 La rang chu ban she, 2005, 133 p.

Sidhu, Jatswan S. *Sejarah sosioekonomi Brunei 1906–1959* [*Socio-economic History of Brunei*]. Kuala Lumpur: DBP, 1995, 148 p.

Song, Kin Koi. *Brunei Cyberpark: The basis for transforming Brunei Darussalam into the knowledge-based economy*. BSB: UBD, 2001, 63 p.

Tan, Siew Ee and Hj. Ismail bin Hj Duraman, eds. *Readings on the economy of Brunei Darussalam*. BSB: UBD, Faculty of Business, Economics and Policy Studies, 2002, 411 p.

______ and Rosnah Opai, eds. *The Economy of Brunei Darussalam: Perspectives & insights*. Singapore: ISEAS, 2008, 386 p.

Tasie, George Okanou (Dr) and (Dr) Rzali Mat Zin. "Globalisation and diversification of economy: The case of Negara Brunei Darussalam". BSB: n.d. (200?), 19 p.

Tisdell, Clem. "Brunei's quest for sustainable development: Diversification and other", *Journal of the Asia Pacific Economy* 33, 3 (1998): 388–409.

Yong, Willi Ching Choon, Wee Han Pang and Pui-Yee Kwok. "Brunei's Proposed Economic Transformation". Final year project. Singapore: Nanyang Technological University, 2003/04, 239 p.

Foreign Trade

Anaman, Kwabena A. and Tuty H. Mahmod. "An analysis of trade flows between Brunei Darussalam and the European Union", *ASEAN Economic Bulletin* 20, 1(2003): 60–72.

______. "Determinants of supply of non-oil exports in Brunei Darussalam", *ASEAN Economic Bulletin* 20, 2 (2003): 144–57.

World Trade Organization. *Trade policy review, Report by the Secretariat, Brunei Darussalam*. Geneva, 21 Jan. 2008, 14 p.

Finance

Abdul Aziz bin Awang Juned. *Monetary issues: Compilation of State Mufti's Fatwa on monetary issues, 1962–1999*. BSB: State Mufti's Office, Prime Minister's Office, xl, 635 and 12 p.

Gunn, Geoffrey. "'Trophy capitalism', Jefrinomics and Dynastic Travail in Brunei", *Japan Focus*, 18 March 2008, reprinted in *Asia Times*, "Brunei fund of wealth and scandal", 1 April 2008a.

______. "Brunei Darussalam: Dynastic Fallout, Economic Crisis and Recovery?", 東南アジア研究年報 *Tonan Ajia kenkyu nenpo—Annual review of Southeast Asian Studies* 49 (2008b): 1–24.

Land Policy

Lim Hooi Siang. "Land policy and development: Case of Brunei Darusssalam". Paper presented at *ASCP-AESOP Joint International Congress*, Toronto, 25–28 July 1996, 17 p.

Hydrocarbons

Brunei Primer Report on Petroleum. Virtual Information Centre, 14 Feb. 2005, 54 p.

Cleary, Mark and Shuang Yann Wong. *Oil, Economic Development and Diversification of Brunei Darussalam*. New York: St. Martin's, 1994, 154 p.

Franz, J.C. *The sultanate of Brunei: Oil Wealth and the problem of development*. Nurenberg: Universtaet Nurnberg, 1980, 335 p.

Hamzah, B.A. "Oil and security in Brunei", *Contemporary Southeast Asia* 2, 2 (1980): 182–91.

———. *The Oil Sultanate: Political history of oil in Brunei Darussalam*. Seremban (Negeri Sembilan): Mawaddah Enterprise, 1991, xvi, 239 p.

Ismail Duraman, Clem Tisdell and John Asafu-Adjaye. "Achieving sustainable development in an oil-dependant economy: The case of Brunei Darussalam", *Asia-Pacific Development Journal* 5, 1 (June 1998): 103–20.

Norhayati Ahmad. *A Survey of technical development of oil and gas industries in Brunei Darussalam and its impact to Brunei economy*. Sunderland: Sunderland Polytechnic, 1988, vii, 133 p.

Education

Abu Bakar Hj. Apong. "The Development of education in Brunei during self-government period". Ph.D. dissertation, unpublished, University of Birmingham, 1980.

Asbol bin Haji Mail, Awg. *Sejarah Perkembangan Pendidikan di Brunei, 1950–1985* [*History of the development of education in Brunei*]. BSB: Jabatan Pusat Sejarah Brunei, 2006, xiv, 217 p.

International Relations

Contested Zones

Buszynski, Leszek and Iskandar Sazlan. "Maritime Claims and Energy Cooperation in the South China Sea", *Contemporary Southeast Asia* 29 (2007–1): 143–71.

Cleary, Mark and Brian Shaw. "Limbang: A lost province of oil-rich Brunei Darussalam", *Geography* 77, pt. 2, no. 335 (Apr. 1992): 178–81.

Emmers, Ralf. "The De-escalation of the Spratley dispute in Sino-Southeast Asian relations". Singapore: S. Rajaratnam School of International Studies, 2007, 31 p.

Haller-Trost, Renate. *The Brunei-Malaysia dispute over territorial and maritime claims in international law*. Durham: International Boundaries Research Unit (IBRU), Department of Geography, University of Durham, Maritime briefing, Vol. 1, no. 3, 1994, 63 p.

Zakaria M. Yatim (High Court, Malaysia). "The Development of the Law of the Sea in relation to Malaysia", *Malaysian Management Journal* 1, 1 (1991): 87–98.

Defence

Defending the Nation's Sovereignty, Defence White Paper 2004. BSB: Ministry of Defence, 2004, 45 p.

Defending the Nation's Sovereignty, Expanding Roles in Wider Horizons. Defence White Paper 2011. BSB: Ministry of Defense, 2011, 59 p.

Huxley, Tim. *Brunei's defence policy and military expenditure*. Canberra: Australian National University, Strategic and Defence Studies Centre, Working paper no. 166, Dec. 1988, 40 p.

Shaping the Force Today, Defence White Paper Update 2007. BSB: Ministry of Defence, 2007, 54 p.

Toh, Ee Loong. "Writing and Exhibiting Small State Capacity Building: The Case of Brunei's Defence White Paper Update and Bridex 2007", in *Small States in the International System Standing Group on International Relations, 6th Pan-European International Relations Conference*, Turin, 12–15 Sept. 2007, 18 p.

Index